# BARRON'S

# AP

# UNITED STATES HISTORY

## 8TH EDITION

**William O. Kellogg, Ed.M.**
Former Head of the History Department
St. Paul's School
Concord, New Hampshire
President, New Hampshire Council on World Affairs

BARRON'S

*Dedication*

*To all those students who have made teaching United States history a pleasure. May they inspire others. And to the grandchildren, Matt, Rachael, Sarah, Emily, Reid and Boden, whose questions continually inspire me.*

*I wish to thank the New Hampshire Historical Society for permission to use photographs from their collection both in the text and on the CD-ROM. The cartoons are largely from the extensive collections of 19th- and early 20th-century magazines in the New Hampshire State Library and St. Paul's School library in Concord, N.H. I appreciate the opportunity to access these collections.*

*All inquiries should be addressed to:*
Barron's Educational Series, Inc.
250 Wireless Boulevard
Hauppauge, New York 11788
**www.barronseduc.com**

Library of Congress Control No. 2007027923

ISBN-13 (book): 978-0-7641-3684-9
ISBN-10 (book): 0-7641-3684-4

ISBN-13 (book w/CD-ROM): 978-0-7641-9334-7
ISBN-10 (book w/CD-ROM): 0-7641-9334-1

**Library of Congress Cataloging-in-Publication Data**
Kellogg, William O.
    AP U.S. history / William Kellogg.—8th ed.
        p. cm.
    At head of title: Barron's
    Rev. ed. of: How to prepare for the AP advanced placement exam, United States history. 7th ed. c2004.
    Includes bibliographical references and index.
    ISBN-13: 978-0-7641-3684-9 (alk. paper)
    ISBN-10: 0-7641-3684-4 (alk. paper)
    ISBN-13: 978-0-7641-9334-7
    ISBN-10: 0-7641-9334-1
    1. United States—History—Examinations, questions, etc. 2. United States—History—Examinations—Study guides. 3. Advanced placement programs (Education)—Examinations—Study guides.  I. Kellogg, William O. How to prepare for the AP advanced placement exam, United States history.  II. Title.  III. Title: Barron's AP U.S. history.  IV. Title: AP US history.

E178.25.K44 2008
973—dc22

                                                                    2007027923

# Contents

# Preface to the Eighth Edition

First writing and then rewriting this book on the Advanced Placement examination has always been most interesting and educational for me. I only hope it proves to be the same for the students and teachers who will use it to further their study and understanding of that always intriguing subject: the history of the United States.

Although the material included in the book is mine and I am responsible for the emphasis and interpretations, more than 4,000 St. Paul's students during 40 years of teaching strongly influenced my understanding and method of presenting history. They, together with the many colleagues with whom I have worked both at St. Paul's and elsewhere, have my heartfelt thanks for providing ideas and the stimulating atmosphere that have made teaching such an exciting endeavor. Special thanks go to many St. Paul's students who wrote responses to questions for this text. Also, my thanks go to students in several classes, especially those in Mike Foley's classes at Belmont, New Hampshire High School, as well as those who have attended the New Hampshire Historical Society's AP program over the years and those who have participated in the World Affairs Council's student programs. They have all provided an important student voice. Also, thanks to the librarians at Boulder's Carnegie Library.

I would also like to express my gratitude to my typist of the first edition in 1977, Judy Morin, who had an uncanny ability to decipher scratchings, turning them into words and to follow arrows making words into sentences. Without her this manuscript would never have emerged, and she is greatly missed. My special thanks go to my daughter, Elli Kellogg Blackwell, who has taken over where Judy began as decipherer and typist. My thanks also go to the several editors at Barron's who have helped with the eight editions. Their patience, advice, and insights are greatly appreciated.

WILLIAM O. KELLOGG
Boulder, CO

# What to Expect from the Book and the Exam

## CHAPTER 1

- Tips for student and teacher alike
- All about the AP exam: types of questions, time allotment, and scoring
- Review of content areas

This book was written to help students prepare for the Advanced Placement examination. It can be used three different ways. First, it can be used as a supplement to a regular course in United States history. The student wishing to take the AP exam and not enrolled in an advanced course can use this book to provide depth of coverage. If the student writes the essays and answers the multiple-choice questions, he or she will be well prepared for the AP exam.

The second way this book may be used is as part of an AP course. The teacher can assign chapters in the book to supplement work in class or a student can pick those chapters where he or she needs help. The suggested essay topics in each chapter can be assigned at the teacher's discretion.

The third way the book may be used is by a student who has already had a course in United States history and wishes to simply review before taking the AP exam. A student using the book in this way should start by taking the Model A Advanced Placement exam to find areas of weakness in the information he or she already has and then develop a review plan.

## ADVICE FOR STUDENTS

The book was designed to provide information on how to prepare for the United States History AP exam. It was not written as a quick review, although the material at the end of each chapter and the sample answers throughout the text provide the factual knowledge you will need to know for the exam.

A careful study of this book will provide you with the skills needed on the Advanced Placement exam. Writing the practice essays will help you develop the skills you need to do well. The questions will require you to act as a historian collecting and organizing information, and the multiple-choice questions will test how well you have absorbed that information. The AP program refers to all essays as free-response questions. The "Document-Based Question (DBQ)" and the "standard essays" are *both* grouped under this designation. The Model AP exams will, if taken in a situation similar to the examination, provide you a rehearsal, which is extremely valuable.

While it is important that you move at your own pace in working through the book, it is also important that you study the material in each chapter.

## SUGGESTIONS FOR TEACHERS

This book can be used to supplement work in class. If you are teaching a regular section of United States history, the book can provide the supplementary stimulation needed to prepare a few interested students to take the Advanced Placement exam. You may in this case wish to suggest additional reading, but it is not necessary, as this book will help those students prepare for the exam. If you are teaching an Advanced Placement course, the book can be broken up in segments and assigned as you find appropriate. The chronological material provides a good overview of important issues in our history, and the essays provide much factual information.

## HOW THE BOOK IS ORGANIZED

**Part One** presents an introduction to this book and to the Advanced Placement examination. It introduces skills needed in the study of history and discusses a method of writing essays. The Seven Steps method has proven very helpful for students preparing for the essays on the Advanced Placement examination or writing any essays.

**Part Two** is organized around periods of time in U.S. history and in each chapter the important issues of the period are listed. Each chapter focuses on a different type of free-response question. Each type is analyzed and sample answers are included. Also in Part Two different types of multiple-choice questions are introduced and analyzed. Included in each chapter are sample essay questions and multiple-choice questions dealing with the time period or with preceding time periods. This is not to suggest that only these types of questions will be asked on that particular era of United States history. As you work through Part Two, your knowledge of United States history will be broadened.

**Part Three** presents two sample Advanced Placement exams. Also included are suggestions on how to take the exam and how to do the final review before the exam.

The book ends with a list of important dates, a glossary, and an index.

This volume was designed to be used in a flexible way. It can be read straight through, or different sections can be chosen to help your review and in-depth study. It has proven very helpful to many students of U.S. history, and it has been used in a variety of courses throughout the country.

## THE AP EXAM

The AP exam is designed to test the information presented in typical college level introductory United States History courses. The AP exam is designed and written by a Development Committee whose members are chosen from among high school and college teachers. Each year there are subtle changes in the exam that reflect changes in the content and emphasis of introductory college courses. One should not rely on previous exams to find out what is being tested today. For instance, recently the committee has slightly reduced the percentage of questions devoted to political history and increased the amount devoted to social history. They have also folded intellectual and cultural history into social history.

## Grading

The AP United States History exam essays are read by college and high school consultants meeting in June. Grades are reported in July.

The readers, referred to as consultants, give a rank to each paper from a scale of 1 to 9. They do not write comments on the papers, nor do they give them a traditional grade. The ranking scale is established at the reading site by a group of teachers called "table leaders" who read student papers and discuss what is included in them. They then develop a set of guidelines for the entire group of consultants. These guidelines reflect what they have found in the student papers. In other words, there is no ideal answer for the question written by the Development Committee. Instead, the table leaders develop the standards by which the papers are to be judged based on student answers. Your essays are ranked against all of your fellow students who take the exam. For the consultants, it is a demanding exercise that has been developed over the years and has proven to produce consistent and accurate results, assuring that the grades sent to colleges from year to year can be accurately compared.

Advanced Placement exams are offered annually in May. Final scores are reported on a five-point scale as follows:

> 5    extremely well qualified
> 4    well qualified
> 3    qualified
> 2    possibly qualified
> 1    no recommendation

**INTERESTING FACT**

AP Exams are **ranked** by the readers. They are not corrected or graded.

In granting credit or advanced placement, many colleges honor grades of 3 or higher. The policies of colleges vary: some automatically grant credit or advanced academic standing; others respond individually to each situation. Be sure to check with the colleges that interest you to find out their AP policies.

Many high school juniors take the AP United States History exam. Having your AP score reported to the colleges to which you apply may help your admission opportunities.

**TIP**

A student who is well prepared to take the AP U.S. History exam should be well prepared to take the SAT Subject Test in U.S. History as well. This test is different in its design, consisting of multiple-choice questions only. To do well on the SAT, a quick review of the multiple-choice questions in this book would be helpful. The multiple-choice questions on the SAT are similar to those in this book.

## Types of Questions

The AP United States History exam consists of three types of questions: multiple-choice, the document-based essay (often abbreviated as DBQ), and the standard essay. **Both types of essays are referred to as free-response questions.** Essay answers account for 50 percent of the grade. It is thus clear that writing skills are extremely important in achieving a good score on the Advanced Placement exam. Minor adjustments have been made to the format of the exam over the years. **Students have 2 hours and 10 minutes in which to answer one DBQ and two** standard essay questions. If you use old exams for practice, it is important to realize they may not follow the format of the current exam.

## MULTIPLE-CHOICE QUESTIONS

**Students have 55 minutes to answer 80 multiple-choice questions.**
The following questions are typical of those that appear on the exam:

1. "A well-regulated militia being necessary to the security of a free state, the right of the people to keep and bear arms shall not be infringed."

   All of the following are true in relation to the above quotation EXCEPT

   (A) It is the second amendment to the U.S. Constitution
   (B) It is considered part of the Bill of Rights
   (C) The "right to bear arms" has become a major political issue
   (D) The National Guard is an example of a "well-regulated militia"
   (E) The statement assumes that all people will serve in the military

2. Among the scandals connected with the Grant administration was

   (A) Whitewater
   (B) Teapot Dome
   (C) Credit Mobilier
   (D) Iran-Contra
   (E) Watergate

3. Which of the following describes the use of neutrality by the United States?

   (A) It has been used to avoid involvement in foreign wars.
   (B) The United States has never declared neutrality.
   (C) Maintaining neutrality was the goal of the Monroe Doctrine.
   (D) It was ignored in the years prior to U.S. entry into World War II.
   (E) It was the basis of U.S. policy in Central America in the 19th century.

Questions in the multiple-choice section of the exam require recall of information and critical analysis of historic information as well as interpretation of information such as political cartoons, tables and charts, maps, or documents presented in the question. These latter questions are often referred to as "stimulus" questions. The multiple-choice section of the examination will draw on information from all aspects of United States history. There is further information on multiple-choice questions in Part Two.

## SCORING MULTIPLE-CHOICE QUESTIONS

In scoring the multiple-choice section of the AP examination, one-fourth of a point is taken off for each incorrect answer. Therefore, you should not guess blindly at answers but rather analyze the choices. If at least one of the five choices can be eliminated, then you may wish to pick an answer from the remaining four options. Statistically, it makes sense. As the sample multiple-choice questions in each chapter are analyzed, practice eliminating incorrect choices.

### *Answers to Sample Questions*

1. **(E)**    2. **(C)**    3. **(A)**

## THE FREE-RESPONSE DOCUMENT-BASED ESSAY QUESTION (DBQ)

The essay or free-response section of the examination consists of two parts: the free-response document-based question (DBQ) and the free-response standard essay questions. The DBQ will be based on documents but not necessarily famous documents such as the Constitution. The documents may include writings by well-known individuals, or individuals representative of their time, journals, Supreme Court decisions, other important national documents, or newspaper articles, and when appropriate will include visual representation such as pictures, charts, graphs, maps, or cartoons.

The document-based question is designed to test your analytical skills **as well as** your ability to relate the material to the major issues of the time period covered by the DBQ. These major issues form what is referred to by historians as the "mainstream" of American history. It includes the topics and chronological overview incorporated in most college survey courses. You must be able to introduce ideas and information from this "mainstream" in your DBQ answer. For example, the question might be on the intricacies of U.S. foreign policy between 1795 and the outbreak of the war in 1812. The documents included would reflect the various aspects of this foreign policy and might include selections from treaties, the XYZ correspondence, or the embargo of 1807. You would then be expected to interpret these documents and show how they relate to the "mainstream" developments of those years. For instance, you should be able to express the views of the Federalists and the Anti-Federalists, of John Adams and Thomas Jefferson, of New Englanders and frontier settlers on the issues raised by the documents. Your answer should not be based simply on the documents.

The DBQ is discussed in greater detail in Part Two, Chapter 8, where a sample question is included. There are also sample DBQs included in the model exams found in Part Three and on the CD-ROM.

> **IMPORTANT FACT**
>
> All the sample essays in this book include accurate information. Reading them provides a review of United States history.

## THE STANDARD FREE-RESPONSE ESSAY QUESTION

The second part of the essay section presents two groups of two questions each for a total of four questions. You are to answer two questions—one from each group. You should choose the questions about which you know the most and pick your facts carefully to support your opinion on the particular subject. In each chapter of Part Two, a different type of essay question is presented and analyzed and sample answers presented. Of course, any type of question can be asked on any period.

**A great deal of United States history is included in these sample essay answers, and although some of it is not presented well, there are no factual errors in these answers, and therefore these sample answers provide a helpful review of U.S. history.** Thus, as you work through this book you will be studying both history chronologically and different types of essay and multiple-choice questions.

This combination of chronology and questions has proven to be an effective and efficient way to review for the Advanced Placement exam.

Following are three essay questions similar to those that appear on the actual AP exam:

1. "The English founded colonies in the new world to escape oppression in England." Evaluate this statement as it applies to TWO of the following colonies:

   Massachusetts Bay Colony
   Pennsylvania
   Virginia

2. Analyze how TWO of the following prepared the way for the United States to emerge as a world leader in the latter half of the 20th century.

   The Spanish-American War
   Woodrow Wilson's Fourteen Points
   The Lend-Lease Act

3. Describe and evaluate the significance of the abolitionist movement in bringing about the Civil War.

## TIME ALLOTMENT

The AP U.S. History exam is 3 hours and 5 minutes. You are given 55 minutes to answer 80 multiple-choice questions. You are then allotted 2 hours and 10 minutes for the free-response or essay section. This is divided so that you have 15 minutes to read and analyze the DBQ and 45 minutes to write it. You will then have 70 minutes to answer two of the four essay questions. It is suggested you spend 5 minutes reading and making notes on each of the two questions you will answer and 30 minutes writing each answer. Thus you have a total of 105 minutes of writing and 25 minutes of reading and analysis on the essay section for a total of 2 hours and 10 minutes.

## Content Covered on the Exam

**TIP**

Forty-five percent of multiple-choice questions come from 1790–1914.

The AP exam is given in May. Since the mid-May date falls at a time when many high school courses have not yet completed their chronological study, the AP exam presently places less emphasis on the period since the election of Ronald Reagan. No essay questions will deal exclusively with the last 27 years but there may be multiple-choice questions specifically on these years. Also, since a number of schools and colleges today devote less time to colonial history and concentrate on the period after 1754, the AP exam has placed less emphasis on pre-1754 American history than on later history, although students should have an understanding of important topics such as the interaction between Native American cultures and that of the European settlers in the colonial period and the development of Hispanic culture in the Southwest. On the multiple-choice section of the exam approximately 20% of the questions come from the period prior to 1789, approximately 45% of the questions deal with the period from 1790 to 1914, and approximately 35% of the questions deal with the period from 1915 to the present.

Following a recent trend toward more social history in college courses, 40% of the exam multiple-choice and essay questions reflect social, cultural, and intellectual history, and 35% reflect political history and government issues. The remaining 25% is split with economic history accounting for 10% and diplomatic and foreign policy issues accounting for 15%. Many questions, especially the essay questions, seek connections between these areas, such as political responses to economic crises or the impact of foreign policy decisions on society.

## SUGGESTED APPROACHES TO THE HIGH SCHOOL AP COURSE

The AP program has always emphasized the independence of each classroom teacher in developing a United States history course. However, the Development Committee has suggested two broad approaches, one chronological and one topical, for designing a course. A third approach is to combine the two. For the chronological they have suggested 28 areas that would cover the "mainstream" of United States history from pre-Columbian to the present. This reflects what is covered in most introductory college courses and reads very much like the table of contents of any standard textbook. Such an approach would be expected to cover material illustrating the following:

Native American cultures

Early European settlement

Social and economic developments in the colonial period

Colonial wars and the crisis of Empire

The revolutionary period

Articles of Confederation and the Constitution

The New Nation in war and peace

Early Westward movement

Social and cultural changes in the pre-industrial period

Expansion and Manifest Destiny

Social and cultural differences in the pre-Civil War period

Political crisis and war 1850–1865

Reconstruction

The rise of industry and the growth of cities

Postwar economic and social development in the South, West, and North

Changing frontiers and Indian Wars

Populism and Progressivism

Overseas expansion, the Spanish-American War, and Theodore Roosevelt

World War I and its domestic impact

Cultural and economic aspects of the 1920s

Depression and the New Deal

World War II at home and abroad

The start of the Cold War

Vietnam and Civil Rights

The Presidency of Richard Nixon

The Reagan Revolution: the New Right and Economic Policy

The end of the Cold War and its international ramifications

Social and cultural tensions at the start of the 21st century

Foreign and domestic challenges of terrorism

**TIP**

The exam breaks down as follows: 35 percent on political activity, 40 percent on social and cultural history, 15 percent on diplomatic history and foreign policy, and 10 percent on economic change.

This list is only one suggestion as to what might be covered in a chronological survey of United States history just as that offered by the AP program is another. Each student and teacher must design an approach that suits his or her teaching style and the student's learning style. It is important, however, to respond to the AP program's announced content coverage.

The Development Committee recently rephrased the topics or themes that might form the basis of a topical approach to United States history. Themes can be expressed briefly, such as immigration or religion, or described more fully, such as expansion on the continent and overseas and its social and economic impact on the nation. Picking several themes and exploring them in depth will provide an effective survey course for the student and an excellent preparation for the AP exam. Among possible themes are the following:

American expansion, both on the continent and overseas, and its social and economic impact on the nation

The changing role of government throughout our history

Economic changes both in business and labor practices and attitudes

Slavery, immigration, and the role of minorities

The cause of major wars and their effect—economic, political, and social

The growth of an American culture in the 19th century and its flowering in the 20th century

**TIP**

Individual teachers or schools have the flexibility to design their own AP U.S. History course. There is no standardized program that must be followed.

Whatever approach is taken, it is important that the four content areas—social, political, foreign policy, and economics—are included in the study. Literature can be effectively used in courses to illustrate changing social and cultural attitudes and to introduce important authors, but the emphasis should not be on the work as art but on its relation to history. Gender, ethnic and racial differences, socioeconomic conflicts, as well as changing historiographic interpretations of major developments in the mainstream of American history should be considered. Although historiography will not be questioned directly on the examination, students should be aware of major interpretations. Of course, not all of this material can be included in a one-year course so choices must be made.

Some students want to approach studying for the AP exam as an exercise in guessing what will be on the exam. It is better to spend your time studying content and developing your analytical skills as they will not only be crucial to doing well on the exam but also will serve you well throughout life. Knowing what types of free-response and DBQ questions have been asked can be of some help. However, as the Development Committee has changed, the type of questions asked has changed, but they all are described within the chapters of this book.

Also, some students want to know just what will be on the exam and what types of multiple-choice questions there will be. Again this book includes samples of different types of questions. Your textbook, together with the chronology in each chapter, is the best guide as to what will be tested. One should be cautious of statements such as "historiography is not tested" because the guidelines published by the College Board clearly state that students need to be aware of changing interpretations. If one just wants to cram in facts, one can read the index of a textbook to learn the "facts" of United States history, but will not have an understanding of that history. That can only be achieved by analyzing and interpreting how events and ideas interrelate throughout history.

One matter that may be of help on the multiple-choice questions is the manner in which they appear. They are presented chronologically in groups of 8 to 14 questions. The groups appear to get harder as the test goes on, but that is a personal judgment that depends on your knowledge and your analytical and logical skills. Realizing that the questions do not come randomly nor strictly chronologically is helpful since it means you will not be continually jumping around in time, which may help focus your thinking.

---

### SUMMARY OF AP EXAM CONTENT

This description of exam content may seem confusing: Just realize that no two courses in AP United States History will be the same; thus you must decide what areas to concentrate on. The core or 75 percent of the exam will cover social and political history with items from diplomatic and economic history making up the other 25 percent. You need to consider the major events in the "mainstream" of the nation's history. You can do this by studying either chronology or themes. There will be less emphasis on the period prior to 1754 and after 1980 than on the other periods, with approximately half the multiple-choice questions covering material between 1790 and 1914.

# Strategies for Studying

---

## CHAPTER 2

- Reading skills
- Note taking
- Vocabulary
- Sources

In studying any subject there are certain study techniques and approaches that make understanding the material easier. However, many students approach all subjects with the same methods and become frustrated when they fail to achieve success in one area with techniques that proved successful in other subjects. For example, the study of history requires a great deal of reading, but if you read history the way you read a novel, you will not find success, since you may miss many of the important details you must know.

Each student studying history will develop his or her own very personal approaches to material. This chapter introduces a number of study techniques that students of history have found valuable.

## READING SKILLS

Any student planning to take the Advanced Placement examination should be a good reader, since he or she will have to read extensively, quickly, and with understanding. Many students read all written material in the same manner—they start at the beginning and go to the end. In a novel or in other literary works and in pleasure reading, this is a satisfactory approach, but another method is more beneficial when you are attempting to learn the details presented in the written material and when the subject is strange or unfamiliar to you. This method is to pre-read the material.

### Pre-Read

Pre-reading involves looking over the material (book, chapter, document) quickly, reading titles and subheadings when they occur and, when they do not, reading the first sentence of paragraphs to get the sense of what will be presented in the reading. Often review questions or a summary appear at the end of a chapter, and these should be included as part of the pre-reading. Once you have looked over the reading, you should have a good idea of what it is about. You should have some questions of your own. These questions should be written down.

If there are questions in the book, these should be noted. These questions should guide your reading.

## Ask Questions

As you read, you should interact with the material. Keep in mind the questions you have developed. Take notes (see below) to help you answer them. Stop after a section and ask yourself, "What was the main point I just read?" Write it down. Remember that the writer is an individual with ideas and a point he or she wants you to believe. You need to know what the ideas are, but you must also decide if you believe them and how the writer has used evidence to convey them. You must ask, "Is the evidence correct? Is it complete? What might have been left out?"

Many students consider history to be nothing but facts. Actually, history is what writers have done with the facts, the evidence from the past. What we have in a history book or a document is what the author thought was important. Not every fact or every bit of evidence from the past is included, any more than we include everything we have done, or thought, when we write a letter. When you read history, you must consider what evidence or facts might have been left out because of the author's viewpoint.

## Analyze Authors' Viewpoints

History is a very personal subject. Every writer has his or her own ideas about the relationship of different events, the importance of certain individuals, the motivations behind various actions, and the significance of each event. No two historians will agree entirely on their interpretations and the evidence they use. For example, if you are reading one of the *Federalist Papers* written by James Madison, it is important to realize Madison's biases in favor of the Constitution, of education, and of wealth, and his biases against the poorer and less educated. When you see Madison quoted in a text, you will want to keep these points in mind.

Likewise, if you are reading Charles Beard, one of the great American historians of the first half of the 20th century, you will want to be aware of his biases. If you are not aware, you might accept without question Beard's interpretation of the Constitution as a document written by wealthy men for the protection of their own wealth. Knowing that Beard was an economic historian and that he interpreted history, as does a Marxist, in terms of economic pressures and class divisions based on wealth, you might not accept all Beard has to present. Charles Beard made many important points in his famous book, *The Economic Interpretation of the Constitution*, but many of his assumptions have been questioned or tempered by later scholars.

The point is that historians interpret events based on their personal viewpoints and the student must learn what these viewpoints or biases are as well as learn the evidence the historian presents. Further reading may make you aware of how much evidence was left out or overlooked by the author of a particular book. This will lead you to develop and identify your own viewpoints or biases.

## Identify Biases

There are many ways to identify biases. Such simple devices as the date of publication and the place of residence of an author will give some insights. Prefaces, biographical sketches, and reviews will also provide information. The most important way to discover bias, however, is through a careful reading of the material. For instance, the words chosen to describe the slave in America may reveal certain attitudes. Is he Sambo, a *shuffling* character who *benefited* from his *master's* religion? Or was he an *exploited* worker—more exploited than those in the factories of England since he could never be *free?* Such words reveal a lot about the author, as will the manner in which various events are described.

As a test of authors' biases, try reading about the same event in several different books. Most historians in considering Lincoln's signing of the Emancipation Proclamation would include the same so-called hard facts or evidence, such as the date (1863), document (Emancipation Proclamation), and events (the signing ceremony). How each uses these facts to explain Lincoln's reasons for signing reveals the author's bias. Textbooks compared this way can reveal a great deal. Textbook authors do have biases.

Not only do writers have biases; everyone has them. You must be aware of these—and particularly your own biases and prejudices—as you study. Also, do not overlook the fact that I, the author, have biases that are incorporated in this text. Can you identify some of them?

Biases and prejudices are not necessarily bad, although we often use the word prejudice negatively. They are simply a part of being human and thus are a part of history. The greater your awareness of the biases of the authors you read, and of your own, the greater your understanding of events will be.

## Post-Read

The final step of effective reading is to post-read. Look at the questions you developed in your pre-reading and be sure you can answer them. This amounts to a review of the chapter. If you are taking a history course, you will want to do this reviewing as close to the class meeting time as possible. If you are studying independently, you will want to look over your questions and the answers you developed at regular intervals. If you have good notes on the material you study, you will find it very helpful to read these during the week before you take the Advanced Placement exam. You will find it exceedingly difficult to review all the reading you do in an advanced level course the week before the exam, so your notes will be most important.

## Read "Nonverbal" Material

Documentary films and videos as well as those created for entertainment, CD-ROMs, charts, graphs, maps, cartoons, paintings, and songs can all be used as sources for historical research. In viewing such sources it is important to apply your reading skills. You may not be able to skim through a film, but you can read about it before seeing it and develop questions. You can look at selected sections of videos after viewing them. Computer information and CD-ROM sources can be printed out or reviewed. For all these sources you should analyze the author's views and biases. If the author, artist, producer, or director is not identified, seek information about the company that produced the item. The maker of a video, the painter of a portrait, and the creator of a chart all have something they personally wish to convey. Be aware of that as you use these sources.

## Underline

Many students who own books develop techniques of underlining or making marginal notes in the books to identify the information that will answer the questions they have developed. This can be a very helpful technique, but one should limit the amount of underlining that is done. Too much underlining is worse than none, since it defeats the purpose, which is to clearly mark those items in a book that you think are important to remember. Underlinings, slash marks through important sentences, and circles around key words are all helpful techniques. Each student fortunate enough to own his or her history books will develop a technique that will make reviewing written material easy and will enable the student to answer questions developed in pre-reading.

# Quick Review

In studying for a history course or exam, you should first pre-read or review all material. While doing this you should develop questions that will provide the focus for your reading. You should then read the material. Be aware as you read (or look) of the author's viewpoints and biases. Finally, before class or before going on to the next reading, you should review the material by checking the answers you have prepared for the questions you developed in your pre-reading. You will also want to review your answers to questions before any test and especially before taking the AP exam.

## NOTE-TAKING SKILLS

Note-taking is an important skill for every history student to develop. There are several approaches. Students should try different methods and use those with which they are most comfortable.

As suggested, one method of note-taking is to develop questions about your reading and then take notes to develop answers. The evidence might be written on a page under the question or on your computer. This method allows you to restructure the material in a book into patterns that you have developed. If you follow this method, you will have put yourself into the role of the historian, collecting and reordering factual information to provide answers to questions of interest to you. If you consider the question as a sort of thesis and the factual information you put in your notes as the data to prove it, this method of note taking will be excellent practice for writing essays.

Many students today use the note-taking technique called "mapping" in which a key word or idea is put in the center of the page and circled. Then, relevant ideas are grouped along lines running out from the circle. The technique, often used in brainstorming, allows the student to reorganize material around key points.

Many students will keep their notes in a notebook. A looseleaf book is suggested since you can add or rearrange pages. This can be helpful. A few students will take notes on index cards. This is a valuable technique when writing a research paper, but can become rather burdensome when simply taking notes on a text. Many students take their notes on the computer using hypercard or a technique they develop such as using the questions you develop.

Another type of note-taking is keeping a list of important individuals. Your notes might group them by activity, such as political leaders, business leaders, reformers, inventors, and the like, or by time periods.

## Make an Outline

Another valuable method of note-taking is outlining. In this approach the student simply summarizes or condenses the information in the book. The summary does not reorder the information, but retains the important data in a short version that can be referred to for review or before the exam. The student is not involved in being the historian in preparing such notes, but will have at hand a brief version of the information he or she needs to discuss issues or to prove given hypotheses.

## Create a Time Line

In addition to taking notes on the general content of the material read, there are several types of specialized note taking that can be invaluable to the student of history. The first involves making a time line. Dates are important in history since they provide the key to the cause-and-effect relationship that is at the heart of understanding history in the Western world. Unless you know the chronological order in which events happened, you cannot explain the relationships among them. Therefore, **as you read it would be wise to keep a list of *major* events and the date on which each occurred**. This can be a simple list in which you merely record the date and the name of the event. For instance, a time line can be as simple as the following:

1763 — Treaty of Paris
— Proclamation Line

1764 — Grenville Program
— Sugar Act

1765 — Stamp Act
— Stamp Act Congress
— Boycott

1766 — Stamp Act Repealed
— Declaratory Act

> **TIP**
>
> Time lines can include other information—names of people and places involved in the event, brief descriptions of the event, even the month and day if that seems significant (for example, September 11, 2001). You must decide how complex you wish to make yours, but good advice is to keep it simple. What you want is something that will jog your memory and be quick to review.

   Part Four includes a time line. You may wish to add to this one or make your own as you study. If you make your own, emphasize what is important to you and not what someone else has decided you should learn. This is an important part of any study—to make the information yours.

## The Importance of Vocabulary

Every discipline has its own vocabulary. We often do not realize this as we study English or history, since most of the vocabulary is familiar to us from our daily usage. However, there are many words that are used in special ways in history. As you study, you should develop a list of words with which you were not familiar when you began your study. In the list, after each word you should write a definition. Such a list is a glossary. A short glossary is included at the end of the book but you should develop your own word list.

   Many words used in history change their meaning during the course of time. You must be aware of the shifting use of words as well as of their meanings today. For instance, a person labeled as a liberal in 1830, in 1912, in 1968, and in 2004 might stand for very different points of view. As you read, be certain you can identify these shifting meanings.

Also, many terms or phrases used in history refer to much more than is meant by the word alone. For instance, the word *frontier* has different meanings and different connotations depending upon how it is used. If by *frontier* one means the edge of unsettled land, you react in one way. However, if you mean *frontier* as understood by the very important American historian Frederick Jackson Turner, then you need to react in many other ways. *Frontier* is simply one example of many words that have particular meanings for history.

## Key Phrases

Historians also have adopted many phrases used by politicians and others through the years to convey certain concepts. For instance, the New Frontier of President Kennedy has a specialized meaning with which you should be familiar. Keep a list of such phrases as you study; you will find them to be invaluable in aiding your understanding of American history. Many questions on the exam will assume a knowledge of such phrases and words.

The sample multiple-choice questions in Chapter 11 deal with vocabulary. By the time you get to those questions you should have developed your own vocabulary list and thus should find these questions easy. Of course, all questions dealing with history require knowledge of the vocabulary of history. Thus, you need to add new words to your vocabulary notes as you study.

---

### STUDY REMINDERS

When studying history, it is very important to take notes on the material. Each student should practice taking notes in different ways to find one that works best for him or her. However, all students should keep their own time lines, lists of individuals and key phrases, and glossary. Reorganizing the evidence presented as answers to questions that are of significance to you, leads you to act as an historian and is strongly recommended as a study skill.

---

## WHAT SOURCES TO USE

When students or teachers first look at the amount of material available in the field of United States history, both in hardcover editions and in paperbacks, on video and film and now on CD-ROMs and the Internet, they are often overwhelmed. The quantity, much of it of high quality by important people and outstanding historians, is so discouraging that the teacher or student often retreats to a safe textbook within the covers of which will be found brief presentations of all the important events of American history, at least as understood by one or several authors. It is hoped that the users of this book will not fall into that trap, but rather will use a variety of sources for the study of American history.

A textbook is often a fine starting place, but for the truly interested student-scholar, it should be only that—a starting place. Documents, cartoons, videos, even well-written novels of a period will supply depth of understanding to your study and will provide important evidence for the answers to your questions. With the greater emphasis on social history on the exam, such supplemental sources will be even more important.

## Books

There are many textbooks from which to choose. A major consideration is length. A brief text will provide the basic structure and allow time for extensive special research. The texts mentioned at the end of the chapter are a sampling of those often used in AP classes.

There are hundreds of specialized works on United States history as any visit to a bookstore will show. Students should consult at least one such work to learn how historians approach particular topics. In addition, don't overlook the specialized encyclopedias and document collections available. These works can be very helpful when investigating a particular question. Let your personal interests be your guide in selecting topics.

## Journals and Magazines

You may wish to consult some of the learned history journals that carry articles on recent research. Consulting such journals is a good supplement to your regular study. The articles are often written by well-known historians and this provides an opportunity to learn who they are.

## Historiography and Changing Interpretations

Historiography, which includes the methodology or way historians work and write, must be understood by each student of history. As already stated, each historian has his or her own viewpoints and biases. From time to time, these personal views change but more importantly, interpretations of past events change both over time and with new authors.

## Internet, Videos, and CD-ROMs

The Internet, videos, and CD-ROMs provide a wide range of helpful information for students of United States history. As a rapidly changing and expanding resource, it is difficult to remain abreast of the most valuable sources since the quality of such resources can vary immensely. For the Internet, .edu web sites are more likely to be accurate and helpful, but that is not always true. The Library of Congress web site as well as state and university sites are important ones to check. The issue in using all three resources is time. The Web can absorb one for hours, and videos and most CD-ROMs must be viewed in real time and cannot be skimmed as printed material can be. Also, web sites and addresses change. However, if you are comfortable on the Internet, you should use search engines to find specific information, especially documents, relevant to your study.

> **POINT TO REMEMBER**
>
> No bibliographies are included in this book. To prepare effectively for the AP exam, you should consult works beyond the text. With the large amount of information available and the great range of topics you can pick to investigate in depth, the choice of books must be left to you or your teacher.

## Suggested Textbooks

There are innumerable textbooks on United States history. Among those that might be used in an advanced-level course are the following:

Bailey, T. A., and David M. Kennedy. *The American Pageant*. Boston: Houghton Mifflin, 2001.

Blum, John, et al. *The National Experience: A History of the United States*. New York: International Thomson Pub., 2000.

Kellogg, W.O. *American History: The Easy Way*. Hauppauge, NY: Barron's Educational Series, Inc., 2003. (A brief overview of American history)

Norton, M. B. et al. *A People and a Nation: A History of the United States*. Boston: Houghton Mifflin, 2004. (Emphasizes the social history of the nation.)

Zinn, Howard. *A People's History of the United States: 1492 to the Present*. New York: Harper/Collins, 2003. (Another text that emphasizes social history.)

# Seven Steps to Make Essay Writing Easy

## CHAPTER 3

- Analyzing the question
- Collecting information
- Developing a thesis
- Writing an introduction
- Preparing the body of the essay
- Drafting a conclusion
- Reviewing your response

**A** good essay style is the key to success on the Advanced Placement United States History exam. This may appear to be an extreme statement, but it is true; *essays count 50 percent of your AP grade*.

You may be well trained at analyzing documents, and you may have mastered the factual content of American history, but if you cannot express yourself in writing, the reader of your exam paper will never know how much you understand and how much work you have done. Over two-thirds of the exam involves writing and determines 50 percent of your grade. The required DBQ is allotted 60 minutes and the two free-response questions 35 minutes each. In determining your score, the DBQ is given a weight of 45 and the two essays 27.5 each. So you can see how important it is to do well on the essays if you want to get a good grade on the exam.

Because of this, in Chapters 4–11 in Part Two we will consider different types of essay questions used on the Advanced Placement examination. There are many ways in which essay questions may be phrased and it is important to understand how they differ.

> **STUDY TIP**
>
> A good thesis is essential for an essay. It sets your essay apart from others.

## THE ESSAY QUESTION

The term *essay* is often used to mean a composition or a piece of writing in which a question is answered. However, by definition an essay is more. It is a literary, analytical composition expressing the writer's viewpoint on a single subject. An essay is not a rambling piece of writing that answers a question.

An essay is

1. literary
2. analytical or interpretive
3. on a single subject
4. the personal viewpoint of the author

All four of these points are important for you to understand about the essay, but the idea that the essay presents a personal viewpoint is most significant. We will refer to this personal viewpoint as the thesis[1] of the essay, and we want you to develop your personal opinion on each essay topic presented in this book. Your thesis will distinguish your essay answer from those of other students and how well you convince the reader that your view is correct will determine the grade you receive for your essay.

## *Evaluate This Statement* Question

Essay questions may be phrased in many different ways using such key words as *evaluate, compare, contrast, analyze,* and *assess.* As an introduction to essay writing, we will first look at an *Evaluate This Statement* question. In the *Evaluate This Statement* question the test designer presents a statement that is controversial. The word *Evaluate* is crucial in this type of question. The student must be prepared to judge the validity of the statement, to weigh the pros and cons, and to reject or accept the truth of the statement after analysis. Therefore, you must first read the statement and be certain that you understand what it says, then you decide what your opinion on the statement is—that is the evaluation. Your opinion provides your thesis, which you must prove using evidence you can recall.

This *Evaluate This Statement* essay question deals with the geography of the colonial regions. Two sample introductory paragraphs are presented and then analyzed. Next, two complete essay answers to the question are presented and analyzed. From these analyses some general guides for the writing of essays are presented. You should follow these guidelines throughout your study.

### SAMPLE QUESTION

"The geographic conditions of the three major areas of English settlement in America—New England, the mid-Atlantic region, and the South—were the primary factors in determining the differences in the colonial way of life in these three areas." Evaluate this statement.

### Sample Introduction 1

Virginia had a fairly mild climate and fertile soil in the tidewater area where many rivers supplied transportation to the plantations. The mid-Atlantic region also had fertile soil, but it lacked the rivers into the interior to aid transportation and the winters were less mild. With cold winters and hot summers, New England was climatically the least attractive of the three colonial regions, and the soil was very rocky. Therefore, New Englanders turned to business and the sea in order to make a living.

### Sample Introduction 2

Geography is an important factor in the lives of all people. However, to say that geography accounts for the differences in the colonial way of life in the three areas of English settlement—New England, the mid-Atlantic, and the South—is an exaggeration. The relations with the mother country, the different reasons for settlement, and especially the different types of settlers had a major impact on the colonial way of life.

---

[1]The American Heritage Dictionary defines *thesis* as "1. a proposition . . . that is maintained by argument. 2. a dissertation advancing an original point of view as a result of research."

## Comments on Sample Introduction 1

Sample Introduction 1 is a poor, ineffective response to the given question. It clearly illustrates the greatest problem students have in writing essay answers—the problem of analysis of the question. Under the pressure of limited time, students too often begin their writing without considering what they are being asked, how they should organize their response, and what their opinion (their thesis) is on the topic. Such a response can lead to disaster on the Advanced Placement examination. Let us look at this introduction and see what the student has done.

The student has immediately grabbed the idea of three regions and focused on an example of one, Virginia, and in the first sentence has proceeded to present three items of information connected with geography—climate, soil, rivers. The student demonstrates good factual information, referring to "tidewater" Virginia and to the plantation economy. In the second and third sentences, general information is presented about the two other regions. There is a structure to the paragraph, to these three sentences, and to the way they are constructed. You might wonder, therefore, why this paragraph is being criticized as an introduction. The problem, of course, is that the writer has not indicated what the question is. There is no evaluation and no personal view or thesis presented. The writer does not understand the purpose of an introduction to an essay.

> **STUDY TIP**
>
> Practice writing opening paragraphs. First impressions are important.

---

### PARAGRAPH POINTERS

An effective introductory paragraph must answer two questions:
1. What is the topic? (for example, a statement of the topic or issue under consideration or, simply, the question rephrased)
2. What is the author's opinion on the topic? (for example, the author's thesis)

An excellent introductory paragraph will also contain
3. a rather broad, attention-catching comment on the topic
4. limited factual information because the facts should be saved for the body of the essay

---

The most effective introductory or opening paragraphs have the thesis as the last sentence of the paragraph, and the earlier sentences present the question and a broad comment on the general topic. Now with these guides in mind look at the last sentence of Sample Introduction 1 and decide what thesis or personal opinion this student is presenting. Is this sentence the thesis of the essay? Reread the paragraph. Is there a statement of what the author believes or is trying to prove anywhere in the paragraph? Can you tell what the topic is? If you cannot determine that the topic is a comparison of the geographic features of New England, the South, and the mid-Atlantic states, and you can find no personal opinion stated, you would agree with the author that this is a poor introduction. This illustration should impress upon you the importance of that first step in writing any essay—*analyzing the question.*

### Comments on Sample Introduction 2

Now consider Sample Introduction 2. What factors distinguish Introduction 2 from Introduction 1? Can you determine what the topic under consideration is for the second introduction? Can you determine what that writer's opinion is on the topic?

Sample Introduction 2 is one type of effective introductory paragraph for an essay. In the first sentence a broad comment on the general topic of the question—geographic influences in history—is introduced. This catches your attention. The specific topic is presented in the second sentence, and the author's personal opinion, or the thesis of the essay, is presented in the last half of that sentence and in the third sentence. This introduction answers the two questions that should be dealt with in every essay in the introductory paragraph.

Now let us look at the body or remainder of the two sample answers to this same essay question. As you read the body of sample essays 1 and 2, first pay particular attention to the organizational structure used by each writer. Second, consider the way specific information is used in each essay.

### Sample Essay 1

The Pilgrims were the first settlers in New England. They farmed, taught by the Indian Squanto, and as a result of their production, they celebrated the first Thanksgiving. The later Puritan settlers based their life around the church and lived very strict and limited lives. Because they believed that God rewarded those who worked hard, the Puritans were very industrious. Boston became a thriving seaport and many merchants were soon involved in the triangular trade with England or Africa, the West Indies, and Boston, trading slaves, sugar, and rum. Lumber for ships of the English navy also made fortunes for many Bostonians.

Tobacco was the crop that produced the wealth of Virginia. Rice and indigo were important in South Carolina as fortunes were made there in the 18th century by plantation owners. The southerners sold their crops to England and in return imported fine English furniture and china. Some of the plantations in Virginia, such as Westover, rivaled the finest English homes and showed that the southern colonies had come a long way from the log houses of Jamestown. The Virginia plantation owners imported blacks from Africa to work the tobacco fields as slaves, while the owners developed the first legislative body in America in the House of Burgesses.

Pennsylvania, in the mid-Atlantic region, had its own system of government. The colony was the private estate of William Penn. He ruled it as such, but because he was a Quaker, he allowed religious toleration in the colony. Pennsylvania prospered, with many small farms producing staple crops. When Ben Franklin came to Philadelphia, he worked as a printer, showing how advanced Philadelphia was as a city. The city was well planned with straight streets and fine buildings.

In this paper I have tried to show how different the colonies were. Virginia was the best place to live because it was easiest to make a living on the plantations. New England and Pennsylvania were not as good, although many people in both colonies made money in trade.

### Sample Essay 2

The majority of settlers in New England came there for religious reasons—the Pilgrims to separate from the Church of England and the Puritans to purify the church. Later settlements such as those founded by Roger Williams and Anne

Hutchinson were established essentially for religious reasons. This fact colored the colonists' outlook on life and led to such events as the great preaching of Cotton Mather in the Massachusetts Bay Colony and the Salem witch trials. The emphasis upon religion and the Bible required that people could read and led to public-supported schools and the founding of Harvard College. The Puritan view of life held that work was essential and success God-given. Therefore, the New Englanders were driven to seek employment and use their abundant resource—lumber—and experience with the sea to become sailors and merchants in the triangular trade. New Englanders sold rum in Africa, brought slaves to the West Indies, and imported sugar or molasses to New England for the production of rum. English mercantilist policies attempted to control this trade. Arguments developed that affected colonial life. Of course, geography provided the harbors and the lumber for ships involved in the triangular trade and for the British navy, but it was their religion that was most important in setting the lifestyle of New Englanders.

Virginia's plantation-based lifestyle was representative of the South. One might consider that soil and climate determined it. That is partly true, but what was crucial in Virginia was the London Company's motivation in founding the colony—to make a profit. Until tobacco was discovered and a market was found in England, Virginians struggled. Once a money-making product was found—it could as easily have been gold, which would have greatly changed the lifestyle—Virginia's future was determined. Slaves, large farms or plantations, a close connection with England—sons were sent there for education and plantation homes such as Westover were built on Georgian models—all developed as a result of economic motivation and the finding of a cash product. Geography may have determined the product, but the type of people and their contacts with England helped determine the lifestyle.

Pennsylvania, in the mid-Atlantic region, was founded at a time of economic prosperity, which allowed the colony to grow rapidly. William Penn, a Quaker, was an idealist who believed in religious toleration. This attracted numerous Germans to the colony. Many became small farmers in the rich valleys—a geographic factor—but it was Philadelphia that typified the colony. Here, merchants flourished in the well-planned port city. The Quakers believed in equality and provided good hospitals and charity for the poor, setting an example followed later by the United States. Because of his religious convictions, Penn set very liberal laws for the colony, and a group of elected officials helped the proprietor run the colony. Thus it was the attitudes of the settlers and of Penn himself, more than the geographic conditions, which determined the colonial way of life in Pennsylvania.

The colonial way of life differed in the three areas of settlement. The types of people who settled and their reasons for colonizing—religious or economic— played a key role in determining these differences. Of course geography—climate, ports, soil, and available crops—affected what people could do, but it was the people themselves who made the difference. The settlers not the geography determined the colonial way of life as we do ours.

## Comments on Sample Essays

It is clear that each writer followed the easy yet effective method of organizing material by geographic areas. It should also be clear that after that, the writer of Essay 1 simply presented factual information as it occurred to him with little attempt to relate the facts to each other and with no attempt to relate these facts to the topic. The writer of Essay 2, however, has organized material within each paragraph to follow the same pattern; motivation for settlement, effect of motivation on lifestyle, an acknowledgment of the role of geography. He or she also continually relates the ideas to the thesis and to the overall topic.

To illustrate this point, prepare an outline of the second answer, following traditional outline form. The form is as follows:

I.  Major Topic 1
  A.  Primary evidence A
    1.  Secondary evidence to support A
      a.  Tertiary evidence to support A-1
  B.  Primary evidence B
    1.  Secondary evidence to support B
      a.  Tertiary evidence to support B-1
II.  Major Topic 2
  A.  Primary evidence A
    1.  Secondary evidence to support A
      a.  Tertiary evidence to support A-1

. . . and so forth.

Basically, outlines simply provide an organizational format or structure. A formal outline of the body of Essay 2 would look like this:

I.  New England
  A.  Why settlement?—Religion
    1.  Cotton Mather
    2.  Salem witches
    3.  read
      a.  public school
      b.  Harvard
  B.  Lifestyle: Success for God
    1.  work
      a.  resources
      b.  sea
      c.  merchants
    2.  triangular trade
  C.  Struggle with England: Mercantilism
  D.  Geography
    1.  harbors
    2.  lumber
II.  Virginia (the South)
  A.  Why settlement?—Profit
    1.  London Co.
    2.  tobacco
  B.  Lifestyle
    1.  slaves
    2.  English education
    3.  plantations
  C.  Geography

III. Pennsylvania
   A. Why settlement?—Penn's idealism
      1. economic prosperity
      2. religious toleration
   B. Lifestyle
      1. Philadelphia
         a. port
         b. equality
         c. hospitals
      2. religion
         a. liberal laws
         b. legislature
   C. Geography
IV. Conclusion
   A. Different lifestyles
      1. types of people
      2. reasons for settling
   B. Geography
      1. climate
      2. ports
      3. soil
      4. crops
   C. Settlers made lifestyle; so do we

As the outline illustrates, Essay 2 has a very clear structure and organization. If you outlined the answer for Essay 1, it would be hard to see the structure. Making outlines, either formal or informal (see Step Two of the Seven Steps in Essay Writing) is an important skill to have and a great help in creating good essay answers. For every question there are different ways to organize an answer. For this question you could organize by geographic region, by lifestyle, or by climate.

## Summary of Comments on Essay Answers 1 and 2

The writers of answers 1 and 2 are both knowledgeable students. They both include the type of effective factual information required for Advanced Placement work. They are aware of details, and their sentence structure is sound. The writer of Essay 2, however, has demonstrated two additional skills that clearly mark him or her as an above-average student. These skills are that of organization and analysis. The writer of Essay 1 clearly demonstrates a lack of analytical work, and the reader is left wondering if the student understood the question. Because of this, the student would receive an average grade on the Advanced Placement examination, while the writer of Essay 2 would receive a very good one.

# Seven Steps in Essay Writing

## STEP ONE—ANALYZING THE QUESTION

**In writing an essay answer, the first step is always to analyze the question.** Without a clear understanding of what the question is, you cannot possibly write an adequate answer. Let us now look at the question again.

### SAMPLE QUESTION

"The geographic conditions of the three major areas of English settlement in America—New England, the mid-Atlantic region, and the South—were the primary factors in determining the differences in the colonial way of life in these three areas." Evaluate this statement.

## The Meaning of Evaluate

The question presents a statement and then asks the student to evaluate the statement. According to the dictionary, *evaluate* means to determine the value of or to appraise carefully. In other words, the question is asking the student to determine the value measured in terms of historical accuracy of the statement. Does it express what you believe happened in the past or is there some truth that must be qualified?

The *Evaluate This Statement* format is a popular type of essay question. It presents a statement or idea and forces the student or writer to judge the suitability of the statement as a thesis. In many ways, it is one of the easiest forms of questions for the student. The statement can be accepted or rejected as the thesis of the essay. The writer is not required to express a personal opinion or thesis in his or her own words. As you will see later, the formulation of one's own thesis is often the most difficult aspect of producing good, effective essay answers.

## The Importance of Geography

This particular question presents a thesis involving geographic influences on the development of patterns of living. The general topic of geography or environmental influences on human activity is an important one historically. Most historians have strong opinions on the topic, and every student of history has confronted the question directly or indirectly at some point. Therefore, it is a good topic for the Advanced Placement examination and a good topic with which to begin a study or review of U.S. history. The quotation suggests that the extreme environmentalist interpretation of history—that the colonial way of life was *determined* by geographic influences—is the correct view.

The quotation assumes there were three different geographic regions in the English colonies and a different way of life in each. It uses general terms for these three regions—South, mid-Atlantic, New England—so the writer is forced either to supply specific names for colonies in these regions or to deal in generalizations. It is always better to be specific, so you should immediately focus on one or two colonies in each region. Most histories of colonial America emphasize Virginia in the South, Pennsylvania in the mid-Atlantic region, and Massachusetts Bay Colony in New England as typical of the three regions.

## The Colonial Way of Life

Thus, having decided on specific illustrations for the three regions mentioned in the question, the next step in the analysis would be to focus on the phrase *colonial way of life*. This phrase suggests social conditions and relations as opposed to political structures. It reflects the Development Committee's interest in social and cultural factors.

What was the colonial way of life in each of these three colonies? That is, how did the people live and make a living? A few ideas should come quickly to mind. Then you must decide if geography was the primary factor in *determining* that way of life or if other factors helped determine it. If you have a strong opinion about geography's importance or lack of importance and some evidence of both the geography and the way of life, then you may decide that this is a question you wish to answer.

You have now completed the analysis of the question. You have taken the question apart, considered the definition of words and decided what is being asked. You have identified some evidence. You are ready to proceed.

This process may have seemed simple or obvious but it is often overlooked in the rush of an exam. It is crucial that you develop the habit of analyzing every question in detail to be certain that you understand

**the words used,**

**the evidence needed,** and

**the question asked.**

## STEP TWO—COLLECTING AND SORTING INFORMATION

**Once you know what the question asks, you must start to collect and sort your information.** The best way to do this is to create an informal outline. For this question, write down on a piece of paper the name of each colony you have decided to use as an illustration. Under each colony write a few simple phrases illustrating the way of life in the colony and a few brief phrases illustrating the geographic conditions. The notes might look something like the box shown on page 28 but you may have a different style, such as mapping, for informal note taking. (The columns and letters are referred to later in the text; they would not be part of your actual note taking.)

## Notes for Answering Question

| **Column M** | **Column O** |
| (Way of Life) | (Geography) |

### Virginia

e. plantations
r. Church of England
   London Co. for Eco. Reasons
e. Slaves
p. House of Burgesses

warm mild
river transport
tobacco
good soil

### Penn.

e. merchants
r. Quakers/Germans
p. Wm. Penn, proprietor
   melting pot

mix of S. and N.E.
little river transport
grains and vegetables

### Mass Bay

e. merchants/sailors
r. Puritans
p. town meetings

cold
rocky soil
lumber
harbors

You have collected your information in this informal outline. You now need to sort it to find a way of using it most effectively in your answer. Your goal is to relate the way of life to the geography and the obvious approach suggested is to write about each colony separately. But how to organize the information in the paragraphs? The idea of including religion, politics, and economics in your answer should jump at you from the notes. As you look at the brief notes in **Column M**, you will see that **r** under each region refers to religion, **p** to political developments or organization, and **e** to economic activities. Within each paragraph you can present evidence from these three areas in the same order, thus giving fine structure to the paragraphs. How would you organize the information in **Column O**?

## Other Ways to Organize the Answer

There are other ways of organizing the answer to this question. You might organize your answer with a section on religion in all three regions, followed by sections on political developments and economic activities. This organization would appear more complicated and less effective, but it illustrates the variety of ways in which one can organize answers. For this answer the best organization is by colony or region as done in Sample Essay 2.

As you collect information and sort through the facts, be sure that you

**write an informal outline,**
**group ideas by letters to provide structure,** and
**consider different organizational patterns.**

After you have analyzed the question and collected and sorted information, you are ready for the third step in essay writing—developing your thesis.

## STEP THREE—DEVELOPING YOUR THESIS

As mentioned previously, every essay *must* have a thesis. **Your thesis is your personal opinion on the given topic and should be included in the opening paragraph.** When you look over the information you have gathered, a thesis will usually, but not always, become clear. You must take the time to think through just what you believe on the topic and how you will prove it with the information you have. On an exam you do not have the luxury of doing further research to gather more information, so you must rely on what you have written down to prove whatever opinion you state as your thesis. What is your opinion on this sample question?

> **STUDY TIP**
>
> The thesis is crucial!!

The writer of Sample Essay 1 agreed with the statement but never clearly stated that in the essay. That is the great weakness of Essay 1. Do you see that? Does this criticism make sense to you?

The writer of Sample Essay 2 did not believe that the statement made complete sense and saw an alternative explanation or cause for the differences in the way of life of the three colonial regions. In the last sentence of the introductory paragraph, the writer presents a personal opinion or thesis on the issue only partly agreeing with the statement. It is very important to realize that **you may disagree** with any given statement. The grade on an essay depends on how well you prove your opinion and not on the opinion. What would your thesis be for this question? Would you accept the view expressed in the quotation after analyzing the question, or would you qualify it, as the author of Essay 2 has done, or would you reject it totally?

As you develop your thesis, remember that you should

**present your opinion in every essay** and
**put your opinion in the opening paragraph.**

## STEP FOUR—WRITING THE INTRODUCTION

**In many ways the introductory or opening paragraph is the most important one of any essay.** It is here that the reader gets the first idea of you, the writer. As in friendships, the first impression remains with one. As stated above, an effective opening paragraph must answer two questions: What is the topic? and What is the author's opinion on the topic? When these two questions are not answered, the reader is confused. Usually, the statement of the topic comes in the first part of the paragraph, and the writer's opinion or thesis is the last sentence of a paragraph.

In Sample Introduction 2, the question is quoted and the author's opinion, without stating it as "my opinion" or "I believe," is clearly stated in the word *exaggerated.* The thesis then follows in the last sentence and is clear to the reader.

This introductory paragraph also illustrates another very important aspect of a good essay introduction. It begins with a broad, general comment on the topic, which is meant to catch the reader's attention, slowly narrows the focus of the topic to the specific question, and then narrows it more to the thesis. The good opening paragraph is like a lighthouse or a flashlight beam.

The beam catches the viewer in its broad beam or sweep and then brings his or her attention to the source of the light. Your introduction should always work like a lighthouse beam, starting broad enough in scope to get the reader's interest, and then pulling attention to a specific point—your thesis.

An effective introductory or opening paragraph is one in which the writer

1. identifies the topic

2. states a personal opinion and

3. catches the reader's attention in a broad beam similar to a lighthouse.

## STEP FIVE—WRITING THE BODY OF THE ESSAY

Once the crucial introduction is completed, you are ready for the fifth step: *the writing of the body of the essay*. **It is in this section that the factual information to prove your thesis should be presented.** The facts should be organized in a logical sequence. Each major set of facts should be presented in a separate paragraph. These paragraphs might be considered as the separate batteries that power a flashlight. Each must work separately, yet they must be connected at the contact point if the light is to work. The batteries are held together by the casing that provides structure and body for the flashlight, just as the facts in paragraphs provide structure for your essay. If the essay is to work, it must have a thesis—the light, paragraphs—the batteries that are connected, and a conclusion—the end cap.

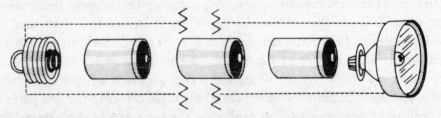

There are many ways to achieve connections between paragraphs—similar ideas, linking words (such as *however, therefore, but*), or repetition of an aspect of the question. Look again at Essay 2. Paragraphs 1 and 2 are linked by repeating the word *lifestyle*; 2 and 3 by the idea of economic conditions; and 3 and 4 by repeating a phrase.

All the paragraphs present information related to the thesis. The essay works. As in a flashlight, the connections are made, the beam shines and catches your attention.

Often, in defending a position, you will come across several arguments that can be used against your view. If you have time and are able to refute any of these arguments, you should introduce them and refute them immediately. Then present your strong facts in the succeeding paragraphs, ending with your strongest point. This is a good lawyer's or debater's technique, and in your essay you are like a lawyer arguing a case. You want the reader to believe your position—your case.

When you jotted down your brief notes as part of Step Two, you were collecting information to prove your thesis. Look at these brief notes and arrange them in the most effective sequence for proving your thesis by numbering the items 1, 2, 3, etc.

> **TIP**
> Brief notes provide a structure.

The notes jotted down on the colony of Virginia might logically be presented in the order numbered 1–6. You might leave out the House of Burgesses and the Church of England, as they seem to have little relation to geography. You could include river transportation as number 7 as a link to Pennsylvania's lack of rivers. This is the way you will use your brief notes to help write the body of your essay.

| Column M | Column O |
|---|---|
| (Way of Life) | (Geography) |
| *Virginia* | |
| 5. plantations | 2. warm mild |
| Church of England | 7. river transport |
| 4. London Co. for Eco. Reasons | 3. tobacco |
| 6. Slaves | 1. good soil |
| House of Burgesses | |

The body of an essay consists of

**separate paragraphs that are connected** and
**information that proves the thesis.**

## STEP SIX—WRITING THE CONCLUSION

When you have completed the body of the paper, you are ready for the sixth step: *writing the conclusion*. **The conclusion of the essay is the second most important paragraph.** The conclusion holds the essay together and might be compared to the cap on the end of a flashlight, that holds the batteries in and forces them into contact. Without a good cap, the flashlight does not work; without a good conclusion, the essay does not work.

> **TIP**
> The conclusion holds the essay together. It is *not* just a summary.

The conclusion should bring the reader back to the question and back to the thesis. An excellent preparation for writing the conclusion is to read through your introduction and the body of your essay before writing the conclusion. Then, keeping in mind what you have said and what your thesis is, write a paragraph that reintroduces the thesis and the topic without merely repeating the introduction. If possible, you should end your conclusion with reference to the broad general idea in the first sentence of your introduction or with an indication of the applicability of your thesis to other situations, thus leaving the reader with the idea that you have proven something of general significance.

**A helpful approach to make certain that your conclusion agrees with your introduction is to go back and read your introduction just before you write the concluding paragraph.** Make sure to include in the conclusion the thesis that you introduced in the opening paragraph. It may be paraphrased or stated exactly the same.

There are two things one should avoid doing in the conclusion. The first thing to avoid is presenting a summary of all you've included. There is nothing worse than the conclusion that begins, "Now I have shown that . . .," yet many students end an essay this way. It is simplistic, boring, does nothing to help your case, and antagonizes the reader. If you have "shown that," then it should be obvious to the reader and you do not have to tell it again. Secondly, do not introduce new evidence in the conclusion—evidence that will help prove your thesis. Get all the evidence into the body of the paper. The conclusion is simply your flashlight cap, and it is not one of the batteries.

With these two negative warnings in mind, you might wonder how you can possibly write a conclusion. The conclusion to Essay 2 provides a good example to look at and follow. The writer rephrases the question, clearly indicates his or her differences with it, and ends emphasizing the significance of people as was done in the opening. The conclusion to Essay 1 is a poor one because the writer begins by saying what he or she had done, introduces new materials, does not reintroduce the topic or the thesis, and makes no attempt to relate his or her ideas to other situations. Other good conclusions will be presented in later chapters.

In summary, when writing a conclusion

1. restate the ideas in the introductory paragraph

2. put a tight "cap" on the essay

3. do not introduce new facts

4. do not merely list what has been said

## STEP SEVEN—READING OVER YOUR ESSAY

**When you have completed writing your essay, there is one step left—reading it over to check the spelling, style, and consistency.** It is very helpful if you start reading with your conclusion and then read the introduction, checking to see that they agree. Often, students who have not analyzed the question well and who have not developed an effective thesis will contradict themselves in these two paragraphs. Make sure you have not done that. Then read the body of the paper and the conclusion again. Correct any spelling or punctuation errors. Finally, check to see if the paragraphs link together smoothly.

The final step in writing a good essay is to read over the essay to check for

1. agreement between opinion expressed in the opening and conclusion

2. clarity of expression

3. spelling and grammar

4. links between paragraphs

> ### ELIMINATE THE "I"
>
> There is one last item to consider about the essay style. Most essayists avoid the use of the personal pronoun *I*. The reader assumes that everything in the essay is what the writer believes, so "I think" or "I believe" is redundant. The usual pronouns used are those of the third-person editorial *we* or the impersonal *one*. Although there are times when an author uses the *I* with great effect, it is rare. Stylistically it is better for the beginner to avoid using *I* in essay writing.

As you work through this book, studying and reviewing for the Advanced Placement examination, use these seven steps to make essay writing easy. They should become habit for you so that you do not have to think about them. This technique will help you to write effective, well-organized, and factually sound essays. Follow these seven steps as you prepare essay answers for questions in this book. Check the organization of your essay by making formal outlines of your answers until you are satisfied that your answers are well organized.

> **TIP**
>
> Use the seven steps for success.

## Quick Review

To recapitulate, the seven steps to make essay writing easy are

1. Analyze the question
2. Collect and sort information
3. Develop your thesis
4. Write the introduction
5. Write the body of the essay
6. Write the conclusion
7. Read over the essay

As you use these seven steps, keep in mind the image of the flashlight. It should prove a valuable image for you as you construct your essays.

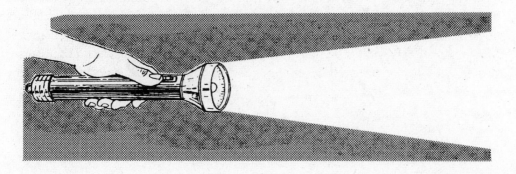

# Colonial America Before 1763

## CHAPTER 4

- The colonial period
- Assessing validity/evaluate questions
- Chronology questions

The foundations for the nation were laid during the colonial period. If this is accepted, then in studying the colonial period an important focus would be to identify these foundations. The more one can identify links among periods and begin to develop meaningful cause-and-effect relationships, the more effective a study of the past will be. The identification of these relationships should provide the basic pattern for the study of the colonial period before 1763 and for all the study done for the AP United States History exam.

The differences between the colonists and the British, which evolved over the 150 years of settlement, reached a climax with the Declaration of Independence. These differences in social, cultural, political, military, and economic attitudes should form the basis of a study of colonial history. It should include information on the Native American cultures and the clash between them and the European cultures, especially the English, Spanish, and French. Today some courses in United States history begin with the Treaty of Paris in 1763, which ended the French and Indian War. In these courses a quick look should be taken at the origin of the differences in the early colonial period. The Advanced Placement examination places less emphasis on the history of America before 1763 than on other periods. However, some information on colonial history before 1763, on pre-Columbian, and on Hispanic culture of the Southwest is expected.

## CONNECTIONS WITH OTHER TIME PERIODS

In studying this period, the connections between the colonial period and later periods of United States history should be emphasized. For instance, the concept of a written constitution is rooted in colonial history as illustrated by such items as the Mayflower Compact, colonial charters, and the Albany Plan. There is therefore an important connection between the U.S. Constitution and colonial history and it is this type of information that you should explore.

There will be multiple-choice questions on the colonial period before 1763, and there may be a free-response question for which information from this period will be necessary. Although the sample essay questions presented below are restricted to the colonial period before 1763, the information required for effective answers is related to many later developments.

Among the important developments of the colonial period that have a bearing on later history are

1. Pre-Columbian Native American social and cultural developments
2. The reasons for European exploration, the areas explored, and the conflicts that ensued
3. The relations between the Native Americans and the colonists in all regions of settlement
4. The geographic differences among the regions of settlement and the motivation for the settlement of the different European colonies, including Spanish and French
5. The economic development of each colony and the English mercantilist system
6. The development of social and cultural attitudes within each colony and the resulting differences among the colonies and the Native Americans
7. The attempts at unity among various colonies
8. The establishment of local political institutions in each colony
9. The westward expansion of each colony
10. The military conflicts between the English settlers and both the Native Americans and other European settlers

> **TIP**
>
> As in each chapter, factual information relating to themes can be found in Part 4.

## SAMPLE ESSAY QUESTION—ASSESS THE VALIDITY/EVALUATE THIS STATEMENT

In each chapter we will present and analyze different types of essay questions. We will also present in each chapter a sample answer to at least one essay question. **As stated above, the information in these sample answers is all accurate. Therefore, each answer provides important knowledge of the time period of the chapter and serves as a review for the exam.** The essay questions presented in this chapter are examples of the *Evaluate This Statement* form discussed in Part One and a very popular variation of that type, the *Assess the Validity* form.

In Part One we presented two sample answers to a question dealing with the colonial period. The following question deals with that era, but it goes beyond the colonial period and calls for information from the period of the American Revolution.

> ### SAMPLE QUESTION
>
> In the 1600s the major issues of U.S. colonial history revolved around theological issues. In the 1700s the major issues revolved around political issues. Assess the validity of this statement.

### Comments on Sample Question

Recalling our Seven Steps in Essay Writing, we must first analyze the statement. For some students the understanding of centuries is difficult, and this would be the first matter to clear up. In the Christian dating method, those dates since the birth of Christ are designated as A.D. Because we must designate the years 1–99 as the first century A.D. or the first 100 years, the second century begins with the year 100 and goes to 199 even though the dates begin with one. All A.D. centuries are one number higher than the first or first two digits of the number of the year. Therefore, dates in the 17th century are those years starting with 16, so that 1607, 1620, 1688 are all 17th-century dates, and 1701 and 1756 are 18th-century dates. Until that matter is clear, the question cannot be analyzed.

The next concern in analyzing this question is to determine the meaning of the words *theological* and *political*. As you study American history, be certain you understand the specialized vocabulary used and build your vocabulary. To help you, a glossary of important terms is included in the appendix of this book.

*Theological* comes from the Greek words *theos*, meaning God, and *logos*, meaning word or speak. *Theology*, therefore, means speaking about God and *theological* is the adjective form of the word. Theological issues are issues dealing with God or religion. *Political* is an adjective. It means pertaining to the conduct of government. It too has a Greek origin, coming from the word *politikos*, meaning of the citizens. Students often find it helpful to learn the origins of words; it is an excellent way to build vocabulary.

Once you are certain of the meaning of the words and time period, it should be clear the statement suggests that the great concerns of one century revolved about religious issues while the concerns of the next were political. You are asked to assess the validity of the statement. *Assess* means to determine the value of something as a tax collector assesses the value of property to determine how much tax a person should pay. You must determine what value or truth there is to this statement. Is it true or only partly true or is it false? What do you think? Following the Seven Steps in Essay Writing, you will next want to jot down information about the theological and political issues in two columns labeled 17th century and 18th century. Once you have done that you'll be ready to write your thesis, since you will have determined your opinion on this topic. Then you will go on to write your essay following Steps Four through Six. You may wish to write your own answer before proceeding to read the following sample answer.

## Sample Answer

Religion and politics always seem to be important issues in people's lives. Beginning with the first colonists in America during the 17th century, theology was an important issue. Indeed, the greatest reason that many of the colonists had for moving to America was the desire to find freedom of religion in a new land. Many of the ideals that developed in the colonies founded for religious reasons were later, in the 18th century, the ideals for which colonists fought political battles.

The Puritans were a prime example of religious development in America. They had become social outcasts in England, where they had little voice in matters, and so they migrated to America. There they set up the Massachusetts Bay Colony, which flourished. With religious motivation to fulfill a "covenant" with God to establish the "New Jerusalem," a successful model colony in America, they laid many of the foundations that would later be of great political importance. They established a two-part representative body or legislature elected by the people and had a single leader, or executive, who for many years was John Winthrop. Winthrop might easily have pre-

**STUDY TIP**

There were important religious issues in the 18th century as seen in the Great Awakening. Do not ignore them.

served all legislative power to himself, but he did not, perhaps inspired by a theological view that believers within the community are all equal.

The Massachusetts Bay Colony had many conflicts that revolved about the meaning of the word *believer*. With the Puritans, if you did not agree with them, you were damned and could not live in their "perfect society." People such as Roger Williams became involved in these conflicts and were forced to leave the colony. He founded Rhode Island. The poor witches of Salem show how theological issues dominated the century.

Other colonies also were involved in theological conflicts; the Quaker William Penn founded Pennsylvania for religious freedom, and the Catholic Lord Baltimore supported religious toleration in Maryland when it was not the popular stand. Even Virginia had religious Blue Laws and the colony grew rapidly as Church of Englanders fled England during the rule of the Puritan Cromwell. The century was full of religious conflict, both in England and the colonies.

Under the influence of Puritan ideas as well as the philosophies of John Locke and leaders of the European Enlightenment, legislatures were formed in each of the colonies, and charters, though requiring approval by the king, were written. Objections began to arise when the lack of power of these representative legislatures was felt.

After 1763, when England had ended its Seven Years' War with France, it turned its attention to America to try to find a way of paying the expense of war. Internal taxes, such as the excise tax on paper (Stamp Act) to which there was strong objection, and external taxes on trade were enacted by Parliament without the consent of the colonial legislatures. Puritan tradition was one force that warned America that "taxation without representation" was wrong. The theological issues of the 17th century—who was a believer and could live in a colony? —gave way to the political issues of the 18th century—who could control the government of the colonies? When the Acts of Trade and Navigation were enforced and other acts were enacted, especially the Declaratory Act, emphasizing the power of Parliament to tax and legislate without the consent of the colonists, the colonists felt that their political rights had been infringed upon, and they revolted.

The period of the Articles of Confederation was a testing period in American history. There was trust in the workability of a true democracy, and though an attempt at this was made, the federal government, unable to tax or enforce any laws, was too weak and could not tie the nation together. The political issue had become one of how to set up a new government.

The Constitution brought all the political ideas of Americans together in compromise. Puritan ideals were certainly present here, but the issues were not theological but political. The political conflicts between financial and agrarian influences would persist for many years, but a new government was formed that allowed the way for political issues to be compromised. This had not been done with 17th-century theological issues.

In the 17th century, theological issues were not compromised, but in the struggle over these issues ideas of identity and self-government were developed that became the great political issues Americans fought for in the 18th century. Religion and politics were important colonial issues.

What is your evaluation of the above essay? What are its strong points and its weak points? You could make a formal outline of the answer in order to identify the structure of the essay. Once you have made your own evaluation of the essay, you should compare your notes with the following teacher comments.

## Teacher Comments on Sample Answer

"The student answering this question on theological and political issues has written an adequate but not an outstanding paper. The paper includes enough factual information to provide a very good answer, but the student fails to use this information to respond to the question asked. The student does not understand the difference between reciting information and using information to support a thesis.

"The student has written an introductory paragraph and has presented a thesis in the last sentence of the introduction. The thesis is interesting and could be developed, but as worded, the thesis does not relate to the 'great issues' of the 17th and 18th centuries. What is suggested is that the 'great' theological issues of the 17th century became the 'great' political issues of the 18th. Unfortunately, in the body of the paper this relationship is not clearly explored. Instead, the student describes important theological incidents in the 17th century, such as the Salem witch trials, and only briefly focuses on issues. Still, the 17th-century material is better presented than the 18th-century information.

"In the 18th century, the student too often loses sight of the relationship he or she is trying to establish between the issues in the two centuries. Although the student refers to Puritan ideas in the section, he or she falls into the all-too-open trap of listing information without using it to advance the argument. When discussing the Articles of Confederation and the Constitution, it seems the student is most interested in presenting his or her knowledge of the struggle over the development of the U.S. government, and that he or she has forgotten the theological issues of the 17th century, which, according to the original thesis, had become the major political issues of the 18th.

"The student has an adequate conclusion in which the thesis is restated. He or she avoids repeating arguments and also makes an attempt both in the conclusion and introduction to relate the question to a broader time period. The organization follows a clear pattern established by the quotation—chronology. Apparently the student did not consider the possibility of organizing the paper around those issues that were theological in the 17th century and political in the 18th century. Such an organization would appear to have a closer connection to the thesis than the organization used, and it might have helped the paper.

"In the future the student needs to be more careful in analyzing the question and relating information to the question. The student had fully adequate information, and the body of his or her paper has an obvious organization. The student should receive an above average but not a top grade."

Did your analysis develop the same points as the teacher's? If you did not agree, then reread the sample answer and see where you and the teacher diverged.

# Quick Review

**TIP**

Popular questions in recent years ask you to pick two or three specific items on which to focus your analysis or evaluation. The items may be time periods, individuals, concepts, events, etc.

The *Assess the Validity* question has appeared on many recent Advanced Placement examinations. It allows the student great freedom of choice in designing the answer, as the statement may be accepted or rejected and the specific information to be used is determined by the writer.

There are many variations of this basic type of question. The directions may ask you to *evaluate* or *discuss* a statement or generalization, and again the writer has many choices as to what position to take and what evidence to use. The important point is to stay on the subject and evaluate or judge the statement if the direction says to evaluate. If you are asked to discuss, be certain to write about the statement in the essay discussing it using historical evidence. Sometimes more directions will be given, as in the following examples of this type of question.

## Variations on the *Assess the Validity* Type of Question

1. Evaluate this statement as it relates to the years 1763–1776 and indicate to what extent you agree or disagree with it.
2. Assess the validity of this generalization for either 1763–1776 or 1800–1815.
3. Discuss the validity of this quotation as it applies to the presidencies of George Washington, John Adams, and Thomas Jefferson.
4. Judging from evidence drawn from the years 1763–1776 and 1850–1861, assess the validity of this viewpoint.
5. Evaluate the applicability of this quotation to three of the following incidents.

You will want to practice your own writing ability and develop your knowledge of the colonial period by writing essay answers to several of the following questions. These questions, as with all of those presented in this book, are not inclusive of all the issues that might arise on the Advanced Placement examination. These questions are representative examination questions, and they will help you organize your knowledge of American history. These five questions will give you practice with the popular *Assess the Validity* and *Evaluate This Statement* type of essay questions. Remember, this type of question can be used to test material from any period of United States history.

# Practice Essay Questions

1. "The English founded colonies to escape oppression in England." Evaluate this statement as it applies to THREE of the following colonies:

   Massachusetts Bay
   Pennsylvania
   Maryland
   Virginia
   Georgia

2. "Economic issues not religion determined the development of the English colonies in North America." Assess the validity of this quotation as it applies to THREE of the following colonies before 1763:

   Virginia
   Maryland
   Pennsylvania
   Massachusetts Bay
   Rhode Island

3. "Before 1763 British mercantilist policy, while restricting colonial economic development, allowed colonial political life to develop unhampered by the Mother Country." Evaluate this statement.

4. "After 1750, the conflict between the British and the French for domination of the North American continent created a sense of national spirit among the British colonies and created the basis for later unity." Assess the validity of this statement.

5. "As long as the French controlled parts of North America, they accepted the Native American population as equal, whereas the British colonists viewed them as hostile." Evaluate this statement as it relates to the years 1608–1763.

## Comments on Question 1

This is a typical evaluation question that gives you a choice of items on which to focus. Be sure you discuss the correct number of items in your answer (i.e. **read the question carefully**). If you pick Massachusetts Bay, Pennsylvania, and Maryland, you might focus on oppression, but picking Virginia and/or Georgia would require you to introduce other reasons. Virginia was founded primarily for economic reasons and Georgia was founded as a penal colony—a type of jail for English criminals. Always pick those items that you know the most about when given choices like this.

## Comments on Question 2

The second question raises the issue of economic determinism, often called the Marxist view of history because it was first articulated by Karl Marx. One does not have to be a Communist to support this concept. Therefore, you should analyze the question as you would any other and decide for your thesis whether religion or economics was more important in colonial development or if there are other factors to consider. You are given five colonies from which you must pick three to write about. Virginia, Pennsylvania, and Massachusetts Bay are discussed at some length in all textbooks; Maryland and Rhode Island are often less well covered but religion was important in each. Pick the three that will best support your thesis.

## Comments on Question 3

A definite time period is set in the third question, which is also a more complex and perhaps more interesting question. It requires an understanding of specific historic terms—Mother Country—and of a particular historical policy, mercantilism. The question involves a double relationship, and therefore it resembles the sample essay in this chapter. Develop your thesis and decide on an organizing method to avoid being overwhelmed with detailed information.

## Comments on Question 4

Question 4 introduces the topic of war and its impact on society. Military events interest many students and provide an important element in U.S. history, but one should not merely study battles. Here the question forces you to deal with the impact of war on the life of the colonies. The AP exam is much more likely to use military history in this way rather than asking about specific battles. It is suggested you know the general strategy used in fighting wars. But you must also know the causes and results, peace terms, and, most important, the psychological impact upon the people. The time period given focuses attention on the French and Indian War (1756–1763) which ended with the French being forced off the mainland of North America.

## Comments on Question 5

The last question raises an interesting and timely topic, that of British and French racial attitudes as expressed in colonial history. The question assumes a difference in the attitudes of two European colonizing powers, and you need to test this difference. The French were essentially forced out of North America in 1763. The question requires information from different sources to properly evaluate the quotation, so do not be trapped by the word *hostile* into discussing wars and massacres only. Hostility can manifest itself in a variety of ways. The answer should include social and cultural history as well as military. The question, then, becomes a complex one and may be more challenging since it does not deal directly with the topics considered in the usual history book.

These brief analyses should start you on your way to writing effective and well-prepared essays on the five sample topics. Be sure and use the Seven Steps in Essay Writing. The questions will force you to study and review key information from colonial history, which is the information you need to know for the Advanced Placement exam. That is **how** one should prepare for the exam.

## MULTIPLE CHOICE—THE CHRONOLOGY QUESTION

As indicated in the introduction, the Advanced Placement examination includes 80 multiple-choice questions. In each chapter of this book, sample questions dealing with information from the different periods will be presented. Different types of multiple-choice questions will be analyzed in each chapter and the correct answer for each question will be discussed. This is done to stimulate your thinking about different periods and to illustrate the many types of multiple-choice questions.

In this chapter we will look at the most obvious type of multiple-choice question—the type that requires a factual recall of chronological information. Many people find historic dates boring and difficult. Some dates are important, however, and in the Western concept of historical cause and effect, a knowledge of the chronological order of events is essential. You should know important dates, but you must also know the order in which events occurred. As suggested in Part One, the making of time lines dealing with related events can be a very valuable device in studying history.

## Advice on Skipping Questions

One thing to remember is you may make marks on the test booklet. As you eliminate possible answers on a difficult multiple-choice question, you may find putting an X beside the choice or crossing it out to be helpful. You should also skip questions you are uncertain of and return to them. A checkmark by the number will alert you to which questions you skipped. However, after skipping a question, be sure and check that you are placing a black pencil mark in the correct oval for the next question.

---

### SAMPLE QUESTION

Which of the following British colonies was founded last?

(A) Plymouth
(B) Pennsylvania
(C) Georgia
(D) Massachusetts Bay Colony
(E) Virginia

---

### Comments on Sample Question

The correct answer is (C) Georgia. The same question could be phrased, "Which colony was founded first?" or the question could involve the chronological order of legislation, publication of major works, time period of leaders—any grouping that has connection, especially that of cause and effect. (See Chapter 6.) In any case, you must know the chronological order and preferably the dates of the founding of the colonies. This is why a time line is helpful. There is very little you can do with a question of chronology unless you know the chronology. This is the simplest type of multiple-choice question you will find. **While this type of question is rare on the AP exam, the knowledge needed to answer such a simple, direct, factual recall question is key for answering other questions on the AP.**

Study the following multiple-choice questions. How well can you do on them? The various types presented will be analyzed in later chapters. Following the 10 questions are brief analyses of each correct answer.

# Practice Multiple-Choice Questions

1. All of the following important colonial cities are correctly paired with the colony EXCEPT

   (A) Williamsburg—Virginia
   (B) Annapolis—Maryland
   (C) Salem—Rhode Island
   (D) Charleston—South Carolina
   (E) New London—Connecticut

2. Which of the following events occurred last?

   (A) Establishment of elected government in Massachusetts Bay Colony
   (B) Signing of the Mayflower Compact
   (C) Expulsion of Roger Williams from Massachusetts Bay Colony
   (D) Salem Witch Trials
   (E) Decline in Puritan immigration to Massachusetts Bay Colony

3. The chief significance of the Great Awakening was that it

   (A) led to the foundation of colleges
   (B) provided Jonathan Edwards with an opportunity to preach
   (C) was the first genuine unified movement of the American colonists
   (D) revived intolerance
   (E) created new interest in the churches

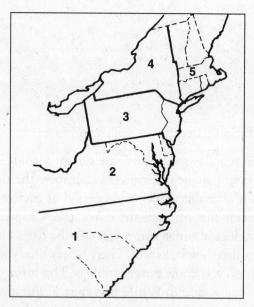

4. In which region was Fort Duquesne colony located?

   (A) 1
   (B) 2
   (C) 3
   (D) 4
   (E) 5

5. The Native Americans did all of the following EXCEPT

   (A) aid the Pilgrims in Plymouth
   (B) split in their support of the French and English in the 18th-century colonial wars
   (C) felt their way of life was threatened by the territorial expansion of the colonists
   (D) converted to Christianity in very limited numbers
   (E) organized effectively to block English expansion west of the Appalachians

6. Which of the following men explored in North America for the French?

   (A) Magellan
   (B) Coronado
   (C) Hudson
   (D) Frobisher
   (E) Champlain

7. The trial of Peter Zenger in New York has often been considered an important step in the development of

   (A) religious toleration
   (B) freedom of the press
   (C) trial by jury
   (D) the right to bear arms
   (E) concepts of privacy

8. Which of the following was NOT an important cause of the French and Indian War?

   (A) Formation of the Ohio Company
   (B) Desire of Massachusetts colonists to clear the French out of Canada
   (C) Washington and Braddock's attack on Fort Duquesne
   (D) trade limitations imposed by the Acts of Trade
   (E) French exploration in the Great Lakes region and westward

9. Which of the following had the LEAST significance in providing experience and concepts that were used by the colonists in their arguments and fight for independence?

   (A) French and Indian War
   (B) New England town meetings
   (C) Use of the Power of the Purse by the Virginia House of Burgesses
   (D) The Albany Plan
   (E) Development by the colonists of crops for export

10. "The hatchet is a hard stone, eight or ten inches in length and three or four in breadth, of an oval form, flatted and rubbed to an edge at one end; near the other end is a groove in which the handle was fastened; and their process to do it was this: When the stone was prepared, they chose a very young sapling, and splitting it near the ground, they forced the hatchet into it, as far as the groove, and left nature to complete the work by the growth of the wood, so as to fill the groove and adhere firmly to the stone. They then cut the sapling off above and below, and the hatchet was fit for use."

The above passage indicates the following about the people who used the process described:

(A) They made tomahawks for military purposes
(B) They had very few tools
(C) They made all their tools from stone
(D) They made intelligent use of their natural surroundings
(E) They were Native Americans

## Answers and Answer Explanations

1. **(C)**    2. **(D)**    3. **(C)**    4. **(C)**
5. **(E)**    6. **(E)**    7. **(B)**    8. **(D)**
9. **(E)**    10. **(D)**

1. **(C)**  Salem in Massachusetts is famous as the location of the colonial witch trials. The other cities are correctly matched.

2. **(D)**  This is a chronological question focusing on Massachusetts in the 17th century. It is testing specific developments in the colony, and the Mayflower Compact (1620) and founding of the Bay Colony (1630) should be familiar. You should know about Roger Williams and the founding of Rhode Island (1636) and about the Salem Witch Trials (1692), but you may not know the exact dates. The Puritan Cromwell led his forces to victory over King Charles in the early 1640s, and with Puritans in control of the government, immigration to the Bay Colony dropped dramatically. You may not know this but it is important to be aware of major changes in England because they did have an impact on the colonies. The Salem Witch Trials came last, after the colony was well established and experienced a new interest in religion.

3. **(C)**  The Great Awakening was the first movement of religious revival experienced in all the colonies. Although each choice offered is true, the chief significance of the Great Awakening would be its unifying nature, and therefore C would be the best answer.

4. **(C)**  Fort Duquesne was founded by the French in western Pennsylvania (area 3). The British changed the name to Fort Pitt when they captured the fort, and it later became the city of Pittsburgh.

5. **(E)**  The Native Americans did all of the items listed except organize effectively to block English expansion westward. Many tribes supported the French in the

French and Indian War. They later tried to block the westward movement of the colonists, but they were not successful.

6. **(E)** Each of these men were early explorers of the New World, but only Champlain, for whom Lake Champlain in New York State is named, explored under the French flag.

7. **(B)** The trial of Peter Zenger is often cited as the true beginning of the free press in America. The trial was one of the most important in the colonies although some historians now believe its significance has been exaggerated.

8. **(D)** There were many causes of the French and Indian War, but the limitation on trade under the British Acts of Trade and Navigation was not one of them. The acts were a major cause of the American Revolution.

9. **(E)** The first four events listed provided the colonists with the experience and/or concepts to be used in the fight for independence. Fighting methods were developed in the war. Town meetings and the Power of the Purse (appropriation of money) gave good arguments for the rights of English subjects. While the development of export crops and subsequent trade was essential in creating viable colonies, the process supplied little experience useful in the fight for independence.

10. **(D)** The passage, from Jeremy Belknap's *History of New Hampshire, 1812,* is a description of the process used by Native Americans in the Northeast to make a hatchet, but there is no indication it is a tomahawk or that the people described are Native Americans. While only one tool is mentioned, there is no indication whether they had many tools or not. Be careful in your reading and do not jump to conclusions that are not clearly stated in quotations. As we know, the Native Americans of the Northeast had a large variety of specialized tools. They were made from many natural materials—bone, stone, wood, shells—but no metal until after contact with Europeans. As the passage clearly indicates, they made intelligent use of their natural surroundings waiting for a sapling to grow around a stone hatchet head to provide a handle.

# The Era of the American Revolution 1763–1789

---

## CHAPTER 5

- Conflicts during this period
- "Describe" and "explain" essays
- Quotation questions

---

The issues and conflicts that led to the independence of the British colonies, the winning of that independence, and the establishment of the new nation—the United States of America—are the major themes of this period. It is a crucial period for understanding United States history and one that should be studied in all United States history survey courses. One can expect questions dealing with various aspects of this era on any United States history examination.

Many issues and ideas from the colonial period had an impact on developments after 1763 and on our independent history. They include Puritanism; attitudes toward slaves, Native Americans, and free blacks; religious toleration; economic independence, especially in trade and manufacturing; self-government; the legal status of the individual and the right to vote; access to free land and the settlement of the West; conflicts between the European powers. These issues and ideas were important immediately after 1763 and should form part of one's study of this period, but their roots can be found in the colonial era.

## THREE TIME PERIODS

The years 1763–1789 logically divide into three separate but related time periods. These are: the steps to independence, 1763–1776; the War of the American Revolution, also called the War for American Independence, 1775–1783; the establishment of an independent government, 1783–1789. This latter period is sometimes referred to as "the critical period," a phrase coined by the American historian John Fiske in the 19th century and used ever since.

In studying this period, there are many points that need to be understood. There are also several important questions that run through all three periods. Among these are

1. Who will control the frontier lands across the Appalachian Mountains?
2. Who has the power of taxation of citizens?
3. Who will control the legislative power?
4. What are the "inalienable rights" of human beings?

5. Should government be democratic, republican, oligarchical, or monarchical?
6. When are protest, civil disobedience, and revolution legitimate instruments of political action?
7. How should slaves and Native Americans be treated?
8. What are the social and cultural differences between the colonists and Europeans?

## SAMPLE ESSAY QUESTION—DESCRIBE . . . EXPLAIN

The following question is a very good question for covering the history of 1763–1789, since it ties two of the three time periods together in a comparison. The question is of the *Describe . . . explain* type, which often gives the writer a wide choice for the content or focus of an answer.

### SAMPLE QUESTION

Between 1763 and 1776, the colonies confronted many issues in their relations with England. Under the Articles of Confederation (1780–1789), the same issues were behind the tensions in state/federal relations. Describe two of these issues and explain how the central government under the Articles of Confederation tried to solve them.

### Comments on Sample Question

First you need to analyze the question. Before you proceed, read the question carefully and decide what is being asked. You may even wish to make a few notes on your ideas so you can compare them with the following analysis and see how well you are doing.

The directions in the *Describe . . . explain* type of essay are clearly stated. The writer is asked to describe one or more particular situations, relationships, or, as in this example, issues and then to explain something about the issue, situation, relationship, or problem described. The question allows the writer to pick the issues. This becomes an important decision, since you must pick issues or situations about which you not only know the facts, but one for which you can describe the relationship. The choice is yours, but the success of your answer will be determined by how wise a choice you make.

There should be no difficulty in understanding the words *describe* and *explain*. The difficulty in this type of essay comes in how well you describe the situation and how valid an explanation you present. In this question it is clear that you must discuss how the central government under the Articles of Confederation tried to solve the issues you have described. Fortunately, Advanced Placement questions are usually very clear because they have been developed and carefully analyzed by a committee over a period of at least a year.

The above general comments on the *Describe . . . explain* type of question apply to all of them. Now let's look closely at this particular question. What are you asked to describe? Obviously it is issues, but what "issues?" The question states "Between 1763 and 1776, the colonies confronted many issues in their relations with England." This should not be too difficult to understand. The colonies are the British colonies in North America. The history of the period 1763–1776 in America is full of issues that created tension and difficulties between these two. This part of the question appears, therefore, to be asking for a rewriting of the history of the 13 years, but be careful! Note the rest of the question, "Under the Articles of Confederation (1780–1789) the

**TIP**

On many AP questions you will be given a choice of several issues from which to choose. In some ways that makes the question easier, provided you have knowledge of those issues listed. If you do not, then you would prefer an open-ended format which allows you to pick the issues.

same issues were behind the tensions in state/federal relations." The question is tighter than the first part would lead you to suspect. *Issues* is the key to the question. You must not simply rewrite the history of 1763–1776; you must identify the issues of that era that recur in the years 1780–1789 *and* recur in state/federal relations as the issues had occurred in relations between colonies and England earlier. You can now begin to determine what issues you will deal with in your answer. You must at the time you pick the issues remember that you are to "explain how the central government under the Articles of Confederation tried to solve them." Therefore, you must pick issues (1) that you can describe; (2) that recurred; (3) that you can explain how they were dealt with under the Confederation. This should not be difficult, but it illustrates how carefully you should analyze even the simplest-appearing question. Finally, you are to discuss only two major issues.

**TIP**

It is crucial you pick only the number asked for in a question. Doing more does not help your grade.

You are now ready for the second step—collecting and sorting your information. You should do that now, following the points mentioned above. You should first make brief notes on as many issues as you can and then, pick the two issues faced between 1763 and 1776 that you wish to write on. Add more specific information about each and, finally, jot down information on how the issues were dealt with between 1780 and 1789. After this, move on to the third step—developing your thesis.

In this type of question, some people would say no thesis is required. If that is the case, you would not be writing an essay, but merely a historic composition. Your thesis or personal opinion might well revolve around the word *tried.* Unlike the *Evaluate This Statement* type of essay question, the *Describe . . . explain* type forces you to write your thesis in your own words. You should do that now. Then follow the remaining four steps in essay writing and write an answer to this question.

After you have written your own essay on this question, read the following student answer. What is your opinion of it? How does it compare with your answer? You may wish to make a brief outline of the two essays to compare their structure. Finally, do you agree with the teacher comments? Why or why not? Outlining the student answer and your own and comparing the outlines can be helpful. You will also want to compare the teacher's comments on this student essay with your own comments on it.

## Sample Answer

Taxation and defense are two problems every government and people must deal with. In the period between 1763 and 1776 they were issues of colonial/English relations. Later, in 1780–1789, these two issues involved relations between the Confederation and the states. All four groups—colonists, England, states, Confederation—had ideas on how the problems should be resolved and attempted to do so, but no real solution was found until the Constitution was written in 1789.

The main problem from 1763 to 1776 was that of taxation. The colonists insisted that as members of the British Empire they were entitled to the same rights that Englishmen living in England enjoyed. They propounded that taxation without representation was unfair and that taxation for the sole purpose of raising revenue was equally unjust. Actually, what they were demanding was Dominion status, something granted to Canada in 1839.

A second issue of disagreement between the colonies and the Crown concerned the raising and housing of troops. Parliament, naturally, assumed that since America was a colony, it needed to be protected. Consequently, British regulars would have to be sent over and housed in the colonies. This situation first arose in the Quartering

Act. This act stated that Americans must house British Regulars and help pay for their maintenance. This seemed absurd to the colonists, who felt that they themselves could, with less expense and more efficiency, raise the requisite troops for protection as they had been doing since 1607. One provision of these "Coercive" Acts stated that the colonists must within 24 hours comply with any troop quartering regulation that might be enacted.

Taxation under the Articles of Confederation was just as important as it was during the colonial period. The Congress's main weakness was that it did not have the power to tax the states. As one can see, the problem was entirely different in substance. Instead of the central government forcing the taxes upon the people, it could only tax with the people's (states') acquiescence. However, the situation is in one respect similar. The states and the people protested against any taxation. When Robert Morris was Secretary of the Treasury, he tried three times to impose taxes but met with failure every time. When he tried to resign from the thankless job, his resignation was not accepted. Under the Articles of Confederation the government could only remedy the taxing problem of 1763–1776 by asking for taxes rather than demanding them. They found, however, that the states were equally as unresponsive as the colonies had been.

Finally, the Articles of Confederation attempted to solve the troop question by leaving it up to the states themselves. Congress was not permitted to raise an army; instead, each state would have its own army or militia that could be called upon by Congress when needed. This, however, created new difficulties. It made it impossible for the country to have a central army, centrally trained and operated. And what was to happen if one state army refused to cooperate with another?

Although these issues of taxation and army were apparently solved in the new Constitution in 1789, the solutions have been questioned at other times in history. These issues seem to reflect continual concerns of the American people.

## Teacher Comments on Sample Answer

> **TIP**
>
> In writing an answer to an essay, carefully select the evidence to support your thesis. Do *not* just present everything you know.

"This essay is an excellent answer to the question. It is very effectively and clearly organized with both introductory and concluding paragraphs. The student's personal view on the question is stated in the last sentence of the introduction and again in the conclusion. Although the body of the paper does not deal specifically with the thesis, it is obvious in the presentation of the information and in the discussion of it that the student believes no solutions to the issues were discovered in either period.

"The factual information presented to describe the two issues is excellent. The student carefully chooses particular events to illustrate the two issues under discussion. Taxation and the army are good choices to illustrate issues.

"Considering the student's thesis, it was wise not to include the problem of western lands or the frontier as an illustration. The issue in this area was settled effectively by the Confederation government with the Northwest Ordinance."

Do you agree with these teacher comments? Overall, this essay is excellent—an 8 or 9. Students should study its organization and the choice of vocabulary and information as both a review of this time period and an example of an answer that would have received a high grade.

# Practice Essay Questions

1. Between 1763 and 1789, the use and control of the frontier regions presented problems to both the British and the Americans. Describe the problems involved in the use and control of the frontier and explain how both the British and the Americans attempted to solve them.

2. "Between 1763 and 1776 the colonists developed a theory of political independence and government." Assess the validity of this statement.

3. Pick TWO of the following acts and explain in what ways the colonial response to each helped the colonists develop a theory of political independence.

   Quebec Act
   Stamp Act
   Intolerable Acts

4. "The Declaration of Independence issued a call for a democratic government of equal citizens that was rejected by the writers of the Constitution, who created an aristocratic government that benefited only the wealthy few." Assess the validity of this statement.

5. "The United States has undergone revolutionary changes throughout its history."

   Discuss the validity of this quotation as it applies to ONE of the following time periods:

   1783–1789
   1828–1836

Before you read the brief comments on the above questions, you may wish to make your own analysis of the questions and write out answers to several of them.

## Comments on Question 1

Question 1 is very similar to the question analyzed above. It narrows the choice of problems to those involved with the frontier, but other than that the format is the same.

## Comments on Question 2

Question 2 uses the *Assess the Validity* format The time period is narrower than for the other questions, thus requiring a more detailed knowledge of the period 1763–1776. Do not just describe all the steps leading to independence, but carefully pick those that can help you illustrate the developing theory of political independence and government if that is your thesis. You may believe no such theory was developed and that position can be argued effectively.

## Comments on Question 3

The third question introduces another type of essay question. Here you are to pick TWO acts from the three listed. Do not pick more than TWO—it will not help you in the reading as you are expected to follow directions. The question requires you to understand the meaning of a theory of political independence. The arguments before the Declaration of Independence did that, as the colonists wrote pamphlets and organized resistance in defense of their understanding of their "rights as Englishmen." These reactions and arguments are what you need to focus on and not just the telling of events. You must decide how or if you agree with the comment, decide on which two acts you know the most about, and organize the material you will use. You may want to write about one act and then the second and then pull your points together, *or* you may find similarities in the responses and write paragraphs on these similarities, referring to each act in each paragraph.

## Comments on Question 4

The fourth question is typical of the *Assess the Validity* type. The issue raised by the statement is one of major interest to historians and one on which you should have ideas. The question basically asks, "Did the Constitution reject the principles set forth in the Declaration of Independence?" You need to understand several key words—*democratic, equal, aristocratic*—in order to answer the question. This illustrates the importance of building your vocabulary.

## Comments on Question 5

You may not be prepared to answer this question now because you may lack knowledge of the 1828–1836 period. It was included here to illustrate how differing time periods can be used.

The wording of this question may seem to force you to accept the political changes as revolutionary. Actually, you always have the option of arguing the other side of a statement and, in this question, you could argue against either period being revolutionary. Do not be trapped into taking positions you do not believe in by the wording of a question, but at the same time, do not lose sight of the point of the question as you defend an unusual position. You should feel free to state and defend your personal opinion or thesis on every question. The question is a variation of the type discussed in Chapter 1.

# MULTIPLE CHOICE—THE QUOTATION QUESTION

Multiple-choice questions on the AP exam test your analytical skills and knowledge. One excellent way this is done is with a so-called "stimulus" question. The question presents a stimulus—a quotation, chart, map, graph, cartoon—and asks a question relating to it. You must be able to analyze the information in the stimulus to answer the question. Often you will also need to call on your general knowledge of the time period in order to fully understand the stimulus. In that sense, stimulus questions resemble the DBQ.

The simplest type of stimulus question is the one in which the student must identify the author or the source of the quotation. Such quotations will either be obvious and well known or the content of the quotation will be easily identifiable with the position or viewpoint of the author or with the content of an important document.

Other multiple-choice questions based on quotations or historical documents will require you to understand the content of the passage in view of the history of the time, to identify the philosophical viewpoint expressed, or to analyze the content of the passage using your own analytical and interpretive skills.

Although we are discussing documents from the era of the American Revolution, you must realize that you may have documents from any period of U.S. history on the examination. We have chosen to present this type of stimulus question here for several reasons. First, there are many documents that are discussed in all history texts dealing with the era of the American Revolution and you should be familiar with them. Using these documents will illustrate how quotations from any period might be used.

The second reason is that quotations are often connected with individuals. In this unit and throughout the remainder of your study, you will read about many important people and as you do, you should relate particular ideas and positions to them. The type of specific information needed to answer many of the quotation-based multiple-choice questions will be acquired as you study your history. Names and authors of documents and important laws, the changing concept and interpretation of the laws as they apply to economic and social activity, major speeches and who delivered them, the changing attitudes of people living in various parts of the country—all of this information can be absorbed as you study the past.

The third reason is that if you begin now to practice reading documents to find key ideas and relate these to the "mainstream" of our history, you will be preparing all through your study or review for the DBQ. Read the quotations looking for the key ideas and connect these to individuals and the history of the time.

As the following examples of quotation-based multiple-choice questions are studied, it should become clear how various types of information will help you respond to such questions.

## SAMPLE QUESTIONS

"So soon as there shall be 5,000 free male inhabitants of full age in the district . . . , they shall receive authority, . . . , to elect representatives from their counties or townships to represent them in the General Assembly: *Provided*. That, for every 500 free male inhabitants, there shall be one representative, and so on . . . until the number of representatives shall amount to 25; after which, the number and proportion of representatives shall be regulated by the Legislature . . . "

1. The above quotation is most likely from

  (A) the U.S. Constitution
  (B) Galloway's Plan of Union
  (C) Quebec Act
  (D) Northwest Ordinance
  (E) Stamp Act

2. The most important concept presented in this passage (from the Northwest Ordinance) that is considered a basic American political concept is the idea of the

  (A) equality of men
  (B) right of representation based on counties and townships
  (C) size of a legislative body
  (D) right of 5,000 free men to have elections
  (E) right of free men to govern themselves using elected legislatures

## Comments on Question 1

Question 1 is a most common form of question. It requires you to be familiar with five acts and be able to understand the passage. The passage states how and when a legislative body will first be set up. You might remember the line "5,000 free male inhabitants," as many books point out that this clause has set the pattern for the government of territories and the admission of states into the union throughout our history. Chances are, however, that you will not recognize the quotation but that you will be able to understand its content and purpose.

You must then look at the choices offered in this question to determine which one most likely contained the quotation. As is often the case, several choices will be very familiar. All students should know the U.S. Constitution well enough to realize that it does not establish the pattern for creating legislatures. State legislatures were in existence and the Constitution establishes the two branches of the U.S. Congress only. The U.S. Constitution can obviously be eliminated.

You should be aware of the Stamp Act. It would then be obvious that the Stamp Act did not deal with legislatures; therefore, it can be quickly eliminated. You are now left with three choices, each of which is a possibility. You should recall the Quebec Act, Galloway's Plan of Union, and the Northwest Ordinance, all of which deal with the establishment of government. The Quebec Act of 1774 extended the Province of Quebec to include all the land north of the Ohio River under the authority of the Provincial government. It also continued the French method of government. There was no place in such an act for the establishment of new legislatures.

The same holds true of Galloway's Plan of Union of 1774. It is probably the least familiar of your choices, but the title alone should identify it as an attempt to unite the already established colonies. The goal of the plan was the union of existing colonies, not the creation of new ones.

By elimination, we come to the Northwest Ordinance, which was designed in 1787 to provide organized government for the land between the Ohio River and the Great Lakes west to the Mississippi River land gained in the 1783 Treaty of Paris, the area known as the Northwest Territory. Various states claimed the land but ceded their claims to the federal government under the Articles of Confederation at the insistence of Maryland and New Jersey. The territory lacked a governmental system, and this ordinance established it. The concept of new and equal legislatures formed by free men when the population of a territory reaches a certain point is one of the great contributions of the American people to the concept of colonial government. You may have been familiar with the document and the idea and have been able to identify the Northwest Ordinance immediately. However, if you find that with such questions you cannot immediately spot the answer, think through the choices and see if you can come to the correct answer.

## Comments on Question 2

Question 2 has been phrased to see if you understand the significance of the content of the question. In this version you need not identify the document as it is given to you in the statement. Even if the name of the document were eliminated (note the parentheses), you could still identify the political concept stated in the passage. The multiple-choice question now becomes one of checking your analytical and reading abilities—those two skills essential for every historian.

You may know that the Northwest Ordinance dealt with the establishment of governments in the territories that were to be free and equal to the governments of the original 13 colonies. In this case you would probably consider choices A and E and eliminate the others. Since A is very general and equality is not mentioned in the passage, you would quickly decide on choice E, which is a summary of the main idea in the quotation.

Simply reading the passage you would realize that choices B, C, and D are all included in the quotation. However, none of these should qualify as a "basic American political concept." It is true that the Northwest Ordinance allowed the governor to set the election date, but governors do not do that today. Again the passage allows 5,000 free men to have an election, but that has no relation to basic American political concepts. The passage does state a rule concerning legislative size, but that also is not a basic American political concept. This leaves you with choice E, which is very basic to American political life. It is the correct answer since choice A, although a basic American political concept, is not mentioned in the passage.

## SAMPLE QUESTION

3. The previous quotation (from the Northwest Ordinance) establishes

   I.  The right of free males to vote for members of a legislature
  II.  The authority of the legislature to set its own size once there are 25 members
 III.  The control of the governor over the legislative body
 IV.  That you need 5,000 free male citizens in a district to establish a General Assembly

  (A)  I and II
  (B)  I and III
  (C)  I, II, and IV
  (D)  I, III, and IV
  (E)  I, II, III, and IV

## Comments on Question 3

The format of this question is somewhat complicated. You not only have a quotation—you have four statements lettered I–IV that state ideas that may or may not be in the quotation. The possible answers are then presented as five combinations of those four Roman numerals lettered A–E. Your task is to determine which combination of statements with Roman numerals is correct. Your reading and analytical skills are being tested. **The best way to answer this type of question is to read the four statements, then read the quotation. When you find information that will confirm one of the statements, mark the statement** with a check (√). Then see which letter lists the numbers of the items by which you have placed marks. If you read the quotation carefully you will find that statements I, II, and IV are correct. The correct answer is thus C. The Northwest Ordinance established the right of free males to vote for a legislative body when there are 5,000 free males in the district. Finally, once the General Assembly (legislature) reaches 25 members, they may decide the future size of the legislative body. The quotation does not set the governor's control over the legislative body.

This format can be used in a variety of questions and not only with quotations. It is an interesting but complicated format. **This format has been used less often in recent years**, but you should be aware of it. If you read the questions carefully, analyze the statements, and think of the history of the stated or implied time period, you will easily master this format.

On the Advanced Placement examination **sometimes** more than one question will be asked about the same quotation, map, chart, or cartoon. Here we have presented three that illustrate various types of questions that could be asked. **As in the case of the essay section, in the multiple-choice section of the Advanced Placement examination the first crucial step toward achieving success on multiple-choice questions is to analyze the question.** The stem is the key to analyzing the multiple-choice question.

Let us look at several other quotation-based multiple-choice questions. Read them carefully, analyze the question, and decide on your answer. Then read the brief descriptions of the questions that follow.

---

### SAMPLE QUESTIONS

"All communities divide themselves into the few and the many. The first are the rich and well born, the other the mass of the people. . . . The people are turbulent and changing; they seldom judge or determine right. Give therefore to the first class a distinct, permanent share in the government. They will check the unsteadiness of the second, . . . Nothing but a permanent body can check the imprudence of democracy. Their turbulent and uncontrolling disposition requires checks."

4. The writer believed all of the following EXCEPT

   (A) the people are poor judges of what is right
   (B) there should be stability in government
   (C) the rich and well born deserve a permanent share in the government
   (D) government should be headed by a king
   (E) government should be designed with checks

5. The above statement is most likely to be found in

   (A) the *Virginia Resolves*
   (B) *Notes on the Debates in the Federal Convention in Philadelphia*
   (C) the Quebec Act of 1774
   (D) an account of the Boston Tea Party
   (E) the Peace of Paris 1783

---

## Comments on Questions 4–5

The passage presents an argument in favor of a position. It is from a speech by Alexander Hamilton at the debates on the Constitution in 1787 and is found in the *Notes on the Debates of the Constitutional Convention.* It briefly summarizes the position held by Hamilton until his death. He believed in government by the few who are rich. Unlike Jefferson, who believed that the people, especially the small farmers, should be the deciding power in government, Hamilton distrusted the people who had no economic stake in society.

Question 4 requires that you understand the paragraph. There is no mention of rule by a king, although it may be implied. The hasty reader might miss this point.

In question 5, "the above statement" would not be suitable for a treaty or for a description of an action-packed event, such as the Tea Party. The remaining three choices must be recognized if you are to analyze them properly. *The Virginia Resolves* presented a pro-people position. The Quebec Act established the form of government for Canada and did not argue a position as does this passage. *The Debates* remains the correct answer and you might have suspected this type of statement would be in a debate where a particular opinion is being expressed.

## SAMPLE QUESTIONS

"Government is, or ought to be instituted for the common benefit, protection, and security of the people, nation, or community; of all . . . forms of government, that is best which is capable of producing the greatest degree of happiness and safety, and is most effectually secured against the danger of maladministration; and that when any government shall be found inadequate or contrary to these purposes, a majority of the community hath an indubitable, unalienable . . . right to reform, alter or abolish it, in such manner as shall be judged most conducive to the public weal."

6. The philosophy expressed in the above quotation most closely resembles that held by

   (A)  Jean-Jacques Rousseau
   (B)  Montesquieu
   (C)  John Locke
   (D)  Voltaire
   (E)  Hobbes

7. The philosophy expressed in the above quotation finds its most famous expression in United States history in the

   (A)  Declaration of Independence
   (B)  Constitution
   (C)  Articles of Confederation
   (D)  Northwest Ordinance
   (E)  Declaration and Resolves of the Continental Congress

## Comments on Questions 6–7

The quotation forms part of the Virginia Bill of Rights, a document adopted in 1776. It is an excellent statement of John Locke's philosophy as stated in his *Two Treatises on Government.* Locke's philosophy was well known to the colonial leaders and provided the philosophical basis of the Declaration of Independence. In the Declaration, Jefferson adopted Locke's ideas about inalienable rights and the "right of revolution." The latter is the main idea in this passage. The other men listed in question 6 were important philosophers of the 17th and 18th centuries and their ideas were important to many of the colonial leaders, but Locke's ideas were crucial in the Declaration.

In question 7 the other choices are all important documents, but all students should recognize the similarity between this passage from the Virginia Bill of Rights and the Declaration of Independence, which is the most famous American document to express Locke's idea of the right of revolution.

## SAMPLE QUESTIONS

"But with the greatest submittion we beg leave to informe your Honours that unles something takes place more favourable to the people, in a little time att least, one half of our inhabitants in our oppinion will become banckerupt . . . the constables are dayly (selling at auction) our property . . . , our land after itt is appraised by the best judges under oath is sold for about one third of the value of itt, our cattle about one half the value . . . . And we beg leave further to informe your honours that sutes att law are very numerous and the atturneys in our oppinion very extravigent and oppressive in their demands . . . What can your honours ask of us unles a paper curancy or some other medium be provided so that we may pay your taxes and debts."

8. The quotation reflects the views most likely held by a typical

    (A)  English gentleman in London in 1783
    (B)  Virginia planter of tobacco in 1787
    (C)  Boston merchant in 1788
    (D)  settler in eastern Kentucky in 1783
    (E)  frontier farmer of western Massachusetts in 1786

9. The quotation discusses a recurrent issue in American history, the concern of the

    (A)  merchant for a fair income from investment
    (B)  farmer for easy credit
    (C)  attorney for a living wage
    (D)  judge for equal justice
    (E)  legislator for fair laws

## Comments on Questions 8–9

The spelling and grammar have not been changed in this quotation. The meaning should be perfectly clear, but the language of the quotation may slow down your reading. The spelling and style will often provide a clue as to the date of the writing.

The quotation is from the Petition of the Town of Greenwich, Massachusetts, in January 1786. It is a post-revolutionary war document and focuses on a new aspect of the taxation/money issue. Here the small farmers of the western part of the state are protesting high prices, tight (or limited amounts of) money, and what seemed to be unfair bankruptcy laws and judges. These farmers were soon to participate in Shays' Rebellion.

The answer to question 8 is, therefore, a frontier farmer of western Massachusetts in 1786. The other choices are not suitable, as these complaints were not issues to an English gentleman, a Virginia planter, or a Boston merchant, and Kentucky was not yet organized enough in 1783 to have farmers' complaints formalized.

The quotation is an early example of a recurrent issue in American history, the farmer's desire for easy credit, and this is the answer to question 9.

# Practice Multiple-Choice Questions

Questions 1–2 refer to the following map

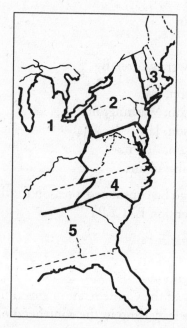

1. The First Continental Congress met in the region numbered

   (A) 1
   (B) 2
   (C) 3
   (D) 4
   (E) 5

2. The region numbered 3 on the map is remembered as including the site of:

   I. the Battles of Lexington and Concord
  II. the settlement of Plymouth
 III. the meetings of the House of Burgesses
 IV. the Battle of Saratoga

(A) I
(B) I and II
(C) I, II, and III
(D) I and IV
(E) I, II, and IV

3. All of the following played a role at the Constitutional Convention of 1787 EXCEPT

(A) George Washington
(B) Alexander Hamilton
(C) Thomas Jefferson
(D) Benjamin Franklin
(E) James Madison

4. The *Federalist Papers* were written by

(A) Hamilton, Jefferson, Jay
(B) Hamilton, Madison, Washington
(C) Hamilton, Madison, Jay
(D) Hamilton, Jefferson, Adams
(E) Madison, Jefferson, Adams

5. All of the following can be considered a reason for the calling of the federal Constitutional Convention EXCEPT

(A) Northwest Ordinance
(B) Shays' Rebellion
(C) Annapolis Convention
(D) Near-bankruptcy of the Confederation government
(E) Lack of executive leadership in the confederation

6. Thomas Jefferson's philosophical position during the period prior to 1789 could best be described as

(A) aristocratic and internationalist
(B) monarchical and agrarian
(C) democratic and mercantilist
(D) democratic and agrarian
(E) socialistic and internationalist

7. The Bill of Rights was added to the Constitution primarily to

   (A) curtail state power
   (B) protect the states from the power of the federal government
   (C) protect individual liberties from the power of the federal government
   (D) protect individual liberties from the power of local government
   (E) protect the states from the power of the church

Questions 8–9 refer to the following quotation

". . . The power of Parliament is uncontrolable, but by themselves, and we must obey. They only can repeal their own Acts. There would be an end of all government, if one or a number of subjects or [and] provinces should take upon them to judge the justice of an Act of Parliament, to refuse obedience to it. . . . Reasons may be given, why an Act ought to be repeal'd, and yet obedience must be yielded to it till that repeal takes place."

8. The argument presented in the above quotation assumes that

   (A) government is a blessing for mankind
   (B) the state of nature is one of conflict and war
   (C) Parliament derives its power from the consent of the governed
   (D) the people are at the complete mercy of the ruling authority
   (E) laws should be obeyed until they are changed by legal means

9. The above statement reflects an opinion most likely held by a(an)

   (A) English gentleman in 1775
   (B) frontier settler in 1763
   (C) Boston merchant in 1773
   (D) moderate colonist in 1765
   (E) Virginia planter in 1776

10. "You are to be diligent in the execution of the powers and authorities given you by several Acts of Parliament for . . . searching of ships, and for seizing, securing and bringing on shore any goods prohibited to be imported into, or exported out of said plantations; or for which any duties are payable, or ought to have been paid."

    The above quotation sets forth the British theory that Parliament had the right to

    (A) dominate the seas
    (B) regulate production in the colonies
    (C) seize missing seamen
    (D) control colonial trade
    (E) issue Bills of Attainder

## *Answers and Answer Explanations*

| | | | |
|---|---|---|---|
| 1. **(B)** | 2. **(B)** | 3. **(C)** | 4. **(C)** |
| 5. **(A)** | 6. **(D)** | 7. **(C)** | 8. **(E)** |
| 9. **(D)** | 10. **(D)** | | |

1. **(B)** The first Continental Congress met at Philadelphia in the colony of Pennsylvania in 1774. Region 2 includes Pennsylvania, New York, and New Jersey.

2. **(B)** The Battles of Lexington and Concord and the settlement of Plymouth by the Pilgrims took place in New England, which is region 3 on the map. The House of Burgesses was the Virginia assembly and met in Williamsburg, Virginia (region 4), and the Battle of Saratoga took place in New York (region 2). This is a good example of the question format that uses four statements, any combination of which may be correct.

3. **(C)** Thomas Jefferson did not attend the Constitutional Convention. He was in Europe. The other men all played crucial roles at the Convention.

4. **(C)** The *Federalist Papers* were written by Hamilton, Madison, and Jay to support the Constitution. The papers helped win votes for the Constitution in New York and elsewhere. They are considered one of the finest analyses of the new federal system of government and they provide excellent examples of 18th-century essay style.

5. **(A)** The Northwest Ordinance was one of the successes of the Confederation government and was not a cause for calling the Constitutional Convention.

6. **(D)** Thomas Jefferson was a strong believer in the yeoman farmer—the agrarian—as contrasted with the mercantilist interest in society. He also supported the people, which would suggest his support for democracy—not yet a commonly used term. His support of the people is illustrated in his writing of the *Declaration of Independence.* Selection D best summarizes Jefferson's philosophical position.

7. **(C)** The Bill of Rights was added to the Constitution to protect the liberties of the individual from the power of the new federal government. The Constitution written without these protections almost failed ratification. Massachusetts ratified the Constitution with the provision that the Bill of Rights be added, and several other states followed ratifying the document with this qualification.

8. **(E)** James Otis, in this selection from his *Rights of the British Colonies,* 1764, bases his argument on the assumption that laws should be obeyed until they are changed or modified by legal means. He believes Parliament has the wisdom to understand when its laws are oppressive and that Parliament will change these laws.

9. (**D**) The argument presented in this document would most likely be held by a moderate colonist, as was James Otis, before the development of major controversies between colonies and the Mother Country. Choice D is the best answer.

10. (**D**) This quotation, from a summary of the British Acts of Trade made in 1769, clearly assumes the right of the British Parliament to control colonial trade.

## CHAPTER 6

# The New Nation 1789–1824

- Recap of important developments
- Who, What, When, Where, Why, and How questions
- Historical thinking skills

The adoption of the Constitution by the United States in 1789 ushered in a new phase of our history. The Constitution is a remarkable document and should be studied carefully by all students. It will be clear that the Constitution established the simplest framework for the new government, a framework that had to be fleshed out with laws, policies, and programs and by the development of customs. This filling out of the framework of the Constitution occurred in the generation after 1789 against a background of international tension and war.

United States foreign policy from 1789 to 1824 often seems confusing. The intrigues of the British, French, Spanish, and Americans brought the nation close to war several times and finally resulted in the War of 1812. The problems of control of the western frontier were as complicated, and throughout this period there were dramatic developments internally, as seen in the Hamilton-Jefferson, Hamilton-Burr, Federalist-Republican conflicts. All of these issues are of importance, but the most important development in the era was the establishment of those laws and the setting of those policies that established the United States as a viable nation. These laws and policies have affected all later United States history and should therefore be understood by every student.

**STUDY TIP**

During Washington's administration, the overall framework of the government was set. The essence of that framework is still the basis of the federal government.

## IMPORTANT DEVELOPMENTS

Important developments of the years 1789–1824 include the following:

1. The creation of political parties or factions
2. The establishment of the judicial system and its functioning, especially under Chief Justice John Marshall
3. The imprint George Washington put on the new government
4. The development of conflicting interpretations of the Constitution as exemplified by Alexander Hamilton and Thomas Jefferson

**TIP**

If you have a factual knowledge of these major developments and are able to see their interrelations and to develop parallels to other periods of our history, you should have an excellent understanding of this era.

5. The continuing conflict with the British over both the 1783 Treaty of Paris and the idea of freedom of the seas, and the political, economic, and social consequences

6. United States relations with the revolutionary government of France and the political, economic, and social consequences

7. The growing sense of nationalism in the country, especially after 1814

8. The physical and economic growth of the United States

9. The beginnings of a cultural identity established through the work of writers and artists.

## SAMPLE QUESTIONS—HISTORICAL THINKING AND QUESTIONS HISTORIANS ASK

The AP program was developed to test the level of historical thinking and understanding achieved by high school students. Historical thinking is the search for an understanding of what happened in the past, of people, events, places, and dates, but it is more. Historical thinking also involves the search for the meaning of past events and requires the development of a set of skills. Over time, historians have developed an approach, the historical method, as a way to organize this search.

In the past several years the AP program has become concerned that some AP courses are more of a survey or a preparation/cramming for the exam rather than an in-depth seeking of historical knowledge using both the historical method and historical thinking. Therefore, they have offered schools the opportunity to have their AP courses audited for quality and have begun a review process to redesign the course description to assure that all AP courses meet the highest standards. These new descriptions will emphasize the use of the type of questions the historian asks. Courses and the exam will be centered on this approach.

### Who? What? When? Where? Why? How?

**TIP**

Because the AP exam is designed to test higher level skills, it is very rare that the exam asks a direct *Who? What? When? Where?* question either in the multiple-choice or the free response sections, but they have on occasion. Instead, almost all AP exam questions will assume you have this information.

As one begins historical research, the questions are simple ones that seek the factual data that must be understood before analysis and interpretation can begin. In the historical method model this is the stage of gathering data. As you seek information, you need to ask questions about all actions and events of the past. The easiest way to do this is to focus on six simple words—often referred to as "The five W's plus *How*." Answers to *Who?*, *What?*, *When?*, and *Where?* provide the basic facts of history. Slightly more complex and leading into historical thinking are the final W, *Why?*, and *How?* For example, question 3 (Practice Essays p. 72) requires that you know **who** George Washington, Alexander Hamilton, Thomas Jefferson, and John Marshall were, **what** their opinions were, and **when** the term "new nation" would apply to the United States. If you do not have that basic factual knowledge, you cannot answer the question. It requires historical thinking, which must be based on factual information. The question asks you to use this fundamental information to determine the impact of an individual's opinions on the new nation. This is the type of question the historian seeks to answer.

# Historical Thinking Skills

Historians use a variety of specific skills. These are:

1.  **Analysis:** collecting pertinent information from a variety of sources, evaluating its significance (strengths, weaknesses, and biases) and drawing conclusions

2.  **Cause and Effect and/or Chronological Relationships:** identifying patterns of change and continuity, of impact of one event upon others, and realizing that different patterns are possible

3.  **Interpretation:** recognizing the multiple causes of historic events and that people from other groups and of different ethnicities may offer different views; judging these views in terms of point of view, historic context, evidence, and argument

4.  **Context:** relating local events to broader global issues and concerns and vice versa

5.  **Comparison:** comparing developments within one society with others, both in the same and different time periods and locations

6.  **Argumentation:** creating a coherent and acceptable argument in answer to a question developed to aid in collecting evidence from a variety of sources; judging the arguments of others in view of the evidence available

7.  **Synthesis:** using, and properly acknowledging, all relevant sources (primary, secondary, archaeological, etc.) to present a historical narrative offering a coherent and logical interpretation of the past

> **TIP**
>
> Skill #2—cause and effect and/or chronological relationships—is a crucial skill.

To prepare for the AP exam and, as you review United States history in this book, you should always be honing your historical thinking skills. Unlike some cultures where history is viewed as cyclical, European and western culture views history as lineal. Historians seek to comprehend the past by finding cause and effect relationships. By their nature, these are chronological—an event in the present cannot affect or cause something to happen in the past.

The following questions are not framed as examples of essay questions that will be on the exam. **However, these questions are the type that historians ask when seeking knowledge** (see #6 above). Read them over. As you review, create such questions to organize your knowledge in preparation for writing essays.

1. How did independence affect the cultural and social development of the United States in the period up to 1824?

2. What steps did the administration of George Washington take to establish the structure of the United States government?

3. How did the United States avoid being drawn into European wars in the period 1789 to 1812?

4. Why did political parties evolve?

> **TIP**
>
> As you study and review facts, be certain to explore patterns of cause and effect. Many questions on the AP exam will require such an understanding. It is unlikely the questions will ask a simple, "What happened first?" but they will require that you have such knowledge as they test your historical thinking.

> **TIP**
>
> To organize your facts, frame broad questions as the historian does.

A more complicated and sophisticated question on political parties would be

5. What were the causes and impact on the nation of the development of political parties and changing political allegiances in the period 1789 to 1824?

6. How and why did the economy of the new nation evolve in the forty years after independence?

In summary, the AP program expects AP courses to be rigorous, not mere surveys. Students are expected to have a full understanding of the historical method and historical thinking and to be able to demonstrate this on the exam.

**TIP**

Historical thinking requires asking questions, collecting evidence, and applying specific intellectual skills to this evidence to seek an understanding of the past.

## SAMPLE QUESTION

How was war with England and France avoided in the years 1793–1810?

For this question we will not present a full answer, but rather concentrate on writing a conclusion. The *How?* question asks the writer to explore the cause-and-effect relationship among events. The aim for the student is to avoid a simple listing of events. Both interpretation of the events and a personal opinion, your thesis, need to be included. Read the opening paragraph, underline what you consider the thesis, read the three conclusions and decide on which you think is best. Did you agree with the teacher comments?

### Sample Opening Paragraph

War is a concern to all people, and avoiding war has been a major desire of the United States throughout our history. The newly independent country avoided war with England in 1794, with France in the years 1797–1800, and with both countries in the early 1800s. The way or reason we were able to avoid war then was that the presidents, unlike recent ones, refused to lead the nation into war. They—Washington, Adams, Jefferson—put domestic concerns ahead of schemes to prove our strength or to right "wrongs," and they were willing to *compromise* on issues of "honor."

**TIP**

Practice writing your own conclusion to sample essays in this book. Conclusions are difficult to write, but a good conclusion is an important part of every essay.

### Conclusion A

Clearly, there is a consistency in the *foreign policy* actions of Washington, Adams, and Jefferson. The three were not to be provoked into war by either the English or the French and were willing to compromise on important issues. By avoiding war they may have sacrificed American "honor," but we owe them a great debt because their astute policies and farsightedness permitted the nation to grow strong. Modern American presidents should study the actions of our first three presidents to learn how to avoid war.

### Conclusion B

As you can see, Washington, Adams, and Jefferson all followed the same type of *foreign policy* actions. I have shown how they compromised and went against popular opinion: Washington with the Neutrality Proclamation and in Jay's Treaty; Adams by arranging the Convention of 1800; Jefferson by pursuing the embargo. These men were great presidents. I hope our president will learn.

## Conclusion C

Washington's, Adams's, and Jefferson's *foreign policy* actions were taken to avoid war. In 1812 the war hawks from the frontier areas gained control of Congress and forced a declaration of war against England. Later presidents also led us into war. These three men were wise presidents and presidents today could learn a great deal from them.

## Teacher Comments on the Conclusions

"Of the three conclusions offered, Conclusion A is the most effective. The writer's thesis and the question are restated but in slightly different ways than in the introduction. The information in the body of the essay is pulled together by the word *consistency*, and the writer's interest in honor, which was a major point of the essay. No new information is introduced. The writer returns to the broad context of the opening when he suggests modern presidents can learn to avoid war from the first three. All of these elements are part of a good conclusion.

"Conclusion B is the poorest. The use of the phrases *as you can see* and *I have shown* belittle the reader, who does not need to be told about what has been read. The writer summarizes what is said in the essay, yet fails to restate either the thesis or the question. Although the writer applies the question to a larger area than early America, she does not clearly state what we might learn from these 'great presidents.'

"Conclusion C also applies the topic to a broader context. This writer refers to his thesis and the topic, but introduces new material about the War Hawks and the War of 1812. The question ended with 1810. If this information were to be introduced, and it is not called for by the question, it should have been presented in the body of the essay. This is a common error in conclusions, and yet it is one the student can easily learn to avoid."

> **IMPORTANT FACT**
>
> A good conclusion pulls the essay together and reaffirms the thesis.

---

**QUICK REVIEW**

An effective conclusion is different from a simple summary in which you repeat what you have already stated in the body of the paper. The best AP papers will have a conclusion that restates the thesis and suggests the larger implications of the thesis. You may wish to refer to Step Six—Writing the Conclusion—in Part One.

In summary . . .

a good conclusion *must* include

- a restatement of the thesis
- an indication of what the question was

a good conclusion *should* include in addition to the above

- a reference to how the thesis affects other broad issues

a good conclusion should NOT include

- new evidence or facts not included in the body of the essay
- the pronoun *I*
- a statement saying "It is now proven" or similar wording
- a simple listing of the evidence included in the essay

# Practice Essay Questions

The following essay questions reflect the type of question the historian asks. They require the use of historical thinking skills. They require analysis, collection of data, and the creation of a historical narrative, skills required on all free response questions. Read the questions over, analyze them, and write down some notes before reading the analyses given below.

1. Explain why and how political parties changed in the years 1791 to 1824.

2. How did events on the frontier impact national history in the years 1789–1829?

3. Each of the following individuals expressed strong opinions concerning the policies of the new nation. What opinions were expressed by TWO of the following? Of the two, whose opinions had the greater impact on the new nation?

   (A) George Washington
   (B) Alexander Hamilton
   (C) Thomas Jefferson
   (D) John Marshall

4. "The economic development of New England in the period 1789 to 1824 affected the nation socially and politically."

   Analyze the accuracy of this statement.

5. Analyze the impact the new Constitution had on THREE of the following in the years 1789–1824.

   Yeoman farmer in Pennsylvania
   New England merchant
   Native Americans in the Northwest Territory
   Frontier family in Kentucky
   Women on a plantation in Virginia

## Comments on Question 1

Question 1 combines a *Why?* and *How?* question with the direction to *Explain* a major development in United States history. You need to develop a thesis after pulling together the information you have on the development and growth of political parties. This is part of the historical method and of historical thinking. You should not study history by simply learning others' opinions or theses. You will retain information better and enjoy the study more if you become personally involved in each topic. That is why you are asked to develop theses and answers to the essay questions presented in the book.

As a study of these years reveals, there was no provision for parties, or factions as they were then called, in the Constitution. In fact, one of the major concerns of George Washington was the growth of these factions during his administration. Then why did they develop and how did they change?

In the dictionary, *why* is defined as, "For what cause, reason, or purpose; on what account . . ." *Why?* demands the establishment of a cause-and-effect relationship among events, ideas, and attitudes.

The issue usually cited as decisive in separating groups in Washington's first administration into what would become parties was Hamilton's economic program, and specifically his plan for a Bank of the United States. This is by no means the only issue that divided citizens into two opposing camps, and you should explore others. There are many subquestions you can ask about these issues. The raising of these subquestions is an excellent illustration of what you do in Step One of essay writing—analyze the question.

Having established what divided parties at the start, you must now explain how over time, the original parties changed and new ones emerged (or you might maintain that while names of parties changed, the ideas that separated people into factions remained the same). This covers a long period of time (29 years), and you cannot possibly list all the differences, so you must make choices as to the differences you will discuss. Major differences occurred over attitudes toward England and France, the interpretation of the Constitution, western settlement, and economic growth. What will you include?

The simplest organizational structure would be chronological, discussing various changes in what parties stood for over time. Or you could trace why parties faded away and new ones emerged at different times. As a general rule, one interrelated answer to double questions makes the best and most sophisticated answer, but it is the most difficult approach.

## Comments on Question 2

Essay question 2 is a *How?* question, the more sophisticated of the little words historians ask. It requires a thesis, an interpretation of how events affected one another. It is one type of cause-and-effect question. The answer again can be presented chronologically and, if you have spent any time on frontier history, you should have sufficient evidence to support your thesis. Among events you might consider are the Whiskey Rebellion of 1794, the need for Jay's Treaty with England, the election of the Congressional "War Hawks" from newly admitted frontier states who supported war with England in 1812, and Indian warfare.

In choosing the events to be discussed you will be able to indicate your personal opinion or thesis. You might even decide that no frontier event had a major impact and thereby produce a rather unexpected answer. The answer should be rather easy to write once you have analyzed the question and determined your thesis. The inclusion of the phrase *years 1789–1829* presents an easy method—chronological—for organizing your answer, although your brief notes may provide other organizational ideas.

## Comments on Question 3

Question 3 combines several types of essay questions. It begins with a statement of fact similar to the *Evaluate This Statement* form, but you are not asked to evaluate the statement, which is very simple and almost noncontroversial. The question then presents a *What?* and a *Who?* (*Whose?*) question. Four individuals are then listed from which you must pick two. It is of utmost importance in this type of question that you choose those items about which you know the most *as they relate to the question asked.* All four men mentioned in question 3 had strong opinions, some of which had a great impact throughout our history, such as Marshall's Supreme Court decisions and Washington's attitude toward "entangling alliances." But what impact did these opinions have "on the new nation"? Then you must decide whose opinions, of the two men you chose, had the greater impact on the nation. It is a sophisticated question of the type historians struggle with.

Perhaps the most difficult point in answering question 3 will be in organizing your material. Chronology is not important. One approach would be to present the opinions of one man followed by the second and then present, in a paragraph, which opinions had the greater impact. Another way would be to present the opinions of the two men on specific policies, such as the chartering of a Bank of the United States, U.S. relations with England and France, or the interpretation of the Constitution (loose or strict construction). As each policy is discussed, you could state which, overall, was the greatest, and indicate which man's opinion had the greater impact.

## Comments on Question 4

Question 4 is a straightforward *Analyze* type of question. The ability to analyze is one of the essential skills for historical thinking. In this question you are given a statement to consider. You may always agree or disagree with such statements. In this case you are asked to think how economic developments in one section of the country affected the other parts of the United States. The question directs you to focus on two aspects of history—social and political—the two from which the AP program states the majority of questions will come. Therefore, if you have followed the directions from the AP program, you should have some sound information to use in preparing your answer.

## Comments on Question 5

Question 5 is a typical type of question found on the AP exam. You are given some flexibility in what you write about. You have five items from which you must pick three. Make the choice carefully. *Analyze* questions have been very popular on AP exams over the years but there is no assurance that they will be used in a particular year. The word invites you to use your skills and knowledge as the historian does. The Constitution impacted the lives of different people in different ways as the new government established its authority. For instance, the suppression of the Whiskey Rebellion indicated, as well as other points, that the government intended to have authority over the frontier. The essay can be organized either by discussing how the Constitution affected each of your choices, using a paragraph for each choice, or by deciding what some of the effects of the Constitution were and discussing the impact of each effect on your three choices. The latter would be a more difficult approach.

## MULTIPLE-CHOICE QUESTIONS—CAUSE-AND-EFFECT

The multiple-choice section of the AP exam rarely contains a question introduced by *Who?*, *What?*, *When?*, or *Where?* but as you study for the exam you must ask these questions in order to fully understand the material. The AP exam will test your factual knowledge using more sophisticated and complicated questions as the examples in this book illustrate.

A very important type of question that tests both your factual knowledge and your historical thinking ability is one that seeks the cause-and-effect relationship discussed earlier. These questions can be worded in a variety of ways but the goal of all is to explore the relationship between events. In your studies, you will often be told to prepare a time line of events, or to memorize the relationship between events such as the British Acts and the colonial reaction to them as the colonists moved toward independence. These assignments are not just exercises in frustration, but are given so you have the cause-and-effect pattern of events. The two sample questions in this section require that you understand this relationship.

Many times a seventh little word, *Which?*, will be used to introduce a *Why?* or *How?* question. *Which?* is an undeclinable, both singular and plural pronoun used to refer to objects, while *Who?* is used to refer to persons or animate objects. Therefore, everything that has been said about *Who?* also refers to *Which?* The word *which* can also be used as an adjective; it then seeks the one or ones out of a group that are most relevant to the question asked.

## SAMPLE QUESTION

All of the following contributed to John Adams's defeat in the presidential election of 1800 EXCEPT

(A) The Alien and Sedition Acts
(B) The XYZ Affair
(C) Alexander Hamilton's disagreement with John Adams
(D) British occupation of forts in the Northwest Territory
(E) The failure of Adams to support war with France

## Comments on Sample Question

This question clearly seeks a cause-and-effect relationship. You need to know the events of the 1790s and how they contributed to John Adams's defeat in 1800 when he was seeking a second term. Choice D did not affect the election. The British continued to occupy forts in what was the Northwest Territory after the area was ceded to the United States in the Peace of Paris in 1783. During Washington's administration, in 1795 John Jay negotiated a treaty, Jay's Treaty, with the British and they finally withdrew from the Northwest Territory. Adams was elected for his first term after that treaty was signed so the British occupation of the forts in the Northwest Territory did not contribute to his defeat in 1800. The other events all contributed to Adams's defeat.

Hamilton and the war faction of the Federalist party wanted to fight France, so Hamilton attacked Adams when he refused to support war. The XYZ Affair in Adams's presidency illustrated the tension in our relations with France, and the Alien and Sedition Acts were part of our preparation for war. The XYZ Affair and the Alien and Sedition Acts antagonized many citizens.

Although the election was different from today's process and the election was resolved by the House of Representatives, the individuals involved in that process were affected by the four events listed. The question is clearly a complex one but it requires an understanding of cause and effect.

The structure of the question is somewhat different from most of those found on the AP exam. Instead of asking you to identify the one correct answer from among the five choices, you must pick the one wrong answer. The AP exam uses such questions, but statisticians do not like to have the questions switch from one format to another. Many teachers prefer the EXCEPT question since it reinforces the positive by providing students four correct statements instead of four wrong ones. In reviewing for the AP exam, it is important to learn the correct information, so in this book there are a few more EXCEPT questions than on the exam. In preparing for the exam, you need experience with the EXCEPT question as the evaluation of the choices requires a shift in usual thinking patterns required on negative-oriented multiple-choice questions. You also need positive reinforcement of the content. (This positive reinforcement approach has been followed in sample free-response answers. The content presented in all these answers is correct. Where low grades are given, it is because the information is poorly presented, the amount is inadequate, or it is irrelevant to the question.)

---

## SAMPLE QUESTION

The vote for a declaration of war against the British in 1812 illustrates the importance of the

(A) establishment of a regular army
(B) Native Americans in the frontier area
(C) Congressional representatives from the newly admitted western states
(D) growth of manufacturing in New England
(E) Department of the Navy

---

## Comments on Sample Question

The question does not use one of the "five W words" nor *How?*, but the question is asking, "How did the declaration of war in 1812 get passed?" The question does not mention the words *cause* or *effect,* but a cause-and-effect relationship is being sought. The student must know what issues led to the War of 1812, and from that knowledge he or she must analyze the choices offered. It requires that the student use his or her historical thinking skills, as with all sophisticated and complex questions.

The correct answer is C. The major force in pushing for war were the so-called War Hawks, the young Congressional representatives from the new western states. Our army and navy were unimportant at the time. The Native Americans were a concern, but their activities did not cause this war—in fact, General William H. Harrison had defeated the Indians at the Battle of Tippecanoe in 1811. New Englanders generally opposed the war and voted against it in Congress. If it had not been for the representatives of the new states, we would not have fought the War of 1812.

## Other Ways to Phrase Cause-and-Effect Questions

The following forms of multiple-choice questions all seek a cause-and-effect relationship. It is important to understand in how many different ways such questions can be asked.

1. The chief reason for the formation of the party known as the Jeffersonian Republicans was . . .

2. All of the following were reasons President Thomas Jefferson made the Louisiana Purchase EXCEPT . . .

3. The impressment of American sailors by the British led the United States to . . .

4. The Hartford Convention of 1815 was a result of . . .

5. The Jeffersonian Republicans supported the French in the years immediately after the start of the French Revolution because . . .

6. Which of the following was most directly responsible for the issuance of the Monroe Doctrine . . .

7. The XYZ Affair affected relations between the United States and France by . . .

8. How did members of the Federalist party respond to Washington's Proclamation of Neutrality in 1793 . . .

9. The chief reaction to Jay's Treaty in 1794 was . . .

Practice making up such questions as you study United States history. Involve yourself in the material as a teacher would. Look for relationships. Remember to use the four W words, *Who?, What?, When?, Where?,* as you study events and actions so you will have the factual information needed on the AP exam. Look for cause-and-effect relationships among the facts you learn. Remember the AP program expects you to act as an historian using historical thinking and the skills it entails.

# Practice Multiple-Choice Questions

1. The Rush Bagot Agreement called for

   (A) the expulsion of the British from Canada
   (B) a new boundary in Florida
   (C) the expulsion of aliens
   (D) mutual disarmament of the Great Lakes
   (E) commemoration of Perry's victory

2. Which of the following treaties granted the right of navigation on the Mississippi to the United States?

   (A) Pinckney's Treaty, 1795 (with Spain)
   (B) Jay's Treaty, 1795 (with Britain)
   (C) Treaty of Greenville, 1815 (with Native American tribes)
   (D) Peace of Paris, 1783 (with Britain)
   (E) Treaty of Ghent, 1814 (with Britain)

3. Which of the following accurately describes the Treaty of Ghent (1814) that ended the War of 1812?

   (A) General Andrew Jackson's victory over the British at the Battle of New Orleans forced the British to sign the treaty.
   (B) The treaty included a clause drawing a new boundary line between the United States and Canada.
   (C) The treaty established a mechanism for continued consultation between the British and United States governments.
   (D) The treaty included no reference to the impressment of United States sailors, which is considered one of the causes of the war.
   (E) The British agreed to pay reparations to cover the cost of restoring buildings they had burned in Washington, D.C.

4. All of the following individuals supported those ideas expressed by the Federalist Party leadership EXCEPT

   (A) Alexander Hamilton
   (B) George Washington
   (C) John Adams
   (D) John Marshall
   (E) Thomas Jefferson

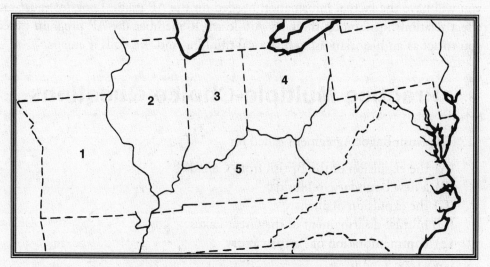

5. The states numbered 2, 3, 4 on the above map of a segment of the United States

   (A) were created from the area referred to as the Northwest Territory
   (B) included the birthplaces of the first five presidents of the United States
   (C) are the location of the largest Native American reservations
   (D) are among the least populated states in the nation
   (E) are considered the birthplace of the industrial revolution in the United States

6. How would one best explain the selection of Washington, D.C. as the capital of the United States?

   (A) It was at a natural ford in the Potomac River.
   (B) The rapids in the river provided power for water mills.
   (C) It was convenient to George Washington's home at Mount Vernon.
   (D) It was selected as a result of a Congressional compromise between the North and the South.
   (E) The land was granted by the state of Maryland to the federal government.

7. Why would a frontier farmer in Illinois in the early 1800s support the United States' acquisition of New Orleans?

   (A) It would keep French and Spanish traders away from his area.
   (B) It would prove the nation supported expansion.
   (C) It would provide convenient access to a large slave market.
   (D) It was where goods coming down the river were transferred to seagoing ships.
   (E) It would provide a cultural center for the region.

"This general principle is inherent in the very definition of government, and essential to every step of the progress to be made by that United States, namely: that every power vested in a government is in its nature sovereign, and includes, . . . , a right to employ all the means requisite and fairly applicable to the attainment of the ends of such power . . . which are not immoral, or contrary to the essential ends of political society . . ."

8. The above quotation expresses the definition of government that would guide the interpretation of the Constitution by

   (A) a supporter of states rights
   (B) John Marshall as Chief Justice
   (C) Thomas Jefferson in the early 1790s
   (D) a strict constructionist
   (E) Patrick Henry of Virginia

9. The major reason for the demise of the Federalist Party in the decade before 1820 was

   (A) their failure to support tariffs and New England manufacturing interests
   (B) public disgust over the duel between the Federalist supporter, Alexander Hamilton, and Aaron Burr
   (C) their support of the spread of slavery into the Northwest Territory
   (D) the popularity of Transcendentalism, which denied the fundamental principles of the Federalists
   (E) the failure of New England Federalists to support the War of 1812

10. The XYZ Affair led to the loss of support for the French in the United States in the 1790s because

   (A) it forced Washington to declare neutrality, which hurt U.S. trade
   (B) it forced the United States to break the Treaty of 1778
   (C) it indicated the French were not willing to sell the Louisiana Territory
   (D) it revealed the French were more interested in obtaining bribes than in negotiating differences
   (E) it showed the French would continue to build forts on the U.S. frontier

### Answers and Answer Explanations

   1. **(D)**    2. **(A)**    3. **(D)**    4. **(E)**
   5. **(A)**    6. **(D)**    7. **(D)**    8. **(B)**
   9. **(E)**    10. **(D)**

These first four questions focus on political and international issues. They are all recall questions of different levels of difficulty.

1. **(D)** The Rush Bagot Agreement between the United States and Great Britain in 1817 established the principle of the undefended border between Britain's Canadian colony and the United States. It called for the disarming of the Great Lakes. It was a result of an arbitration committee established under the terms of the Treaty of Ghent in 1814 and illustrates the growing cooperation between the United States and Great Britain.

2. **(A)** Pinckney's Treaty with Spain, signed in 1795, permitted navigation on the Mississippi. At the time Spain owned the Louisiana Territory and controlled the city of New Orleans, so Spain controlled navigation by owning one side of the river and the port at the mouth. France later acquired Louisiana from Spain and we bought the territory from France in 1803. The other treaties dealt with various international issues in the years 1783–1814.

3. **(D)** The Treaty of Ghent in 1814 essentially reestablished the situation as it existed before the war. Those issues that had led to war, including impressment, were not mentioned, and the British made no offer to repair damages inflicted during the war, such as their burning of the nation's capital. It is ironic that Jackson's victory at New Orleans, one of the few major victories the United States had in the war, came after the treaty was signed, because communication across the Atlantic was so slow.

4. **(E)** Thomas Jefferson held views opposite to those of the Federalists and became the leader of the opposition party, the Jeffersonian Republicans. The differences between Jefferson and Hamilton (considered the spokesman for the Federalist viewpoint), expressed in their letters to Washington concerning the Bank of the United States, are considered the initial clear presentation of the ideas of these first two parties in the United States. The other four men supported Federalist ideas of a strong central government and support for the merchant and business communities and Great Britain.

5. **(A)** This question requires that you have a knowledge of the map of the United States, that is, basic *Where?* knowledge. You should recognize the states numbered 2, 3, and 4 as Illinois, Indiana, and Ohio, which were formed from the area known as the Northwest Territory. The line forming their southern border is the Ohio River and that is a clue for you. These states today are highly industrialized, but the start of the industrial revolution in the United States took place in New England. There were important struggles with the Native Americans in the region but there are few reservations there today—the large ones are west of the Mississippi River. These two incorrect answers illustrate how answers will often have elements of truth in them.

6. **(D)** The decision to locate the national capital on the banks of the Potomac River—a southern location—came as a result of a Congressional compromise in which Alexander Hamilton, Secretary of the Treasury, gained southern votes for his economic plans in return for northern votes for the location of Washington, D.C. on the Potomac. It is true the state of Maryland granted the site of Washington, D.C. to the federal government but that is not the reason the capital is located there. It did not grow up as so many cities did because of fords or water power. Being close to Washington's home in Mount Vernon had no bearing on the situation, as New York City served as the capital throughout Washington's presidency. This question and question 7 both require an understanding of the cause-and-effect relationship discussed in this chapter.

7. **(D)** A frontier settler in Illinois would most likely support the acquisition of New Orleans because it was the place goods coming down the river on boats were transferred (the "right of deposit") to oceangoing vessels, thus giving the farmer access to markets on the East Coast, in Europe, and in the Caribbean. Illinois was a non-slave state, so there would be no interest in the slave market. The French and Spanish were not a threat to Illinois in the early 1800s, and while New Orleans was a cultural center, it was a long distance away for the average frontier farmer. The "right of deposit" is often mentioned in relation to New Orleans. It is a term from International Law that permits goods from one country to be changed from one mode of transportation to another in a second country with no taxes or import duties paid to that second country.

8. **(B)** This question provides a quote as a stimulus. You do not need to recognize its source but must use your historical thinking skills to interpret its meaning. Then you must use recall of factual information to decide which of the five choices would most likely support the view expressed. In this case it would be John Marshall as Chief Justice. The court under Marshall interpreted the Constitution in a broad manner, often referred to as "loose construction," or the doctrine of implied powers. It says that if a power is *not* specifically *denied* in the Constitution, is not immoral or opposed to the ends of political unity, and is needed to carry out one of the powers expressly mentioned in the Constitution, then the federal government should have that power. Loose construction has been advocated by different parties and individuals at different times. Usually the party in power supports the concept. The Federalists did in the 1790s, but opposed loose construction at the time of the Louisiana Purchase and after 1812. The Jeffersonians opposed it during John Adams's administration. States-

righters oppose loose construction, as it gives more power to the federal government.

9. **(E)** Both this question and number 10 are seeking a cause-and-effect relationship. The major reason for the demise of the Federalist Party was the failure of Federalists in New England to support the War of 1812. The Hartford Convention is often cited as an example of their attitude—an attitude that suggested New England might be better off if it withdrew from the Union since its merchant and manufacturing interests did appear to have national support. Failure to support the government in wartime has often led to political isolation. The Federalists did support tariffs and trade. Slavery was abolished in the Northwest Territory under the government of the Articles of Confederation so it was not an issue. Transcendentalism did not emerge as an important intellectual movement until later in the century and had a limited effect on politics. The Hamilton-Burr duel occurred in 1804 and while shocking, it did not seem to affect the party the way some recent scandals have affected political parties.

10. **(D)** The XYZ Affair led to the loss of support for the French in the United States. It revealed the French were more interested in obtaining bribes than in negotiating differences. John Adams had sent envoys to Paris to resolve differences with the French government concerning their interference with United States shipping and other issues. The French Foreign Minister, Talleyrand, sought a bribe and loan before negotiations began and the United States refused. Two envoys returned and when a report on the situation was published in 1798, there were calls for war against the French. The other choices, except the French building of forts on the frontier, reflect different aspects of relations with France. You need to know how these relations developed and then separate out the one that affected relations in the late 1790s.

# Jackson, the West, and Manifest Destiny 1824–1850

## CHAPTER 7

- Review of events
- Sample essay questions and responses
- Questions involving maps

Jacksonian Democracy and Manifest Destiny are the two chief issues of the years 1824–1850. Andrew Jackson, the dominant figure, is in the eyes of one historian, J. W. Ward, the symbol of an age. Other historians, while acknowledging the significance of the era, question the contributions Jackson made and the amount of democracy present. However, Jackson's name has been given to the period 1824–1837, the Age of Jackson, which is considered by some historians as the adolescence of the nation. In preparation for the Advanced Placement examination, every student should have a thorough understanding of Jackson's career and of the meaning of Jacksonian Democracy. Also, the concept of Manifest Destiny must be understood and the way Americans followed it to expand the nation.

## AGE OF JACKSON

The Age of Jackson was a period marked by many social and economic changes. The age is recognized as the start of the operation of the political system as we know it today. It was a time of contrasts—of great intolerance and of great concern for the underprivileged. Jackson's presidency was followed by economic depression and then by a decade of expansion for which the slogan became Manifest Destiny.

Manifest Destiny culminated in the acquisition of Oregon and the Mexican War. These events in turn opened up the issue of the spread of slavery, which was temporarily settled at the end of this time period with the Compromise of 1850.

Among the topics one would want to consider in studying these years would be the following:

1. The reasons for the breakup of the Era of Good Feelings, which culminated in the election of 1828

2. Jackson's "War on the Bank of the United States"
3. The tariff issue and Calhoun's ideas on nullification
4. The growth of sectionalism and the distinguishing features of the three sections—Northeast, South, and West
5. Emerging social concerns and attitudes as exemplified by educational, institutional, and literary developments
6. The Panic of 1837 and its impact upon the nation
7. Manifest Destiny and the presidency of James K. Polk
8. The Mexican War and its aftermath
9. The spread of slavery to new territories.

## SAMPLE ESSAY QUESTION—IN WHAT WAYS...?

The question that begins *In what ways . . . ?* is a common type of essay question and one that has many variations, such as *In what manner . . . ?* or *In what respects . . . ?* or *To what extent . . . ?* Basically, this form is a version of the simple *What?* type, but with the addition of the other words, the writer is given more specific direction as to what must be done. Therefore, in the *In what ways?* type, the important word becomes the one after *what.*

How do you approach answering an *In what ways?* question? The key word in this type of question is *ways.* The word *ways* implies a progression or movement from one point to another and suggests a chronological organization by which the writer can illustrate how an event or idea led to other events or ideas.

What do you do when you are asked to focus on the *manner* in which something occurred? The word *manner* means a mode of procedure or customary way of acting. The focus of the answer to this type of essay would be less on the sequence of events and more on what lay behind them. Why did they occur, or what made people act the way they did, would be the important part of the answer.

If you are asked *In what respects?* you are being asked about relationships again. *Respect* is defined as relation or relationship, regarding an act of noticing with attention. This version of the basic type is very similar to the *In what way?* version and would require a cause-and-effect approach with events carefully related together. You would want to dwell on the reasons, paying strict attention to all the *whys* and *wherefores* you can consider. There are other variations of the *In what ways?* type of question such as *to what extent?* The key is always to look at and analyze the word after *what.*

**TIP**

"Do you agree or disagree" means you must argue your position.

Sometimes the *To what extent?* variation will have added the phrase *Do you agree or disagree?* This phrase can be attached to many essay questions and simply reinforces the invitation to argument. **Remember, in every essay answer you are arguing a case as a lawyer or debater does**. You may take any personal view you wish on any issue, and the quality of your paper will be judged on how well you argue and prove your personal opinion or thesis. The *Do you agree or disagree?* phrase simply makes it clearer that your personal opinion is being sought. The phrase is another way of asking the writer to evaluate the statement, and much of what was said about that type of essay question in Part One applies to any essay question in which you are asked to agree or disagree.

A typical *In what ways?* essay question is the following:

## Comments on Sample Question

The question asks you to consider the "ways"—that is, the stops or progression or events in which "the emerging sectional conflicts within the United States manifested themselves" in two time periods—the time leading to the election of Jackson and the time during his presidency. In order to answer the question you must know that the word *manifest* means to reveal or else you would be in trouble. You must deal with the two periods and it is important that both areas be treated.

You will want to begin your analysis by deciding what the sectional conflicts were. If you cannot remember them, then this is not a question for you. If you do know them, then list the issues of the election of 1828 and Jackson's domestic policies. Then you are ready to answer the question. After you have worked up notes or written your answer to this question following the Seven Steps in Essay Writing, you will want to read and judge the following student answer to the question.

Some people may think that questions starting with "To what extent" or "In what ways" do not require a thesis. Of course that is not correct. Every essay requires a thesis, and individuals will differ on what they consider the extent or the ways in which certain issues or events impacted other issues or events. This leads to the thesis statement—the statement of your point of view.

## Sample Answer

Andrew Jackson was elected president in 1828, having run and been defeated in 1824 by J. Q. Adams, whom he beat in 1828. The campaign was a dirty one, the first really dirty campaign. In fact, Jackson later felt that the accusations against his wife and her divorce from her first husband were the cause of her death, which took place early in his first administration.

J. Q. Adams was a very intelligent man, but he was not a very good president. This helped defeat him, as some members of his own party, including the later president, Van Buren, left Adams to support Jackson. Jackson, on the other hand, had proven himself a fine general by winning the Battle of New Orleans He was called Old Hickory and his supporters claimed he was born in a log cabin. Actually, Jackson was wealthy and had a beautiful plantation home, the Hermitage, but the log cabin idea caught on and many men running for office during our history have capitalized on their log cabin backgrounds.

When Jackson became president, he used the Spoils System to put his friends in office. He did not start the system, as was once believed, but he used it extensively. Jackson believed any American could operate the government, and since the government was the people's, he appointed ordinary citizens to fill important posts. Jackson also believed, since he was the only official in the federal government elected by all the people, that he represented the people. This encouraged him to act as a strong president. An example of this position was when Chief Justice Marshall declared in a case that Georgia had no claim to Indian territory in the state. Rather than enforce the ruling, which he disapproved of, Jackson said, "Marshall made the decision; let him enforce it." Along with the Spoils System, Jackson was known for the Kitchen Cabinet, which was made up of a group of his friends who gave him advice on various domestic and foreign issues. They did not hold government positions, yet they were more important than the regular cabinet.

During Jackson's administration, the sale of western lands was important. There was a lot of speculation in the land sales and this led to inflation, which Jackson didn't like. He therefore issued the "specie circular," which forced people to pay for lands with gold or silver. This was a cause of the Panic of 1837.

The name Jackson is connected with the word *democracy*. Many historians believe the nation really became democratic during the 1830s. To support this idea they report the spread of universal male suffrage. Also, behind this coming of age of democracy are many other important developments, such as the spread of free public schools, the growing rate of immigration, the growth of industry, and the rise of labor unions, which supported the common man. Industry grew the most in the North, and the South remained agricultural. The West wanted roads and transportation. The idea emerged to have a high tariff on imports to help the North's industry and to use the money to build roads. The South didn't like the high tariff since they imported many goods. The tariff was a major issue during Jackson's presidency. Another issue of Jackson's time was the bank issue, which involved a long fight with Nicholas Biddle and a refusal to recharter the Second Bank. Then there were problems with Indians, England, and picking Jackson's successor. These all affected different people and sections.

## Questions About the Sample Answer

As in the case of the other sample essays, reflect on this one before you read the teacher comments. The making of a formal outline of this answer will help you better understand what the writer has done. What are its good features? What are its bad features? Do you think the writer followed the Seven Steps in Essay Writing? On a scale of 1 to 9 with a 9 being the top, where would you rank it? This is what the readers of your exam will be asked to do. What advice do you have for this student? Have you ever written an essay similar to this one? What did the teacher tell you?

## Teacher Comments on Sample Answer

"The writer of this essay has plenty of important and accurate factual information at his or her command, but he or she has simply spewed it out with no reference to the question at all. It is an unfortunate case of rushing into answering a question. The writer has focused on a few words in the question, in this case *election* and *Andrew Jackson*, and written what he knew about them with no reference to how the words are used in the question. The student's references to Van Buren's desertion of Adams, to the "specie circular," to the purchase of western lands, to the North, South, West split over internal improvements, and to the tariff reveal that he or she has valuable information to develop a viewpoint on "emerging sectional conflicts." Unfortunately, in no place does the student present a personal viewpoint or thesis on the topic under consideration, nor is the topic of the question mentioned. A thesis is badly needed. The writer has left out the two essentials of a good opening and has clearly not analyzed the question.

"The writer presents detailed information on the Spoils System, the Kitchen Cabinet, and Jacksonian Democracy. All of these items could have been used to illustrate sectional differences, although the Kitchen Cabinet may be a little farfetched as an illustration. Still, the idea of the use of friends and the common people to run the government could be used to illustrate the change in government brought about when the West took the presidency from the more aristocratic East.

"The writer of the essay uses several paragraphs, but the last one includes several ideas—democracy, industry, tariff, and Bank—which should be presented in separate paragraphs. There is no clear linkage of the paragraphs and the organization—a mixture of topic and chronology—is confusing and seems to follow a free association of ideas rather than any formal structure. Finally, the essay just stops; there is no conclusion. Therefore, in spite of the fine information this writer has, the failure to answer the question and the poor essay style earned a low grade—a 5 on a 1–9 scale. It is an all too common failure among students. It is particularly unfortunate in this case since the student obviously is bright and knowledgeable. If the student had thought before writing and used the Seven Steps, with the information presented, he or she should have been able to write a fine essay and to earn an outstanding grade."

## Practice Essay Questions

The above student essay clearly demonstrates the importance of the Seven Steps in Essay Writing. Before you read and prepare the answer to the following essay questions, you may want to check back to Part One and review the Seven Steps in Essay Writing. Also, as you prepare to deal with these five essays, do not forget our image of the flashlight. Your essay needs a beam to catch the reader, connected batteries to make the beam shine, and a cap to hold the batteries in contact and to make the whole flashlight work.

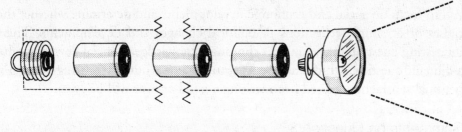

1. In what ways did the concept of Manifest Destiny affect the foreign and domestic policies of the United States in the years 1840–1850?

2. To what extent did the Jackson presidency reflect the social and economic developments in the nation at that time?

3. In what respects did TWO of the following represent in their expressed opinions and actions the viewpoint of the section of the nation from which he came?

   Calhoun—The South
   Clay—The West
   Webster—New England

4. "Both the Jacksonian Democrats between 1828 and 1836 and the Populists between 1890 and 1896 wanted to eliminate special privilege in American society. The Jacksonian Democrats succeeded; the Populists failed."

   Assess the validity of this view.

5. In what manner did the Jacksonian Revolution mark the establishment of democracy in America, whereas the Jeffersonian Revolution merely marked the arrival of a new party in political power?

## Comments on Question 1

Question 1 is typical of the *In what ways?* type of question. It is seeking a cause-and-effect relationship as in a *What?* question, and implicitly it asks you to present the manner in which this relationship came about. This particular question is dependent upon your understanding the concept of Manifest Destiny.* This is one of those phrases students should know; it summarizes a whole series of attitudes and beliefs held by the Americans at a particular point in history. Once you have the meaning of the phrase clear in your mind, then you should list some of the foreign and domestic issues of the years 1840 to 1850. Once you have done that, you will want to ask yourself the question, "How did Manifest Destiny relate to the issues listed?" Your answer to that question will be your thesis; your list of issues should provide organizational clues, and so you should be ready to write.

## Comments on Question 2

The second question is one variation on the *In what ways?* type discussed above. The *To what extent?* form is a *What?* question seeking cause-and-effect relations, but it clearly asks for your personal opinion about the question and in that sense it is asking you to agree or disagree with the material. This particular question seeks your judgment on the relationship between Jackson's presidency and social and economic development. It is a good example of a question dealing with social history. It asks you to focus on social and economic developments and determine whether they are causes of or simply reflections of political changes and developments. This is an interesting question that requires a thorough knowledge of social developments. It is a difficult question, which may be hard to organize, but if you struggle with it, the personal satisfaction gained from writing a good answer will be great.

## Comments on Question 3

The third question, an *In what respects?* form, is another variation on the *In what ways?* type. It is another one of those questions in which a personal opinion may appear not to be needed, but as always, you must make and express a judgment. In this case you must know the opinions and actions of at least two of three important leaders of the period before 1850 and you must know the viewpoints of the major sections of the nation in those years. Finally, you must decide if two men's opinions and actions reflect the ideas of their section of the country. If you are in command of details involving all of these points, then you can develop your thesis and prepare to answer the question. In this question the obvious organizational format would be to discuss each man in turn and write introductory and concluding paragraphs that tie the two men together with the general topic.

## Comments on Question 4

This is a typical *Assess the Validity* (*Evaluate This Statement*) type of question discussed in Chapter 3. The quotation asks you to deal with two specific movements in

---

* Manifest Destiny summarizes the idea that it was the destiny of the United States to control the continent and was an important idea in U.S. foreign policy in the late 1830s and 1840s.

American history in two different periods. They are major movements that all students should be familiar with, but the focus of the question is on eliminating "special privilege" in American life—an aspect of these movements that may not be as familiar. The question illustrates how an AP examination question may focus on an unusual aspect of the period. If you are not in control of such information, it would be wise not to attempt the question, but if you are, it is not a difficult question. In this case, once you have analyzed what you know about eliminating special privilege in these two eras, you must decide if you agree that the Jacksonians were successful and the Populists were not. Obviously, your decision on this issue will provide you with the thesis statement. There are several ways to organize the answer. You can write about the Jacksonians and then the Populists separately or you might find issues, such as the monopoly of transportation, that appeared in both time periods and discuss how each group handled it.

## Comments on Question 5

The last question presents the *In what manner?* variation of the *In what ways?* form. The question asks for a comparison of time periods, and in this case you are comparing two periods with which you should be familiar by now if you are studying American history chronologically as you read this book. The issue raised—when did the United States become a democracy?—is one investigated in most U.S. history courses. The Jackson and Jefferson revolutions are often compared. The question takes an extreme position, and you should be able to react strongly with a personal opinion. The facts should then follow, and they should supply you with an organizational framework. Finding such a framework may be the most difficult task with this question.

# MULTIPLE CHOICE—MAPS

As indicated when discussing the sample essay in Part One, many historians believe that geography or environmental factors are at the heart of history. They believe these factors determine and control the choices people can make about their lives. This is perhaps an extreme interpretation, but it does illustrate how central geography is for understanding history. For you, as a student of United States history, geography must be learned and understood. A knowledge of the location of states and of geographic features, such as rivers and mountains, and of their importance in the development of the nation and of the movement of people must be understood. Your knowledge of this information may be needed in essay answers (see question 3 on page 87), or it may be tested in multiple-choice questions.

Map questions are a good example of a stimulus question. They also provide an excellent way to gain fundamental information about United States history and to help the student review basic information. Map questions have already been included in the sample multiple-choice questions in Chapters 4, 5, and 6, and will be included in the remaining chapters. These examples of multiple-choice questions involving maps will illustrate the wide range of questions that can be asked based directly on maps and on the analysis of maps. Many other questions might be asked in addition to these. These questions should make you realize the importance of geography, of studying the maps in the textbooks, and of locating places **where** events took place as you read about those events.

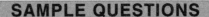

**SAMPLE QUESTIONS**

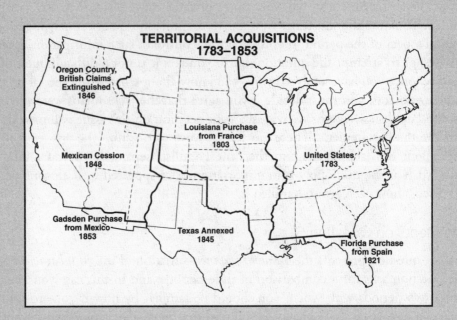

TERRITORIAL ACQUISITIONS
1783–1853

Oregon Country, British Claims Extinguished 1846

Louisiana Purchase from France 1803

United States 1783

Mexican Cession 1848

Gadsden Purchase from Mexico 1853

Texas Annexed 1845

Florida Purchase from Spain 1821

1. The map indicates our largest single territorial acquisition after independence was the

(A) Oregon Country
(B) Mexican Cession
(C) Gadsden Purchase
(D) Louisiana Purchase
(E) Florida Purchase

2. The Gadsden Purchase was particularly important because it

(A) gave us a more defensible border with Mexico
(B) included a new source of gold
(C) included the best southern route for a railroad to the West Coast
(D) provided land for an Indian reservation
(E) smoothed our relations with Mexico after the strain of the Mexican War

3. The map indicates the period of greatest territorial growth of the United States was in the decade

(A) 1790–1800
(B) 1800–1810
(C) 1820–1830
(D) 1840–1850
(E) 1850–1860

Comments on Questions 1–3

Question 1 (D) assumes that you can read a very familiar map. There should be no question that the Louisiana Purchase was the largest single territorial acquisition shown on the map. You may want to say Alaska, but it is *not* on the map and *not* offered as a choice. Sometimes your recall knowledge will *not* be offered as a choice for an answer, and then you must analyze the data given to pick the best answer from the choices.

Question 2 (C) tests learned knowledge. However, by studying the map and the five choices, there is a good chance you would pick the correct answer (C) even if you were not familiar with the Gadsden Purchase. Reading choice C might remind you of the main reason for it. **You will often find the choices given in a multiple-choice ques-**

tion trigger your thinking and help you with the answer. **Do not skip reading the choices just because the information in the stem is unfamiliar. Multiple-choice questions are constructed to help you in your analysis.** You might also have figured it out by eliminating the other choices or by realizing railroads were of growing significance in the 1850s and the purchase is on the extreme southern border. Some map questions, as the ones used in the book so far, will simply test your factual recall.

Question 3 requires that you combine territories acquired in the same decade to determine in which decade the nation grew the most. Although the largest single territory acquired was Louisiana in 1803, we acquired more territory in three different sections in the decade of the 1840s. The question is an easy test of map-reading skill.

## SAMPLE QUESTIONS

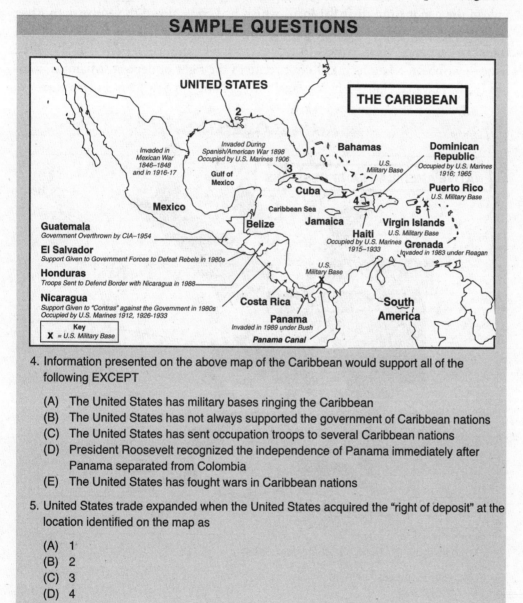

4. Information presented on the above map of the Caribbean would support all of the following EXCEPT

(A) The United States has military bases ringing the Caribbean
(B) The United States has not always supported the government of Caribbean nations
(C) The United States has sent occupation troops to several Caribbean nations
(D) President Roosevelt recognized the independence of Panama immediately after Panama separated from Colombia
(E) The United States has fought wars in Caribbean nations

5. United States trade expanded when the United States acquired the "right of deposit" at the location identified on the map as

(A) 1
(B) 2
(C) 3
(D) 4
(E) 5

## Comments on Questions 4–5

The map of the Caribbean is included here to remind you that you must know not only the geography of the United States when studying United States history but also that of areas where the United States has been involved overseas, such as Europe, the Pacific, and the Asian Rim. The map of the Caribbean presents information that would confirm all but D of the statements given in question 4. The United States has military bases around the Caribbean and has sent troops to occupy several nations. The United States supported the Contra rebels against the government of Nicaragua. The United States invaded Mexico in the Mexican War and attacked Spanish forces in Cuba during the Spanish-American War. This information is placed on the map in addition to the geographic features one normally expects to find. While this map includes more information than found on most maps, it illustrates the variety of information one can find on a map.

Question 5 (B) is a straightforward identification question that requires you to recall the meaning of the "right of deposit" and to connect it with the city of New Orleans, which is number 2 on the map. The right of deposit allowed Americans to unload the goods from their flatboats, which had come down the Mississippi River onto oceangoing vessels without paying import duties on the goods. This allowed trade to expand. The other locations are all important ones for United States–Caribbean relations but do not relate to the right of deposit. Miami is number 1; 3 is Havana, Cuba; 4 is Port-au-Prince, Haiti; 5 is San Juan, Puerto Rico.

## SAMPLE QUESTION

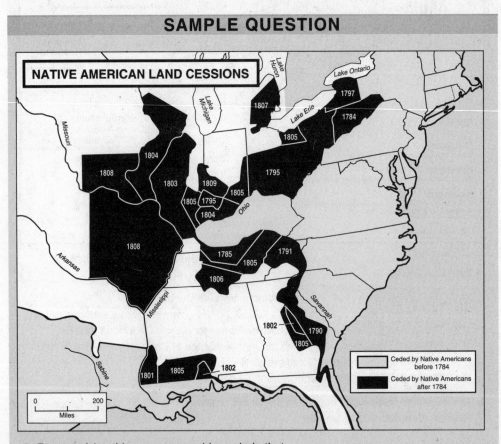

6. From studying this map, one could conclude that

   (A)  Native Americans ceded land along the Atlantic coast prior to the writing of the Constitution.

   (B)  Native Americans and white settlers believed in treaties.

   (C)  white settlers were greedy for land.

   (D)  the Native Americans made money from the sale of lands.

   (E)  the Supreme Court under Marshall protected the Cherokee lands in Georgia.

## Comments on Question 6

Question 6 (A) offers several choices that are true statements but for which there is no evidence on the map. It is important to realize there are limits as to what can be proven by a map. The Supreme Court under Marshall did protect Cherokee lands and white settlers were greedy, but the map doesn't prove it—it may suggest it, but there may have been other motivations for the Native American cession of lands. Belief in treaties and money is not mentioned on the map. You can, however, prove that Native Americans ceded land to the colonists along the mid-Atlantic seacoast prior to the writing of the Constitution. The map key indicates that statement A is true.

## SAMPLE QUESTION

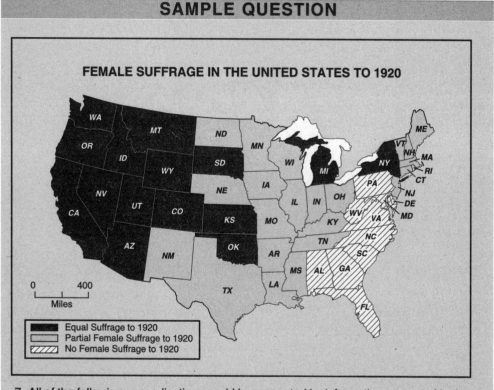

**FEMALE SUFFRAGE IN THE UNITED STATES TO 1920**

■ Equal Suffrage to 1920
☐ Partial Female Suffrage to 1920
▨ No Female Suffrage to 1920

7. All of the following generalizations could be supported by information presented in the map EXCEPT

(A) The western half of the nation was more responsive to the issue of women's suffrage than the eastern half.

(B) States created from the Louisiana Purchase and Mexican Cession all had at least partial female suffrage by 1920.

(C) It would be impossible in 1919 to get a constitutional amendment passed giving the vote to women.

(D) In 1920, states along the eastern seaboard would be most likely to reject a constitutional amendment that gave the vote to women.

(E) New York was the most liberal state of the original 13 on the issue of votes for women.

## Comments on Question 7

Question 7 again asks you to confirm generalizations or speculations based on evidence from a map. It is a good test of map-reading ability. The map on female suffrage would support all the generalizations given, except that it would be impossible to get a constitutional amendment passed in 1919 giving the women the right to vote (C). You might assume this, but there is no way of knowing how the states with partial female suffrage would vote. You would *suspect* the states with equal suffrage would support the amendment and those states with no female suffrage would vote against the amendment, but there is no way to be sure from the map how they would vote or how that crucial group of 24 states with partial suffrage would vote. One must be careful not to assume too much from the map. The other four assumptions would appear quite safe. The states created from the Louisiana Purchase and the Mexican Cession, all west of the Mississippi River, had either granted equal or partial suffrage by 1920. Only states in the East had granted no suffrage by then. Of the original 13, only New York allowed women to vote equally with men. The western states all had granted female suffrage. If liberal means to grant suffrage, then the West and New York are liberal.

## SAMPLE QUESTIONS

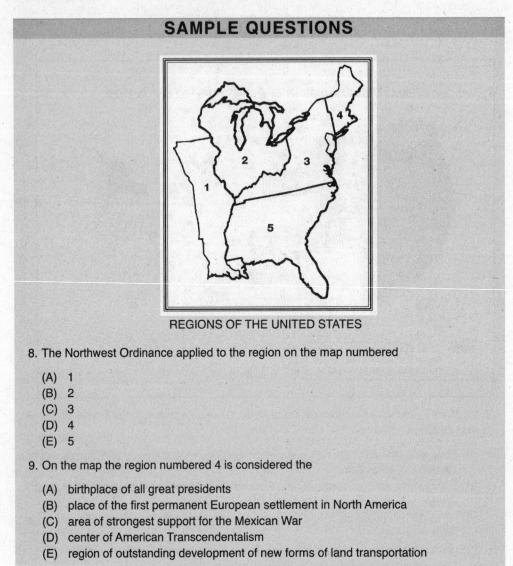

REGIONS OF THE UNITED STATES

8. The Northwest Ordinance applied to the region on the map numbered

(A) 1
(B) 2
(C) 3
(D) 4
(E) 5

9. On the map the region numbered 4 is considered the

(A) birthplace of all great presidents
(B) place of the first permanent European settlement in North America
(C) area of strongest support for the Mexican War
(D) center of American Transcendentalism
(E) region of outstanding development of new forms of land transportation

## Comments on Questions 8–9

The map for questions 8 and 9 is a type commonly used in multiple-choice questions. The type requires that you know the geography of the United States so that you can identify regions, states, major cities, and territories. In question 8 (B) you must know that the Northwest Ordinance applied to the Northwest Territory and be able to recognize this region on the map. It is 2—the area east of the Mississippi River, north of the Ohio River, south of the Great Lakes, and west of Pennsylvania. The question tests recall and factual geographic knowledge. Question 9 (D) does the same but it is a little more sophisticated, requiring you to identify a region with an activity. It also tests literary knowledge—an example that map questions can be used to bring about a recall of all types of information. In this question, area 4 is New England, the center of Transcendentalism. Its leaders were Emerson and Thoreau, but many other intellectual leaders of New England, such as Hawthorne and Parkman, were connected with Transcendentalism. Some people may believe that all great presidents are New Englanders, but that is ridiculous. The first permanent European settlement was the Spanish settlement at St. Augustine, Florida. New Englanders opposed the Mexican War, and new land transportation was developed in the West while New Englanders concentrated on clipper ships and the sea. Question 9 is a good use of the simple map question where you need to know the geography of the country and to recall factual information about it.

## SAMPLE QUESTIONS

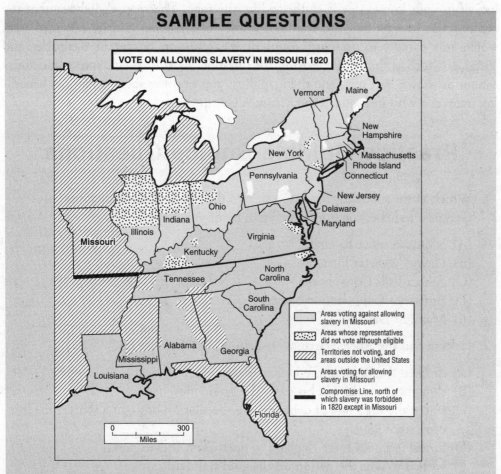

10. According to the map, which one of the following statements is true?

   (A) There were no southern states in favor of the extension of slavery into Missouri.
   (B) Of those eligible, only delegates from slaveholding states failed to vote.
   (C) No New Englanders favored extending slavery into Missouri.
   (D) Florida was a non-slaveholding territory.
   (E) The North and the South were essentially divided on the issue of the extension of slavery to Missouri.

11. The map illustrates that

   (A) Henry Clay proposed the Missouri Compromise
   (B) the South always voted as a block
   (C) the North could not unite on issues
   (D) the Missouri Compromise line continues approximately at the southern border of Virginia and Kentucky
   (E) there were many territories about to be states

Comments on Questions 10–11

Questions 10 and 11 are good tests of map-reading skill. For number 10 (E) the map clearly shows that there were some New Englanders in favor of the Missouri Compromise and that some delegates from all regions failed to vote. Of course the map shows nothing about slavery in Florida. Choice A of question 10 is very tricky. You might read it quickly and say it was true, but, of course, it is just the reverse of the truth. Be careful in your reading. The map shows there was a decided division between the North and the South on the issue of the extension of slavery into Missouri, which is the correct answer for question 10. You might have known this, but again your knowledge is confirmed by the map. The map also shows that the compromise line follows the southern border of Missouri and, if extended east, would run parallel to and just south of the southern border of Kentucky and Virginia, which is the correct answer for question 11 (D). Block voting and unity cannot be shown by a map and the map illustrates nothing about territories becoming states nor who introduced the Missouri Compromise.

# Practice Multiple-Choice Questions

1. Which of the following was a reaction to the desire of some members of Congress to lower the price of western land?

   (A) Mormon move to Utah
   (B) Hayne-Webster Debate
   (C) Seneca Falls Convention
   (D) American Colonization Society
   (E) Manifest Destiny

2. Jackson had the "specie circular" issued in 1836 because he

   (A) disliked the Bank of the United States
   (B) thought it would win his party the presidency
   (C) feared the high rate of debt and the speculation brought about by the sale of western land.
   (D) hoped it would force England to open West Indian ports
   (E) wished to take the nation off the gold standard

3. Of the 19th-century inventions listed below which is incorrectly paired with its inventor

   (A) Reaper—Fulton
   (B) Vulcanization of rubber—Whitney
   (C) Sewing machine—McCormack
   (D) Steamboat—Howe
   (E) Telegraph—Bell

Questions 4–5 refer to the following quotation:

"If we must have a bank with private stockholders, every consideration of sound policy . . . admonishes that it should be *purely American*. Its stockholders should be composed exclusively of our own citizens, who at least ought to be friendly to our Government and willing to support it in times of difficulty and danger . . . To a bank exclusively of American stockholders, . . . subscriptions for $200,000,000 could be readily obtained . . .

"It is maintained by the advocates of the bank that its constitutionality in all its features ought to be considered as settled by precedent and by the decision of the Supreme Court. To this conclusion I can not assent."

4. The author of the above quotation appears to believe all of the following EXCEPT

(A) the Bank is not constitutional
(B) it is dangerous to have foreign stockholders
(C) stockholders should be friendly to the government
(D) $200,000,000 cannot be raised by Americans
(E) the Bank is not consistent with personal liberty

5. The opinion expressed in this quotation proved to be that held by the American people as indicated by

(A) the victory of Andrew Jackson in the 1832 election
(B) Nicholas Biddle's support of New England manufacturing
(C) the Webster Ashburton Treaty
(D) Calhoun's doctrine of nullification
(E) the essays of Ralph Waldo Emerson

6. All of the following are true statements about the Monroe Doctrine EXCEPT

(A) was first proposed by the British government to the United States
(B) was presented by President Monroe in a State of the Union message
(C) has always been adhered to by European nations
(D) has been used to protect American business interests
(E) stated that the United States would not become involved in European affairs

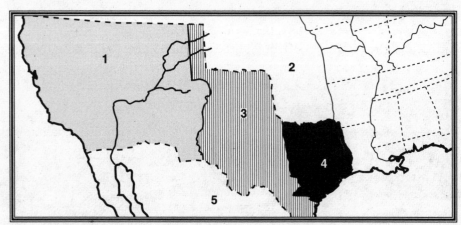

SOURCE: U.S. Bureau of the Census *Historical Statistics of the U.S., Colonial Times to 1957.*

7. On the map above the area numbered 4 was the

(A) land of the Cherokee nation
(B) Republic of Texas
(C) southern area of the Louisiana Purchase
(D) site of the Oregon boundary dispute
(E) great cattle-grazing region of Oklahoma

Questions 8–9 refer to the following chart

## Immigration to the United States

| Year | Total | Gr. Britain | Ireland | Scandinavia | Germany | Poland |
|------|-------|-------------|---------|-------------|---------|--------|
| 1820 | 8,385 | 2,410 | 3,614 | 23 | 968 | 5 |
| 1830 | 23,322 | 1,153 | 2,721 | 19 | 1,906 | 2 |
| 1840 | 84,066 | 2,613 | 39,340 | 207 | 29,704 | 5 |
| 1850 | 369,980 | 51,085 | 164,004 | 1,589 | 78,896 | 5 |

8. According to the chart on immigration, all of the following are true EXCEPT

   (A) more immigrants came from eastern Europe than from the British Isles
   (B) the total number of immigrants more than doubled each decade
   (C) Polish immigration remained rather constant
   (D) there was a very significant increase in immigration in the 1840s
   (E) the smallest number of immigrants from Great Britain arrived in the 1830s

9. The figures in the chart on immigration suggest that in the period 1820–1850

   (A) the total immigration remained constant
   (B) Polish immigration increased in the 1830s
   (C) in each decade, the Irish formed the largest group of immigrants
   (D) British immigration declined over these years
   (E) many immigrants came from Scandinavia

Fort Laramie, Wyoming, lithograph from *Fremont's First and Second Expeditions 1841–2–3*. Washington, D.C., Blair and Rives, 1845.

10. All of the following are indicated by the picture EXCEPT

    (A) U.S. civilians are using or staying near a Native American-type tepee
    (B) The large square structure left of the center of the picture is a fort
    (C) People may be living in tepees outside the large square structure
    (D) Carts and horses are available for transportation for U.S. civilians
    (E) Traditional farming is not practiced in the area shown

## Answers and Answer Explanations

1. **(B)**    2. **(C)**    3. **(E)**    4. **(D)**
5. **(A)**    6. **(C)**    7. **(B)**    8. **(A)**
9. **(C)**    10. **(B)**

1. **(B)** The Hayne-Webster Debate had as its start a proposal to reduce the price of western land. It was one of the most important congressional debates of the 19th century. Its focus became the role of the federal government as opposed to that of state government.

2. **(C)** Although Jackson disliked the Bank of the United States, he also disliked paper currency, speculation, and the increase in the level of private debt. The "specie circular" required payment for western lands in gold or silver and was meant to cut down speculation and inflation.

3. **(E)** Inventions were important in stimulating the economic and industrial growth of the nation, especially of the Northeast. Except for the telegraph, which was invented by Morse and not Bell, these inventions were made before 1850 by the men indicated. Bell invented the telephone later in the century.

4. **(D)** An analysis of this quotation from Jackson's veto message of the bill renewing the charter of the Second Bank of the United States reveals that he believed $200,000,000 *could* be raised in the United States without foreign support. From the quotation it is clear that he believed the other four choices.

5. **(A)** The American people apparently supported Jackson's position on the Bank since they overwhelmingly voted for him in 1832, and the Bank was a major issue of the campaign.

6. **(C)** The Monroe Doctrine was presented in a State of the Union message by President Monroe, developing a concept suggested by the British government. President Monroe indicated that the United States would stay out of the affairs of Europe just as he expected the European nations to stay out of the affairs of the Americas, an idea not always adhered to. United States business interests developed in the Americas often under the protection of the Monroe Doctrine.

7. **(B)** Region 4 was the pre-Mexican War independent Republic of Texas.

8. **(A)** An understanding of immigration from different sections of Europe is an important aspect of the analysis of immigration to America and of this question. The question requires an understanding of European geography as does

any analysis of European immigration. If you do not have this information, you would have difficulty with this question. It is therefore important to study maps of Europe and other parts of the world as you study United States history that has connections to those regions. Before the 1890s the majority of immigrants came from western and northern Europe, England, Ireland, Scandinavia, and Germany, as this table clearly shows. Therefore, A is incorrect. Poland is the only eastern European country listed, and the number of immigrants is insignificant.

9. **(C)** The chart reveals that in each year reported, the Irish were the largest single group of immigrants. Scandinavian and Polish immigration was less than that from the British Isles, which makes choice A incorrect. Later in the century, immigration from eastern Europe did increase. Total immigration greatly increased. British immigration, except for one small drop reported in 1830, did also. Irish immigration remained large through these years. This is a good example of a stimulus question that requires good reading of charts and some general background knowledge.

10. **(B)** The picture is of a lithograph of Fort Laramie, Wyoming, found in *Fremont's First and Second Expeditions 1841–2–3*, Washington, D.C., Blair and Rives, 1845. J. C. Fremont, a captain in the army, led exploratory expeditions through the West in the early 1840s. He later ran for president. In the picture there is no clear indication that the large square structure is a fort; there are no soldiers, no guns, not even any flags flying on it. There are some men dressed in civilian clothes near a tepee, a type of Native American dwelling found in the Great Plains area. Next to the tepee are some carts and a horse. The U.S. flag is flying from a flagpole identifying the individuals and carts and horse as being from the United States. There are a number of tepees near the large square structure indicating a number of people may be living outside the structure. There is no indication whether those living in the tepees are Native Americans, although the three figures in the foreground suggest they might be. Nowhere in the picture is there any indication of farming of any kind, which suggests it was not practiced in the area at the time of the picture. Chapter 9 includes a discussion of the use of photographs in multiple-choice questions.

# Coming of the Civil War, Civil War, and Reconstruction 1850–1877

## CHAPTER 8

- Important developments
- DBQs
- Sample essays
- Charts and graphs

The Civil War has often been considered the great transitional point in American history. In this view the prewar period was one of territorial growth and the establishment of the framework of the nation. The Civil War intensified all the previous developments and precipitated rapid growth of the nation, growth that made the United States an industrial giant and a world power by 1900. Whether this view is valid you need to decide. It certainly is a thesis worth testing in your study of the history of this period.

## THREE TIME PERIODS

This thesis permits a focus on the Civil War era and as is the case with the era of the American Revolution, the years 1850–1877 logically fall into three time units. The first, 1850–1860, covers those years when the union appeared to be moving inexorably toward war. The second unit encompasses the war years 1860–1865, and the third unit includes the postwar or Reconstruction era, 1865–1877. Factual information from all three periods will certainly be needed on any United States history exam. Questions on these years may cover the entire time span, may require intensive knowledge of one period, or may ask for comparison among the three periods. In your study you may wish to break the time into the three units mentioned above, but be certain you understand the relationship between events in one period and the next.

Although historians place events in time units or periods as they attempt to make sense of the past, you must remember that the events occurred with no division between them. History occurs as a flowing stream. The image of pouring concrete to form a wall comes to mind. The historian sees the solid wall and draws lines on the concrete wall to make the wall appear to be a brick one. In history books we write as

> **INTERESTING FACT**
>
> Many historians consider the era of the Civil War to be the turning point in U.S. history that created the nation the United States is today.

though the wall were made of separate bricks, but in reality the wall is one solid mass of material. The bricks help us to analyze, compartmentalize, and master details, but they are not the real history. If you keep this image in mind as you study the periods to which historians have assigned the events of history, you will never lose sight of the Western concept of the chronological interrelatedness of all historical developments.

Among the developments you will want to study in detail from the years 1850–1877 are the following:

1. Events leading to war, 1850–1860—political, economic, social, intellectual
2. Secession and the outbreak of war
3. Military and naval war strategy
4. The strengths and weaknesses of the Confederacy and the Union
5. International relations in the war and post-Civil War period
6. Reconstruction plans and policies
7. The presidency of Ulysses S. Grant
8. The social and intellectual changes that took place in both the South and North during the war and Reconstruction
9. The growth and development of the West
10. The election and compromise of 1876

## SAMPLE ESSAY QUESTION—THE DBQ

The DBQ or document-based question became a required part of the essay or free-response section of the Advanced Placement examination in 1973. The DBQ is a unique type of free-response question and a very important part of the examination. The DBQ essay answer receives 45 percent of the score given for the free-response section of the exam. The remaining 55 percent is divided between the two required standard essays, which thus count 27.5 percent each. Your total score on the free-response section counts for 50 percent of the exam score.

The DBQ is a special type of essay question. In the free-response questions we have discussed so far you must recall all the data or factual material to use in your answer. In the DBQ some of the information you need is presented in documents. These documents may include maps, graphs, cartoons, photographs, and art as well as the printed word from many different sources—speeches, newspapers, diaries, novels, laws, legal decisions. **For the DBQ in its present format, you are expected to analyze and interpret the documents and *at the same time* relate the information in the documents and your analysis of it to the "mainstream," that is, the main chronological development, of United States history as agreed to by most historians. This includes important dates and events, people, ideas, and art, as well as the interpretation different historians have made of this information. You must include in your answer information from this chronology that is not found in the documents.**

The question asked concerning these documents may be of any essay type. The fact that the form or wording of the DBQ may be the same as any essay type illustrates how important and widely applicable are the methods of question analysis presented in previous chapters and in the next three chapters. In answering the DBQ, you must begin by analyzing the question, the familiar first step in essay writing. After that step, the second step becomes slightly different. You will still need to make an outline or brief notes, but for the DBQ you should first read the documents, analyze them, and identify the key points being made. Then, take notes on them and

> **STUDY TIP**
>
> Throughout your study, practice asking "What does it mean?" That question forces you to analyze the information, and that is a key to understanding the past.

jot down a few brief notes about what you recall from the mainstream of United States history that is relevant to the documents presented and to the question asked.

**TIP**

Use your analytical skills to succeed on the DBQ.

The reading and understanding of documents lies at the heart of the DBQ, but the real test of your ability is in how well you, the student, relate these documents to your understanding of the mainstream of United States history. The DBQ was added to the Advanced Placement examination as a means of testing your understanding of the role of the historian and to test your analytical and interpretive skills rather than merely to test your memory or recall skills. Many multiple-choice questions have been designed to test analytical skills, but they can test skills in a very limited way. The DBQ provides a much greater, in-depth test, since you are allowed 15 minutes to read, analyze the documents, and make notes, and 45 minutes in which to write your answer. For multiple-choice questions you have less than 1 minute to read, analyze, and decide on your answer for each question.

The goal of the DBQ is to present a question that will force students to combine their historical research and analytical techniques with their recall of historical data in order to answer the question. The AP directions indicate that you cannot expect the documents to be those studied in all courses such as the Declaration of Independence and the Gettysburg Address. There is no way a student can memorize or become familiar with all the documents that might appear on the DBQ. The only way to prepare for it is to practice being a historian as you study—practice analyzing documents of all types, questioning statements made by the authors, seeking cause-and-effect relationships to illustrate your personal opinion on issues, and continually relating the information in documents you read to the "mainstream" issues in United States history. Reference to historical facts and developments not mentioned in the documents must be included in your answer. In addition, when referring to the documents it is best NOT to quote the material but rather to paraphrase, putting the key ideas in your own words. You should identify the document you are using. For Document B on page 105, you could refer to it as "Lincoln letter to Robertson," "Lincoln writing in 1855," or "Lincoln letter of 1855"—all would be acceptable. You may also refer to it as Document B by putting the phrase "Document B" **in parentheses** after you have referred to the document in your text. This is similar to using footnotes in a research paper. However, the more sophisticated papers will use a reference such as "Lincoln writing in 1855 . . ." The student who approaches all of the material in this way will do well on the DBQ.

---

**QUICK REVIEW**

In summary, the DBQ tests your ability to work with historical documents and your knowledge of the mainstream of United States history. You are asked to do two related things in a unified essay: to formulate an answer derived from the evidence contained in the documents, as it relates to and has bearing on events in United States history that you must recall from your study; and where relevant to your answer, to assess the value of the documents as historical sources.

---

## Sample Document-Based Question

The election of Lincoln and its relation to the abolition of slavery is the topic of the following sample DBQ. All courses in American history will include information on the abolitionist movement, the election of Abraham Lincoln, and the secession of the Confederate states and Lincoln's attitude toward slavery. This is "mainstream" information. The sample question requires that you have this information, but the documents also present other information that you might not have had at your command. In this question there are ten documents. Under the present DBQ format the number and length of documents and the type of documents will vary but there would rarely be more than ten.

Read the directions, the question, and the documents carefully.

**Section II**
**Part A**
**Suggested Writing**
**Time—45 minutes***

Directions: The following question requires you to construct a coherent essay that integrates your interpretation of documents A–J *and* your knowledge of the period referred to in the question. High scores will be earned only if you cite important evidence from the documents and include information from your knowledge of the period.

1. Analyze the following question as it apples to the period 1835–1865.

   To what extent was the election of Abraham Lincoln a mandate for the abolition of slavery in the United States?

## Document A

> *Source:* **Dan Stone and Abraham Lincoln, representatives from the county of Sangamon. Entry in the *Journal of the House of Representatives of Illinois* on March 3, 1837**
>
> The following protest was presented to the House, which was read and ordered to be spread on (put in) the journals, to-wit:
>
> "Resolutions upon the subject of domestic slavery having passed both branches of the General Assembly at its present session, the undersigned hereby protest against the passage of the same.
>
> "They believe that the institution of slavery is founded on both injustice and bad policy; but that the promulgation of abolition doctrines tends rather to increase than abate its evils.
>
> "They believe that the Congress of the United States has no power, under the Constitution, to interfere with the institution of slavery in the different States. . . .
>
> "The difference between these opinions and those contained in the said resolutions, is their reasoning for entering this protest."

## Document B

*Source:* **Letter from Abraham Lincoln to George Robertson in Lexington, Kentucky—August 15, 1855**

My dear Sir, . . . experience has demonstrated, I think, that there is no peaceful extinction of slavery in prospect for us. The failure of Henry Clay and other good and great men, in 1849, to effect anything in favour of gradual emancipation in Kentucky . . . extinguishes that hope utterly. . . . When we were the political slaves of King George, and wanted to be free, we called the maxim that "all men are created equal" a self-evident truth; but now when we have grown fat, and have lost all dread of being slaves ourselves, we have become so greedy to be masters that we call the same maxim "a self-evident lie." . . .

Our political problem now is, "Can we as a nation continue together permanently—forever—half slave, and half free?" The problem is too mighty for me. May God in his mercy superintend the solution.

## Document C

*Source:* **Abraham Lincoln in the Lincoln-Douglas Debate at Freeport, Illinois, September of 1858**

I should be exceedingly glad to see Slavery abolished in the District of Columbia. I believe that Congress possesses the constitutional power to abolish it. Yet as a member of Congress, I should not, with my present views, be in favor of endeavoring to abolish Slavery in the District of Columbia, unless it would be upon these conditions: First that the abolition should be gradual; second, that it should be on a vote of the majority of qualified voters in the District; and third, that compensation should be made to unwilling owners. With these three conditions, I confess I would be exceedingly glad to see Congress abolish Slavery in the District of Columbia, and in the language of Henry Clay, "sweep from our Capitol that foul blot upon our 'nation.'"

## Document D

*Source:* **Comments on the Lincoln-Douglas Freeport Debate from the *Louisville* [Kentucky] *Journal,* as quoted in the *Chicago Tribune*—September 4, 1858**

According to Senator Douglas, the Territorial Legislatures, though prohibited by the Constitution from abolishing slavery within their respective jurisdictions, may lawfully abstain from enforcing the rights of slaveholders and so extinguish the institution by voluntary neglect . . . In the name of common sense and common fairness, if slavery is to be prohibited or abolished in the Territories by any legislative tribunal, let it be done by one in which the whole nation is represented, . . . let it be done by the people of the United States. . . . not squatter sovereignty. Senator Douglas, as we have seen, gives us the latter—Mr. Lincoln the former. Between the two, no intelligent, discerning patriot can hesitate a moment. Mr. Lincoln's position . . . is infinitely less unfriendly to the constitutional rights and just interests of the South.

## Document E

*Source:* **Editorial from the Springfield, Illinois,** *Register*—**November 7, 1860**

### THE QUESTION OF DISUNION

At the hour we write these lines, the American people, in all parts of the United States, are exercising their constitutional privilege of electing a president and vice-president of the United States for the next four years . . .

But, much as we may deplore the election of Lincoln, because of its calamitous consequences, . . . under no circumstances, can disunion be the remedy or redress for the unfortunate choice. Mr. Lincoln may obtain a majority of the election (i.e., electoral) college, and yet receive less than one-third of the popular vote, yet he will nevertheless be constitutionally elected.

. . . It has been proposed by those who seek a disruption of the Union, that in case Mr. Lincoln shall be elected president the southern states shall withdraw from the Union; . . . We wish to place on record now, that . . . such secession . . . will become rebellion and treason . . .

If Mr. Lincoln shall in any manner . . . violate the constitution . . . the constitution provides: "The president . . . shall be removed from office, on impeachment for, and conviction of treason, bribery, or other high crimes and misdemeanors." . . . We believe . . . the Senate would, upon a constitutional form of trial convict Abraham Lincoln and dismiss him from office . . .

Should Mr. Lincoln be elected, great as the calamity will prove to be, still we think it is the duty of every democrat to give to his administration (not his party) every aid and support that the government can constitutionally demand of citizens.

## Document F

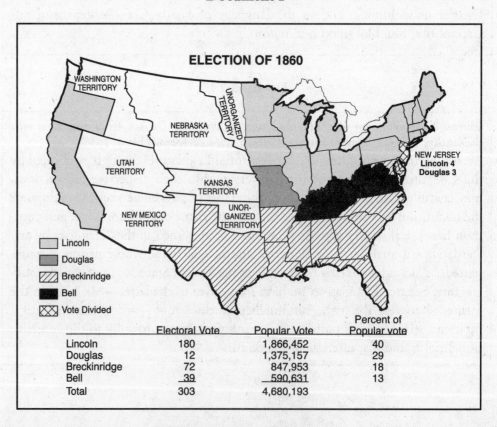

**ELECTION OF 1860**

|  | Electoral Vote | Popular Vote | Percent of Popular vote |
|---|---|---|---|
| Lincoln | 180 | 1,866,452 | 40 |
| Douglas | 12 | 1,375,157 | 29 |
| Breckinridge | 72 | 847,953 | 18 |
| Bell | 39 | 590,631 | 13 |
| Total | 303 | 4,680,193 | |

## Document G

*Source:* **Editorial from the Reading, Pennsylvania,** *Berks and Schuylkill Journal*—**December 15, 1860**

"It is much to be regretted that in the present crisis of our national affairs, the disposition of events will be, to a great extent, in the hands of mere politicians; and that the sentiments of the masses will be scarcely known. The present unfortunate state of public feelings has, to a great extent, been created by ultra men on both sides, while we believe that the great body of the people, North and South, love the Union, and would deplore its dissolution as the greatest of earthly calamities, and a death blow to the cause of freedom throughout the world. . . . In so large a party as the Republican, it cannot but be supposed that a great variety of sentiment exists. . . .

"The great mass of the Republican party hold the conservative views so often expressed by Lincoln himself."

## Document H

*Source:* **South Carolina** *Declaration of Causes of Secession*—**December 24, 1860**

. . . A geographical line has been drawn across the Union, and all the States north of that line have united in the election of a man to the high office of President of the United States whose opinions and purposes are hostile to Slavery. He is to be intrusted with the administration of the common Government, because he has declared that "Government cannot endure permanently half slave, half free," and that the public mind must rest in the belief that Slavery is in the course of ultimate extinction.

We, therefore, the people of South Carolina . . . have solemnly declared that the Union heretofore existing between this State and the other States of North America is dissolved . . .

## Document I

*Source:* **Abraham Lincoln's First Inaugural Address**—**March 4, 1861**

Apprehension seems to exist among the people of the Southern States that by the accession of a Republican administration their property and their peace and personal security are to be endangered. There has never been any reasonable cause for such apprehension. . . . (There is) ample evidence to the contrary. It is found in nearly all my published speeches. I quote from one of those speeches, "I have no purpose, directly or indirectly, to interfere with the institution of slavery in the States where it exists. I believe I have no lawful right to do so, and I have no inclination to do so." Those who nominated and elected me did so with full knowledge that I had made this and many similar declarations, and had never recanted them.

## Document J

---

*Source:* **New Jersey Peace Resolutions—March 18, 1863**

1. *Be it Resolved by the Senate and General Assembly of the State of New Jersey,* That this State, . . . believed and confided in the declarations of the President of the United States, in his inaugural address . . .

. . . . (now we) make unto the Federal Government this our solemn

### PROTEST

Against the power assumed in the proclamation (Emancipation Proclamation) of the President made January first, 1863, by which all the slaves in certain States and part of States are for ever set free; and against the expenditures of the public moneys for the emancipation of slaves or their support at any time, under any pretence whatever; . . .

---

## Comments on the DBQ

All DBQs include three parts. First are the general directions, second is the question itself, and third are the documents, which in this question include a map. Let us consider each of these three parts in turn.

First, the directions specify the time allotted, which is 45 minutes for writing. The directions on the examination will indicate that you are to take 15 minutes to read the documents and to make notes. At the examination you will not be allowed to start writing your answer during these 15 minutes. If you finish reading and organizing your answer before the 15 minutes end, you may start preparing your other essay answers but do not rush your DBQ preparation. The examination papers you will be given include space for you to take notes, another indication that the Advanced Placement program strongly supports Step Two in Essay Writing. Incidentally, the directions also tell you where you are to write your answer—keep alert to such details in the directions for any exam. **Read all directions carefully; do not rush over them to get to the question.** This is a fundamental rule of all test taking. After taking notes and organizing your information, you have 45 minutes in which to write the answer.

The directions also indicate the purpose of the DBQ—when they state, ". . . a coherent essay that integrates your interpretation of documents A–J *and* your knowledge of the period referred to in the question." This idea is then repeated in the second sentence and links it to obtaining a "high score." These directions should leave no doubt as to what is wanted. **The DBQ is designed to test your ability to analyze the documents presented, to relate the material to "mainstream" United States history, and to write a unified essay expressing your personal opinion on the question raised.** The readers of the exam want you to show that you have knowledge of the important events and people of the time period covered in the question—the events and people generally accepted by historians as the heart of United States chronological, intellectual, social, political, economic, and diplomatic history. The DBQ does *not* ask you to simply describe what each document includes. Writing the essay should present no difficulty once you have analyzed the question and the documents and taken notes.

The second part of the DBQ is the question itself. The question is a *To what extent?* type and, as indicated in Chapter 7, the key word here is *extent*. You are to determine, on the basis of the evidence presented and of your recall of United States history, whether Lincoln's election as president of the United States was a mandate for the abolition of slavery in the United States. The word *mandate* may provide some difficulty for you. A mandate is an order. It may not be voiced directly, but rather it is implied by the circumstances. With this interpretation of the word, you can see that the question is asking you to determine if the people of the United States were ordering the abolition of slavery when they voted for Abraham Lincoln. As you will recall from your study, and as the documents imply, there were many different views as to what Lincoln stood for and what the election of 1860 meant. You must determine what your opinion is, and from this decide on a thesis for the essay. You will have the limited evidence from the documents and the information you can recall to help you to determine your thesis. As you read the documents and take notes on them, as in Steps One and Two in Essay Writing, a thesis should emerge that will determine your approach to the question.

The third part of the DBQ is made up of the documents. As you look at them, remember that you are to write a unified essay and **not** a mere summary of what is in each document. What would you look for in making your brief notes? One important piece of information is the source of the document. How biased would it be? Next, note the date of the document if given. How will that affect its accuracy? Finally, you must read the document carefully and determine exactly the point(s) being made. What is the key point—the main idea—in the passage? Are there any secondary points being made? Sometimes the language can be confusing. The following comments on the documents are more extensive than you need to make. However, are there points you would add?

## DOCUMENT A

The first document is an entry dated March 3, 1837 in the Journal of the Illinois House of Representatives in which Lincoln and his fellow representative from his home county protest the legislature's support for the idea of the U.S. government abolishing slavery. **The key point is that Lincoln clearly states that he believes the federal government has no power to abolish slavery in the nation.** Is this view a surprise to you? Did Lincoln believe this in 1860? How does this affect your response to the question? Would the journal of a legislative body be biased? Why might Lincoln have supported this view in 1837? What was happening in the country?

## DOCUMENTS B AND C

Document B (as indicated above you may identify documents this way in your answer, but a better way is to identify documents by the author or source) gives a view on slavery expressed privately by Abraham Lincoln in a personal letter. Letters are not meant for publication and writers can be expected to express their true thoughts when writing them. **The key point is that Lincoln clearly indicates that he is torn by the question of slavery and yet is not prepared to come up with a clear solution.** This document is dated 1855. What events have taken place in the 18 years since 1837 that might have affected Lincoln?

The quotation (Document C) from Lincoln's address at Freeport, Illinois, in 1858 as part of the famous Lincoln-Douglas Debate in their race for the U.S. Senate gives another view from Lincoln. **The key point is that Lincoln believes Congress has**

**the power to abolish slavery in the District of Columbia, i.e., Washington**. He adds that he would not do so unless the people vote for it, that freeing of the slaves is gradual, and that there is compensation. Has Lincoln changed his mind since 1837? What events occurred in the 1850s that would have an impact on one's view of slavery? On the basis of this speech, how do you think he will act as president? How honest a statement of his beliefs would this be? Remember that Lincoln is running for a political office—United States senator. The speech would be reported widely. These are the type of questions you should address as you read the documents, relating them both to the question and to the "mainstream" of American history.

## DOCUMENT D

The comments (Document D) from a southern newspaper on the Lincoln-Douglas Debate were quoted in a northern newspaper, the *Chicago Tribune* from Chicago, Illinois, and this suggests that some people in both the North and the South might be in agreement on this particular interpretation of the famous Freeport Debate. The editor opposes "squatter sovereignty" as a way to determine the future of slavery in the territories. **The key point is that he supports Lincoln's idea of congressional action—action by the people as a whole represented in Congress.** The Supreme Court had already declared such action unconstitutional. Do you remember the case? The Dred Scott Decision of 1857 declared the Missouri Compromise, outlawing slavery in Missouri, and passed by Congress, unconstitutional. The editor is supporting the Southern view even though he is writing in Chicago—a northern city. He is supporting Lincoln because he believes his idea will not happen since the Supreme Court has ruled that Congress does not have the power to abolish slavery. This is a backhanded argument that supports a viewpoint that you know will not happen. Did you see that? It is believed that Lincoln's position lost him the Senate race but endeared him to the Republicans and thus won for him the presidential nomination. How would you use this information in your answer?

## DOCUMENT E

The editorial presented in Document E is from another Illinois newspaper—one that opposed the election of Lincoln. **The key point is that this editorial supports the Constitution and opposes secession as a way to deal with Lincoln's election.** Does this support or reject the idea of Lincoln's election as a mandate for the abolition of slavery? This 1860 editorial can be a most important document in developing your case.

## DOCUMENT F

The map (Document F) can easily be understood. You may have this information in your head, but if not, this could be of benefit to you in developing your argument. Is the document biased? **A key point on the map shows Lincoln won overwhelmingly in the Electoral College yet received only 40 percent of the vote.** Is that a mandate from the people to do something? What states did he carry?

## DOCUMENT G

**The key point in the editorial (Document G) is that there was not unified support for Abraham Lincoln even in the Republican Party.** The date is after

Lincoln's election. Does this help explain his actions during his first months in office? How does this information relate to the idea of a "mandate"?

## DOCUMENT H

A passage from the secession document of South Carolina is presented. It is a document that you may never have read before, but the issue presented should be familiar to you. **The key point is that South Carolinians believed Lincoln's election furthered the idea that slavery was on a course towards extinction.** Do the authors interpret the election of Lincoln as a mandate to abolish slavery in South Carolina? What is the bias of the authors?

## DOCUMENT I

In his first Inaugural Address in 1861 Lincoln revealed how he viewed his election. He states as the **key point that he has no intention to interfere with the institution of slavery.** Does it suggest that Lincoln or the Republicans viewed the election as a mandate for the abolition of slavery? Does the fact that Lincoln states this mean that the entire Republican Party would feel, and therefore vote, the same way? This is the issue that you must resolve in your reading and analysis of the documents.

## DOCUMENT J

The final document (Document J) is from a series of resolutions passed by the legislature of New Jersey in 1863 after the Emancipation Proclamation was issued. It clearly suggests New Jersey was not in full support of the war effort.

The **key point is that New Jersey does not support the Emancipation Proclamation that freed the slaves in areas still in rebellion.** How does this document fit into the overall question? You may not have studied the Emancipation Proclamation in detail, but you should have general knowledge of it. Was New Jersey in favor of the abolition of slavery?

## Writing Your Own DBQ Response

These brief comments on the documents raise many issues. What are your answers to the questions suggested? What other questions do these documents raise in your mind? During the 15 minutes allotted for reading and analyzing the documents and taking notes, you will want to go over documents in this manner. From your notes you should then develop your thesis. **You need not refer to all the documents in your answer.** You should pick *only* those that help you to present your case and to prove your thesis. However, if you have time, you should refute a document that does not support your thesis. If you can do this with evidence from outside sources, it would be to your credit. In answering the DBQ the greatest danger is in merely describing or listing what is in each document and not writing an essay answering the question. Too many students write only a summary of each document. You can clearly see that this would not answer the question and is ineffective.

At this time you should write your own answer for this DBQ. Use the documents by grouping common ideas found in them. Do not quote what is said verbatim. Identify the source of the document. Remember to include information from the "mainstream" of American history during the years 1837–1863.

For this question we have not included a sample answer. Instead, we have focused on the introductory paragraph. After writing your own answer to this question, read the sample introductions provided here and make your judgment of them. Rank them 1–9 with 9 being the best. Recall what was said in Part One about a good introduction. If you have forgotten, go back and read that section again. **A good introduction is crucial for a good essay.**

## Sample Introductions

### Sample Introduction A
Lincoln's election as President of the United States was not a mandate to abolish slavery in the United States. It took Lincoln a long time to get around to freeing any slaves. In the Emancipation Proclamation he only freed slaves in the areas of Confederate states still in rebellion against the Union government. The New Jersey Peace Proposals were opposed even to this move.

### Sample Introduction B
Abraham Lincoln was known as the Great Emancipator, and he deserves the title since he freed the slaves.

### Sample Introduction C
The political process in America is often confusing. To determine clearly what the results of an election mean is a difficult task. Although slavery appears to be the major issue in the election of Abraham Lincoln, there were others including transportation to the West and the tariff issue. Considering these factors and Lincoln's personal comments on the issue of slavery, it is clear that the election of Lincoln was not a mandate for the abolition of slavery in the United States.

### Sample Introduction D
Slavery was a divisive issue at the Constitutional Convention and had been throughout the years of our history to 1860. Compromise after compromise was tried, but as Lincoln asked, "Can a nation continue together permanently half slave and half free?" The answer was certainly no, and the election of Lincoln in 1860 was a mandate for the abolition of slavery in the United States.

### Sample Introduction E
These documents have a lot of conflicting viewpoints. It is very hard to see that anybody agreed on anything. Although Lincoln was consistently opposed to slavery in the District of Columbia, he was not prepared to abolish it. The election in 1860 was viewed in different ways by South Carolina and by the Reading, Pennsylvania, newspaper. Since Lincoln had said that the nation could not be half slave and half free, he must have thought he should abolish slavery. When he did this in the Emancipation Proclamation, which was in agreement with what he had said at Freeport, the country could truly say it was free and all men were created equal.

## Teacher Comments on Sample Introductions

As should be very clear, the writers have interpreted the question in a variety of ways. Each position could be defended based on the evidence of the documents and outside information.

**Sample B**

"Considering the merits of these five introductions, Sample B is the poorest. The writer fails to set a broad context and fails to introduce the question. This viewpoint on Lincoln does not really relate to the question except indirectly. Sample B confirms the point that a one-sentence introduction is usually not sufficient to set the broad context of the question and to state your thesis. It deserves a 1.

**Sample E**

"Sample E is also poorly written. The author has included a good deal of information, much of it from the documents, but there is no clear organization. Instead, a shotgun-spatter approach has been used, and the topic of the question is not included. A thesis is implied in the last sentence, but it is not clearly stated, nor is it related to the election of 1860. This introduction would deserve a 3 in spite of all the information.

**Sample A**

"In Sample A a thesis is clearly stated in the first sentence, and the question is introduced. Unfortunately, since there is no broad context set, the reader is somewhat taken aback by the opening. The author then elaborates on the thesis in the second sentence. Unfortunately, the last sentence introduces information that could be better used in the body of the paper. It almost appears as if the author of Sample A, just like the author of Sample E, did not take time to organize the material before starting to write. In Sample A one can understand the way the writer's thoughts are moving, but the three sentences do not make as effective an introduction as in Samples C and D. It deserves a mid-range grade of 6 as it has a good thesis.

**Samples C and D**

"These two introductions are both good and can be ranked highly. Sample D is a bit more concise and clear and would rank as a 9. Sample C would deserve an 8. Remember, readers of the exam rank all the papers on a 1 to 9 scale, finding hundreds of papers in each rank. Each begins with a broad topic related to the question, moves from this topic to the specific topic of the question (Lincoln, his election, slavery), and ends with a clearly stated thesis. The two writers disagree completely about their interpretation of the meaning of the election of Lincoln. Either thesis could be defended. Both Samples C and D conform most closely to what has been set in this book as the pattern for good introductory paragraphs."

Do you agree with the above analysis? Do you see why Samples C and D are considered the best of the five? Do you now have this pattern of an introductory paragraph established in your mind?

## Sample Introduction and Conclusion

Introductions and conclusions are always important. They are the bookends that hold together the essay. They *must* relate to each other. Below is an example where they clearly do.

**Introduction**

Slavery was an issue in American history starting in 1619. The leaders of the country in the first half of the 19th century shared many different opinions on the topic. Beginning in the 1830s, the Abolitionist sentiment was fanned by many events. These events culminated in the election of Abraham Lincoln. Based on his personal views and those of the North, Lincoln's election was a mandate for the abolition of slavery.

**Conclusion**

Slavery was abolished as a result of the Civil War. The election of Lincoln determined that this would be so, since it was understood by the Republican Party and its leader, Abraham Lincoln, that slavery must not spread to the territories and that ultimately it should be abolished. The election of 1860 ended years of attempted compromise and eliminated slavery as an issue for the American nation.

**Comments**

You see how well they relate together: The introduction sets a broad issue (i.e., slavery), presents the question (i.e., to what extent was the election of Lincoln a mandate for the abolition of slavery?), and concludes with a thesis. The conclusion returns to the question and presents the writer's thesis in the second sentence. It then goes on to bring the question back to the broad issue of slavery paralleling the first sentence in the introduction. This neatly frames the entire essay.

Some teachers suggest that students not write the opening paragraph until after they have written the essay and the conclusion. They tell the student to read over the essay and write the introduction. You may want to try this, but this approach has you writing an essay without developing that crucial bit of all essays—a thesis. The method described in Seven Steps of Essay Writing—going back and reading your opening paragraph before writing your conclusion—seems a much wiser and logical approach. It also means that if you run out of time in your writing—something that does happen—you have written a good introduction. Practicing writing essays in a 30-minute time period will prepare you for writing under the time limit of the AP exam.

---

### QUICK REVIEW

The following five points summarize the key concepts to remember when writing the answer to the DBQ.

1. Remember that you are writing a **unified essay** *answer* involving the documents and events in the "mainstream" of United States history.

2. Some documents will be more valuable or reliable than others. Pick and choose the documents you use and rearrange the order. Group documents with similar ideas together and dismiss the less valuable. Be imaginative! **Do not merely summarize the content of each document.**

3. **Identify the documents** by source or letter.

4. Summarize or paraphase the key idea(s) found in the document, but **do not quote the full document**.

5. Refer to other events of the age, and **clearly indicate how these documents relate to these events and help you gain a better understanding of events in the generally accepted "mainstream" of United States history**.

If you keep these five points in mind and remember the Seven Steps in Essay Writing, you should have little difficulty in writing a good answer for any DBQ.

# Practice Essay Questions

1. Pick TWO of the following and explain to what extent each may be considered a cause of the Civil War.

   Westward expansion
   Social differences between the North and South
   Economic growth and development

2. To what extent do you agree or disagree with the idea that the North had won the Civil War before it began?

3. Pick THREE of the following and analyze in what ways they affected the decision of South Carolina to secede in 1860.

   Nullification Crisis of 1832–1833
   Kansas-Nebraska Act of 1854 and its aftermath
   Dred Scott Decision 1857
   Lincoln-Douglas Debates 1858
   Election of Lincoln 1860

4. In what ways are the issues that led to the Civil War similar to those that led to the American War for Independence?

5. "The Civil Rights legislation of the 1960s recaptured for African Americans the social and political status they held briefly under Reconstruction." Assess the validity of this generalization.

## Comments on Question 1

Question 1 is a straightforward *To what extent?* question. It gives you three choices and you must pick the two about which you know the most as they would apply to the outbreak of the Civil War. Westward expansion led by the Gold Rush in California would be difficult to relate to a cause of the Civil War. However, Westward expansion in Texas and the southwest and in Kansas provides many ideas that link to the war—the actions of John Brown in "Bleeding Kansas," for example. Social differences, which of course would include slavery in the South and the Abolition Movement in the North, provide many issues of division and tension between the two regions. Economic growth and free factory labor in the North, divisions over tariffs, and the building of a cross-continental railroad fueled antagonisms between the two regions. Pick the two items with which you feel most comfortable. Writing on the two items separately and then pulling the two together in the conclusion would be a reasonable approach.

## Comments on Question 2

The second question illustrates the *To what extent?* type of question used in the DBQ example in this chapter. It adds those familiar words *agree or disagree,* which invite a strong statement of personal opinion. The idea presented is an intriguing one—the idea that the South had lost the war before it began. Considering the length of the war and the difficulty Lincoln had in finding a general to win the war, you might wonder how this could be true, but some historians have suggested that the railroad network of the North plus its industry made it undefeatable. What do you think? This question requires good factual knowledge and good insights into how facts from different sources can be put together to defend a position. The question is completely open as to organizational format and the organization would depend entirely on what you put down in your brief notes. This question illustrates the importance of organizing your essay from the brief notes you make.

## Comments on Question 3

Question 3 combines an *Analyze?* and *In what Ways?* question that needs a personal opinion or thesis that bridges a long time span in which many changes in attitudes, people, and problems occurred. The five choices all relate to states' rights issues and that is one key to their connection to the secession of South Carolina. The last four relate to slavery and are always given as steps leading to the Civil War but that is not the question. If you are to discuss slavery or the coming of the war, you must connect your ideas to secession. When you have your thesis, an organizational scheme should emerge. This is a difficult question.

## Comments on Question 4

The fourth question is a very broad question directly in the mainstream of U.S. history. You are asked to relate two of the most important periods. The question asks you to find the similarities, but, of course, you could disagree with the premise of the question and state that there is no similarity. Among the issues you might describe are economic issues, majority-minority political issues, and social issues involving differences in lifestyles. These three issues should give you some ideas of how these two periods could be compared in terms of similarities. The essay might be best organized around similarities—relating first the Revolutionary War situation and then the Civil War situation before moving on to the next similarity to be treated. Remember that it is an *In what ways?* question so you must concentrate on how the issues are similar or different and not merely retell events.

## Comments on Question 5

The last question is the broadest question we have had so far in the book. It takes one situation—the treatment of the African American—and asks you to compare the status of African Americans in two periods. You must know something about the way African Americans were treated in the South socially and politically during Reconstruction. You also must know some of the details of the civil rights legislation of the 1960s. If you know both, then you may wish to answer this question. You will need to define status and this will help you develop a thesis. The question combines social and political history and you must include examples from each to have a top answer. The question also illustrates how you may be asked to compare different time periods.

## MULTIPLE CHOICE—CHARTS AND GRAPHS

A popular type of multiple-choice question used to test analytical skills is one based on charts and graphs. It is an excellent type of stimulus question. Many textbooks today present large amounts of information in this manner. Summaries of voting patterns of different social groups, attitudes of minorities, economic issues, votes on various issues in Congress, the pattern of immigration, manufacturing growth, even the numbers of enlistees compared to draftees in World War I can be presented in this way. There are a variety of types of charts and graphs—ranging from simple statistical tables presenting raw numbers to complex bar and line graphs where several items are presented for comparison. Today in texts, as well as in magazines and newspapers, we are presented with a great variety of statistical data that we need to understand. As you study, be certain you look at the charts and graphs in your books and learn how to interpret them and get information from them. Do not skip over such items because they form an important method of presenting historical information, and your ability to understand and interpret information in this way will be tested on the Advanced Placement exam. Also, learning to read and interpret charts and graphs and applying this information to the mainstream history you are studying will help you prepare for analyzing documents presented on the DBQ.

Study the following examples of multiple-choice questions based on charts and graphs. There will be other examples in the sample multiple-choice questions in succeeding chapters. The charts and graphs present information from later than 1870 but you should be able to understand the context even if you have not yet studied the time period.

## SAMPLE QUESTIONS

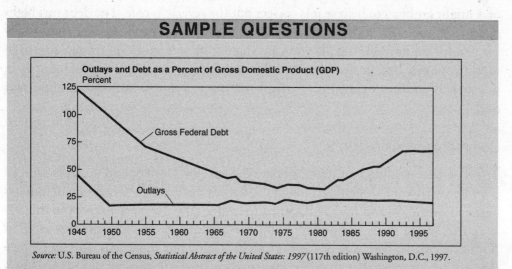

*Source:* U.S. Bureau of the Census, *Statistical Abstract of the United States: 1997* (117th edition) Washington, D.C., 1997.

1. According to the graph, all of the following statements concerning the Gross Federal Debt as a percentage of the Gross Domestic Product (GDP) are true EXCEPT

   (A) The Gross Federal Debt was largest in 1995.
   (B) The Gross Federal Debt began to increase in the 1970s.
   (C) The Gross Federal Debt declined until 1966.
   (D) The Gross Federal Debt has more than doubled since 1981.
   (E) The Gross Federal Debt has been approximately steady since 1992.

2. The graph clearly indicates that

   (A) government outlays (expenditures) have always been under 20% of GDP
   (B) debt and outlays have never increased at the same time
   (C) there was economic prosperity in the 1990s
   (D) the Gross Federal Debt declined steadily from the end of World War II until United States involvement in Vietnam
   (E) Reagan economic policies had no impact on the debt

## Comments on Questions 1–2

Questions 1and 2 are based on information presented in a line graph—one of the most common graphs used to present information visually. The graph presents data concerning the Gross Federal Debt and government outlays in the period from 1945, the end of World War II, to 1997. The graph presents information as a percentage of the Gross Domestic Product or GDP. The GDP is the total of all goods and services produced in the country. Information on the debt, government outlays, and GDP provide important economic insights into the changing patterns of American life.

## Comments on Question 1

Question 1 (A) requires you to read the graph to get your information. You need to know how to read the graph. In the graph the left-hand or vertical column represents the percentage of the Gross Domestic Product (GDP) and the bottom or horizontal line represents years from 1945 to 1997. The graph compares the total or Gross Federal Debt to the total of government outlays as they reflect a percentage of Gross Domestic Product (GDP). It is a measure of national productivity. The question requires that you read only one line of the graph—the top line representing the debt. There is nothing in the question relating to outlays. A quick reading of A might lead you to believe it is correct but the reverse is true. The debt was highest in 1945, not 1995. The other answers are all correct. This question requires simple graph reading skills—skills you can practice as you study the graphs found in most textbooks, but, in case your text does not have graphs, you can find graphs in newspapers and news magazines. Graph reading is a simple skill yet an important one.

## Comments on Question 2

This question requires you to both relate the two lines—debt and outlays—and to have knowledge of several periods in United States history. Government outlays began at over 25% and rapidly declined to under 20% but have been close to 25% since the 1980s. Debt and outlays both increased in 1967 (Vietnam) and in 1974 (OPEC Crisis). There was prosperity in the 1990s but the graph does not prove that—it proves only that the debt appeared to level off and outlays very slightly declined. It has been assumed that Reagan's economic policies were the cause of the rapid increase in debt after 1981, but the chart cannot prove that. The statement itself states the reverse of that common interpretation of Reaganomics. That leaves D as the correct choice. The Gross Federal Debt declined steadily from the end of World War II until the United States became heavily involved in Vietnam. You must know that World War II ended in 1945 and that United States involvement in Vietnam peaked in 1966–1967 when the debt jumped for a brief period.

## SAMPLE QUESTION

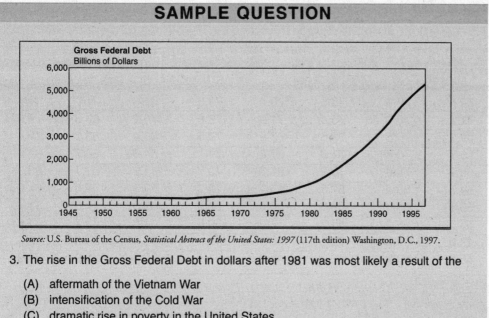

**Gross Federal Debt**
Billions of Dollars

*Source:* U.S. Bureau of the Census, *Statistical Abstract of the United States: 1997* (117th edition) Washington, D.C., 1997.

3. The rise in the Gross Federal Debt in dollars after 1981 was most likely a result of the

   (A)   aftermath of the Vietnam War
   (B)   intensification of the Cold War
   (C)   dramatic rise in poverty in the United States
   (D)   supply-side economic policy of Reaganomics
   (E)   decline in immigration

## Comments on Question 3

Questions based on charts and graphs are testing skills similar to those tested in the DBQ—skills of analysis and interpretation—and you need to know the mainstream conditions surrounding the question. For example, in question 3, you need to know the dates of the Vietnam War and World War II as well as something about Reaganomics. Using your knowledge of these topics from the mainstream of U.S. history, you would conclude that the supply-side economic policies known as Reaganomics adopted during Reagan's first term in 1981 had the greatest impact on increasing the debt after 1981. Also, choice D is the only choice that is clearly related to economic policy. Question 3 illustrates how a multiple-choice question based on a graph can test not only a skill but also factual knowledge.

## Life Expectancy at Birth

| Year | Total | | | White | | | Nonwhite | | |
| | Both Sexes | Male | Female | Both Sexes | Male | Female | Both Sexes | Male | Female |
|------|------------|------|--------|------------|------|--------|------------|------|--------|
| 1995 | 75.8 | 72.6 | 78.9 | 76.5 | 73.4 | 79.6 | NA | NA | NA |
| 1986 | 74.7 | 71.2 | 78.2 | 75.4 | 71.9 | 78.8 | 70.9 | 66.8 | 74.9 |
| 1976 | 72.9 | 69.1 | 76.8 | 73.6 | 69.9 | 77.5 | 68.4 | 63.7 | 72.4 |
| 1966 | 70.1 | 66.7 | 73.8 | 71.0 | 67.6 | 74.7 | 64.0 | 60.7 | 67.4 |
| 1956 | 69.6 | 66.7 | 73.0 | 70.2 | 67.3 | 73.7 | 63.2 | 61.1 | 65.9 |
| 1946 | 66.7 | 64.6 | 69.4 | 67.5 | 65.1 | 70.3 | 59.1 | 57.5 | 61.0 |
| 1936 | 58.5 | 56.6 | 60.6 | 59.8 | 58.0 | 61.9 | 49.0 | 47.0 | 51.4 |
| 1926 | 56.7 | 55.5 | 58.0 | 58.2 | 57.0 | 59.6 | 44.6 | 43.7 | 45.6 |
| 1916 | 51.7 | 49.6 | 54.3 | 52.5 | 50.2 | 55.2 | 41.3 | 39.6 | 43.1 |
| 1906 | 48.7 | 46.9 | 50.8 | 49.3 | 47.3 | 51.4 | 32.9 | 31.8 | 33.9 |

*Source:* U.S. Bureau of the Census, *Historical Statistics of the U.S., Colonial Times to 1970* U.S. Bureau of the Census, *Statistical Abstract of the United States 1981,* 2nd 1997, Washington, D.C.

## SAMPLE QUESTIONS

4. According to the statistics presented in the table, the individual with the shortest life expectancy at birth was a

   (A) white male in 1995
   (B) nonwhite female in 1936
   (C) white female in 1926
   (D) nonwhite male in 1906
   (E) white male in 1906

5. The statistics indicate all of the following to be true EXCEPT

   (A) The greatest increase in life expectancy for all people occurred between 1936 and 1946.
   (B) Male life expectancy for white and nonwhite males has always been shorter than for females in the same year.
   (C) Life exptectancy for both sexes of the white population has always been longer than the life expectancy for both sexes of the nonwhite population.
   (D) White female life expectancy in 1986 was over twice that of nonwhite females in 1906.
   (E) For all whites the smallest increase in life expectancy occurred between 1966 and 1976.

6. The statistics in the chart could most effectively be used to support the idea that

   (A) more females are born than males
   (B) life is harder for males who have to work more years
   (C) it is better to be born nonwhite than white
   (D) life expectancy reflects the social and economic condition of nonwhites
   (E) whites are always older than nonwhites

## Comments on Questions 4–6

Questions 4, 5, and 6 are based on a statistical table, another very common method of presenting a large amount of information. The table deals with life expectancy at birth for the total population, the white population, and the nonwhite population.

These three divisions or headings appear at the top of the table identifying three wide columns, each of which in turn is divided into three parts representing life expectancy for both sexes, for males and for females. The careful reading of column headings will save you from many silly errors. The years to be compared are presented in the left-hand column. For 1995 NA appears in the boxes under Nonwhite. This means this information was not available at the time the graph was produced. You will see N/A (not available or not applicable) from time to time in charts and graphs. The Bureau of the Census has made changes in the way information is collected and reported. The information is presented by decades except for 1986–1995. While a great deal of information is presented in the table, this is a rather simple lineal table. There is no accumulative data to be presented in peripheral boxes as you sometimes find in statistical tables.

## Comments on Question 4

Question 4 offers five choices for the individual with the shortest life expectancy at birth. Looking at the appropriate column for each choice, you see that the life expectancy of a white male in 1995 was 73.4 years, of a nonwhite female in 1936 was 51.4 years, of a white female in 1926 was 59.6 years, of a nonwhite male in 1906 was 31.8 years, and of a white male in 1906 was 47.3 years. If you have located these same numbers, then you can read the table. The answer is clearly the nonwhite male in 1906, choice D.

## Comments on Question 5

Question 5 involves a comparison of data in the table and you are asked to locate the one untrue statement. It is that for all whites, the smallest increase in life expectancy occurred between 1966 and 1976, which is choice E. Choices A through D are all true and you can prove this by looking at the boxes suggested in each of the choices given. This chart is complex and the questions require that you study and compare different boxes.

## Comments on Question 6

Question 6 moves beyond the statistics in the table and asks you to figure out how they might be used. Five possible theses or ideas are presented, and you are asked to decide which would be most effectively supported by these statistics. The best choice would be D—life expectancy reflects the social and economic condition of nonwhites. The statistics do not prove more females are born—only that they live longer. In fact, more males are born. Life may be harder for males, but the statistics do not prove it. Unless you find life unattractive and wish to die young, it is certainly not better to be born nonwhite and, of course, whites are not always older than nonwhites—a ridiculous statement, but one you might accept if you read too quickly! Living conditions and life expectancy— are related, and these statistics could be used effectively to support this idea. This question thus tests your ability to understand the statistics, to apply them to historic situations, and to make judgments as to the best use of given data. It is a good type of multiple-choice question based on charts.

## SAMPLE QUESTIONS

**U.S. Merchandise Trade With Japan**

Billions of Dollars

☑ U.S. exports
■ U.S. imports

1960　1970　1980　1984　1988　1992　1993

7. In reading the bar graph all of the following are accurate statements EXCEPT:

(A) U.S. imports from Japan have increased throughout the years shown.
(B) The graph presents information on U.S.-Japan trade relations.
(C) At no time have U.S. exports to Japan exceeded U.S. imports from Japan.
(D) The number of years between bars are not always the same.
(E) The greatest increase in U.S. exports came between 1988 and 1992.

8. According to information presented in the graph, you can conclude that

(A) the U.S. trade deficit was a problem from 1960–1984
(B) the Vietnam War forced the United States to buy from Japan
(C) the wages paid to Japanese workers are lower than those paid to Americans
(D) the Reagan tax cut program hurt our trade balance with Japan
(E) the exports of the United States grew more rapidly from 1970 to 1984 than in any other period

## Comments on Question 7

Question 7 simply asks you to read the graph. It is a test of your ability to read and understand the information in the key. The numbers at the bottom on the horizontal represent years, and billions of dollars are presented on the vertical. U.S. imports, beginning very small in 1960, have increased throughout the years shown. The title tells you that the graph is about *U.S. Merchandise Trade with Japan*. The number of years between bars vary. The greatest increase in U.S. exports, represented by the hatch marks, came between 1988 and 1992. You may need to measure this using the edge of a piece of paper. This leaves choice C as the wrong statement—U.S. exports to Japan exceeded imports in 1960. This is a good test of your ability to read all parts of a graph.

## Comments on Question 8

Question 8 asks you to interpret the graph and relate information in it to some ideas in recent mainstream history. The only point you can clearly conclude from the graph and not from outside sources is choice E, "the exports of the United States grew more rapidly from 1970 to 1984 than in any other period." The U.S. trade deficit was not a problem in 1960, as we exported more than we imported, so choice

A is inaccurate. Choices B, C, and D cannot be proven from the graph. We did not have to buy from Japan as a result of the Vietnam War and you can learn nothing about Japanese wages or Reagan's tax cut from the graph, although both have been suggested as reasons for the imbalance of trade. They are ideas from mainstream history that are important but cannot be proven from the graph.

These sample multiple-choice questions based on charts and graphs should illustrate the range of questions that might be asked. The analysis should provide you assistance in reading the charts and graphs you find as you study. Several of these charts contain more complex information and the questions require more analysis than may be needed on the exam. However, they provide good practice in analysis. Charts can provide helpful information on the United States. Do not skip over such information—spend time interpreting complex charts and graphs.

# Practice Multiple-Choice Questions

1. After the South seceded, the Congress passed legislation that benefited the North and the West, such as the

   (A) Kansas-Nebraska Act
   (B) Pacific Railroad Bill
   (C) Underwood Tariff
   (D) Sherman Anti-Trust Act
   (E) Chinese Exclusion Act

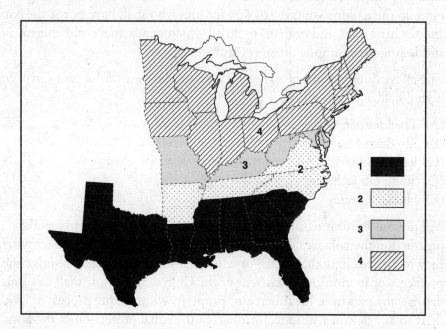

2. On the map, the Confederate States of America are those included in the area numbered

   (A) 1 and 4
   (B) 1 and 3
   (C) 1, 2, and 3
   (D) 2 and 3
   (E) 1 and 2

3. The so-called border states at the time of the outbreak of the Civil War were those states

   (A) bordering the Atlantic
   (B) bordering on but not members of the Confederacy
   (C) bordering the Mississippi River south of Missouri
   (D) bordering Canada from where Confederate sympathizers raided the North
   (E) bordering Mexico

4. All of the following comments would apply to *Uncle Tom's Cabin* EXCEPT

   (A) It was written by a talented woman.
   (B) It originated a common phrase used in race relations—*Uncle Tom*.
   (C) It is a story of living conditions under slavery.
   (D) It was an important element in creating antislavery feeling in the North.
   (E) It was not widely read until ten years after publication.

5. The purpose of the Freedman's Bureau was to

   (A) gain the vote for the freed slave
   (B) provide 40 acres and a mule for each slave
   (C) get Radical Republicans in positions of power in the South
   (D) feed and educate the former slaves
   (E) work against the Black Codes

6. "With malice toward none, with charity for all, with firmness in the right as God gives us to see the right, let us strive on to finish the work we are in, to bind up the nation's wounds, to care for him who shall have borne the battle and for his widow and orphan, to do all which may achieve and cherish a just and lasting peace among ourselves and all nations."

   The above quotation from a speech expresses the view of the post-Civil War period held and initiated by

   (A) Thaddeus Stevens
   (B) Abraham Lincoln
   (C) Jefferson Davis
   (D) Stonewall Jackson
   (E) Horace Greeley

7. "All persons born or naturalized in the United States, and subject to the jurisdiction thereof, are citizens of the United States and of the states wherein they reside. No state shall make or enforce any law which shall abridge the privileges or immunities of citizens of the United States; nor shall any state deprive any person of life, liberty, or property, without due process of law; nor deny to any person within its jurisdiction the equal protection of the laws."

   The above quotation is a key clause in the

   (A) Black Code of South Carolina
   (B) Gettysburg Address
   (C) Thirteenth Amendment to the Constitution
   (D) Fourteenth Amendment to the Constitution
   (E) Fifteenth Amendment to the Constitution

## Value of Selected Exports From the United States

| Year | Total Value* Millions of Dollars | Cotton Millions of Dollars | Leaf Tobacco Millions of Dollars | Wheat Millions of Dollars |
|------|------|------|------|------|
| 1850 | 101 | 72 | 10 | 1 |
| 1853 | 124 | 109 | 11 | 4 |
| 1855 | 151 | 88 | 15 | 1 |
| 1858 | 157 | 131 | 17 | 9 |
| 1860 | 270 | 192 | 16 | 4 |
| 1863 | 74 | 7 | 20 | 47 |
| 1865 | 154 | 7 | 23 | 30 |
| 1868 | 206 | 153 | 23 | 30 |
| 1870 | 359 | 227 | 21 | 47 |

*Selected Exports

Source: U.S. Bureau of the Census, *Historical Statistics of the U.S., Colonial Times to 1957.*

8. According to information presented in the above table, all of the following would appear true concerning United States exports EXCEPT

    (A) Export of leaf tobacco was not affected by the Civil War the way the export of cotton was.
    (B) The export of wheat grew during and after the Civil War.
    (C) The total value of U.S. exports rapidly recovered from the disruption of the Civil War.
    (D) Except for the period of the Civil War, cotton accounted for over 50 percent of total U.S. exports.
    (E) The total value of selected exports from the U.S. increased at a steady rate from 1850 to 1870.

9. Which one of the following individuals is incorrectly paired with his area of contribution to the arts?

    (A) Herman Melville—novelist
    (B) Walt Whitman—orator
    (C) Ralph Waldo Emerson—essayist
    (D) William Sydney Mount—artist
    (E) Henry Hobson Richardson—architect

*Source: Harper's Weekly,* May 17, 1862

10. The above sketch done by the artist Winslow Homer clearly indicates

    I.   U.S. cavalry on the move
    II.  a tent encampment possibly of Native Americans
    III. the troops had no guns or gunpowder
    IV. a time period after the invention of the telegraph

    (A) I and III
    (B) I, III, IV
    (C) I, II, III
    (D) I, II, IV
    (E) II, III, IV

## Answers and Answer Explanations

| | | | | |
|---|---|---|---|---|
| 1. **(B)** | 2. **(E)** | 3. **(B)** | 4. **(E)** | 5. **(D)** |
| 6. **(B)** | 7. **(D)** | 8. **(E)** | 9. **(B)** | 10. **(D)** |

1. **(B)** The Pacific Railroad Bill, providing federal financial aid and land grants for a railroad from St. Louis west, was passed after the South seceded. Until then no bill could be passed because of controversy concerning whether a northern or southern route should be followed. The other four choices are important congressional acts from other times.

2. **(E)** The Confederate States are 1 and 2 on the map.

3. **(B)** The border states at the time of the Civil War were those states that might have seceded but did not. They are identified as 3 on the map in question 2.

4. **(E)** *Uncle Tom's Cabin,* written by Harriet Beecher Stowe, was published in 1854 and immediately became popular. Its tale of slavery was a major factor in stirring up Northern anger at the South's "peculiar institution."

5. **(D)** The Freedman's Bureau was formed to help the newly freed slaves adjust to their new condition. It was especially important in supplying food and education until it fell under the control of the Radical Reconstructionists, who used it for political purposes.

6. **(B)** The quotation is from Lincoln's Second Inaugural Address and is often considered a summary of his view for Reconstruction. Certainly the plans for Reconstruction initiated by Lincoln reflect this view. None of the other men, except possibly the *New York Tribune* editor Horace Greeley, expressed such conciliatory sentiments, and Greeley was in no position to initiate action.

7. **(D)** The question asks you to identify a section of the Fourteenth Amendment. It is a clause you should know. The Thirteenth Amendment abolished slavery and the Fifteenth granted the vote without regard to color or previous condition of servitude. "Black Codes" restricted rather than granted liberty, and the famous Gettysburg Address was delivered at the dedication of a cemetery and would not include such language or ideas. The Republicans felt they needed to incorporate their ideas in the Constitution and made ratification of this amendment a condition for re-entry of the seceded states into the union.

8. **(E)** Question 8 asks you to read a simple statistical table dealing with U.S. exports in the years 1850–1870. In studying the table you will see that all the statements except the last, "The total value of selected exports from the U.S. increased at a steady rate from 1850 to 1870," are true. U.S. exports dropped during the Civil War. You must know that the Civil War years were 1861–1865 in order to interpret the other four choices.

9. **(B)** Walt Whitman was a noted poet whose reputation was guaranteed by the publication of his work *Leaves of Grass* in 1855. He was not an orator. The other men are correctly identified. Herman Melville was a novelist and his most famous novel, *Moby Dick,* was published in 1851. Ralph Waldo Emerson of Concord, Massachusetts, a Transcendentalist, was noted as an essayist and orator. His Phi Beta Kappa lecture at Harvard in 1837 titled *An American Scholar* is considered a wake-up call for cultural independence for a United States free

from the restraints of European culture. William Sydney Mount was an important genre painter noted for his scenes of daily life in the period 1836–1867. His scenes of farm life, country dances, and horse trading are especially noteworthy. He was the first artist of note to include African Americans in his paintings of daily life. Henry Hobson Richardson, born in Louisiana and educated at Harvard and the Ecole des Beaux Arts in Paris, was an architect noted for his revival of Romanesque designs. Trinity Church in Boston (1872–1877) was an early work in what became known as Richardson Romanesque.

10. **(D)** Winslow Homer, later famous for his seascapes and scenes of late 19th-century life, was sent as a young artist to portray events of the Civil War when cameras were relatively new. Homer's sketches appeared in *Harper's Weekly.* This one is from May 17, 1862, and shows "The Union Cavalry and Artillery Starting in Pursuit of the Rebels up the Yorktown Turnpike." Homer portrays Northern cavalry; see the large "US" on the rump of the horse in the foreground. There is a collection of tents in the background that may be Indian tepees. The wires, whether telegraph (1844) or telephone (1876), indicate it was *after* the telegraph was invented. This demonstrates a need for careful reading of information. While the weapons portrayed on the cavalry are swords, there is no indication the troops did not have guns. In fact, a careful study of the sketch will show a cannon in the center left.

# Growth of Industrial America, Populists, and Progressives 1877–1916

---

## CHAPTER 9

- Key developments and movements
- Essays based on comparisons
- Visuals: cartoons, photos, and paintings

---

The two related yet separate reform movements—the Populist and Progressive movements—that bridged the turn of the century should be studied in any survey course either in their own right as significant developments in our history or as part of a general study of reform movements in America. These would include, in addition to these two movements, the Jacksonian period, the New Deal, and Lyndon Johnson's War on Poverty. Changes continually occur in human affairs, but at certain periods these changes seem to occur more rapidly and are, in some cases, the result of deliberate decision. The periods in United States history when changes came rapidly have been of particular interest to historians.

## IMPORTANT FACETS OF THIS PERIOD

The years 1877 to 1916 include many important developments. Some were causes, some results, and some had no real connection to the reform movements. Such issues include literary and artistic developments, growth of manufacturing methods, our changing relations with England and other European nations, the establishment of the United States empire in the Pacific, immigration concerns, and changing lifestyles as a result of economic and social developments. These years saw the nation grow to be the world power it was in the 20th century.

Among those items you should consider in studying this period are

1. The meaning of Populism
2. The effect of the closing of the frontier on American life
3. The impact of the growth of manufacturing and the railroads on the farmer
4. The economic or business cycles
5. The causes and results of the Spanish-American War

> **STUDY TIP**
>
> Build your study of the years 1877 to 1916 around the Populist and Progressive Movements as they have links to almost all of the developments of the period.

6. American expansion in the Pacific and U.S. relations with the European powers
7. The growth of cities and resulting changes in social patterns
8. The changing status of African Americans, both in the South and throughout the country
9. The changing patterns of immigration and Americans' response to it
10. The meaning of the Progressive movement, especially through a comparison of Theodore Roosevelt and Woodrow Wilson
11. Developments in American literary and artistic expression

## SAMPLE ESSAY QUESTION—COMPARE

One type of essay question often found on Advanced Placement examinations asks you to compare several items, which can be people, events, or ideas. The word *compare* means to represent as similar, to examine the character or qualities of two or more items for the purpose of discovering their resemblances **or** differences. Usually you will be asked to compare two items but at times, more items may be included. In the definition, it is suggested that *compare* implies similarity, but note that the word *differences* is used as well as *resemblances*. In a question asking you to compare, you may stress either differences or similarities.

Often in such questions another word is included. You will often find the word *contrast* used, so the question reads *Compare and contrast. . . .* In this situation you must discuss both the differences and similarities between the items since contrast means to show the differences between objects. However, compare alone does require you to consider both similarities and differences and this should not be forgotten. Another word that might be added to a *Compare* question to clarify what you are to do is *explain*, which we discussed in Chapter 5 with the *Describe . . . explain* question. You may find *Compare* questions that include *discuss, defend,* or *analyze*. It should be clear by this point that many essay questions are combinations of several other type questions, and that within every type there are many variations possible.

---

### SAMPLE QUESTION

Compare the contributions of TWO of the following to the economic well-being of the United States in the period 1881 to 1915:

Ida Tarbell
John D. Rockefeller
Theodore Roosevelt
Henry Ford

---

### Comments on Sample Question

The question is quite straightforward. It is a *Compare* question without any additional words, so you are to find the similarities and/or differences in the contributions of the two individuals you pick to the economic well-being of the United States in the years 1881 to 1915. Before you pick the two individuals you will write about, it is important that you understand the question. It is somewhat loosely worded as to just what is meant by well-being. The idea behind the phrase is that which makes a situation healthy. The question focuses on economic history and events related to it and not political history, but you will need to include some political history especially if you pick Ida Tarbell and Theodore Roosevelt. The dates given are interesting. In 1881 John D. Rockefeller established the Standard Oil Trust. By 1915 war had broken out in Europe and Henry Ford was making an attempt to stop the war. He had already introduced the Model T car and the eight-hour work day. The time span thus covers the period of rapid industrial growth in the United States and its emergence as a world power. You will need to be aware of those events.

Once you have analyzed the question, the next step is to pick the two individuals about whom you will write. Assuming that you know something about all four choices, you should make brief notes about what you know and then decide which two to pick. As you make the notes, you will want to begin thinking of the approach you will take to the question.

In a *Compare* question you can either weave together information about the items being compared showing how they are similar or different on various points, or you may present information on the items separately and then write an analysis of the ways they are similar and different. In the former approach you would want to decide on the points for comparison first and organize material around them. In the latter approach, you need first to decide what you know of the individuals. Then, decide what you will include in the paragraphs where you present your analysis. Whatever approach you take, you will want to have notes on the items to be compared.

The four choices in this question are interesting individuals. Two, Rockefeller and Ford, are clearly related to economics. Each made major contributions to the development of business in the United States. Theodore Roosevelt is remembered as a political leader of the Progressive Era. A link to economic well-being may seem tenuous but he had views on trusts, supported legislation regulating food and drugs in the United States, and intervened in the Coal Strike of 1902. These events are related to both politics and economics and are the type of information to include in your answer. Ida Tarbell made her reputation as a muckraker, exposing the Standard Oil Trust and other evils as she saw them in U.S. society at the turn of the century. If you pick her, you need to connect her social concerns with their economic impact on the United States. This is a particularly good question on which to practice writing an answer, doing additional research if needed. When you have written your essay, read the following student essay. Again, if you make a formal outline of the answer before you read the teacher comments on the essay, you will be able to see how the student organized the answer, and it will help you review the history of this time period and to judge the quality of your essay.

## Sample Answer

Economic well-being, which would include not only business prosperity but also the quality of that prosperity for all the people, is an important aspect of life in any society. Many individuals contributed to the economic well-being of the United States between 1881 and 1915. Their contributions were of different types from presidential to business leadership. Ida Tarbell and Henry Ford represent two very different contributions to that well-being, but they both had the best interests of the nation as their guiding principle.

During the early part of the 20th century, a group of journalists, called *Muckrakers,* prompted the reform of government and big business. Particularly important among these journalists was Ida Tarbell, whose work was significant in opening the eyes of America to problems facing the country and led to the reform of business and government. What she is most famous for is the writing she did on Standard Oil and its president, the business genius, John D. Rockefeller. Her series in *McClure's Magazine* revealed that the Standard Oil Company was selling its oil at lower prices than other oil producers, yet it was still making a larger profit. Tarbell showed that the company had established a horizontal integration of the oil industry. In her articles, Tarbell revealed that Standard Oil had conspired to monopolize trade by getting rebates and preferences from railroads and by controlling pipelines, and had used local price cutting and espionage to eliminate competition.

Tarbell's work was revolutionary; she had exposed the most powerful corporation in America, and she was a *woman* no less! It was easy for the oil workers to see the evil in what Rockefeller had done, but for the average American who knew of Rockefeller only as the man who gave enormous sums of money to universities and who employed thousands of people, this evil was difficult to believe and comprehend.

There was no denying that the information that Tarbell had uncovered was valid; thus, Rockefeller was forced to reform. State government passed bills to control railroad and pipeline rates. The federal government became involved, and in response to the company's monopolization, Congress passed a bill creating a Bureau of Corporations, which had the authority to oversee the accounts and activities of corporations. In 1907 the government charged Standard Oil with violating the Sherman Anti-Trust Act of 1890 (which declared trusts illegal and gave the government the right to dissolve them) as the company and its related associates had conspired to monopolize interstate commerce in oil. Other charges brought against the company were ones that Tarbell had revealed. In May of 1911 the Standard Oil Company was dissolved by the Supreme Court. The hard work of Ida Tarbell had been rewarded, and the economic well-being of the country improved as people benefited.

After years of tinkering and experimentation, by 1903 Henry Ford had raised enough capital to incorporate the Ford Motor Company. Attempting to construct a car for the "great multitude," Ford introduced the Model T in October 1908 and fulfilled his vision of an affordable automobile. Although there were roughly 20 established automakers at the time, Ford was successful because of his low price. Once seen as a luxury perk, the automobile soon came within the grasp of the common man and the revolution was underway.

From an economic standpoint, the development of the Model T and the rise of the automotive industry provided the nation with a uniquely "American" product. In the years of Model T production, millions of cars were sold in the United States and abroad, thus, the Model T began to symbolize globally the quality of American industry. With this rapid production came the need for various raw materials and products. The automobile became the main stimulant of the American economy. Industrially, coal, steel, and rubber companies benefited greatly from Ford. Agriculturally speaking, the abundant use of the automobile rendered the horse obsolete and the rapid shift from hay production to other crops caused a major farming change. The car made long trips short and tied the country into one community, so highways became essential and America responded with the best road system in the world. With every industry now cross-related, big business and industry boomed between 1896 and 1915.

Through his work with the Model T, Henry Ford revolutionized manufacturing. He used a constantly moving assembly line, which increased car production. He paid his workers $5 a day, twice the industry average. Ford kept his workers happy and thus more productive. To finance these absurd salaries, Ford slashed prices and increased production.

Socially, the birth of the automobile changed America drastically in a few short years. Readily available to the working man, automobiles led to the rise of the middle class. Suburbs sprouted, as commuting was made easy. The country gained a stronger sense of unity, as it became easier to travel. Americans became quite proud of their automobiles. The auto became a symbol of quality and Henry Ford became a folk hero. A true American success story that inspired others throughout the nation. Certainly he changed the economic well-being of the United States.

Ida Tarbell and Henry Ford made dramatic but very different contributions to the economic well-being of the United States at the start of the 20th century. Just think what this country and the world would be like if monopolies ran all businesses and we did not have the automobile. These two individuals changed the economic lives of all Americans for the better.

## Teacher Comments on Sample Answer

"The organization of the essay around Tarbell and Ford is fine, but the writer fails to make an effective comparison between the two. The writer merely presents information, all of which is very good, about the two individuals and makes no attempt to relate it to the thesis or to find common or contrasting points for comparison, which is what is expected in a *Compare* question. For instance, the writer might have compared how both Ford and Tarbell wished to change industry or how the work of both benefited the nation by reducing prices. The writer might have preferred to concentrate on the dissimilarities, which might range from the contrast of Tarbell's working through the press and Ford working in factories to the fact that Tarbell was destroying a large company and Ford was creating one.

"In conclusion, this essay is very satisfactory in terms of information. There is an obvious organization, but it does not focus on a comparison and, although it has a thesis, the body of the essay does not support it. It is an example of an essay with many possibilities that are not fulfilled. In spite of its defects, because of the quality of the information the essay would qualify for a good score—a 7."

Do you agree with these comments? The introductory paragraph of the sample student essay is a good one and could be used as a model in your writing.

# Practice Essay Questions

The following essay questions will test your knowledge of this period, and in addition, question 5 forces you to relate this period of time to an earlier one you have studied. Types of essay questions we have discussed in previous chapters are used in these five sample questions to provide practice with different type questions.

1. "In understanding the nature of a reform movement it is as important to know what it seeks to preserve as to know what it seeks to change." Compare the Populist and Progressive Reform movements of the late 19th and early 20th centuries in light of this statement.

2. "The nation (United States) whose Constitution is so perfect that no man suggests change and whose fundamental laws as they stand are satisfactory to all . . . The nation in which the right of the minority, the right of property and . . . of free labor are most secure."

   To what extent is this statement an accurate summary of the situation in the United States at the end of the 19th century for TWO of the following groups?

   Women
   African Americans
   European immigrants
   Native Americans

3. "The closing of the frontier in 1890 had a profound effect on the social and economic development of the United States in the succeeding 20 years." Evaluate this statement.

4. In what ways did THREE of the following affect the development of the West?

   Introduction of barbed wire
   Building of the railroads
   Introduction of the McCormack reaper
   End of the Indian Wars

5. "In the period 1793–1812 the United States was a small nation pushed around by the big powers; in the period 1895–1911 the United States was a big power that pushed around small nations."

   Compare the foreign policy of the United States in these two time periods to test the validity of this generalization.

## Comments on Question 1

Question 1 is a straightforward *Compare* question. The quotation is an interesting one that could be applied to any reform movement. In this case you are asked to compare two movements that sometimes appear rather similar, but that are quite different. These differences should be clarified in an essay based on this quotation. Your thesis would have to state what you believe each movement sought to preserve, assuming, of course, you don't take the extreme position that the movements tried to preserve nothing. An organization based on similarities and differences in the two movements would seem more satisfactory than a chronological organization. If you have studied these two important reform movements, the question should be rather easy, since there are no unusual words or twists to the question.

## Comments on Question 2

In question 2 you first need to read and analyze the quote. The author of the quote is very optimistic about the United States. He believes everything is fine for everybody. He mentions particularly the security of the rights of the minority, of property, and of free labor. These three form an interesting combination. Who are the minority in the speaker's eyes? What is property? What is free labor? These three terms are crucial in understanding the meaning of the quotation and in determining what you will have to say about the situation for two of the four groups in the United States at the end of the 19th century. Your thesis may well state the quotation applied only to men. The factual information can be organized in different ways to answer the question. The question suggests an interesting approach to the period of time at the end of the century.*

## Comments on Question 3

Question 3 is a straightforward *Evaluate This Statement* type. The quotation uses a familiar idea from the Bureau of the Census report for 1890. The *closed frontier* is the phrase that Frederick Jackson Turner used to develop his important thesis on the significance of the frontier in America. If the thesis is not familiar, you can still develop an interesting essay on the issue of the impact of the frontier on social and economic developments. This essay would best be organized around the various social and economic effects and *not* by chronology.

## Comments on Question 4

This is a straightforward *In what ways?* question in which you are asked to discuss three of four items. As in all questions with a choice of this type, you must pick the three items carefully. For instance, you may know a lot about the fighting of the Indian Wars but if you cannot connect this information to the development of the West, do not pick that item. The four choices all changed the way life in the West was lived. Barbed wire allowed cattle to be controlled, the McCormack reaper made it possible to harvest large fields of wheat, and railroads opened markets. You may know all these facts, but the key to the question is to connect them to the development of the West and not simply describe the three items you pick. An organization focusing on how the items interconnect would be better than a chronology or a description of each item separately. As always, you must express your opinion on the topic.

## Comments on Question 5

The fifth essay question again combines several types of essay questions. There is a statement about U.S. foreign policy, but then, instead of being asked to evaluate the statement, you are asked to compare the two time periods mentioned in the statement with the goal of testing the validity of the generalization. What the writer of this question is seeking in the way of an answer is very close to an evaluation of the statement, but the writer has given directions as to how this is to be achieved—by a comparison. Your thesis will reflect how true you believe the statement to be. Examples of the United States being pushed around in the years 1793–1812 contrasted with the examples of the United States pushing small nations or not pushing them, depending on your personal thesis, in the years 1895–1911, would provide an effective organization.

In analyzing the statement, you will no doubt recall many examples of U.S. foreign policy activity from which you may choose. In the years 1793–1812 the United States had innumerable dealings with France and England, to say nothing of Spain and the Barbary Pirates, while in the later period we were involved in the

*The author of the quote is not given in the question. You may be interested to know that the author was Andrew Carnegie, writing in 1873.

annexation of Hawaii, the Spanish-American War, incidents in Panama and Venezuela, and several incidents involving European powers, such as the Algeciras Conference, the Russo-Japanese War, and the Second Hague Disarmament Conference. Again, you will have many examples of foreign policy activity to choose from, so the major difficulty in this question will be in picking information to support your thesis and being certain to refute any major piece of evidence that does not agree with your thesis. For instance, if you do not believe the United States pushed small nations around in the 1895–1911 period, you must not ignore Theodore Roosevelt's use of the "big stick," but either explain that this was an exception to your thesis or that T. R. had certain larger goals in mind. As mentioned in Part One, when defending a thesis, you are being a lawyer or debater; they often concede points before going on to make their main argument. This technique is important if you wish to win readers to your side.

## MULTIPLE-CHOICE QUESTIONS—VISUALS: CARTOONS, PHOTOGRAPHS, AND PAINTINGS

In Chapter 8 we discussed multiple-choice questions based on charts and graphs and indicated that the primary purpose of such questions was to test your analytical skills. Another popular type of multiple-choice question designed to test analytical skill is the multiple-choice question based upon a visual stimulus—a cartoon, photograph, or painting. The cartoon is often a politically oriented one. As is true in the case of multiple-choice questions based on charts and graphs, when dealing with questions based on visuals, you will often be expected to know about the history of the period in which the cartoon or picture was produced. Therefore, although the primary purpose of such multiple-choice questions is to test analytical skills needed by the student of history, there is also an element of factual recall involved. As in the case of the DBQ, in these questions you will often be required to relate the visual to the mainstream of American history.

The following multiple-choice questions are examples of what you might find on an examination. The cartoons are all from *Harper's Weekly.* There are many other sources for cartoons and sketches, but those that appeared in *Harper's Weekly* are typical of 19th-century cartoons. Many textbooks today use such cartoons to illustrate points. It is wise to take time to look carefully at the cartoons and other illustrations as you study. The old expression, "A picture can convey a thousand words," is often true. These sample questions and comments will supply some practice in developing your skill in *reading* illustrations. If your text or the books you are using to study history lack cartoons and pictures, you can practice by analyzing the cartoons and photographs in the daily papers, in newsmagazines, or in special books of cartoons. You can also look at books on different schools of art such as the Hudson River School, or at different artists such as Benjamin Rush (18th century), William Sydney Mount (19th century), and Andy Warhol (20th century).

## SAMPLE QUESTIONS

DON'T SWAP HORSES

JOHN BULL. "Why don't you ride the other Horse a bit? He's the best Animal."
BROTHER JONATHAN [Uncle Sam]. "Well that may be; but the fact is, OLD ABE is just where I can put my finger on him; and as for the other—though they say he's somewhere out in the scrub yonder—I never know where to find him."

*Source: Harper's Weekly,* November 1864

1. Considering the topic of the above cartoon, in which of the following years was it most likely published?

   (A) 1844
   (B) 1860
   (C) 1864
   (D) 1940
   (E) 1968

2. In the cartoon the words in the bushes refer to

   (A) John Bull's economic policies
   (B) the horse trader's promises
   (C) the charter of the city of Chicago
   (D) the main planks in the Democratic Party's Chicago Platform
   (E) the goals of the Republican Party of "Old Abe"

## Comments on Question 1

The cartoon is from *Harper's Weekly* of November 1864. The artist is not identified. The subject is Abraham Lincoln's campaign for reelection to the presidency. To answer the question you must be able to recall several items that are suggested by points in the cartoon. The biggest point for identification is the reference to "Old Abe" which should lead you to identify the face on the horse as Lincoln's. If you recall the years of Lincoln's elections and presidency—1860–1865—you have narrowed the choices down to 1860 and 1864. You then need to decide what the title of the cartoon means. *Don't swap horses* is a western expression meaning "don't change." When was Lincoln or the country, represented here by Brother Jonathan, involved in changing? There were times Lincoln changed generals, but this was not a decision made by the country (Brother Jonathan) or of interest to other nations (John Bull representing England). Another change, one involving the years given as possible answers, was that offered to the country in the election of 1864, choice C. Abe was president (note the horse being ridden) and the other choice or candidate (see the figure in the bushes) was an "unknown" quantity as Brother Jonathan says. This is further confirmed, if you recognize the face in the bushes as McClellan, Lincoln's Democratic opponent, or if you know the Democrats held their convention at Chicago and their platform called for peace and compromise. Perhaps you were able to identify the years without such a detailed analysis, but this analysis illustrates how you can read cartoons using your knowledge of history to understand what is being presented. Incidentally, the *Don't swap horses* slogan was also used by the Democrats in 1940 to support the third-term election of Franklin D. Roosevelt, with the idea being that we should not change presidents at a period of such international crisis. The year 1844 has no connection to the cartoon; 1968 was the year of turmoil at the Democratic Party Convention in Chicago, where peace and compromise in Vietnam were major issues, but this is irrelevant to the cartoon.

## Comments on Question 2

In answering the second question about the 1864 cartoon, you would have to know what the Democrats stood for in 1864. It is a question based more on recall than on analysis, but you might be able to arrive at the correct answer by eliminating the other choices. John Bull's economic policies have nothing to do with the topic of the cartoon, and the cartoon is *not* about horse trading, so you should be able to eliminate those two choices. Although Lincoln was from Illinois and Chicago is in that state, choice C about the charter of the city has no obvious connection to the conversation between Brother Jonathan and John Bull, so it should be eliminated. Finally, you are left with two choices involving political parties. If you have identified "Old Abe" as Lincoln, then you could probably eliminate the words in the bushes as the goals of the Republican party. The Republicans were ready to fight the Civil War and not compromise for peace. Thus, even with a limited amount of knowledge of the period, by careful elimination, you could arrive at the correct answer, D. In preparation for the exam, practice this type of analysis and elimination as you look at cartoons, and as you practice doing multiple-choice questions, see how often you guess correctly.

> **TIP**
>
> Statistically the odds are in your favor to guess at answers, provided you can eliminate one or more of the five selections.

**SAMPLE QUESTION**

With permission of the NH Historical Society, Concord, NH

3. The above late 19th-century photograph could most accurately be used to illustrate the point that in the 19th century

   (A)  houses lacked central heating
   (B)  electricity was not widely used
   (C)  beards were not fashionable
   (D)  barbershops were available
   (E)  apprentices were widely employed

## Comments on Question 3

The only choice that can be proven by the photograph is D. The photo, taken around 1888, shows the interior of a barbershop located across from the state capitol in Concord, NH. It is typical of barbershops of the period. The chairs facing mirrors, the towels over the chairs, the shaving mugs on the counter, and the individual mugs on the wall above the sink in the corner with the pitcher for rinsing hair are all bits of evidence to help prove that barbershops were available. It does not answer how available they were. The stove suggests no central heating but pipes running across the ceiling may be for heat. The lamps appear to be gas but even if they were, it is not appropriate to jump to the conclusion that electricity was not widely used. The same is true of the fashion of beards. Two men have mustaches and no beards, and the third is clean shaven but may be so young that he doesn't even shave. He may well be an apprentice learning the trade of barbering but, again, there is no proof that he is or that apprentices were widely used in the barbering trade. This is a tricky question in some ways and it requires careful thought and analysis. The choices all describe situations in the late-19th-century that you may have studied, but can the photograph be used to support the idea without further information? A picture may be worth a thousand words, but those words must be carefully chosen.

## SAMPLE QUESTION

With permission of the NH Historical Society, Concord, NH

4. This painting by 19th-century artist Thomas Hill most clearly illustrates his interest in

(A) the desirability of creating national parks in mountain areas
(B) the appeal of the mountains in developing the tourist industry
(C) the glory and power of nature compared to the works of man
(D) the importance of developing water power
(E) the significance of conservation for mountain areas

## Comments on Question 4

This 1872 painting of the Willey Home in Crawford Notch in the White Mountains of New Hampshire by Thomas Hill clearly illustrates his sense of the overwhelming power and grandeur of nature when compared to the insignificance of the home built by the Willey family—early settlers in the Notch. The house is overpowered by it surroundings. Throughout much of the 19th century, from the transcendentalists to the great painters of the western Rockies to the Hudson River and White Mountain Schools, this sense of the power of nature was a recurring aspect of artistic and intellectual thought. All the other choices were also of interest at different times in the century, but none of them are illustrated by the painting. However, it is interesting to note that a mud slide killed all of the Willey family in 1826, but left the house intact. Newspaper publicity, which brought many visitors to the notch, is credited with starting the tourist industry in the area. This region of the White Mountains is now a national park, and conservation is a top priority in the area but that is not illustrated by this painting. Also, water power was important in New England, but again, this is not clearly illustrated by the painting (in spite of the roaring stream). Question 4 requires careful analysis of the painting and recall of some interests of 19th-century artists and the public.

## SAMPLE QUESTIONS

SOURCE:  Library of Congress

5. The photograph most likely portrays

    (A)   workers on an automobile assembly line
    (B)   child laborers in a factory
    (C)   Civil War recruits waiting for uniforms
    (D)   two boys preparing hot dogs at a baseball game
    (E)   recent illegal immigrants

6. The conditions presented in the above photograph were largely eliminated by

    (A)   exporting production to foreign countries
    (B)   the Child Labor Amendment to the Constitution
    (C)   Supreme Court decisions before World War I
    (D)   legislation under the New Deal
    (E)   the Great Depression

## Comments on Question 5

The photograph used for questions 5 and 6 is of two young boys working in a glass factory in 1908. It is an example of child labor and reflects factory conditions at a time when the ideas of the Social Darwinists and trust builders dominated American business. By studying this photograph it would be clear that it is not an assembly line or a hot dog stand. The caps may make you think of Civil War recruits, but the chimney tongs and work table make it appear more a factory than a recruiting station. If the boys are immigrants, the photo cannot prove they are illegal. There are limits to the use of photos as evidence. The photograph is a good thought provoker and is typical of what might be found on an exam. Choice B is correct.

## Comments on Question 6

Question 6 illustrates how a photograph may lead to a multiple-choice question requiring both analysis and factual recall. For question 6 you must recognize the conditions as being those of child labor in a factory, and then you must know how the conditions of child labor were changed. Exporting production abroad has in many cases simply moved the working conditions out of the U.S. without eliminating them. The Child Labor Amendment to the Constitution was never ratified by the states, and though it may have had some impact on child labor, it did not eliminate it. Before World War I the Supreme Court was conservative and would not interfere in private business matters, and depressions generally create worse situations for workers; they do not eliminate bad conditions. It was not until the New Deal labor legislation that child labor was largely eliminated, choice D.

## SAMPLE QUESTIONS

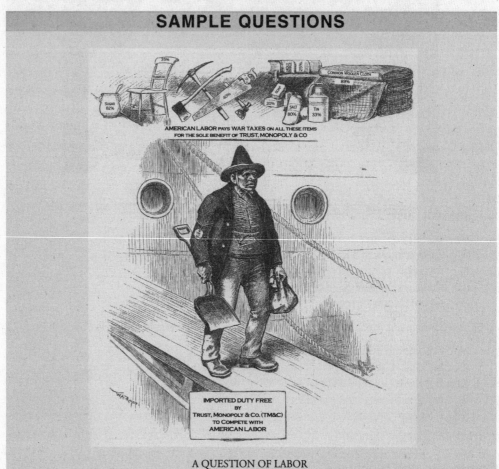

A QUESTION OF LABOR

"This question is from first to last, from the beginning to the end, from skin to core and from core back to skin again, a question of labor."—James G. Blaine at Madison Square, August 10, 1888.

*Source: Harper's Weekly,* September 29, 1888

7. The cartoonist is protesting all of the following EXCEPT

   (A) free immigration
   (B) high taxes on manufactured items
   (C) the power of trusts and monopolies
   (D) James G. Blaine's comment that the immigration issue is "first to last . . . a question of labor."
   (E) the poor-quality work of American labor

8. The T. M. & Co. tag on the immigrant's arm and in the box under his feet stands for Trust, Monopoly and Company, which is

   (A) John D. Rockefeller's company
   (B) a fictitious organization representing the power of trusts
   (C) a company created by the U.S. Congress
   (D) a worldwide conglomerate
   (E) a government corporation formed to aid immigrants

## Comments on Question 7

W. A. Rogers' cartoon titled "A Question of Labor" provides the basis for questions 7 and 8. It is from the September 29, 1888 issue of *Harper's Weekly.* Question 7 asks what Mr. Rogers is protesting about in the cartoon, and the question is phrased in that very common way that seeks the one point that is incorrect. This phrasing, "all of the following EXCEPT," has been used in many multiple-choice questions in this book. It provides a positive approach to the information because four out of the five choices are correct, rather than the reverse where four choices are wrong. In this cartoon you can tell Mr. Rogers is unhappy about free immigration since the sign indicates that the immigrant is imported "duty free . . . to compete with American labor." *Compete* is the key word here. He also opposes high taxes he believes only help the trusts. Implied in both these points is Rogers's dislike of the power of the trusts and monopolies, as such phrases as *compete* and *sole benefit* indicate. He is also protesting James G. Blaine's comment, although that is not as easy to see. The title of the cartoon, "A Question of Labor," picked up Blaine's comment, and the impact of the entire cartoon is to indicate that the question is *not* merely a question of labor, it is also a question of labor competition, monopoly control, and high taxes. Rogers is thus protesting the points indicated in the first four choices and he is not protesting "the poor-quality work of American labor," choice E, which is the correct answer for this all-but-one type of multiple-choice question. The answer was arrived at simply by analyzing the cartoon, and there was no need to understand the historical circumstances in which it was placed. These circumstances were a presidential campaign in which Benjamin Harrison, the Republican, was running against Grover Cleveland, the Democrat, whom he defeated. Blaine had been defeated by Cleveland in 1884. Blaine was considered the leading Republican. He was appointed Secretary of State by Harrison, he was a supporter of trusts and big business, and was a U.S. Senator from Maine.

## Comments on Question 8

In question 8 the T. M. & Co. tag stands for Trust, Monopoly and Company, which is mentioned in the sign under the immigrant's feet. It is a fictitious organization created by Rogers to represent the power of the trusts and is the correct answer, B. The other choices given are all possibilities, and you might pick one of them unless you know a little of the history of the period. The cartoon gives you the date so you do not have to figure that out. Rockefeller's company was Standard Oil; the U.S. Congress was not creating companies at this time—it was done by private enterprise; worldwide conglomerates are a later historic development (in the pre-1900 period national trusts were being created); the United States government did very little to aid immigrants in this time period.

These illustrations of multiple-choice questions based on cartoons and photographs should help you in your study and analysis of such items in your texts. As you can see, many types of questions can be based on cartoons and pictures, some of which will require a simple analysis of the illustrations, some of which require pure recall, and some of which require both. There will be examples of such multiple-choice questions in the following chapters.

# Practice Multiple-Choice Questions

OUR PRESIDENT PUTS HIS FOOT DOWN, AND THE BRITISH LION WILL HAVE TO WRIGGLE OUT.

*Source: Harper's Weekly,* June 6, 1872

1. The cartoonist is making a point concerning the *Alabama* claims, claims that

   (A) resulted from the attack of the *Alabama* on Northern shipping
   (B) were presented against British shipping in the West Indies
   (C) were British complaints against the quality of *Alabama's* cotton
   (D) involved *Alabama* businessmen and the British government
   (E) resulted from Union attack on the South during the Civil War

## Vote of the State of Connecticut 1872–1886

| Date | Office | Parties | | | | Plurality* | |
|------|--------|------|------|------|------|------|---|
| | | Dem. | Rep. | Gr. | Pro. | | |
| 1872 | President .... | 45,880 | 50,638 | ... | ... | 4758 | R. |
| 1874 | Governor...... | 46,755 | 39,973 | ... | 4942 | 6782 | D. |
| 1876 | President..... | 61,071 | 59,034 | 774 | 378 | 2900 | D. |
| 1878 | Governor...... | 46,385 | 48,867 | 8314 | 1079 | 2482 | R. |
| 1880 | President..... | 64,415 | 67,169 | 863 | 448 | 2656 | R. |
| 1882 | Governor...... | 59,014 | 54,853 | 697 | 1034 | 4161 | R. |
| 1884 | President..... | 67,167 | 65,893 | 1684 | 2489 | 1284 | D. |
| 1884 | Governor...... | 67,910 | 66,275 | 1379 | 1636 | 1636 | D. |
| 1886 | Governor...... | 58,817 | 56,920 | 4687 | 2792 | 1897 | D. |

*Source: Harper's Weekly,* 1888
**KEY**
Dem.—Democratic Party
Rep.—Republican Party
Gr.—Greenback Party
Pro.—Prohibition Party
*Majority.

2. For the years 1872 to 1886, according to the information presented in the table, one might conclude that all of the following are true EXCEPT:

   (A) There were only two third parties from 1876 to 1886.
   (B) The Prohibition Party (Pro.) obtained its largest number of votes when it was the only third party.
   (C) The Republican presidential candidate would have won all of Connecticut's electoral college votes in 1884 if all third party votes had been cast for him.
   (D) Election for governor and president never occur in the same year.
   (E) Democratic Party nominees won more often in Connecticut.

3. "The millionaires are a product of natural selection acting on the whole body of men to pick out those qualified few who can meet the requirements of certain work to be done…"

   The author of the above quotation is most likely

   (A) Woodrow Wilson
   (B) William Graham Sumner
   (C) William Jennings Bryan
   (D) Eugene V. Debs
   (E) Theodore Roosevelt

4. The ideas of natural selection and survival of the fittest, when applied to business and economic activity, are referred to as

   (A) Communism
   (B) Trust-busting
   (C) Anarchism
   (D) Dollar Diplomacy
   (E) Social Darwinism

5. In 1895 President Cleveland turned to J. P. Morgan and a Wall Street syndicate to borrow gold for the U.S. Treasury because

   (A) the government could not otherwise redeem its outstanding paper money
   (B) Cleveland had Morgan's support in the election and wished to help him
   (C) Congress refused to repeal the Sherman Silver Purchase Act
   (D) the government needed the money to build the Panama Canal
   (E) it was the only way Wall Street could recover from the Panic of 1893

6. The major point of difference between Booker T. Washington and W. E. B. Du Bois was over their view of

   (A) the need for education
   (B) the importance of better race relations
   (C) the need for immediate equality for African Americans
   (D) the significance of independence for Africa
   (E) using white institutions to help the African Americans

7. The Populist Party platform in 1892 called for all of the following EXCEPT

   (A) a graduated income tax
   (B) government ownership of railroads
   (C) a gold-based currency
   (D) support for initiative and referendum legislation
   (E) direct election of United States senators

8. Among the major political issues on which Congress passed legislation during the years 1877–1892 were all of the following EXCEPT

   (A) civil service reform
   (B) civil rights
   (C) control of the trusts
   (D) the coinage of silver
   (E) tariffs

THE FINISHING TOUCH
Drawn by B.W. Kemble

*Source: Harper's Weekly*, November, 1912

9. The above cartoon is commenting upon the fact that

   (A) Woodrow Wilson was a skilled bullfighter
   (B) campaigns are like bullfights
   (C) there were few issues in the 1912 campaign
   (D) lectures delivered by Woodrow Wilson always had a point
   (E) the "Prof" Wilson defeated Theodore Roosevelt's Bull Moose Party

10. The U.S. Supreme Court in the case of *Lochner v. New York* declared a law limiting the hours of labor in a bakery unconstitutional because it

   (A) discriminated against women workers
   (B) increased the cost of bread
   (C) interfered in the worker's right of free contract
   (D) gave an advantage to the owners
   (E) compromised the health of the workers

## Answers and Answer Explanations

1. (**A**)    2. (**D**)    3. (**B**)    4. (**E**)    5. (**A**)
6. (**C**)    7. (**C**)    8. (**B**)    9. (**E**)    10. (**C**)

1. (**A**) Question 1 refers to a cartoon about the *Alabama* claims. It appeared in *Harper's Weekly* on June 6, 1872. One piece of paper in the foreground, titled the

"Alabama Claims," suggests the topic of the cartoon and requires that you know what the claims were. The *Alabama* was a warship built in Great Britain for the Confederacy during the Civil War. It raided Northern shipping. The immediate situation almost led to the North declaring war on Great Britain. The Northern financial losses resulting from ships sunk by the *Alabama* were blamed on the British who had built the ship. The situation after the war was referred to international arbitration during Grant's presidency when he "put his foot down." The lion has been a common symbol for Great Britain. Note how, in the cartoon, Grant has his foot on the British Lion's tail. This is a good example of a multiple-choice cartoon-based question requiring both recall and analytical skill.

2. **(D)** Question 2 requires that you read the Table. You will see when you do that all the choices are correct except that there were elections for governor and president in 1884. This question requires that you understand the operation of the electoral college at that time. In 1884 the party with the largest number of votes won *all* the electoral college votes from that state.

3. **(B)** The quotation in question 3 is from William Graham Sumner, a Yale sociologist who became the chief spokesperson for the philosophy of Social Darwinism. The other men were not active supporters of Social Darwinism.

4. **(E)** Social Darwinism is briefly described by the two terms used in question 4. Social Darwinists believed that Darwin's laws of evolution—natural selection and the survival of the fittest—also apply to social and economic activity. They held that government should not interfere in such activity but should allow business and social activities to progress naturally.

5. **(A)** Question 5 touches on the monetary problems of the government. A major political issue in 19th-century history involved a freer and more flexible currency. One solution to the problem called for coinage of silver in a ratio with gold and the issuance of paper money redeemable in either gold or silver. When the Panic of 1893 hit, the gold reserves dropped to what Cleveland considered a dangerous level. The only way he could see to keep the U.S. credit good was to go to J. P. Morgan and his associates on Wall Street to get a loan of gold to redeem outstanding paper money. It created an enraged outcry from the Democrats and Populists, but it maintained America's credit.

6. **(C)** Booker T. Washington and W. E. B. Du Bois were two outstanding African American leaders at the beginning of the 20th century. They agreed on many issues, but they disagreed strongly on the need for immediate equality. Washington, the president of Tuskegee Institute, was more popular with whites and was entertained at the White House. He held that first African Americans should prove their economic importance and then equality would follow. Du Bois, a graduate of Harvard and an outstanding scholar, wanted immediate equality, and to gain this equality, he helped found the N.A.A.C.P. Both men saw a need for education, but of different types; both men would use white institutions to help African Americans and saw the importance of good race relations; African independence was not an issue in their lifetime, so the other choices can be eliminated.

7. **(C)** The Populist Party platform in 1892 seemed to many a very radical document, but most of its provisions were adopted by 1935. Since the Populists desired a more flexible currency, they did *not* want a gold standard. Instead, they wanted silver and gold as the basis of the currency. They supported a graduated income tax, which would tax the millionaires more heavily than the poor; the government ownership of railroads; the initiative and referendum, which they felt would put more political power in the hands of the people, and the direct election of U.S. senators. The platform of 1892 provides an excellent statement of the goals of the Populists.

8. **(B)** Question 8 lists four areas in regard to which Congress passed legislation in the years 1877–1892. All the issues except civil rights were major political issues of these years. Congress passed civil rights legislation immediately after the Civil War, but not again until after World War II.

9. **(E)** The cartoon in question 9 was drawn by E. W. Kimble in November 1912, as a comment on Theodore Roosevelt and his Bull Moose Party's defeat in the presidential election by Woodrow Wilson, then the governor of New Jersey and a former professor at and president of Princeton University. Wilson is portrayed in the cap and gown of the college professor while Theodore Roosevelt is portrayed as a Bull Moose stuck in the sand and stopped by the bullfighter Wilson. The cartoon makes use of such symbols as the Bull Moose representing Roosevelt's Progressive Party and the college cap and gown. If you recognize these symbols from your study, interpreting the cartoon would be easier, but if you did not, you still might be able to eliminate several choices.

10. **(C)** In the case of *Lochner v. New York* in 1905 the U.S. Supreme Court declared a law regulating the number of hours a worker could work in a bakery unconstitutional because it interfered with the worker's right of free contract. This decision reflects the support of the Court for the concept of laissez-faire and support of business, which, in general, opposed government regulation and guidelines. The law's intent was to protect workers' health. It might have increased the cost of bread but the Court did not consider that. The law more likely would have given an advantage to the workers in that they could demand fewer hours of work. Later, in *Muller v. Oregon* in 1910, the Supreme Court accepted a law regulating hours of work for women.

# World War I, the Interwar Period, and World War II 1916–1945

---

## CHAPTER 10

- Important facets of this period
- Analyze essay questions
- Questions based on EXCEPT

## MAJOR EVENTS

The years 1916–1945 include several major events of American history with which every student should be familiar. These are World War I, the stock market crash of 1929 and the Great Depression that followed, the New Deal, and World War II. Every United States history Advanced Placement exam would include multiple-choice questions involving these events and often the exam will have essay questions about them. The Great Depression and the New Deal responses to it are two of the major historic developments of the 20th century. These events had tremendous social impact on America as well as political, economic, and international impact. They should be considered from each of these viewpoints. Other events that occurred in these years are also very important but did not have the impact the above-listed events had.

The *Roaring Twenties* is a phrase describing the 1920s used to cover a variety of events from the political policy of Normalcy, advocated by President Harding, to the Florida land boom. The phrase *New Deal* incorporates many events in the 1930s, largely economic, social, and political. Phrases such as these are important and help to summarize periods but there are other developments of the twenties and thirties that you should be aware of. The division of the country between isolationists and internationalists and the growth of the urban population are two such developments that should be understood, but that are not strictly part of the Roaring Twenties or the New Deal.

The two world wars and the international relations connected with them involve many issues. **Some specific events of each war—general strategy and major battles—are important, but of greater significance are the events surrounding the** wars—the causes, the economic and social consequences, and the efforts at peacekeeping. Information on some of these aspects of the two wars appears in Chapters 9 and 11. This illustrates how difficult it is to compartmentalize history into units and chapters.

As we move closer to the present, there seem to be more and more details that are included in the history texts. If you look in the average text you will usually discover that the chapters devoted to recent history (such as the last half of the 20th century) are more detailed and cover shorter periods of time than the earlier chapters. The closer we are to events, the more information we have. For instance, eyewitness accounts are still available, and it is more difficult to see the important and crucial patterns that later historians develop. Therefore, do not be overwhelmed by the factual details of the history of these years, but use your skills to organize the details into your interpretation of the events. In other words, practice being a historian as you work through the history of recent years, establishing your theses and organizing material to support them as you have been doing in writing essays throughout your study. Studying these recent years should be an enjoyable culmination to your study of United States history and to your development of skills of historical research. Be your own historian as you pursue information on the following issues:

1.  The reasons for the United States' entrance into World War I, the war strategy, and the Treaty of Versailles
2.  The Red Scare of the early 1920s
3.  The scandals of the Harding administration
4.  The effect of the automobile on the economy of the United States and the social habits of its citizens
5.  The causes of the Great Crash of 1929 and the Great Depression
6.  The New Deal legislation and its impact
7.  The New Deal as an economic, social, and political revolution
8.  The social changes in America between World Wars I and II
9.  The isolationist policies of the United States after World War I and our relations with Europe and the League of Nations
10. The most significant contributions to American social, intellectual, and cultural history in the years between World War I and World War II including the Lost Generation and the Harlem Renaissance
11. The impact on the United States of the origins and start of World War II in Europe and Asia
12. The strategy of fighting World War II, including wartime conferences, domestic organization, and the founding of the United Nations

## SAMPLE ESSAY QUESTION—*ANALYZE*

| TIP |
| --- |
| Spend your time studying and not guessing what will be on the exam. |

Some individuals spend lots of time analyzing the content of released AP exams in hopes of guessing what will be on the next exam. The time would be better spent practicing your historical skills and writing practice essays of any type. The AP program is constantly under review and changes are continually being made to reflect what is being taught in the colleges, what are presently considered the best methods to teach history, and what is thought to be the clearest way to phrase a free-response question. Special committees have been used to consider changes and new members of the United States History Development Committee constantly offer new and different perspectives. For instance, in the 1970s there were many free-response questions that asked *Explain* type questions while in the 1990s, one year, all the directions for the free-response questions included the phrase, *Analyze*. Questions of this type are still used frequently.

## The *Analyze* Question

The term *analyze* requires that you "examine methodically" a situation or issue. In doing so, you "separate into basic parts" the material being examined in order to determine the meaning of the whole. This is an excellent summary of the Historical Method. It is what you have been doing in all of your study of history. The *Analyze* type of question tests your historical thinking skills—remember the first of those special skills listed on p. 26 was **analysis**.

Several of the free-response questions already presented have been of the *Analyze* type so you should already be familiar with the approach. Sometimes these questions include an added direction that will more clearly focus your analysis. These can include phrases such as *"In what ways…"* or *"To what extent…"* or a word such as *validity*.

Rather than present a question followed by sample answers, in this chapter, two student answers are given before a question. Read Sample Answer A *before* you read the question. After reading it, write down what you think the question is. This is a very good test of how well the student has understood the question and has responded to it in the essay. When you have written down your ideas about what the question was, read Sample Answer B. You can try this exercise with classmates or friends or a parent.

### Sample Answer A

Roosevelt had to face a big crisis. He had to stop a severe depression and had no precedents with which to work. Many of the measures he took provided both relief and long-range reform, which have proven important for the democratization of American life. His first action was to pass the Emergency Banking Act, closing the banks, and thus stop the serious runs on the banks. He allowed them to reopen only after passing tests of stability and gave them loans if needed to prevent the run from occurring again. He provided for insurance of up to $5,000 on future bank deposits.

To help business recover and to provide jobs, Congress passed the NIRA (National Industrial Recovery Act), which gave management wide powers of operation, including the suspension of antitrust cases, as well as assuring labor's rights to collective bargaining. For the farmers, Roosevelt developed two agricultural acts (AAA) that paid farmers to reduce and store crops.

To help Americans get jobs several acts were passed. The CCC (Civilian Conservation Corps) employed 500,000 workers, especially young men from urban areas, on conservation projects. The FWA (Federal Works Administration) provided work for thousands making parks and sidewalks. The WPA (Works Projects Administration) was established to coordinate the various programs. He also set up the TVA (Tennessee Valley Authority) to provide cheap electric power. When the Supreme Court nullified some of what he thought was his greatest legislation, he tried to get Congress to pass a law allowing him to pack the Supreme Court.

Roosevelt also cleverly supported the British while keeping the nation out of war until the Japanese bombed Pearl Harbor. He then provided strong leadership to the nation and the alliance. Although he died before the final victory, his wartime conferences with Churchill and Stalin paved the way for the unconditional surrender of the Nazis and Japan and for the United Nations.

Obviously, Roosevelt was a great autocratic and democratic president, as shown in how he handled these big crises.

**Note:** Before you read on, write down what you think the question was for this essay.

## Sample Answer B

The power of government has two appearances, one during calm and another during crises. In time of crisis the president seems to be all-powerful and the way in which he acts reveals much about his ability and stature as a president. Franklin D. Roosevelt faced two crises successfully and by the way he handled them should be considered our greatest president.

Of course, other presidents have faced crises and handled them well to preserve our freedom and our nation. For instance, George Washington, while establishing the office of president, had to avoid war with England, and Woodrow Wilson kept us out of World War I for three years before finally entering and winning a victory for democracy. Other presidents faced domestic crises. Andrew Jackson faced the nullification issue and Abraham Lincoln had to fight the Civil War, but only Roosevelt successfully confronted major domestic and international crises and thus deserves the title of greatest president.

Roosevelt ruled the country with an iron hand because he realized his New Deal program had to be instigated if America was to recover economically from the Great Depression. His programs, such as the CCC and the WPA, gave Americans an opportunity to work while improvements in the country were also being completed. Roosevelt set up a program to rebuild the banks, including emergency banking legislation and the FDIC to insure private deposits in banks. He also started reforms of agriculture with the AAA and of business with the NRA. The Supreme Court declared much of the legislation unconstitutional and Roosevelt threatened to pack the Court. The Court soon accepted his measures to combat domestic crises. The United States was in need of a strong man who could understand the circumstances and take definite steps toward improving the nation's conditions. FDR was such a man—a great president.

Hitler had come to power at the same time as FDR. Hitler rejected the Treaty of Versailles and re-armed Germany. FDR saw the threat but the American people were devoted to neutrality. FDR aided the British secretly after World War II began in 1939 and some say that he set the stage for the Japanese attack on Pearl Harbor. In any case, once America was attacked, he led the Allies to victory. His foresight laid the foundations for the United Nations, which was set up in San Francisco in 1945 just after his death.

There have been many types of men who have sat in the White House— intellectuals, lawyers, professional soldiers—some of whom have been strong and some weak. But during certain times, years of war or depression, the man who heads the government must be strong. Franklin D. Roosevelt was such a man. He faced both a major war and a major depression and found solutions to both, thus revealing his great ability. He definitely deserves the title of our greatest president.

## SAMPLE QUESTION

The essays on pages 153–154 were written as answers to the following question:

"The true ability of a president is revealed by the manner in which he responds to crises."

Analyze the validity of this statement as it applies to ONE president of the United States.

## Comments on Sample Question

How close to this question did you come in formulating a question for Sample Answer A? Where did you differ? Did the answer in Sample A seem to relate to this question? You will want to read the teacher comments to see how they relate to your own analysis of the two student answers.

*Answer A:* "The writer has no introduction and it is not clear just what is being discussed until the final sentence of the essay, when he or she presents a statement indicating that Franklin D. Roosevelt was a great president. In the body of the essay there is a lengthy discussion of the actions of FDR and the information is accurate. On the basis of the answer, it is hard to know what the question is, yet the answer has sound information that could be related to the question. From a strictly factual viewpoint, this is a more than adequate answer, but it is a listing of information rather than an interpretation of a question. From that point of view it is a poor answer. It is hard not to reward the student who knows facts but this essay lacks a clear thesis or restatement of the question and would be fortunate to receive a grade in the mid range."

*Answer B:* "The writer of this essay is more of a generalist than the writer of Answer A. There is an interesting introduction with a broad opening and a clearly stated thesis. The writer then goes on to consider other presidents who might be considered, but rejects their claims while focusing on Franklin D. Roosevelt. Accurate specific information on the New Deal and the war is presented. The writer thus covers the two crises, one domestic and one foreign, mentioned in the opening. More detailed information might be produced but it is clear that the writer has understood the question and knows the presidency of Franklin D. Roosevelt. The conclusion returns to the general philosophical statement at the opening and restates the thesis. The essay clearly was written by a knowledgeable young writer and deserves a score in the top range on the AP rating scale."

Do you agree with these comments? Do you see how the writer in Answer A missed the question yet had very good information? Essay A is an excellent example of what *not* to do when you are smart and have knowledge. It reinforces the importance of analyzing the question. Both writers organized the material well but, as you are aware, there is more to writing an essay than that. Writer B clearly demonstrates that he analyzed the question and is using information to prove his thesis. Writer A is simply spilling out information about Franklin Roosevelt and has made no effort to analyze the question.

**TIP**

Presentations of information without thought are often referred to by Advanced Placement readers as "laundry lists." They are reflections of good memorization but not of great thinking.

# Practice Essay Questions

The following essay questions require information from the years 1916–1945 and one other period in American history. They provide a good review of materials studied earlier as well as of the years covered in this chapter. These questions provide you an excellent review of three very important issues of United States history.

1. "European culture fascinated Americans in the period 1789–1801 and in the period between World Wars I and II."

   Analyze the validity of this statement.

2. "War has united Americans more closely than any other activity."

   Discuss the validity of this statement as it applies to ONE of the following periods

   1800–1820
   1900–1920
   1960–1980

3. "The social changes of the Jacksonian Period were greater and more profound than the social changes of the period between World War I and World War II."

   Assess the validity of this statement.

4. "Republicans have been the party of Big Business and depression; the Democrats have been the party of the Common Man and of war."

   Analyze in what ways this statement applies to TWO of the following events:

   Panic of 1893 and Spanish-American War
   Panic of 1907 and World War I
   Great Depression and World War II

5. Analyze to what extent the economic and political reform proposals of the Populists and Progressives in the period 1890 to 1912 were enacted during the New Deal in the 1930s.

## Comments on Question 1

Question 1 is a typical *Analyze the validity* . . . question of the type discussed in this chapter. You are given specific directions as to the two periods you are to discuss. There should be no difficulty understanding what is expected. There may, however, be difficulty in finding factual information. When you find yourself in that situation you have two options: first, not to write on the question and, second, to take the view that the position is not valid and use what limited information you have to show that. However, **it is always better to pick the question about which you know the most**.

The word *culture* is one of those commonly used words that is rarely defined. It is important to have a concept about what culture is before answering this question. Culture is defined in *Webster's Eleventh New Collegiate Dictionary* as "a particular state of advancement in civilization and the characteristic feature(s) of such a stage or state." Usually we think of culture as the "arts," as those aspects of society that are not related to economic or political life. However, the definition says it includes "characteristic feature(s) of" and these often have to do with economic and social developments. In history we often use the expression *economic, political, and social* in describing events or developments. Many people consider social in this phrase as equivalent to culture, but it is not, since culture is the inclusive term under which economic, political, social, and intellectual all fit as the following diagram illustrates:

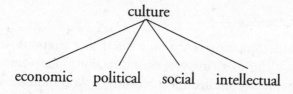

Therefore, you should include political and economic ideas in your answer, although the usual approach to this question would be to discuss those ideas we usually consider as social and intellectual—matters concerning manners, attitudes, lifestyles, literary and artistic development, religious attitudes, and the like. Certainly these latter matters should be discussed in your answer to this question but you would not want to narrow your answer to these matters only.

For example, in the United States, much of our culture reflects and/or is determined by our economic attitudes of free enterprise, competition, and individualism.

## Comments on Question 2

Question 2 is a typical *Discuss* question. There should be no confusion about what is wanted in an answer. As it states, you are to discuss the validity of the statement as it applies to ONE of three periods. The time periods may be difficult, but as mentioned above, the questions in this chapter cover different time periods and are thus excellent review questions for United States history since 1789. How well you can respond to these questions without doing research will provide a good indication of how well prepared you are for the Advanced Placement exam.

The generalization in question 2 is an interesting one. If you do not agree with the statement, you can create a thesis by substituting another idea for war, such as cultural developments, and argue in favor of it. That is an effective way to develop a thesis provided you have evidence to support your idea and evidence to refute the idea presented.

## Comments on Question 3

Question 3 is a typical *Assess the validity* question. The question focuses on social change and, therefore, unlike the question on culture, you should *not* include economic and political changes except as they might cause social changes. The two periods—the Jacksonian and the interwar period, especially the 1920s—were times of great change in the American way of life. Which period do you feel had the more profound and greater changes? In a way this becomes a comparison question without using that word. Certainly a comparison of the changes provides the obvious organization for this question. Questions asking for your opinion based on a comparative value such as "more profound" can be difficult. It is important that you **understand the value**, in this case *more* profound, and make it **clear to the reader**

**that you understand it**. There are many ways a question may seek a value judgment. Among them are the words *least, primarily, most important, probably, generally*. They will appear both in multiple-choice questions and in essay questions. On essays they require a personal judgment and that will lead to your thesis. In multiple-choice questions they will help guide you to the correct answer as the words or phrases will be chosen to reflect the generally accepted interpretation of events.

## Comments on Question 4

Question 4 is another question based on a quote as a stimulus. It asks you to *analyze in what ways . . .* , thus giving you clear direction. The events listed in the three choices are those you have studied most recently, so you should have the facts about the six items. However, with six items in three combinations, it may be difficult to decide which two pairs to use. As always, **pick the two about which you know the most and form your thesis using those four items**.

The major problem in question 4 is the baldness and simplicity of the generalization. It is the type of statement we often hear, but it is so blatantly broad and unthinking that it is hard to deal with. Is there truth in it? Your introduction will probably include general comments on the generalization; that is, such matters as its simplicity and the meaning of "Common Man" and "Big Business." Your thesis will then present your interpretation of the generalization. How to organize this question is a challenge. When you make your brief notes on the information, a pattern should emerge that will supply the organization. The question itself supplies no simple, obvious pattern. This is a difficult question in many ways, but the information should be readily at hand.

## Comments on Question 5

Question 5 is another variation of the *Analyze* question. The generalization is quite straightforward, and the question should not be difficult to understand. There should be no difficulty developing a thesis. An obvious organization is to state a Populist or Progressive proposal and follow with a discussion of how the New Deal used or failed to use the proposal. This format would give an excellent structure to the essay.

The major problem in this question centers on how specific your knowledge is of the Populist or Progressive proposals. The chances are you will have detailed knowledge of the New Deal response to the economic conditions of the 1930s. How well can you relate these to the earlier proposals? This again is an excellent review question.

On the Advanced Placement exam essays, most detailed information that is required will come from the mainstream of United States history and should be familiar to you if you have studied the periods described in this book. Many questions require information from "mainstream" social history or the history of minorities.

# MULTIPLE-CHOICE QUESTIONS—IMPORTANCE OF HISTORIOGRAPHY; THE *EXCEPT* QUESTION

Historiography or the study of history written by different people, each with her or his own bias, should be an important aspect of any in-depth course in history. As stated many times, the AP exam focuses on what is considered the "mainstream" of United States history. This includes what historians consider the major events of that history but also what different historians have to say concerning them. Since all history is an interpretation of past events, scholars differ on their interpretations. Scholars who offer new or different insights into events are referred to as revisionists since they see the past in new ways and ask others to accept these revised views. This has led to many interesting discussions among scholars, and acceptance of several different interpretations of the past within the mainstream of much of United States history. Historiography entails the study of these different interpretations.

> **TIP**
>
> While the AP exam is on U.S. history, it is still important to know major events of world history that have impacted the U.S.

The AP United States History Development Committee expects you to have an understanding of the various views and interpretations of United States history presented by the most distinguished scholars both present and past. In your study so far, you will have been exposed to differing interpretations as you read different sources. You may be tested on specific interpretations. Also understanding different interpretations will help you identify biases in certain documents and sources. This can be very helpful on the DBQ and on stimulus based multiple-choice questions.

As your study of United States history has progressed, you should have learned of **various interpretations of the facts** by the leading historians of the different periods, and **not just the facts**. There are recent revisionist schools on causes of the American Revolution and the Civil War, on the character and politics of Abraham Lincoln, on the Turner thesis concerning the significance of the frontier in American history, and on other events. **History is NOT a monolithic subject that never changes. It is a living, ever changing, record of the past that reflects the biases and prejudices of the historians and the people.**

Realizing this, different publishers over the years have published works that include conflicting opinions on important topics. One of the earliest, designed for college freshmen, was the "Amherst Series" on *Problems in American Civilization,* published by D. C. Heath & Co. Works of this type can be very helpful in discovering how historians differ in their interpretations of the past.

## Multiple-Choice Question with EXCEPT

The two questions below indicate two ways multiple-choice questions can require a knowledge of historiography. Question 1 is in the EXCEPT format mentioned in Chapter 6. As stated there, more of this type of question has been included in the text than may appear on the exam, because the type provides positive reinforcement of information with its four correct answers to one wrong answer. The change in format can be disrupting but this change is signaled on the AP exam by the placement of the word EXCEPT in caps and almost always at the end of the sentence. Be sure to look for this as you take the exam—both the practice ones and the exam itself in May.

## SAMPLE QUESTION

1. In the 1970s revisionist historians of the Cold War reinterpreted events to suggest that all of the following are true EXCEPT

   (A) Truman overreacted to the postwar developments in Greece.
   (B) The Yalta Agreement was a fair document based on historic circumstances.
   (C) The Communists carefully followed a master plan to bring on the Cold War.
   (D) Blame for the Cold War should be split between the Soviet Union and the Western allies.
   (E) Churchill's goal was more the preservation of British power than world peace.

Question 1 tests your understanding of historiography. In this question you must know what the Cold War is and you must know what that group of historians who are revising the interpretation of the Cold War are saying. The question tests factual knowledge of a very particular kind and reveals the types of sources you have used in your study. The Cold War historians reinterpreting the Cold War suggest that, except for C, the choices given are correct.

## SAMPLE QUESTION

2. Which one of the following statements most closely reflects the interpretation or thesis presented by the 20th-century historian, Charles Beard, as to the motivation for the writing of the United States Constitution?

   (A) to provide military protection for all citizens
   (B) to provide economic stability for the wealthy
   (C) to provide equal rights for all men
   (D) to provide life and liberty for all people
   (E) to provide cultural cohesion for the 13 states

Question 2 also requires that you have some knowledge of historiography. As you study, you should identify the theses, biases, and interpretation of the most famous historians of the past, especially those few who have affected the understanding Americans share of their past. In this case, Charles Beard wrote a very important study of the writing of the Constitution in which he suggested it was written for economic reasons by wealthy men to protect their wealth—(B). The view was very popular during the Depression and affected many people and historians. In the latter half of the 20th century, other scholars questioned Beard's thesis, suggesting writers of the Constitution had many motives. In your study of the Constitution, did you get any sense of the motivation for this writing? Since it is the most important document for understanding the United States government, the reason(s) for its writing is/are important for all Americans. The other choices, while possible reasons some of the Founding Fathers wished to write a constitution, do not present Beard's interpretation.

# Practice Multiple-Choice Questions

1. "The world is so deeply divided into opposing classes that social wrongs can be corrected only by revolution" summarizes a position held by traditional supporters of

    (A) Socialism
    (B) Nazism
    (C) Isolationism
    (D) McCarthyism
    (E) Communism

2. All of the following New Deal programs provided work opportunities or direct aid to unemployed or disabled individuals EXCEPT

    (A) Civilian Conservation Corps
    (B) Federal Emergency Relief Administration
    (C) Works Progress Administration
    (D) National Recovery Administration
    (E) Social Security Program

From the collection of the New Hampshire Historical Society with permission.

3. The photograph of a home interior suggests

    (A) the affluence of a late 19th-century upper class home
    (B) a typical late colonial living room
    (C) a 1950s pre-TV recreation room
    (D) the popular 20th-century style referred to as Shaker
    (E) a frontier home in Kentucky

4. All of the following had an impact on the social and cultural life of the 1920s EXCEPT

   (A) The first "talking" motion picture
   (B) The development of commercial radio
   (C) Views on evolution expressed at the trial of John Scopes
   (D) The end of Prohibition
   (E) The rebirth of the Ku Klux Klan

5. All of the following events influenced the decision of the United States to enter World War I EXCEPT

   (A) the Zimmerman Note to Mexico
   (B) the sinking of the passenger ship, *Lusitania*
   (C) the Japanese invasion of China
   (D) unrestricted submarine warfare by the Germans
   (E) the Russian Revolution of March 1917

6. The United States in the 1920s refused to cancel the war debts of its European allies because the United States

   (A) wanted to force Germany to pay the wartime reparations
   (B) needed the money to help pay for economic development at home
   (C) believed the money paid was needed for loans to Germany
   (D) considered that all honestly incurred debts should be paid
   (E) thought debt payment would reduce the arms race in Europe

7. The United States issued a Declaration of Neutrality in 1937 in response to all of the following EXCEPT

   (A) outbreak of the Spanish Civil War
   (B) growing strength of Hitler in Germany
   (C) Nye Committee's Report on War Profiteering in World War I
   (D) invasion of Ethiopia by Mussolini's Italy
   (E) the domestic economic slowdown in 1937

8. All of the following involved United States military forces EXCEPT

   (A) Battle of Stalingrad
   (B) invasion of Iwo Jima
   (C) Battle of Midway
   (D) defense of Bataan
   (E) Battle of the Bulge

9. According to his presentation in the above cartoon, you could assume the artist would support

(A) the Republicans' not providing direct aid to the unemployed
(B) the need for slum clearance in Washington
(C) the Republican interpretation that the depression would be quickly over
(D) specific action to aid the unemployed
(E) the Democratic Party's program of reform of business

*That's Why It's Not Time for a Change*

*Source: Richmond Times Dispatch,* November 12, 1944

10. In the cartoon, the cartoonist, Fred O. Seibel, is suggesting that

(A) the colonel has an old-fashioned record player
(B) Dewey is a poor record salesman
(C) Virginia will not vote for the Republican candidate for the White House
(D) Virginia has its own record and is not interested in changing it
(E) the White House is a loudspeaker for ideas of Virginians

## Answers and Answer Explanations

| 1. **(E)** | 2. **(D)** | 3. **(A)** | 4. **(D)** |
|---|---|---|---|
| 5. **(C)** | 6. **(D)** | 7. **(E)** | 8. **(A)** |
| 9. **(D)** | 10. **(C)** | | |

1. **(E)** The statement in question 1 summarizes a view held by Communists in the tradition of Marx and Lenin. There has been some shift away from this "classical view" in recent years in China and Vietnam and in the Soviet Union before its disintegration in 1991. Traditionally, socialists have not supported revolution.

2. **(D)** One aspect of the New Deal was to provide immediate relief for the unemployed, and each of these acts, except the National Recovery Administration, which dealt with business recovery and conditions of labor, provided either direct relief in the form of unemployment benefits or jobs for the unemployed.

3. (**A**) This question is centered on a photograph as a stimulus. It is of a late 19th-century Victorian parlor and reflects the life style of the affluent upper class of the "Gilded Age." The room is crowded with objects and furniture, indicating there is money to spend on extras and comfort. There is a gas chandelier for lighting and a stove behind the center table. The other choices would have living spaces that look quite different, for example, with different furniture styles. For instance, the Shaker style developed by the Shaker religious communities in the 19th century and popularized in the late 20th century emphasized simple, utilitarian pieces.

4. (**D**) Prohibition was ended in 1933; it was in effect during the 1920s. The other developments listed all occurred in the 1920s and reflect different aspects of that very interesting period, the Roaring Twenties. They all had an impact on the beliefs, attitudes, behavior, and thoughts of the people.

5. (**C**) The Japanese invasion of China soured U.S.- Japanese relations in the 1930s and led indirectly to the U.S. involvement in World War II not World War I. Japan was an ally during World War I. The Russian Revolution in March 1917—the first, non-Bolshevist revolution—established a "democratic" government in Russia that made Russia more appealing as an ally than the authoritarian Tsarist regime that had ruled Russia at the start of the war. Russia was an ally of Great Britain, France, and Italy at the time the United States entered World War I. The Zimmermann Note was a secret message sent by the German Foreign Minister to the German Ambassador in Mexico on March 1, 1917, suggesting an alliance between Mexico and Germany in case the United States entered World War I on the side of the Allies. The message was decoded by the British and heightened American sentiment against Germany. When a German submarine sank the British passenger liner, *Lusitania,* 128 Americans lost their lives. After an exchange of messages, Germany agreed to curtail submarine warfare but its resumption in February 1917 led directly to the Declaration of War on April 7, 1917.

6. (**D**) The United States under the Republican leadership of Harding, Coolidge, and Hoover insisted that honestly incurred debts should be paid. With the stock market crash in 1929, Hoover allowed a one-year moratorium on debt payment, but by then it was too late to renegotiate the debts and they were never paid except by Finland.

7. (**E**) Question 7 seeks reasons for the U.S. Declaration of Neutrality in 1937 and choices A through D were used as reasons to justify the declaration. While there was an economic slowdown in the United States in 1937, it was not a direct factor in declaring neutrality.

8. (**A**) The Battle of Stalingrad was a turning point in World War II. The Russians at Stalingrad stopped the German advance into the Soviet Union without U.S. forces, but with the aid of U.S. supplies. The other four choices involved U.S. troops and are among the most important battles fought. Iwo Jima was a major step on MacArthur's path back to the Philippines and Japan. The naval Battle of Midway stopped a Japanese advance across the Pacific and is considered the turning point of World War II in the Pacific. Bataan, a

peninsula in the Bay of Manila, fell to the Japanese after a significant defensive action that allowed the United States to recover from Pearl Harbor and prepare to wage war in the Pacific. The Battle of the Bulge was the final attempt by the Germans to prevent the Allied invasion of Germany.

9. **(D)** The artist, Barclay, is making a comment on the apparent blindness of the Republicans to the fact that there are 15 million unemployed and that living conditions, as depicted in Hooverville, are terrible. He portrays the Republican elephant as blind and insensitive to these conditions. If this is Barclay's idea, then it would seem logical that he would support specific action to aid the unemployed. The other choices do not appear to reflect the viewpoint expressed in the cartoon.

10. **(C)** The cartoon, drawn by Fred Seibel in November 1944, refers to the Dewey-Roosevelt presidential campaign of that year, when Franklin Roosevelt defeated Dewey winning an unprecedented fourth term. Seibel suggests that the state of Virginia did not vote for Dewey, the G.O.P. candidate because Virginians were happy with the "record" of Franklin Roosevelt and the Democrats and did not want to hear the "record" of the G.O.P. (Grand Old Party or Republicans), which they had heard before from President Hoover.

# The Postwar Period, the Cold War, and After 1945–2007

## CHAPTER 11

- Interpreting recent history
- Review of essay writing
- Questions based on vocabulary

The period after World War II presents many problems for the student of history and for the creators of the Advanced Placement examination. As indicated in the Introduction, since the exam is given in May, those schools that present a chronological history and that continue in session until mid-June will most likely not have studied much of this time period before the May examination. Responding to the problem created by this situation, **the Advanced Placement test creators have indicated that, although one-third of the multiple-choice questions will be on the time after 1914, very few questions will be on the period after 1980. Likewise, the test creators have indicated that no essay question will focus exclusively on the time after 1980, although in some cases an essay will ask for knowledge of that era as it relates to earlier United States history**. The 1980 date was set recently. It means that such major events as the Reagan presidency, the end of the Cold War, the Persian Gulf War, the economic boom of the Clinton years, and the war on terrorism, including the wars in Afghanistan and Iraq, will not be the *exclusive* subject of an essay. However, as the years pass, this date may be changed. Presently there are multiple-choice questions on post-1980 history. The sample essay questions in this chapter indicate how history after 1980 may be included in essay questions.

## INTERPRETING RECENT HISTORY

Another problem these years present to the student of history is that mentioned in the previous chapter concerning the interpretation of recent events and historic perspective. Until a generation or two has passed it is difficult to be certain what events are important and particularly how these events have truly affected the course of history. For instance, everyone believes the Vietnam War has had a profound impact on

U.S. life, but what the impact will prove to be by 2025, when today's high school students are in their 40s, is hard to determine. In the meantime, we have a great deal of data about the war to absorb. You need to know the details of war activities, of domestic protest, of presidential politics, of social changes, and all the rest, yet by 2025 the social changes, for example, may have been totally reversed, and we will consider them of little historic significance. Thus, as events recede into the past, we simplify and interpret them to make them more manageable and, we think, more understandable.

Since we lack historic perspective on the developments of recent years we must consider all events with equal care. This means there is much more factual information to absorb. One can easily become overwhelmed with the details of the recent past and lose sight of any interpretation or themes that are emerging. This is particularly true of the years since World War II, during which time the methods of recording information have multiplied so rapidly.

## U.S. History Since 1941

Another matter that makes recent U.S. history more difficult to study is that **from 1941 on, U.S. history has really become world history, and economic globalization and the Internet have intensified this trend**. No longer can we study developments such as those on the frontier and feel we are learning United States history. Since 1941 the student must not only know domestic developments, but must also be aware of what has happened to the former Soviet Union, what the map of Vietnam looks like, where and when the United States has come under terrorist attacks, why the Arab-Israeli conflict seems unresolvable, how the independence of African nations has affected African Americans in the United States, and many other points involving nations throughout the world. Until 1941 many Americans and many U.S. decisions ignored these areas. It was probably wrong to do so, but it certainly made United States history up to 1941 much easier to study and to understand.

Although the problems stated above make recent United States history more complex, they also offer the student a chance to be an active historian analyzing primary sources and seeking new information and interpretations. As World War II recedes in time, more definitive interpretations of its aftermath are becoming available, and with the end of the Cold War, many historians are offering new interpretations of it.

## Major Trends Following World War II

Many of the trends and concerns of recent years began in the immediate post-World War II era or in the time between the two world wars. Since you are expected to know these time periods on the examination, one helpful way to study the post-World War II period is to analyze it by comparing events and trends with those following World War I. Then you should focus your study on the direction the trends took in the more recent past. The following trends are some of those that have been identified as significant ones in the post-World War II era. Note how many of the trends are contradictory, reflecting the dynamic tension that has existed in the post-World War II world.

1.  Move toward internationalism—the United Nations—and multilateralism, as shown in treaty commitments and concern for undeveloped nations

2. Emergence of the United States as the sole superpower, of unilateralism, and of the United States as policeman of the world
3. The emergence of the Cold War and fear of communism
4. The desire for détente
5. Greater government control of the business cycle, including the role of the Federal Reserve Bank
6. Desire for deregulation of business and industry
7. Development and growth of service industries, advertising, computers, and e-commerce
8. The continuation of poverty within a generally affluent society
9. A general distrust of, and disillusionment with, the political process
10. Expanding globalization, growing awareness of environmental issues and spaceship Earth, concerns about international terrorism and use of weapons of mass destruction
11. Increasing frankness in human relations, sexual freedom, and intellectual and artistic expression, as well as government support for the arts
12. Desire to restore "family" values, to control education and stamp out drug use
13. Struggle for the civil rights of all
14. Increasing isolation from and fear of those who are different

> **TIP**
>
> Review the chronology in Part 4 for factual information.

In addition to these major trends there are issues that need to be considered. How are the above trends illustrated with information from the following?

1. The Cold War
2. Specific foreign policy actions by each postwar president from Truman to George W. Bush
3. The Civil Rights Movement and the emergence of minority organizations
4. The Vietnam War and its impact on government and society
5. Johnson's Great Society
6. Changing economic policies of the federal government, including Reaganomics, welfare, health care, Social Security, and taxes
7. Social, economic, and political divisions in the nation manifested in such issues as civil rights, abortion, the widening gap between rich and poor, legislative gridlock in Washington, the "politics of personal destruction," and the aftermath of the terrorist attack of September 11, 2001
8. The most significant contributions to and changes in American social and intellectual history, including the Internet and changing technology

Some of your study may have to be done in contemporary sources, as some texts will not go up to the present. In fact, if you get in the habit of reading the newspapers and newsmagazines, this reading will give you a lot of information on recent history, will help your understanding of charts, graphs, and maps, and will often make you aware of past events, since such events are often referred to in articles. Such reading of newspapers and newsmagazines is strongly recommended.

## SAMPLE ESSAY QUESTION—REVIEW

In Chapters 4 through 10 we have presented and analyzed different types of essay questions. We have illustrated the fact that different types of questions are often combined. This means there are innumerable combinations of questions and directions, but in what we have discussed so far, you have been presented with the most important types of essay questions found on the Advanced Placement exam. Rather than discuss and analyze another type of essay question in this last chapter, we will present two different questions and one student answer to each. As in all cases so far, we suggest that you write an answer to the question before you read the sample answer and the teacher comments.

---

### SAMPLE QUESTION

"The Supreme Court's interpretation of the Constitution in the thirty years before the election of Franklin Roosevelt in 1932 made it difficult for the federal government to legislate social and economic policy at the national level, yet from 1937 until the resignation of Richard Nixon in 1973, the situation was reversed." *Assess the validity* of this quotation.

---

### Sample Answer

The Supreme Court is a very powerful part of the federal government, perhaps the most powerful, since the president and Congress must abide by its decisions. These decisions are based on the Court's philosophy and interpretation of the Constitution and that changes from time to time. Before the New Deal the Court was conservative on social issues but after 1937 it became more liberal in its interpretation.

Until the late 1930s the philosophy of the Supreme Court judges and their interpretation of the Constitution made it almost impossible to have any social legislation —laws regulating individual and employer and employee social and economic conditions—passed by the federal government upheld by the Court.

In 1916 Congress passed the first child labor act forbidding a company to ship goods in interstate commerce if the company employed children. In *Hammer v. Dragenhart*, a year later, the Court struck down the law as an unjustifiable use of the commerce power to control local labor conditions. A year after that, Congress passed a law taxing companies employing child labor. In *Baily v. Drexel Furniture Company*, the Court again struck down the social legislation. Most states eventually forbade child labor, but the Supreme Court had effectively blocked national social legislation in this area.

Even in 1934, at almost the peak of our country's depression, the Court struck down Roosevelt's NIRA in *Schechter Poultry v. United States*. The NIRA had among other things set a minimum wage and a code of fair labor and price policies. This was needed and was beneficial social legislation for the United States, but the Court again seemed to interpret only the literal meaning of the Constitution. The Court said that Schechter's poultry business didn't affect interstate commerce directly and therefore the law, which was derived from Congress's commerce power, was unconstitutional.

There were two reasons why the Court had not let Congress pass social legislation. One was because in almost all the laws for social reform, some part or wording of the Constitution was being stretched or broadened. For example, Congress claimed that because the Constitution said "Congress shall have the power to regulate interstate commerce," they had the right to regulate any company involved in interstate commerce. The Court believed that if they once gave such a loose interpretation to the Constitution, Congress would soon be able to justify any law it wished to pass, which would be wrong.

The other reason was that the Court was dominated by rather conservative justices who were influenced by the philosophy of Social Darwinism and a laissez-faire approach to economics. These attitudes prevented the Court from regarding social legislation as beneficial to the country.

In the early 1930s the Court continued to uphold its rather literal interpretation of the Constitution. Thus, almost no social legislation was approved but most of the decisions were by a 5–4 vote. After the Court invalidated several other items of New Deal legislation, such as the AAA in 1937, Roosevelt threatened to increase the number of judges or pack the Court. Although not passed by Congress, the threat seemed to work. Also, one of the elder judges retired and was replaced by a supporter of FDR; thus we began to see 5–4 and 6–3 decisions in favor of Roosevelt's social legislation.

The most obvious change in the Court's decisions was in the Bituminous Coal Board case, which said that Congress could regulate the working hours of miners, their pay, and the price of coal. In 1941, in *Darby v. United States*, the Court validated a law forbidding child labor, thus reversing its previous position. *Commerce* was now defined as totally under congressional control, thus breaking down barriers between state and federal areas of control.

The climax in the Court's change of opinion as to how to interpret the Constitution probably is marked by *Brown v. Board of Education*, which struck down segregated schools. Although the decision did not involve federal legislation, it involved the social relations between individuals as established by state and local laws. The Court interpreted the Constitution loosely and largely based its decision on psychological evidence. Under the leadership of Chief Justice Warren several important decisions, such as that in the Gideon case, gave strong protection to the rights of the individual in opposition to the rights of the state. Later in *Roe v. Wade*, a woman's right to an abortion was upheld. This case continued the trend established in the 1930s of using the power of government, in this case the courts, to support the individual. After his election, Ronald Reagan called for more conservative decisions, and with his court appointments the court began to reverse itself. The abortion cases of the 1980s and early 1990s clearly illustrate the conservative trend.

The Supreme Court effectively prevented national social legislation in the first third of the 20th century. After an apparent total reversal of opinion, the Warren Court appeared to be ready not only to approve social legislation passed by Congress, but even to take the lead in bringing on social change, which illustrates that the Court is an important and powerful branch of the federal government.

## Teacher Comments on Sample Answer

"This is a very interesting answer to the question on social legislation and the Supreme Court. It is well organized, presents a thesis that is well developed, and contains fine factual details from one of the more specialized areas of U.S. history—legal history. The student's definition of social legislation is adhered to in the essay and his or her thesis on the philosophy of the judges and their interpretation of the Constitution is well supported. The cases used are good, but there is a shift of emphasis from economic to more social issues towards the end. The conclusion is well presented as is the introduction, both of which follow well-established techniques for essay writing. This essay would have received a top grade—8 or 9—as an answer to this question."

Did you agree with the teacher comments? It is longer than those usually written on the AP but was included to illustrate how legal history can be used and to provide you with information on the Court. This answer is one of the better sample essay answers in the book and was placed here to provide a high standard for comparison now that you have almost completed your study and you have had extended experience writing essays. How did your essay compare with this one?

This is a typical *Assess the validity* type of question. What the question was asking for should not have been difficult for you to analyze. Whether you were as well prepared to discuss Court cases and decisions as the writer of the sample essay will depend on how much time you devoted to legal history. You could write an effective answer putting greater emphasis on social legislation and explaining why you believe the trend changed. The directions to the question illustrate how information from the most recent period covered on the exam may be included. It does not ask you to deal with changes in the Court's decisions that began with the appointment of several conservative judges by President Reagan.

Now let us look at another question and a sample student answer. This question is a good example of the type of essay question you might get on recent history. The question is confined to the post-World War II era and is a clear indication of what a student is expected to know about the period after 1945.

## SAMPLE QUESTION

To what extent did the administrations of TWO of the following presidents continue the containment policy of President Truman?

Eisenhower
Kennedy
Johnson
Nixon

### Sample Answer

Americans seem to have a basic fear of those who are different. The foreign policy known as *containment,* developed in the Truman years following the ideas expressed in the famous "X" article in *Foreign Affairs,* was a reflection of the fears of the American people and government that the Communist Soviet Union (and later China) was a threat to America. The containment policy set by the Truman administration remained the basic foreign policy of the Eisenhower and Kennedy administrations.

The containment policy held that the West should meet every aggressive Communist move with equal pressure. It became clear that Europe would have to be rebuilt if it were to help in applying this pressure. The Marshall Plan was developed in 1947 to do this. The first clear statement of containment was the Truman Doctrine, which, following an apparent Soviet threat to Greece and Turkey, essentially stated the United States would aid any nation in Europe threatened by Communist power internally or externally. When the Soviet Union blocked the land transportation routes to Berlin in 1948, the Truman administration pushed for the establishment of the North Atlantic Treaty Organization, a mutual defense pact eventually subscribed to by most of the nations ringing the Atlantic area and extending through the Mediterranean to Turkey.

The Korean War was a major test of the containment policy and moved its focus of application from Europe to Asia. Truman responded to the invasion of South Korea by sending U.S. troops into battle. Later the United Nations approved of this act and war was fought under the auspices of the U.N. But it was really a U.S. act of containment of Communism.

One primary proponent of the policy of containment was John Foster Dulles, Eisenhower's secretary of state. It was Dulles who formed the Southeast Asia Treaty Organization and the Central Treaty Organization, both modeled after NATO and devoted to the purpose of surrounding the Soviet Union and China with U.S. allies.

It was under Eisenhower that the Domino Theory was first expressed. The theory held that if one country in Southeast Asia fell to Communism, the other countries would fall like dominoes. The French in Indochina were aided under this reasoning. This was the beginning of the long U.S. involvement in Indochina to prevent a Communist government in Vietnam, Laos, and Cambodia. Other examples of containment at work under the Eisenhower administration were the rearmament of Germany and its admittance into NATO, the maintenance of Chiang Kai-shek on Formosa, the sending of Marines to Lebanon in 1957, and the development of extensive spying techniques such as the U-2. Although there were moves for rapprochement with the Soviet Union toward the end of Eisenhower's administration, the basic foreign policy of the Eisenhower administration was containment by *Brinkmanship*, Dulles' idea of threatening nuclear retaliation for any aggressive Communist moves. We were guided by fear of those who were different from us.

Kennedy moved away from the emphasis on fear by enlarging the foreign aid program first used by President Truman to win friends in undeveloped countries. The Peace Corps and an increased emphasis upon the Good Neighbor Policy in South America were part of the aid policy. However, it too was rooted in fear, America's fear that Castro's Cuban Communism would spread to South America if not blocked by U.S. money. The Cuban missile crisis brought the world to the brink of war, but Kennedy proved that the United States would not permit the Soviet Union to establish a military base in this hemisphere. It was a classic example of the containment policy at work and was designed to keep those who are different out of the hemisphere.

In conclusion, then, the Eisenhower and Kennedy administrations saw the enlargement of the containment policy to include not only Western Europe and the Far East, but Southeast Asia, and South America as well. The motive behind the policy was to block the spread of that fearful quantity known as Communism. The policy established America's position as "police officer of the world." America's motivation in this move to a police officer's role began in fear—fear of international Communism.

## Teacher Comments on Sample Answer

"The student essay is a very fine answer. His definition of containment is well presented and the examples are well chosen. However, there are many examples from the Truman years, and actually, the question does not require them. They do illustrate his knowledge but on a peripheral topic. He then picks the Eisenhower and Kennedy administrations as his topics for discussion and presents excellent examples from both. The student states the thesis in the introduction and develops the essay to support it all the way through. The conclusion brings the reader back to the thesis and completes a very effective organization for the paper. Although there are some foreign policy developments in these years that negate the thesis, the student has chosen to ignore them and to pick very effectively a variety of factual details that do support the thesis. The essay is perhaps a bit longer than the average one, but it is the quality of expression and argument, not the length, that makes this an outstanding answer."

Would you have made the same comments as the teacher did on this answer? As with the first essay, it is a good answer—in the 8–9 category—and was placed here to provide a high standard for you as you finish the book. It demonstrates what a student can do with a question based on post-World War II material.

As you realize, this question is a version of the *To what extent?* type of essay question. You should have had no difficulty in analyzing and answering the question. By now, with our consideration of basic types of essay questions and with the many essays you have written, you should be well prepared for the free-response—both the standard essays and the DBQ—part of the Advanced Placement exam. You can test your readiness by taking the sample exams in Part Four and on the CD-ROM. While you are using them and when you take the Advanced Placement exam in U.S. History, never fail to use the Seven Steps in Essay Writing:

**First—Analyze the question**
**Second—Collect and sort information**
**Third—Develop your thesis**
**Fourth—Write the introduction**
**Fifth—Write the body of the essay**
**Sixth—Write the conclusion**
**Seventh—Reread the essay: Introduction, Body, Conclusion**

And do not forget the flashlight image.

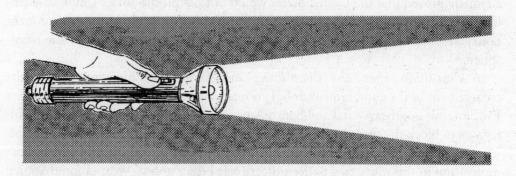

# Practice Essay Questions

The following practice essay questions require knowledge of the period since 1945 and one other period from United States history. The questions represent different types of essay questions presented in the text. These five questions thus provide an excellent review for the Advanced Placement examination.

1. ". . . [A]lmost all the defects inherent in democratic institutions are brought to light in the conduct of foreign affairs."

   Analyze this statement from *Democracy in America* by Alexis de Tocqueville (1835) and evaluate to what extent the statement applies to the conduct of U.S. foreign affairs in ONE of the following periods:

   1929–1941
   1961–1974

2. "In the Populist Era both state legislation and federal Supreme Court decisions went against the civil rights of minorities, whereas in the period 1954–1980, both national legislation and federal Supreme Court decisions supported the civil rights of all Americans."

   Analyze the validity of the above quotation.

3. To what extent and in what ways did reforms instituted under the New Deal in TWO of the following areas continue to impact the nation in the period 1968–2000?

   Civil Rights
   Business/labor relations
   Unemployment
   Banking

4. Compare and contrast the efforts and successes at international cooperation and peace in the 20 years after World War I with those efforts and successes at international cooperation and peace in the 20 years after World War II.

5. "Americans have learned that, when the nation is divided in its support of military activity, the social fabric of a democratic society is weakened, which results in moral and ethical decline."

   Assess the validity of this quotation by using information from TWO of the following:

   World War I
   World War II
   Vietnam War

## Comments on Question 1

The first sample essay question is a standard combination type in which an *Analyze* question is combined with a *To what extent?* question. You first must decide what the quotation is saying and then determine to what extent it applies to one period of time. As always, pick the time you know the most about but also the one in which you can find examples of defects in democratic institutions (unless you decide the quote is inaccurate and does not apply to the period of your choice). The two time periods are very interesting. The 1930s were Depression years domestically, and the nation attempted to remain neutral toward the European crises precipitated by Hitler and Mussolini and the Asian crisis developing around Chinese-Japanese relations. The 1960s were the period of the Civil Rights Movement and the Vietnam War. How the United States responded to these dramatic foreign policy events provides a lot to consider. You may want to organize the time period chronologically. However, a more sophisticated approach would be to focus on defects in democratic institutions, such as the military, Congress, or CIA, in the time period you pick.

The quotation is an observation by that most astute and perceptive Frenchman, Alexis de Tocqueville, who wrote an outstanding commentary on the United States in 1835. His *Democracy in America*, although rather slow reading for present-day students, should be read by all who consider themselves scholars of America's past. This quote is typical of his sharp analysis and perception of life in the United States in the Jackson era, much of which is still applicable to the nation today. Do you agree with this statement of de Tocqueville's? What will your thesis be?

## Comments on Question 2

The second question is the familiar *How do you account?* type. This question asks about the change in attitude toward civil rights and minorities as seen in legislation and Supreme Court decisions between the Populist Era (1890–1898) and the period 1954–1974. Two words—*state, national*—in the question provide a key to analysis. For the Populist Era, *state* legislation is mentioned; for the more recent period, *national* legislation is referred to. Why? When you decide on your answer to that, you will probably have both your thesis and very likely your organizational pattern. The question focuses on a very important aspect of recent history. You will want to include the 1896 *Plessy v. Ferguson* Supreme Court decision that accepted the "separate but equal" concept in race relations as established in state law, thus making it national policy. At the time, Social Darwinism with its idea of "survival of the fittest" still prevailed in the nation. In contrast, you should include both the civil rights legislation of the Johnson era and the Supreme Court decision in the 1954 *Brown v. Board of Education* case (desegregation of schools). An exciting answer would extend civil rights to include the rights of the suspect, the Miranda case, and women's rights to privacy and abortion upheld in *Roe v. Wade* in 1974.

## Comments on Question 3

Question 3 is a combined *To what extent?* and *In what ways?* question involving the link between the New Deal and the postwar era in two areas of reform. Although you have a choice, you do need to know in some detail two of the areas of New Deal reform. There was limited Civil Rights activity under the New Deal but there was some which picked up in the postwar period. You probably are aware of the labor laws of the New Deal and should realize that the Taft Hartley Act cut back on some of them. There was considerable legislation in the other two areas. The wording of the question is not complicated, but this is not an easy question. One assumes continuity in history but that is not always the situation. With the Republican ascendancy at the end of the 20th century, there was general discussion of the New Deal legacy and whether it was being abandoned. Do not worry if you are not ready to answer this question. **On the free-response section you can assume there will be at least one question on a topic with which you are not familiar, so do not get upset when you find a question you cannot answer.**

## Comments on Question 4

The fourth question focuses on the important issue of international cooperation and peace and uses a *Compare . . . Contrast* type of question to get you to make decisions about international cooperation after the two world wars of the 20th century. The information needed to answer the question should be part of your knowledge of the history. What your thesis will be, however, and how you organize the materials is open to many possibilities. The question falls easily into a description of post-World War I and then post-World War II periods and should include actions of the League of Nations and the United Nations as well as information on United States actions. This is a good question for 20th-century foreign policy.

> **TIP**
>
> Remember don't just list events. You must defend a viewpoint.

## Comments on Question 5

The last sample question is based on a quotation dealing with the social and moral as well as the political life of our nation. The familiar directions *Assess the validity* have been expanded to include directions to use information from two wars chosen from a list of three. The wars divided the nation in varying degrees. The nation is still experiencing the aftermath of the very divisive Vietnam War. There was widespread opposition to U.S. involvement in World War I and also in World War II until the Japanese attack on Pearl Harbor brought general support to the war effort. Thus, all three wars had divisive aspects, but did they weaken the social fabric and lead to moral and ethical decline? That you need to decide. The 1968 riots at the Democratic Convention and the Watergate incident suggest changes in the social fabric after the Vietnam War. What about after World Wars I and II?

The question should not be hard to analyze, although the phrase *social fabric* may not be familiar. It refers to the underlying structure of society—all those elements that weave it together. No dates are given so you must recall the time period of each war—this is why a timeline is important. The question focuses on social aspects of military history rather than the more familiar economic or political history. The question certainly invites a range of theses and a variety of organizations. It is a wide-open question dealing with the important issue of war and social life and morality—crucial and recurring issues in history and thus a very good one with which to end this study of essay questions based on United States history.

These five questions, as well as those in Chapter 10, provide an excellent review of U.S. history. If you are able to answer them in effective, well-organized essays without additional research, you should be suitably prepared for the Advanced Placement exam.

## MULTIPLE CHOICE—VOCABULARY

Throughout this book we have taken care to define special words used in the questions. Every student of history must know the vocabulary used by the historian. In Part One we suggested keeping a vocabulary list. Throughout the book, questions, both essay and multiple-choice, have been introduced that indirectly tested your specialized history vocabulary.

Every subject has its own vocabulary. You become particularly aware of this when you study a foreign language or begin studying a new field—biology, for instance, has a very specialized vocabulary. Often, students studying history or English do not realize that there is a specialized vocabulary for these subjects because they have usually used or heard the words all their lives. We have saved this topic for last because most of the vocabulary you will need will have been absorbed without effort, and there is no need to make an issue of an obvious matter. To aid you in your vocabulary development, there is a Glossary included at the end of the book. It is not a list to memorize, but it illustrates the types of words you should know and provides a starting place for expanding your vocabulary. If you followed the suggestions for vocabulary building in Part One, you should have your own extensive list by now that should enable you to answer the sample questions below.

The following multiple-choice questions illustrate several ways in which your knowledge of historical terms may be tested directly on the Advanced Placement exam. It should be obvious, however, that your vocabulary will be tested throughout the exam on every question.

---

## SAMPLE QUESTION

1. One who moves from place to place seeking agricultural employment is referred to as a (an)

   (A)  displaced person
   (B)  serf
   (C)  migrant worker
   (D)  agriculturist
   (E)  veteran

---

## Comments on Question 1

Question 1 is a straightforward one in which a definition of a word is presented followed by five choices of words for which you are to pick the correct word for the definition. You are probably familiar with this type of question from English examinations. In this question the correct answer is "migrant worker." If you did not know the term, you might have known other words related to *migrant,* such as *migratory, migration,* or *immigration.* In all three words, movement is involved; the phrase *moves from place to place* in the definition might lead you to the word *migrant.* Combining with this the fact that *employment* means work, you would have a good chance of picking "migrant worker" as the correct answer. You might also know the meaning of the other words, thus eliminating them. You can check the meaning of these other words in the Glossary.

## SAMPLE QUESTION

2. A scalawag was a Southern white who, after the Civil War, believed

    (A) in segregation
    (B) in cooperation with former slaves and Northerners
    (C) all Southern whites should be paid for their freed slaves
    (D) secession was still legal
    (E) all former slaves should be sent back to Africa

## Comments on Question 2

The second question reverses the order of the first and provides a term in the question and five choices for a correct definition. The term *scalawag* was applied to Southern whites who cooperated with the former slaves and Northerners in the period after the Civil War. The term is often used in discussing the Reconstruction period. The chances are that to answer this question you would have to know the term *scalawag*. It is specialized, but you might have been able to deduce the definition by eliminating several of the choices.

## SAMPLE QUESTION

3. Which of the following terms is used to refer to the attitude toward expansion held by many United States citizens in the years 1844–1850?

    (A) Manifest Destiny
    (B) Détente
    (C) Alliance for Progress
    (D) Isolationism
    (E) Brinkmanship

## Comments on Question 3

The third question combines a knowledge of historic periods with a definition of terms. In order to answer the question you must know that during the years 1844–1850 many United States citizens held the view that it was the God-given destiny of the United States to expand to the Pacific. This attitude guided much United States policy, both domestic and foreign, in these years. All the choices relate to United States foreign policy at different periods. You should recognize them and thus you would have no trouble identifying "Manifest Destiny" as the correct answer. This is a very common expression used in texts to describe U.S. policy of the mid-1840s. The other words can be found in the Glossary. Before studying United States history you were probably not familiar with these terms and you would have had difficulty with the question, but the chances are you know all or enough of them now so that you could eliminate most of the choices.

## SAMPLE QUESTION

4. If you lived in a city slum in the 1890s, the building in which you lived would most likely be a

(A) megalopolis
(B) condominium
(C) skyscraper
(D) trust
(E) tenement

## Comments on Question 4

Again, question 4 combines a knowledge of specific historic periods with an understanding of words. As in the first and third questions, the definition is given in the question and the choices are of words to fit the definition. In this question the words *city, slum, 1890s,* and *building* should combine to give you the answer—"tenement." *Condominium* is a more recent word for middle- and upper-class apartment houses. A skyscraper, a particular type of tall building usually used for offices, was developed in the 1890s, but not in slums. Trusts were formed in the 1890s, but they were large businesses, and *megalopolis* is a 20th-century term used to describe a huge, sprawling urban center and not a building. If you could not immediately identify "tenement" as the correct answer, you could probably arrive at the answer by eliminating the other terms, which should be part of your specialized history vocabulary.

## SAMPLE QUESTION

5. Since the Civil War, those individuals supporting states' rights have most often turned to which of the following for support of their position?

(A) The federal bureaucracy
(B) The Defense Department
(C) The Tenth Amendment to the U.S. Constitution
(D) The National Democratic Party
(E) The Civil Rights Movement

## Comments on Question 5

The last question is a little more complicated in form, but essentially it does what question 2 did. A word is presented in the question and the choices test your understanding of the word. States' rights advocates believe each state is sovereign—has the right to rule itself. They believe the Constitution was formed and ratified by the states. Since the Civil War, which affirmed the union of the states and denied the right of secession, supporters of states' rights have emphasized the 10th Amendment of the Constitution, which reserves powers not delegated to the federal government to the states. State vs. federal power has always been an issue in U.S. history. The federal bureaucracy, national Democratic Party, and Civil Rights Movement have all supported the power of the federal government over that of the states. This question tests a very specialized understanding of a very important concept.

These five examples illustrate ways in which vocabulary can be specifically tested on the Advanced Placement examination. It is important to remember, however, that **all questions on the exam will require a history vocabulary, so be sure to study the Glossary and develop your own vocabulary list.**

## Practice Multiple-Choice Questions

The following questions illustrate the type of questions one might be asked concerning events since World War II. Remember, however, that only one-third of the multiple-choice questions on the examination will be on the post-1914 period (1915–present) and that not many will be on the post-1980 era although there may be questions up to the present.

These are the last practice multiple-choice questions in the book. As you begin this final set of practice questions, remember that it is important to read the entire question and all the answers carefully. Do not guess at answers unless you can eliminate several of the possible choices.

1. All of the following individuals are correctly paired with the organization with which they are usually connected EXCEPT

   (A) Martin Luther King, Jr.—Southern Christian Leadership Conference
   (B) Ralph Nader—Black Panthers
   (C) Malcolm X—Black Muslims
   (D) César Chavez—United Farm Workers of America
   (E) Betty Friedan—National Organization for Women (NOW)

2. Since World War II, U.S. troops have been sent to the Middle East to protect U.S. interests in Lebanon and the Persian Gulf by all of the following presidents EXCEPT

   (A) Eisenhower
   (B) Nixon
   (C) Reagan
   (D) George H. W. Bush
   (E) George W. Bush

3. In retaliation for a supposed attack on U.S. destroyers, the U.S. Congress authorized President Johnson to take any action he deemed necessary to deal with the crisis when they voted for

   (A) My Lai
   (B) the Marshall Plan
   (C) the Patriot Act
   (D) the Point Four Program
   (E) the Tonkin Gulf Resolution

4. On the map at the right, Vietnam is numbered

   (A) 1 and 2
   (B) 2, 3, and 4
   (C) 2 and 4
   (D) 1, 2, 4, and 5
   (E) 4 and 5

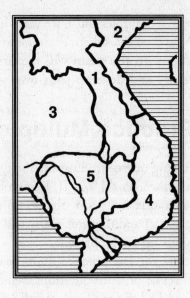

5. The 1973 Supreme Court decision in the case of *Roe v. Wade*

   (A) marked the end of the Court's liberal view in support of the rights of suspected criminals
   (B) was strongly opposed by the National Rifle Association
   (C) was very controversial and precipitated strong political reactions both pro and con
   (D) has been supported by each president since 1973
   (E) was the Court's most sweeping decision in favor of the civil rights of African Americans

6. The event that has come to symbolize the end of the Cold War is the

   (A) seizure of power in Cuba by Fidel Castro
   (B) overthrow of the Shah of Iran
   (C) Iran-Contra Affair
   (D) fall of the Berlin Wall
   (E) Vietnam War

7. All of the following were characteristic of the 1960s EXCEPT

   (A) the rapid growth of the computer industry
   (B) the development of "Pop Art"
   (C) the popularity of the Beatles
   (D) the rise of anti-Vietnam War protests
   (E) the rapid expansion of cable T.V.

## Persons in Poverty

| Family Situation | Number of persons in millions in given family situations living in poverty over total number of persons in that situation. | | |
| --- | --- | --- | --- |
| | White | Nonwhite | Total: All Races |
| Individuals Living Alone | 4.0 / 10.8 | .8 / 1.6 | 4.8 / 12.4 |
| Members of Family Units | 16.3 / 159.6 | 8.5 / 21.4 | 24.8 / 181.0 |
| TOTAL Both Situations | 20.3 / 170.4 | 9.3 / 23.0 | 29.7 / 193.4 |

8. According to the table above for 1966 during Lyndon Johnson's "War on Poverty," all of the following statements are true EXCEPT

   (A) There were more whites living in poverty than nonwhites.
   (B) If you are nonwhite and live alone, you have a 50-50 chance of living in poverty.
   (C) Your best chance of avoiding poverty is to be born in a white family.
   (D) More unrelated individuals live in poverty than do members of families.
   (E) Although the total number in poverty for whites is greater, there is a higher percentage of poverty among nonwhites.

9. Which of the following events most directly led to the resignation of President Nixon?

   (A) the end of the Vietnam War
   (B) the Watergate break-in and consequent Congressional hearings
   (C) the resignation of Vice President Agnew
   (D) diplomatic overtures to the People's Republic of China
   (E) the maintenance of an "enemies list"

10. Which of the following occurred during the presidency of Ronald Reagan?

    (A) A large decrease in the trade deficit
    (B) A large increase in the national debt
    (C) A steady decline of the Dow Jones stock index
    (D) A rapid increase in the rate of inflation
    (E) An agreement to reduce military expenditures during his presidency

## Answers and Answer Explanations

1. **(B)**   2. **(B)**   3. **(E)**   4. **(C)**
5. **(C)**   6. **(D)**   7. **(E)**   8. **(D)**
9. **(B)**   10. **(B)**

1. **(B)** Ralph Nader founded Public Citizen, Inc., an organization that focused on consumer protection. He was not connected with the Black Panthers, who were organized as an activist Black Power group by H. Rap Brown. The other individuals are correctly linked with their organizations, all of which were very important in the Civil Rights Movement of the 1960s and 1970s.

2. **(B)** Since World War II, U.S. troops have been sent to Lebanon and the Persian Gulf by Presidents Eisenhower, Carter, Reagan, George H. W. Bush, Clinton, and George W. Bush. Nixon and Ford did not send troops to these areas. Eisenhower declared the Eisenhower Doctrine to protect our interests in the Middle East and sent troops to Lebanon. Carter sent a helicopter mission to rescue American hostages in Teheran, Iran, but it was brief, unsuccessful, and not as significant as the military missions sent by Eisenhower, Reagan, both Bushes, and Clinton. Reagan intervened in Lebanon, sending troops to stop Palestine Liberation Organization (PLO) activities, but withdrew them when terrorists blew up a marine barracks that killed hundreds. George H. W. Bush organized Operation Desert Storm through the United Nations and sent troops to force Iraq out of Kuwait. After the end of hostilities, United Nations Weapons Inspection Teams were expected to destroy the nuclear and biological weapons of Iraq. When President Saddam Hussein refused to cooperate with the United Nations, President Clinton sent U.S. forces to join Great Britain in a massive bombing attack on Iraq in December 1998. This proved unsuccessful, and George W. Bush, after failing to gain full U.N. support, attacked Iraq in March 2003 with the military support of Great Britain and Australia, and the support of a number of smaller nations, called the coalition of the willing.

3. **(E)** The Tonkin Gulf Resolution, passed by the U.S. Congress in August 1964 after it was reported that two U.S. destroyers were attacked in the Tonkin Gulf, gave the president authority to take any action he deemed necessary for dealing with the crisis. The resolution was used to justify the entire U.S. involvement in Vietnam without a declaration of war. The other items relate to different foreign policy issues.

4. **(C)** On the map of the Indochina Peninsula, 2 is the former North Vietnam and 4 is the former South Vietnam so the correct answer is C—Vietnam consists of both the former North and South Vietnam. It does not include Cambodia, which is number 5, and Laos, which is number 1. Number 3 is Thailand.

5. **(C)** The Supreme Court decision in *Roe v. Wade* supported a woman's right to abortion during the first trimester of pregnancy. It was a very controversial decision and brought reaction in the political arena where pro-life and pro-choice groups became active. The decision was based on the "right to privacy" and not civil rights. It had nothing to do with the rights of suspected criminals. The National Rifle Association, although an active pressure group, has not lobbied against this decision. Presidents Reagan and the two Bushes opposed the decision and worked to have it overturned.

6. **(D)** These items relate to the Cold War and concern over Communism. Fidel Castro took power in Cuba in 1959 turning Cuba into a Communist nation and posing a potential threat to American security during the Cold War. The overthrow of the Shah of Iran in 1979 meant the loss of an American ally in the Persian Gulf area and threatened the oil supplies from the area. A strict Islamic Republic was established. Members of Reagan's administration developed the idea of Iran-Contra in the mid-1980s. The plan called for supplying arms to Iran for its use in its war against Iraq. The goal was to gain favor with Iran, to obtain the release of hostages in Lebanon, and to use secretly the money obtained from the sale of weapons to support the Contras fighting against the government of Nicaragua. That government was seen as too supportive of Communist ideas and potentially another Cuba. Congress had refused to fund the Contras. The Berlin Wall fell in 1989 and its fall has become symbolic of the end of the Cold War. The Vietnam War, a hot aspect of the Cold War, was fought to stop the spread of Communism in Southeast Asia.

7. **(E)** Increased use of computers, Pop Art, the Beatles (rock and roll), and anti-Vietnam War protests were all characteristic of U.S. culture in the 1960s. The rapid growth of cable television began in the 1980s with such stations as CNN.

8. **(D)** The table presents information in nine categories—white and nonwhite, living alone and in family units. Information about the totals in these categories is presented for all races and both living situations and finally, in the lower right-hand corner, there is a grand total indicating all those in poverty. If you read the titles of each column carefully and understand that the fraction represents the total number of persons in each category as the denominator (bottom number) and the number of persons in poverty in each category as the numerator (top number), then you would realize that all the choices except D, "more unrelated individuals live in poverty than do members of families," are correct. Choice E requires that you convert fractions to percentages—a useful mathematical skill for reading charts. It was information of the type presented in this question that led President Johnson to undertake the War on Poverty as part of his Great Society.

9. **(B)** President Nixon was forced to resign as a result of the Watergate break-in at the Democratic Party headquarters and the resulting Congressional hearings that revealed his knowledge of the affair and involvement in a cover-up. Nixon had secretly taped White House conversations, and when they were revealed, it clearly indicated he had been lying about his involvement. The other choices were part of his presidency but had little direct bearing on his resignation.

10. **(B)** The supply-side economic policies adopted by the Reagan administration are considered the cause of a large increase in the national debt. Budgets remained unbalanced until 1998. The trade deficit increased, the Dow Jones stock index rose, although somewhat erratically, and the rate of inflation declined during Reagan's presidency. Reagan increased military expenditures.

# Points to Remember About the Exam: A Summary

## CHAPTER 12

## MULTIPLE-CHOICE SECTION

### The Questions

The exam consists of 80 multiple-choice questions. You have 55 minutes in which to answer them. You should keep moving through the questions at a steady pace. If you come to a question that is difficult or confusing, make a checkmark by the question in your question booklet and go on to the next question. When you have finished the 80 questions, you can come back to those you have skipped. The checkmark by the question will help you quickly identify those you skipped. **When you skip a question, be careful to mark the answer to the next question in the correct space on your answer sheet.**

### Material Covered

The questions will test factual knowledge and, in the "stimulus" questions, analytical skills. Approximately **35 percent** of the questions will cover **political** history, **40 percent** will cover **social**, **intellectual**, and **cultural** aspects of history, **15 percent** will cover **foreign policy**, **international affairs**, and **diplomatic** history, **10 percent** will cover **economic** history. The exam is designed to cover three time periods and questions on those periods are distributed as follows:

| | |
|---|---|
| **Earliest inhabitants to 1789** | 20% |
| **1790 to start of World War I** | 45% |
| **1915 to today** | 35% |

The multiple-choice questions on the exam are presented chronologically in groups of 8 to 14. The pattern is repeated throughout the exam and may help you in identifying the time period of a question. Model Exams A and B follow such a pattern.

### Grading

The multiple-choice questions are designed to present a range of difficulty. The level of difficulty is such that if you answer about 60 percent correctly, you'll receive a grade of three, which ranks you as "qualified" on the AP examination.

Thoughtless guessing of answers should be avoided, as one-fourth of a point is deducted for each incorrect answer. However, if in analyzing the question you can eliminate one or two of the five possible choices, selecting what appears to be the best answer from the three or four choices remaining is recommended.

## The Answer Page

Answers to the questions are indicated on your answer page by filling in a small space with a number 2 lead pencil. You should bring at least two sharpened number 2 pencils with erasers to the exam. **When you skip a question, be sure to leave that space blank on the answer sheet until you come back later.**

## FREE-RESPONSE SECTION OR ESSAY

## Time

There are three essays to be written in Section 2 of the examination. There is a total of 2 hours and 10 minutes devoted to the free-response section. At the start of the exam there is a 15-minute required period in which you should read the questions, analyze the documents, and briefly outline your answer(s). You then have 45 minutes to write your answer to Part A—the DBQ—and 70 minutes to write your answers to Parts B and C—two essay questions, one from Part B and one from Part C. You should use 5 of the 35 minutes allotted for each of the two free-response questions for taking notes and outlining your answer. You should bring two pens to the exam, since **you should write the essays in ink**.

## Free-Response DBQ: Section 2, Part A

Remember, the purpose of the DBQ is to test your analytical skills *and* your understanding of "mainstream" American history. You must analyze the question, then read the documents and determine how they relate to the question and to the traditional, chronological history of the period from which they come. In your answer you need to weave together information from **both** these sources. You should not simply recite what is in the documents.

In writing your DBQ answer you should refer to the documents by the author, source, or letter of the document in parentheses. Do not quote long passages. Paraphrase the main ideas and discuss **how** they relate to the question and to the economic, diplomatic, political, or social history of the period. A listing of the documents and recitation of what each one says is referred to by the correctors as a "laundry list" and is not well regarded by these readers.

## Standard Essays or Free-Response Questions— Section 2, Parts B and C

**Remember that you are to select one question from Part B and one from Part C.** The purpose of the questions is to test your knowledge of United States history, your ability to think as an historian, and your writing skills. Read and analyze the four questions carefully before making your choice. You will have 5 minutes to make a brief outline and 30 minutes to write each answer. Follow the suggestions presented in this book. **Remember the Seven Steps in Essay Writing and the image of the flashlight as you prepare and write your essay.**

## Ranking the Answers

Remember, the consultants who read your exams in June are not grading them—they are ranking them. The top rank is a 9. The consultants will be reading many papers each day, so a concise, well-structured answer with a clear thesis and conclusion that supports the thesis and includes pertinent information is well received and ranked highly.

# DEVELOPING A STUDY PLAN TO ACE THE EXAM

This book is designed to use throughout the academic year as you study United States history. It is not a quick answer on how to beat the exam. If you have worked through the book as you study the different time periods and events, you will be well prepared, you will understand what is on the examination, and you will learn how to achieve your best work.

The most important thing to remember as you begin to review for the AP examination is that you have been preparing since you first picked up this book or began your study of U.S. history. Have confidence in yourself and rely on the work you have done all year. **A planned review can be helpful but cannot replace the confidence gained by systematic work over a year. Last-minute cramming of factual information can be counterproductive and confusing.**

Develop a plan that fits your own time schedule. **A little review each day or evening is best**—an hour should be plenty of time if used well. If you have not yet taken the practice Advanced Placement exam that follows, you should begin your review by doing that. First read this section and then set aside at least three hours in which to take the model exam.

In planning a five-day review, an easy approach is to review two chapters in Part Two each day and use the fifth day for an overview. Each day of the four, begin by going over the sample multiple-choice questions in the two chapters and see how well you do. Then read the appropriate sections in Part Four or study your own time line and notes. Do *not* try to reread the whole text but use *your* notes. Finally, you will want to read over the sample essay questions that day and think about answers to them. What your goal is for this review is to get your mind turning as you think over material you studied several months ago.

One excellent way to review is to work with a friend. If this can be arranged, after you have both read over your own notes and answered the multiple-choice questions, discuss possible approaches to the essays. Share your knowledge. **Remember that your AP examination results will be reported by the College Board as a ranking on a scale of 5 to 1. You are not competing with your friends for the one top grade in the class.** Instead you are going to be ranked in five categories with more than 200,000 students who will take the Advanced Placement exam. A score of 5 means you are "extremely well qualified" and there will be many who achieve this score. Therefore, work together to support each other's efforts to reach a rank of 5. Thirty minutes a day spent reviewing your notes and multiple-choice questions and 30 minutes spent discussing the essay questions and your notes with a friend will prove an excellent five-day review pattern. On the fifth day you can review whatever information seems appropriate at that time—your own notes, your lecture notes, old tests.

**TIP**

Study with a friend.

## TAKING THE EXAM

### The Night Before the Exam

The night before the exam is a time to relax and get a good night's sleep. Some students have found seeing a good movie or watching a favorite TV show a better preparation than last-minute studying. Other students look over special notes or review the chapters that gave them the most difficulty in the final week's review. Another excellent option for this last-night review is to read again one of the model Advanced Placement exams included in Part Three or on the CD. **What is most important on this night is to get a good rest and have confidence that you have prepared well throughout the year.** There is nothing worse than to spend all night before the exam cramming facts into your head—facts that only end up being jumbled by morning.

### The Day of the Exam

Just as a good night's sleep is most beneficial, **a good breakfast is important**. If you are a coffee-only, non-breakfast person, take time to eat something on the morning of the exam. Three hours of exam taking is very draining and you need the energy a good breakfast will supply.

**Plan to be at school or the exam location in plenty of time.** Hunting for a parking spot can be distracting and you want to be focused on United States history on this day. Follow whatever directions you have been given by your teacher or guidance counselor about when to report and what to bring to the exam in the way of I.D. material or other information. Remember you will need several number 2 pencils and two pens.

Once you arrive at the exam room, find a seat where you will feel comfortable. Sitting toward the front often makes it easier to hear all the directions and there will be many instructions given by the person administering the exam. You will have identification material to fill out before beginning the exam. There will normally be a short break between Sections 1 and 2 of the examination. Instructions will be given for both sections. Pay attention but do not hesitate to ask if there is something you do not understand.

For many students the 3 hours and 5 minutes of the Advanced Placement exam will be the longest exam time they have experienced. Both the body and mind can get tired. You want to keep your blood circulating and plenty of oxygen coming into your lungs while you are working on the examination. There are several simple exercises you can do that help to achieve these goals during long examinations. While writing, you can clench your fists several times and release them quickly, and squeeze your toes hard and release them several times. Another excellent exercise is to make what is known in yoga as the Lion's Face. Stick your tongue out as far as you can and open your mouth and eyes as wide as you can. **These three exercises will get circulation going in your face and extremities.** They can be done while you are writing. A fourth exercise is a gentle finger massage of the temples and over the eyes and cheeks; this will help relieve tension and focus your thoughts. It requires putting the pencil or pen down and gently rubbing your fingers over your temples and then the palm of your hands gently over your eye sockets. Some find gently rubbing the cheekbones and forehead also helpful. **A minute or less doing this simple tension-releasing exercise will be time well spent.** These simple exercises should be done

**TIP**

Give yourself enough time in the morning to have breakfast and get to the exam on time.

**TIP**

Do some simple exercises to stay alert and focused on the exam.

when you seem to be getting tired. They are not distracting to others and can be helpful to you. If you are allowed to stand at the break between sections of the examination, bend over to touch your toes several times and stretch. Such simple exercises between sections of the examination, plus some good deep breathing spaced through the exam, can make taking the exam much easier.

Some people bring several pieces of hard candy or a candy bar to eat at the break for quick energy. As we now know, **a sugar high does not have a long-lasting effect but can be very helpful in the middle of the examination**. However, check whether eating is permitted by the test administrator before opening your candy bar.

These hints may seem strange and you may feel awkward making a Lion's Face in the middle of the Advanced Placement examination, but such actions can keep you fresher and your mind working, which is important during the long 3 hours and 5 minutes. You should practice these exercises as you take the model exams that follow.

## After the Exam

**Follow the directions given by your test administrator at the end of the examination.** Ask any questions you have before leaving.

The essays on the Advanced Placement examination are read in June by a large group of experienced college and high school teachers. The multiple-choice questions are machine corrected. Then the Chief Reader, working with a team, determines where each exam ranks. **You will hear your results in the summer so you should relax and get on with the rest of your schoolwork.** Do not worry about how you did on the Advanced Placement examination. **If you have worked steadily all year and reviewed with this book, you have done all you can to do well on the examination.** Now practice taking an examination.

# Practice Test A
## ANSWER SHEET

1. Ⓐ Ⓑ Ⓒ Ⓓ Ⓔ
2. Ⓐ Ⓑ Ⓒ Ⓓ Ⓔ
3. Ⓐ Ⓑ Ⓒ Ⓓ Ⓔ
4. Ⓐ Ⓑ Ⓒ Ⓓ Ⓔ
5. Ⓐ Ⓑ Ⓒ Ⓓ Ⓔ
6. Ⓐ Ⓑ Ⓒ Ⓓ Ⓔ
7. Ⓐ Ⓑ Ⓒ Ⓓ Ⓔ
8. Ⓐ Ⓑ Ⓒ Ⓓ Ⓔ
9. Ⓐ Ⓑ Ⓒ Ⓓ Ⓔ
10. Ⓐ Ⓑ Ⓒ Ⓓ Ⓔ
11. Ⓐ Ⓑ Ⓒ Ⓓ Ⓔ
12. Ⓐ Ⓑ Ⓒ Ⓓ Ⓔ
13. Ⓐ Ⓑ Ⓒ Ⓓ Ⓔ
14. Ⓐ Ⓑ Ⓒ Ⓓ Ⓔ
15. Ⓐ Ⓑ Ⓒ Ⓓ Ⓔ
16. Ⓐ Ⓑ Ⓒ Ⓓ Ⓔ
17. Ⓐ Ⓑ Ⓒ Ⓓ Ⓔ
18. Ⓐ Ⓑ Ⓒ Ⓓ Ⓔ
19. Ⓐ Ⓑ Ⓒ Ⓓ Ⓔ
20. Ⓐ Ⓑ Ⓒ Ⓓ Ⓔ

21. Ⓐ Ⓑ Ⓒ Ⓓ Ⓔ
22. Ⓐ Ⓑ Ⓒ Ⓓ Ⓔ
23. Ⓐ Ⓑ Ⓒ Ⓓ Ⓔ
24. Ⓐ Ⓑ Ⓒ Ⓓ Ⓔ
25. Ⓐ Ⓑ Ⓒ Ⓓ Ⓔ
26. Ⓐ Ⓑ Ⓒ Ⓓ Ⓔ
27. Ⓐ Ⓑ Ⓒ Ⓓ Ⓔ
28. Ⓐ Ⓑ Ⓒ Ⓓ Ⓔ
29. Ⓐ Ⓑ Ⓒ Ⓓ Ⓔ
30. Ⓐ Ⓑ Ⓒ Ⓓ Ⓔ
31. Ⓐ Ⓑ Ⓒ Ⓓ Ⓔ
32. Ⓐ Ⓑ Ⓒ Ⓓ Ⓔ
33. Ⓐ Ⓑ Ⓒ Ⓓ Ⓔ
34. Ⓐ Ⓑ Ⓒ Ⓓ Ⓔ
35. Ⓐ Ⓑ Ⓒ Ⓓ Ⓔ
36. Ⓐ Ⓑ Ⓒ Ⓓ Ⓔ
37. Ⓐ Ⓑ Ⓒ Ⓓ Ⓔ
38. Ⓐ Ⓑ Ⓒ Ⓓ Ⓔ
39. Ⓐ Ⓑ Ⓒ Ⓓ Ⓔ
40. Ⓐ Ⓑ Ⓒ Ⓓ Ⓔ

41. Ⓐ Ⓑ Ⓒ Ⓓ Ⓔ
42. Ⓐ Ⓑ Ⓒ Ⓓ Ⓔ
43. Ⓐ Ⓑ Ⓒ Ⓓ Ⓔ
44. Ⓐ Ⓑ Ⓒ Ⓓ Ⓔ
45. Ⓐ Ⓑ Ⓒ Ⓓ Ⓔ
46. Ⓐ Ⓑ Ⓒ Ⓓ Ⓔ
47. Ⓐ Ⓑ Ⓒ Ⓓ Ⓔ
48. Ⓐ Ⓑ Ⓒ Ⓓ Ⓔ
49. Ⓐ Ⓑ Ⓒ Ⓓ Ⓔ
50. Ⓐ Ⓑ Ⓒ Ⓓ Ⓔ
51. Ⓐ Ⓑ Ⓒ Ⓓ Ⓔ
52. Ⓐ Ⓑ Ⓒ Ⓓ Ⓔ
53. Ⓐ Ⓑ Ⓒ Ⓓ Ⓔ
54. Ⓐ Ⓑ Ⓒ Ⓓ Ⓔ
55. Ⓐ Ⓑ Ⓒ Ⓓ Ⓔ
56. Ⓐ Ⓑ Ⓒ Ⓓ Ⓔ
57. Ⓐ Ⓑ Ⓒ Ⓓ Ⓔ
58. Ⓐ Ⓑ Ⓒ Ⓓ Ⓔ
59. Ⓐ Ⓑ Ⓒ Ⓓ Ⓔ
60. Ⓐ Ⓑ Ⓒ Ⓓ Ⓔ

61. Ⓐ Ⓑ Ⓒ Ⓓ Ⓔ
62. Ⓐ Ⓑ Ⓒ Ⓓ Ⓔ
63. Ⓐ Ⓑ Ⓒ Ⓓ Ⓔ
64. Ⓐ Ⓑ Ⓒ Ⓓ Ⓔ
65. Ⓐ Ⓑ Ⓒ Ⓓ Ⓔ
66. Ⓐ Ⓑ Ⓒ Ⓓ Ⓔ
67. Ⓐ Ⓑ Ⓒ Ⓓ Ⓔ
68. Ⓐ Ⓑ Ⓒ Ⓓ Ⓔ
69. Ⓐ Ⓑ Ⓒ Ⓓ Ⓔ
70. Ⓐ Ⓑ Ⓒ Ⓓ Ⓔ
71. Ⓐ Ⓑ Ⓒ Ⓓ Ⓔ
72. Ⓐ Ⓑ Ⓒ Ⓓ Ⓔ
73. Ⓐ Ⓑ Ⓒ Ⓓ Ⓔ
74. Ⓐ Ⓑ Ⓒ Ⓓ Ⓔ
75. Ⓐ Ⓑ Ⓒ Ⓓ Ⓔ
76. Ⓐ Ⓑ Ⓒ Ⓓ Ⓔ
77. Ⓐ Ⓑ Ⓒ Ⓓ Ⓔ
78. Ⓐ Ⓑ Ⓒ Ⓓ Ⓔ
79. Ⓐ Ⓑ Ⓒ Ⓓ Ⓔ
80. Ⓐ Ⓑ Ⓒ Ⓓ Ⓔ

# Practice Test A

## CHAPTER 13

The following is a typical Advanced Placement examination in United States history. You may use it as a **pre-test to see how much recall you have of United States history, or you may use it as a practice test during your study**. There is a chart on page 224 that, when filled in, will indicate what areas are weakest at the start of your study or whenever you take the test.

## SECTION 1

You will be allowed 3 hours and 5 minutes for the entire examination. Section 1, the Multiple-Choice Section, includes 80 questions to be answered in 55 minutes. This gives you 45 seconds for each question. Since preparation varies from school to school, very few students can answer all the questions, so do not be discouraged. Be sure to use the answer sheet on the previous page because it does take a little longer to mark answers on a separate sheet. If you skip a question, be sure to note it on your answer sheet so you will not mark your answers incorrectly.

Questions are presented in groups of 8 to 14 questions in chronological order and then the pattern is repeated. This will help you identify the time period from which the questions come and will also help you analyze the answers to each question.

## SECTION 2

Section 2, the Free-Response or Essay Section, includes the DBQ and two other essay questions to be selected from four questions. These are to be answered in 2 hours and 10 minutes. The first 15 minutes consist of a reading period in which you will read the DBQ and prepare notes for your answer. At the examination you will be supplied a small booklet of $8\frac{1}{2}" \times 11"$ lined pages on which to write your answers. For this sample examination you will want to use your own paper. You should write your essay answers in black or blue ink. Pencils should not be used as they make reading difficult.

Now tear out the multiple-choice answer sheet or make a copy of it. Get some lined paper, pencils and pens, and a timer, and sit down ready to spend 3 hours and 5 minutes on this practice exam. If you need to, you may take breaks between the sections and/or between the three essays. It would be best to find a quiet place with a desk and to work uninterrupted.

# Practice Test A

<hr />

## SECTION I: MULTIPLE-CHOICE QUESTIONS

TIME: 55 MINUTES

Number of Questions—80 MULTIPLE CHOICE

**Directions:** Each of the questions or incomplete statements below is followed by five suggested answers or completions. Select the one that is best in each case and then blacken the corresponding oval on the answer sheet.

1. The English colony first settled by the Dutch was

   (A) New York
   (B) Jamaica
   (C) Canada
   (D) Pennsylvania
   (E) Delaware

2. "... and he [the president] shall nominate, and by and with the advice and consent of the Senate, shall appoint ... judges of the Supreme Court ..."

   The passage above from the Constitution best illustrates the concept of

   (A) the power of the purse
   (B) executive privilege
   (C) checks and balances
   (D) judicial review
   (E) due process

3. The principal reason for the "Era of Good Feeling" during the presidency of James Monroe was

   (A) lack of international tension and conflict
   (B) economic development and domestic prosperity
   (C) a religious revival that de-emphasized political considerations
   (D) a weakened, unorganized opposition political party
   (E) his strong stand in favor of Latin America stated in the Monroe Doctrine

4. The main purpose of Henry Clay's American System was to

(A) advance and implement Manifest Destiny
(B) develop an interdependent economic system tying the East, West, and South together
(C) curtail immigration in favor of large native population growth
(D) integrate the Native American into U.S. society
(E) expand American investment abroad

5. Transcendentalist writers found their major source of truth and inspiration in

(A) church dogma
(B) the Bible
(C) the political situation of the time
(D) nature
(E) history

6. The event in the western theater during the Civil War that had the effect of splitting the Confederacy in half was the

(A) Battle of the Wilderness
(B) Capture of Vicksburg
(C) Battle of Antietam
(D) Battle of Gettysburg
(E) Siege of Petersburg

7. Of his Fourteen Points, Wilson was most concerned with establishing

(A) Point I: Open covenants, openly arrived at
(B) Point II: Absolute freedom of navigation upon the seas
(C) Point IV: Adequate guarantees given and taken that national armaments will be reduced to the lowest point consistent with domestic safety
(D) Point V: A free, open-minded and absolutely impartial adjustment of all colonial claims
(E) Point XIV: A general association of nations formed to provide political independence and territorial integrity of all nations

8. Which of the following transportation developments took place in the 20th century?

(A) Opening of the transcontinental railroad
(B) Organization of local canals to support manufacturing
(C) Introduction of steamboats on the Mississippi River
(D) Establishment of air mail service
(E) The Pony Express mail service

9. "We had a chance to gain the leadership of the world. We lost it, and soon we shall be witnessing the tragedy of it all."

Which American leader during the 20th century would most likely have made the above statement?

(A) Theodore Roosevelt
(B) Woodrow Wilson
(C) Franklin Roosevelt
(D) John F. Kennedy
(E) Lyndon B. Johnson

THE BEST THEY HAVE TO OFFER.

*Source: World Telegram,* August 11, 1934

10. In the cartoon above the artist is

   (A) suggesting the Republican Party has no effective solution to the depression
   (B) supporting the anticommunist crusade of the 1920s
   (C) advocating Social Darwinism as a policy
   (D) indicating he believes in nonviolent protest
   (E) implying that the GOP is being robbed by Wall Street and Rugged Individualism

11. "With millions of men and women still unemployed and the whole industrialized world critically dependent upon the scope and vigor of the American economic recovery, a veto of the tax cut would be poor public policy, which political headline-hunting could not justify."

   The quotation suggests all of the following EXCEPT

   (A) The United States continues to be in a depression.
   (B) A presidential veto would be harmful to the nation.
   (C) Other nations are heavily affected by the U.S. economy.
   (D) In determining policy, the president should be guided solely by the political impact of the policy.
   (E) The unemployment rate is high in the nation.

12. The political leader most responsible for securing the passage of the Civil Rights Act of 1964 was

    (A) John F. Kennedy
    (B) Lyndon B. Johnson
    (C) Adam Clayton Powell
    (D) Andrew Young
    (E) George Wallace

13. The principal motivation for the settlement of the Plymouth Bay Colony was

    (A) economic
    (B) political
    (C) religious
    (D) social
    (E) cultural

14. Which of the following events occurred under the government of the Articles of Confederation?

    (A) The repeal of the Stamp Act
    (B) Shays' Rebellion
    (C) The Whiskey Rebellion
    (D) Daniel Boone's first trip to Kentucky
    (E) The Boston Massacre

15. All of the following occurred during George Washington's two terms EXCEPT

    (A) the election of John Adams to the presidency
    (B) the resignation of Thomas Jefferson as Secretary of State
    (C) the XYZ Affair
    (D) Hamilton's and Jefferson's letters on the constitutionality of the Bank of the U.S.
    (E) the negotiation of the Jay Treaty

16. In the years immediately after 1825 the pattern of western settlement was greatly affected by the

    (A) aftermath of the Battle of the Little Big Horn
    (B) opening of the Erie Canal
    (C) purchase of Alaska
    (D) discovery of gold in South Dakota
    (E) clipper ship trade with China

17. In the 40 years following the end of Reconstruction, fundamental changes in the American system were brought about as a result of federal legislation in all of the following EXCEPT

    (A) immigration
    (B) civil service
    (C) civil rights
    (D) interstate commerce
    (E) monetary policy

18. All of the following contributed to the decision of the United States to declare war on Spain in 1898 EXCEPT

   (A) The sinking of the battleship Maine
   (B) The De Lome Letter
   (C) The stimulation of public opinion by the Yellow Press
   (D) The acquisition of Pago Pago
   (E) The need to protect American economic investments

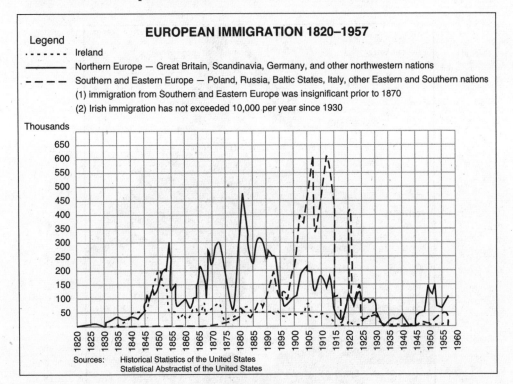

**EUROPEAN IMMIGRATION 1820–1957**

Legend
...... Ireland
——— Northern Europe — Great Britain, Scandinavia, Germany, and other northwestern nations
– – – Southern and Eastern Europe — Poland, Russia, Baltic States, Italy, other Eastern and Southern nations
(1) immigration from Southern and Eastern Europe was insignificant prior to 1870
(2) Irish immigration has not exceeded 10,000 per year since 1930

Sources:    Historical Statistics of the United States
             Statistical Abstractist of the United States

*Source:* U.S. Bureau of the Census, *Historical Statistics of the U.S., Colonial Times to 1957.*

19. According to the chart showing European immigration,

   (A) the period of greatest yearly immigration from northern Europe was 1905–1910
   (B) more Irish came to America in 1850–1855 than in 1885–1890
   (C) immigration from southern and eastern Europe was insignificant prior to 1930
   (D) northern Europe includes Great Britain, Scandinavia, and the Baltic States
   (E) the period of greatest immigration from southern Europe was after 1945

20. The Palmer Raids are significant because they

   (A) created a climate of opinion in which Senator Joseph McCarthy could capture the attention of the American people
   (B) identified over 400,000 Communists who were exiled to the Soviet Union
   (C) exposed the attorney general to such publicity that he was able to capture the Republican nomination for president in 1924
   (D) united the country in opposing the Fascist threat of Italy and Germany in the 1930s
   (E) reflected the anticommunist hysteria of the post-World War I period

21. Which of the following was NOT offered by Americans as a solution to the problems of the Great Depression?

   (A) Works Progress Administration
   (B) "Share the Wealth" proposal
   (C) Agricultural Adjustment Act
   (D) Good Neighbor Policy
   (E) National Recovery Act

22. On the above map, the areas colored black illustrate the

   (A) region divided into camps at the Yalta Conference
   (B) members of the Common Market
   (C) Central Powers in World War I
   (D) greatest extent of Nazi control in World War II
   (E) regions subjected to terrorist attacks during the Cold War

23. All of the following are characteristic of the African slave trade in the 18th century EXCEPT

   (A) Kings of African nations along the coast sold slaves to white traders.
   (B) During the "middle passage" slaves were chained and kept below deck most of the time.
   (C) Degradation and psychological damage occurred to all those involved.
   (D) The colonists relied on the English traders to supply slaves.
   (E) Most of the slaves sold in the Southern colonies were imported directly from Africa.

24. Under the Articles of Confederation, sovereignty was in the hands of the

    (A) executive
    (B) Congress
    (C) states
    (D) town meetings
    (E) revolutionary army

25. Which of the following best explains why the earliest factories in the United States were located in New England?

    (A) Its easy access to large quantities of coal
    (B) Abundant water power
    (C) A well-developed railroad network
    (D) A well-developed system of canals
    (E) Good harbors

26. Jefferson is often accused of political inconsistency since he apparently supported states' rights in the Kentucky and Virginia resolves but acted as a supporter of federal power and loose construction of the Constitution when he did all of the following EXCEPT

    (A) arranged the Louisiana Purchase
    (B) sent the United States Navy to attack the Barbary Pirates
    (C) ordered Lewis and Clark to explore the West
    (D) proclaimed the Embargo in 1807
    (E) supported the French in the XYZ Affair

27. Which of the following acts established the concept of surveying land into six-square-mile townships and the sale of land at public auction?

    (A) Homestead Act
    (B) Pacific Railway Act
    (C) Land Act of 1796
    (D) Desert Land Act
    (E) Surplus Revenue Act

28. All of the following were actions by the United States federal government to deal with the money supply EXCEPT the

    (A) Sherman Silver Purchase Act
    (B) Social Security Act
    (C) Gold Standard Act
    (D) Federal Reserve Act
    (E) Specie Circular

*THE DEFENDER OF TRUSTS*
*J.G.B. "This is only a little private matter, officer, with which you have nothing to do."*

Source: *Harper's Weekly*, September 1, 1888

29. All of the following are suggested by the cartoonist EXCEPT

(A) Several American industries are organized as trusts
(B) The American market at the time the cartoon was drawn was operated under the emblem of freedom and equality
(C) Trusts are limiting competition in the American market
(D) A well-dressed gentleman does not believe the police officer should interfere with the robbery
(E) The law is not prepared to become involved

30. All of the following ideas were incorporated in Frederick Jackson Turner's thesis on the influence of the frontier on America EXCEPT

(A) "The complex European life" had continual impact on America since the "Atlantic Coast . . . was the frontier of Europe."
(B) There is a "new product that is American."
(C) The frontier is the "outer edge . . . the meeting point between savagery and civilization."
(D) A "frontier settlement" had existed until 1890.
(E) "Democracy born of free land, strong in selfishness and individualism," has its "dangers as well as its benefits."

31. Which of the following would be considered part of United States domestic policy during the Cold War?

    (A) The U-2 incident
    (B) The Truman Doctrine
    (C) The U.N. intervention in the Congo
    (D) The attempts to impeach Earl Warren
    (E) The Bay of Pigs invasion of Cuba

32. Which of the following is a correct statement regarding the Vietnam War?

    (A) U.S. involvement in Vietnam began with John F. Kennedy.
    (B) President Lyndon Johnson decided to withdraw from the presidential race because of his position on Vietnam.
    (C) U.S. forces never attacked outside the borders of Vietnam.
    (D) The Gulf of Tonkin Resolution declared war on North Vietnam.
    (E) Throughout the war the areas controlled by each side were clearly identifiable.

33. The economic program introduced during the presidency of Ronald Reagan and often referred to as Reaganomics resulted in which one of the following items?

    (A) Tax increases for all payers of federal income taxes
    (B) Decreased expenditures for military defense
    (C) Elimination of government cabinet-level departments
    (D) A rapidly increasing federal deficit
    (E) Large increases in federal expenditures for social services

34. All of the following are true of the 1994 Congressional elections EXCEPT

    (A) The Republicans gained control of the House of Representatives for the first time since Eisenhower's presidency.
    (B) The Democrats lost control of the Senate.
    (C) President Clinton refused to campaign for members of his party.
    (D) The Republicans based their campaign for the House of Representatives on a Contract with America
    (E) Newt Gingrich, the Republican House Minority Leader, organized the Republican campaign.

35. ". . . we, being willing to . . . secure them [the people] in the free exercise and enjoyment of all their civil and religious rights . . . do hereby publish, grant, ordain, and declare . . . that no person with the said colony, at any time hereafter, shall be any wise molested, punished, disquieted, or called in question for any differences in opinion in matters of religion."

    The above quotation is most likely taken from

    (A) the Mayflower Compact
    (B) the Rhode Island colonial charter
    (C) a speech to Parliament by King James I
    (D) the Albany Plan of Union
    (E) the transcript of the trial of Peter Zenger

36. An economic system in which a nation seeks to accumulate precious metals by maintaining a favorable balance of trade is most descriptive of

    (A) capitalism
    (B) socialism
    (C) mercantilism
    (D) feudalism
    (E) fascism

37. "Having deprived her of this first right of a citizen, the elective franchise [right to vote], thereby leaving her without representation in the halls of legislation, he has oppressed her on all sides.

    "*Resolved,* That it is the duty of the women of this country to secure to themselves their sacred right to the elective franchise."

    The above statement would NOT be needed to have been written after

    (A) 1828
    (B) 1848
    (C) 1870
    (D) 1919
    (E) 1963

38. "(T)he occasion has been judged proper for asserting, as a principle, . . . that the American continents, by the free and independent condition which they have assumed and maintain, are henceforth not to be considered as subjects for future colonization by any European powers . . ."

    The principles articulated in the above passage are often considered the key point in the

    (A) Stimson Doctrine
    (B) Eisenhower Doctrine
    (C) Roosevelt Corollary
    (D) Monroe Doctrine
    (E) Truman Doctrine

39. All of the following reform movements of the pre-Civil War period are correctly paired with a leader of the movement EXCEPT

    (A) Care of the insane—Dorothea Dix
    (B) Abolition—Harriet Beecher Stowe
    (C) Women's Rights—Lucretia Mott
    (D) Education—Brigham Young
    (E) Prohibition—Susan B. Anthony

40. The Pendleton Act was passed by Congress as a response to

    (A) the assassination of President Garfield
    (B) the Cross of Gold speech by William Jennings Bryan
    (C) the declaration by the Supreme Court that the Granger Laws were unconstitutional
    (D) the election of Theodore Roosevelt as vice president
    (E) the annexation of Hawaii

41. Which of the following is NOT true regarding Dollar Diplomacy?

    (A) Investments were encouraged in both the Far East and in countries near the Panama Canal.
    (B) It allowed Taft to spend less on the Navy.
    (C) It eliminated armed intervention by United States forces in the Caribbean.
    (D) Woodrow Wilson reluctantly continued the policy after his election to the presidency.
    (E) United States money was used to support governments in the Caribbean and Central America.

42. " . . . surplus wealth is but a trust to be administered during life for the good of the community."

    The above statement from the end of the 19th century describes the attitude held by

    (A) a Social Darwinist
    (B) Andrew Carnegie
    (C) a successful businessperson
    (D) William Jennings Bryan
    (E) Eugene V. Debs

43. All of the following are characteristics of the era of Prohibition in the 1920s EXCEPT

    (A) A general breakdown or change in the moral attitudes of Americans
    (B) An increase in the number of gangsters and bootleggers
    (C) The establishment of "speakeasys" and brewing of "moonshine"
    (D) Strong support for Prohibition in urban areas
    (E) The weakness of the federal government in controlling private habits of its citizens

44. When the New Deal program of Franklin D. Roosevelt was threatened by Supreme Court decisions against New Deal measures, the president responded by

    (A) giving his famous "my dog Fala" speech
    (B) calling on Congress to increase the size of the Supreme Court
    (C) ordering impeachment proceedings against members of the Court
    (D) ignoring the Court decisions following Andrew Jackson's precedent
    (E) calling on the American people to elect only Democrats to Congress

45. United States society in the period from the end of World War II until the election of President John F. Kennedy was characterized by all of the following EXCEPT

    (A) a new attitude toward segregation precipitated by Supreme Court decisions
    (B) a concern over Communist (Soviet) infiltration into the U.S. government bureaucracy
    (C) the start of a new movement of popular music
    (D) a mood of conformity and uncritical support of government policies
    (E) a major economic recession with high unemployment for all Americans

46. In considering the writing of the Constitution, which of the following events occurred last?

    (A) The rejection of the Articles of Confederation
    (B) The presentation of the Connecticut Compromise
    (C) The introduction of the Virginia Plan
    (D) The election of Washington as chairman
    (E) The offering of the New Jersey Plan

47. A person supporting the concept of implied power in regard to the U.S. Constitution would be a believer in

    (A) limited executive power
    (B) strict constructionism
    (C) Jeffersonianism
    (D) loose constructionism
    (E) states' rights

48. The term *impressment* as used by the United States in the period before the War of 1812 referred to

    (A) the foreign policy concept of shunning alliances with other countries
    (B) the allying of nations to provide greater protection from attacks
    (C) the British practice of forcing American sailors into service on British warships
    (D) an agreement temporarily uniting two or more countries
    (E) a written plea from an individual protesting a wrong

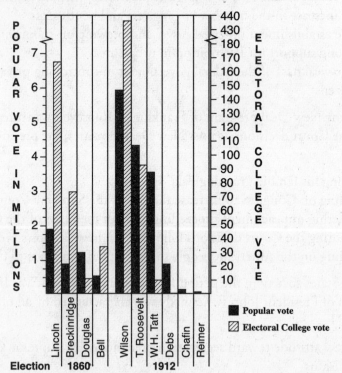

49. The bar graph on page 208 proves that

   (A) the electoral college is unjust
   (B) any of the three top candidates in the 1912 election, if they had run in 1860, would have defeated Lincoln
   (C) popular candidates cannot win in the electoral college
   (D) Bell was a better candidate than Douglas
   (E) Lincoln and Wilson were both minority presidents according to the popular vote, but received a majority of votes in the electoral college

50. The political Reconstruction of the South was ended after

   (A) the impeachment of President Johnson
   (B) the Democratic presidential victory in 1884
   (C) an agreement was arranged that allowed Republican Rutherford B. Hayes to become president
   (D) the Southern states indicated they welcomed military occupation
   (E) the grandfather clause as a voting requirement was outlawed by the Supreme Court

THE IRREPRESSIBLE INDEPENDENT

*Source: Harper's Weekly,* October 20, 1888

51. In the cartoon above, the Spoils System referred to on the Tammany booth indicates the political system of

   (A) honoring opponents with at least one appointed office
   (B) rewarding supporters with appointed offices
   (C) declaring openly who one's political supporters have been
   (D) appointing one's campaign manager to the cabinet
   (E) pointing out how one's opponents spoiled one's opportunity for election

52. Which of the following helped to improve relations between Native Americans and the U.S. government in the 40 years following the Civil War?

(A) The slaughter of the buffalo
(B) The corruption of many Indian Agents
(C) The discovery and exploitation of gold in the Black Hills of South Dakota
(D) The publication of Helen Hunt Jackson's *A Century of Dishonor*
(E) The disregard of treaty arrangements

53. Which of the following events finally precipitated the military activity of the Civil War?

(A) The establishment of the state of West Virginia
(B) Secession of South Carolina
(C) The action at Fort Sumter
(D) The first election of Lincoln to the presidency
(E) The Emancipation Proclamation

*Getting Back to a Competitive Basis*

Source: *Saturday Evening Post*, June 6, 1914

54. The most important political point being made in this cartoon is that

(A) organ grinders are popular
(B) animal rights is popular
(C) Theodore Roosevelt and Woodrow Wilson must appeal for popular support of their reform programs
(D) every product in America is advertised as "new"
(E) political candidates must have a named program

55. The Creel Committee during World War I represented the United States' first successful attempt at large-scale governmental

(A) armament manufacture
(B) food production
(C) shipbuilding
(D) propaganda
(E) railroad management

56. Which of the following New Deal legislation was a basic reform measure dealing with banking?

(A) Public Works Administration
(B) Federal Deposit Insurance Corporation
(C) Civilian Conservation Corps
(D) National Industrial Recovery Act
(E) Agricultural Adjustment Administration

57. "I will not give up my belief that America must, for the happiness of her own people, (and) for the moral guidance . . . of the world, be permitted to live her own life. . . . the tie which binds a man to his country (is crucial), and all plans . . . which would entangle and impede . . . her freedom of action I unhesitatingly put behind me."

The writer is making a statement that could best be summarized as in favor of

(A) isolationism and Christianity
(B) sovereignty and socialism
(C) freedom and nationalism
(D) socialism and Christianity
(E) isolationism and nationalism

58. "If the *British* Parliament has a legal authority to issue an order that we shall furnish a single article for the troops here, and to compel obedience to *that* order, they have the same right to issue an order for us to supply those troops . . . every necessity; and to compel obedience to *that* order also; . . . What is this but taxing us to a certain sum, and leaving us only the manner of raising it?"

The argument presented by the author of the above statement could best be summarized as

(A) The British Parliament has no authority to compel Americans to supply goods for troops.
(B) The Stamp Act is intolerable and should be repealed immediately.
(C) Americans should supply British troops with all necessities.
(D) Americans should determine the sum by which they will be taxed by Parliament.
(E) Americans should pay more taxes to help the British.

59. According to the Constitution, in an impeachment trial of a president

   (A) the evidence against the president should be gathered by an independent counsel
   (B) the president may be impeached by a majority vote of the Senate
   (C) punishment for an impeached and guilty president is removal from office and disqualification to hold other offices
   (D) witnesses against the president must be questioned before the entire Senate
   (E) the House of Representatives must approve the Articles of Impeachment by a two-thirds vote

60. The Age of Jackson is noted for all of the following events EXCEPT

   (A) Jackson's refusal to accept the Supreme Court's decision concerning the land claims of the Cherokee Indian Tribe
   (B) the publication of the South Carolina "exposition and protest"
   (C) the veto of the bill rechartering the Second Bank of the United States
   (D) the meeting of the Hartford Convention
   (E) the passage of the Force Act

61. The purpose of the "gag rule" adopted by the U.S. Senate was to

   (A) encourage full participation in debate by all members of the Senate
   (B) control unlimited filibuster
   (C) limit debate on attempts to override presidential vetoes
   (D) prevent debate of abolitionist proposals
   (E) discourage criticism of U.S. foreign policy

62. "For upwards of half a century the republics of the Western Hemisphere have been working together to promote their common civilization under a system of peace. That venture, launched so hopefully fifty years ago (in 1889), has succeeded; the American family is today a great co-operative group facing a troubled world in serenity and calm . . ."

   To which of the following organizations is the author referring?

   (A) UNESCO
   (B) Pan-American Union
   (C) Contradora Group
   (D) League of Nations
   (E) NATO

63. The industrial revolution in the United States after the Civil War benefited from all of the following EXCEPT

   (A) the development of new business structures
   (B) a rapid increase in immigration
   (C) the abundance of natural resources
   (D) the expansion of the railroad network
   (E) federal regulation exercised by the Interstate Commerce Commission (ICC)

64. All of the following would be considered a victory for organized labor EXCEPT the

    (A) Taft-Hartley Act
    (B) Wisconsin Unemployment Insurance Law
    (C) establishment of a national minimum wage
    (D) Wagner Act
    (E) Anthracite Coal Strike of 1902

65. William Jennings Bryan's Cross of Gold speech addressed economic issues and helped him

    (A) be appointed Secretary of State
    (B) express his views on evolution at the Scopes Trial
    (C) gain support of Republican business leaders
    (D) win the Democratic Party presidential nomination
    (E) found the Populist Party

66. The fundamental thesis of Keynesian economics is that

    (A) the government should tax highly in times of inflation and the government should spend extensively in times of deflation
    (B) the government should keep "hands off" all economic activity
    (C) successful businessmen should run the government
    (D) the wealth of a nation is measured by the amount of gold it holds
    (E) the Federal Reserve Board should control economic policy

67. Which of the following events connected with the Civil Rights Movement of the post-World War II period first brought to national attention the issue of segregation?

    (A) The lunch counter sit-ins
    (B) The decision in *Brown v. Board of Education*
    (C) The assassination of Martin Luther King, Jr.
    (D) Montgomery, Alabama, bus boycott
    (E) The twenty-fourth Amendment (anti-poll tax) to the Constitution

68. Which of the following best describes the events of the Cuban Missile Crisis during John F. Kennedy's presidency?

    (A) The presence of Soviet missiles in Cuba had been known for several years.
    (B) The president of the United States precipitated the crisis.
    (C) Both sides displayed a sober approach and made concessions.
    (D) Nikita Khrushchev refused to accept a U.S. naval quarantine of Cuba.
    (E) Fidel Castro was forced to accept the missiles from the Soviets.

**IMPROVEMENTS IN AMERICAN HOMES**

**TOWN AND CITY HOMES**

| | WITH IMPROVEMENT | WITHOUT IMPROVEMENT |
|---|---|---|
| Running Water | | |
| Electric Lighting | | |
| Private Indoor Water Closet | | |
| Bathtub or Shower | | |
| Central Heating | | |

**FARM HOMES**

| | WITH IMPROVEMENT | WITHOUT IMPROVEMENT |
|---|---|---|
| Running Water | | |
| Electric Lighting | | |
| Private Indoor Water Closet | | |
| Bathtub or Shower | | |
| Central Heating | | |

Each unit represents 10 percent of all homes

*Source: Building America*

69. Considering the items chosen for comparison in the above chart and the quantitative relationship between farm and city homes, one would assume the information in the chart dates from the

    (A) post-World War II period
    (B) Populist Era
    (C) Civil War years
    (D) Great Depression
    (E) Jacksonian period

70. Which of the following was undertaken during the presidency of Ronald Reagan?

    (A) Negotiations to end the Iranian hostage crisis
    (B) Sending of troops to Iraq
    (C) Funding the Contras in Nicaragua
    (D) SALT negotiations
    (E) Recognition of the government of Communist China

71. *The Sovereignty and Goodness of God or Narrative of the Captivity and Restoration of Mrs. Mary Rowlandson* was

(A) an account of the Salem Witch Trials
(B) a sermon by Jonathan Edwards, which precipitated the Great Awakening
(C) an argument used by the Abolitionists in attacking slavery
(D) the most popular story about Native Americans written in the English colonies
(E) a statement in favor of temperance

72. Which of the following groups includes individuals both of whom supported the ratification of the U.S. Constitution by the states?

(A) Thomas Jefferson and Patrick Henry
(B) Alexander Hamilton and Patrick Henry
(C) James Madison and Alexander Hamilton
(D) Thomas Jefferson and Andrew Jackson
(E) James Madison and Daniel Webster

73. Which of the following accurately describes the president's cabinet?

(A) It is fully described in the United States Constitution.
(B) Members are not approved by the United States Senate.
(C) Members of the cabinet serve at the pleasure of the Chief Executive.
(D) The cabinet must meet every Thursday.
(E) The number of Executive Departments headed by cabinet officers can be changed by the president as he wishes.

Source: *Harper's Weekly,* March 9, 1912

74. The tall building in the middle of the photograph reflects the architectural style of

(A) English Georgian architects
(B) the Greek Revival movement
(C) Frank Lloyd Wright
(D) Henry Hobson Richardson
(E) Eero Saarinen

75. Which statement is correctly paired with its author/speaker?

    (A) John C. Calhoun—"The only thing we have to fear is fear itself"
    (B) Patrick Henry—"Our federal union, it must be preserved"
    (C) Thomas Jefferson—"We hold these truths to be self-evident"
    (D) Andrew Jackson—"Liberty and union, now and forever, one and inseparable"
    (E) Franklin D. Roosevelt—"Give me liberty or give me death"

76. All of the following major U.S. Supreme Court decisions are correctly paired with the decision handed down by the Supreme Court in the case named EXCEPT

    (A) *McCulloch v. Maryland*—upheld Maryland's right to tax the Bank of the United States
    (B) *Schechter v. United States*—declared the NIRA invalid, thus ending the first phase of the New Deal
    (C) *Plessy v. Ferguson*—upheld Louisiana law requiring segregated trains
    (D) *Munn v. Illinois*—upheld an Illinois law fixing maximum rates for grain storage
    (E) *Mueller v. Oregon*—upheld an Oregon law limiting the maximum working hours for women

77. "Now the trumpet summons us again—not a call to bear arms, though arms we need—not a call to battle, though embattled we are—but a call to bear the burden of a long twilight struggle, year in and year out, 'rejoicing in hope, patient in tribulation'—a struggle against the common enemies of man: tyranny, poverty, disease and war itself."

    Based on the above quotation, the author would most likely have supported all of the following EXCEPT

    (A) the War on Poverty
    (B) the Peace Corps
    (C) the establishment of Communist rule in Vietnam
    (D) Medicare
    (E) the SALT disarmament agreements

78. Which of the following American authors was LEAST concerned with social criticism of America?

    (A) John Steinbeck
    (B) Frank Norris
    (C) Ernest Hemingway
    (D) Upton Sinclair
    (E) Jacob Riis

79. All of the following occurred during the presidency of Jimmy Carter EXCEPT

    (A) the imposition by OPEC of its first oil embargo to force oil prices to rise

    (B) the seizure of Americans by Iranians and the holding of them as hostages in Teheran

    (C) the signing of the Camp David Peace Accord

    (D) the strong support for human rights and the Helsinki Accord by the president

    (E) the negotiation of a treaty with Panama that would return the Canal to Panama

80. The Treaty of Tordesillas signed in 1494 in Spain

    (A) divided the New World between the Spanish and the Portuguese

    (B) established Spanish as the official language of South America

    (C) resolved the French and Spanish claims to Hispaniola

    (D) determined the border between Florida and Georgia

    (E) ended warfare between the Spanish and the Aztecs

## SECTION II: FREE-RESPONSE

The free-response section consists of three parts. All students must answer the DBQ in Part A. Parts B and C include four essay questions and students must answer one question from each Part.

**You have a 15-minute reading period to read the documents and prepare your answer.**

## PART A: DOCUMENT-BASED ESSAY QUESTION (DBQ)

WRITING TIME: 45 MINUTES

**Directions:** The following question requires you to construct a coherent essay that integrates your interpretation of documents A–H **and** your knowledge of the period referred to in the question. In order to earn a high score you must cite key pieces of evidence from the documents and draw on your knowledge of the period.

1. Between 1900 and 1918 to what degree did the attitudes expressed in Supreme Court decisions concerning government regulation of business and working conditions reflect the attitudes of the people and the national political leaders? Why or why not were they in agreement?

### Document A

*Source:* **Oliver Wendell Holmes' Dissenting Opinion in U.S. Supreme Court Case *Lochner v. New York*, 1905. In this case the majority of the Court declared unconstitutional a New York State law limiting the number of hours bakers could work each week.**

It is settled by various decisions of this court that state constitutions and state laws may regulate life in many ways which we as legislators might think as injudicious or if you like as tyrannical.

The liberty of the citizen to do as he likes so long as he does not interfere with the liberty of others to do the same, which has been a shibboleth (accepted truth) for some well-known writers, is interfered with by school laws, by the Post Office, by every state or municipal institution which takes his money for purposes thought desirable, whether he likes it or not.

A constitution is not intended to embody a particular economic theory, whether of paternalism and the relation of the citizen to the State or of laissez-faire. It is made for people of fundamentally differing views.

## Document B

> **Source: John Spargo, The Cry of the Children, 1906**
>
> . . . in the spinning and carding rooms of cotton and woolen mills, where large numbers of children are employed, clouds of lint-dust fill the lungs and menace the health. The children have a distressing cough, caused by the irritation of the throat, and many are hoarse from the same cause. In bottle factories and other branches of glass manufacture, the atmosphere is constantly charged with microscopic particles of glass.
>
> The children who are employed in the manufacture of wall papers and poisonous paints suffer from slow poisoning. The naphtha fumes in the manufacture of rubber goods produce paralysis and premature decay.

## Document C

> *Source:* **United States Senator Nathan B. Scott of West Virginia, from a Speech in the U.S. Congress, 1906**
>
> . . . A gentleman by the name of Markham, writing a magazine article not long ago, said that he had visited the glasshouses and had seen children—boys and girls—with emaciated forms, with their eyes, as it were, protruding from their sockets, all due to overwork. He spoke of their little bodies being blistered by the hot furnaces, and a lot more of that kind of magazine stuff, for it is nothing but stuff.
>
> I have been engaged in the manufacture of glass for thirty-five years and if Mr. Markham had come to see my factory . . . (he) would not (have seen) anything like that which he described in his magazine article.
>
> . . . The glasshouse boy of today becomes the glass manufacturer of tomorrow.

## Document D

*Source:* **Library of Congress**

Young boy working in canning factory. Early 1900s.

## Document E

*Source:* **Majority opinion in Supreme Court *Mueller v. Oregon*, 1908. In this case the Court upheld an Oregon law limiting to ten a day the hours of labor for women employed in a laundry. Scientific, psychological, and sociological evidence was introduced by Louis B. Brandeis in winning the case.**

Constitutional questions are not settled by even a consensus of present public opinion, for it is the peculiar value of a written constitution that it places in unchanging form limitations upon legislative action, and thus gives a permanence and stability to popular government which otherwise would be lacking.

As argued in this case, the two sexes differ in structure of body, in the functions to be performed by each, in the amount of physical strength, in the capacity for long-continued labor, particularly when done standing, in the influence of vigorous health upon the future well-being of the race. This difference justifies a difference in legislation.

For these reasons the act in question is not in conflict with the federal Constitution as it respects the limitation of the hours of work done by a female in a laundry.

## Document F

*Source:* **Speeches by Woodrow Wilson, 1912 and 1913**

—We used to think in the old-fashioned days when life was very simple that all the government had to do was to put on a policeman's uniform, and say, "Now don't anybody hurt anybody else." We used to say that the ideal of government was for every man to be left alone and not be interfered with, except when he interfered with somebody else. But we are coming now to realize that life is so complicated that we are not dealing with the old conditions, and that the law has to step in and create new conditions under which we may live, the conditions which will make it tolerable for us to live.

—We have been proud of our industrial achievements, but we have not hitherto stopped, thoughtfully enough to count . . . the fearful physical and spiritual cost to the men and women and children upon whom the dead weight and burden of it all has fallen pitilessly the years through.

## Document G

*Source:* **Speeches by Theodore Roosevelt, 1910 and 1912**

The American people are right in demanding that new nationalism, without which we cannot hope to deal with new problems. . . . This new nationalism regards the executive power as the steward of the public welfare. It demands of the judiciary that it should be interested primarily in human welfare rather than in property, just as it demands that the representative body shall represent all of the people rather than any one class or section of people. . . .

One of the fundamental necessities of a representative government such as ours is to make certain that the men to whom people delegate their power shall serve the people by whom they are elected, and not the special interests . . . The object of government is the welfare of the people . . .

## Document H

*Source:* **Majority opinion in U.S. Supreme Court [*Hammer v. Dagenhart*], 1918. In this case the Court declared unconstitutional the Keating-Owen Child Labor Act.**

. . . In the present case . . . The Act, in effect, does not regulate transportation among the states, but aims to standardize the ages at which children may be employed in mining and manufacturing within the states.

That there should be limitations upon the right to employ children in the mines and factories in the interest of their own and the public welfare, all will admit . . . [However,] in our view, the necessary effect of this Act is, . . ., to regulate the hours of labor of children . . ., [which is] a purely state authority . . . The Act . . . is repugnant to the Constitution. It not only transcends the authority delegated to Congress over commerce, but also exerts a power as to a purely local matter to which the federal authority does not extend.

# SECTION II: FREE-RESPONSE QUESTIONS 2–5

## ESSAY QUESTIONS

WRITING TIME: 70 MINUTES

> **Directions:** You are to answer *two* of the following questions—one from Part B and one from Part C. Carefully choose the question that you are best prepared to answer. Cite relevant historical evidence in support of your generalizations and present your arguments clearly and logically. When you finish writing, check your work if time permits. Make certain to number your answer as the question is numbered below. You should write your answer in pen.

**Part B:** Choose ONE question from Part B. It is suggested that you spend 5 minutes organizing your answer and 30 minutes writing it.

2. "Events on the frontier between 1763 and 1788 and the development of government policies in response to them were more significant for the development of the United States than the events that took place in the settled areas of the eastern seaboard between 1763 and 1788."

   Evaluate this statement.

3. "American history reveals that government by the majority can be divisive and that the views of the minority must be considered in executing policy."

   Assess the validity of this statement for the period 1793–1812.

**Part C:** Choose ONE question from Part C. It is suggested that you spend 5 minutes organizing your answer and 30 minutes writing it.

4. In what ways was the change in the political control of the federal government a result of economic issues in TWO of the following presidential elections?

   McKinley's defeat of Bryan in 1896
   Wilson's defeat of Taft in 1912
   Roosevelt's defeat of Hoover in 1932
   Reagan's defeat of Carter in 1980

5. Compare and contrast the issues that led to reform and the reforms that were introduced in TWO of the following periods.

   The Jacksonian Era
   The New Deal period
   The Kennedy/Johnson years

End of Examination

At the end of the exam you will be directed to circle on the back of your essay answer booklet the numbers of the two questions you answered.

## Pretest Analysis

Time Periods and Content Analysis for Multiple-Choice Questions when Practice Test A is used as a **Pretest**.

**Directions:** The questions are presented in the exam in chronological groupings. The question numbers are listed below under their respective time periods. After each number, letters are listed, indicating the general content area for that question.

**E = economic**
**F = foreign policy and diplomatic policy**
**P = political**
**S = social and cultural**
**Many questions cover several content areas.**

Put a check mark after each number where you had the correct answer. The degree of difficulty increases but, of course, difficulty is a personal matter depending on what you studied and what interests you. Look over the content areas and time periods where you had incorrect answers. These are the areas of weakness and the areas you should concentrate on in your study.

### Colonial Period

| Question # | Content | Check if Correct |
|---|---|---|
| 1 | P/E | |
| 2 | P | |
| 13 | S | |
| 14 | S | |
| 23 | E/F | |
| 24 | P | |
| 35 | S | |
| 36 | E | |
| 46 | P/S | |
| 47 | P/S | |
| 58 | P/F | |
| 59 | P | |
| 71 | S | |
| 72 | P | |
| 80 | F | |

## 19th Century

| Question # | Content | Check if Correct |
|---|---|---|
| 3 | S/P | |
| 4 | E | |
| 5 | S | |
| 6 | P | |
| 7 | F | |
| 8 | E/S | |
| 15 | P | |
| 16 | S | |
| 17 | P | |
| 18 | F/P | |
| 25 | E | |
| 26 | P | |
| 27 | P/S | |
| 28 | E | |
| 29 | S/E | |
| 37 | S | |
| 38 | F | |
| 39 | S | |
| 40 | P/S | |
| 41 | F/E | |
| 48 | P/S | |
| 49 | P | |
| 50 | P | |
| 51 | S | |
| 52 | S | |
| 60 | P/S | |
| 61 | P/S | |
| 62 | F | |
| 63 | S | |
| 64 | E | |
| 73 | P | |
| 74 | S | |
| 75 | P/S | |
| 76 | S/P | |

## 20th Century

| Question # | Content | Check if Correct |
|---|---|---|
| 9 | P/F | |
| 10 | P | |
| 11 | P/E | |
| 12 | P | |
| 19 | S | |
| 20 | S/P | |
| 21 | P/S | |
| 22 | F | |
| 30 | S | |
| 31 | F/P | |
| 32 | P/S | |
| 33 | E | |
| 34 | P/S | |
| 42 | E/S | |
| 43 | S | |
| 44 | P | |
| 45 | S | |
| 54 | P | |
| 55 | P | |
| 56 | E/P | |
| 57 | S/P | |
| 65 | E/P | |
| 66 | E | |
| 67 | S/P | |
| 68 | F | |
| 69 | E/S | |
| 70 | F | |
| 77 | S/P | |
| 78 | S | |
| 79 | P/E | |

# ANSWER EXPLANATIONS FOR PRACTICE TEST A

In this section you will find answers and answer explanations for the 80 multiple-choice questions of the practice test. The explanations of the multiple-choice questions indicate which answer is most correct and, in most cases, why the other choices should be eliminated. By reading all 80 statements, you will get a quick summary of the highlights of United States history.

| | | | |
|---|---|---|---|
| 1. **(A)** | 21. **(D)** | 41. **(C)** | 61. **(D)** |
| 2. **(C)** | 22. **(D)** | 42. **(B)** | 62. **(B)** |
| 3. **(D)** | 23. **(D)** | 43. **(D)** | 63. **(E)** |
| 4. **(B)** | 24. **(C)** | 44. **(B)** | 64. **(A)** |
| 5. **(D)** | 25. **(B)** | 45. **(E)** | 65. **(D)** |
| 6. **(B)** | 26. **(E)** | 46. **(B)** | 66. **(A)** |
| 7. **(E)** | 27. **(C)** | 47. **(D)** | 67. **(B)** |
| 8. **(D)** | 28. **(B)** | 48. **(C)** | 68. **(C)** |
| 9. **(B)** | 29. **(E)** | 49. **(E)** | 69. **(D)** |
| 10. **(A)** | 30. **(A)** | 50. **(C)** | 70. **(C)** |
| 11. **(D)** | 31. **(D)** | 51. **(B)** | 71. **(D)** |
| 12. **(B)** | 32. **(B)** | 52. **(D)** | 72. **(C)** |
| 13. **(C)** | 33. **(D)** | 53. **(C)** | 73. **(C)** |
| 14. **(B)** | 34. **(C)** | 54. **(C)** | 74. **(D)** |
| 15. **(C)** | 35. **(B)** | 55. **(D)** | 75. **(C)** |
| 16. **(B)** | 36. **(C)** | 56. **(B)** | 76. **(A)** |
| 17. **(C)** | 37. **(D)** | 57. **(E)** | 77. **(C)** |
| 18. **(D)** | 38. **(D)** | 58. **(A)** | 78. **(C)** |
| 19. **(B)** | 39. **(D)** | 59. **(C)** | 79. **(A)** |
| 20. **(E)** | 40. **(A)** | 60. **(D)** | 80. **(A)** |

## Multiple-Choice Answers Explained

1. **(A)** New York was first settled by the Dutch. Delaware was first settled by Swedes, Pennsylvania by the English, Jamaica by the Spanish, and Canada by the French.

2. **(C)** The quotation from the Constitution is a clear example of checks and balances.

3. **(D)** The presidential years of James Monroe have often been referred to as the *Era of Good Feeling*. The Federalists, the opposition political party, had been badly weakened by its failure to support the War of 1812. Thus, President Monroe had little resistance to his measures, something that made his presidency appear as a period of "good feeling."

4. **(B)** The main purpose of Henry Clay's American System was to develop an interdependent economic system tying the East, West, and South together. He offered it after the Era of Good Feeling at a time when sectionalism was beginning to grow. The other four choices had nothing to do with his American System.

5. **(D)** The Transcendentalist writers of New England, of whom Ralph Waldo Emerson is the most noteworthy, found their major source of truth and inspiration in nature. The writers—centered in Concord, Massachusetts, in the 1830s and 1840s—are considered to have begun the first truly American philosophical movement, although this movement had close connections with the Romantic Movement in England.

6. **(B)** After the capture of Vicksburg in the West, the Confederacy was split in half. The other four choices are important battles of the Civil War in the East.

7. **(E)** Wilson announced his Fourteen Points as a possible formula for peace at the end of World War I. He was most concerned about establishing a League of Nations, as suggested in Point XIV. The League was incorporated into the Treaty of Versailles, and the Treaty was rejected by the Senate. The other points are important ones, but Wilson was more prepared to compromise on them than on the League. He believed that if there was a League, other issues could be resolved by it before war broke out.

8. **(D)** Air mail service was not developed until the 20th century. The other four choices were developed in the 19th century or earlier.

9. **(B)** Woodrow Wilson would most likely have commented on the lost opportunity of the United States to take world leadership. He had hoped the United States would take the lead in the League of Nations after World War I, and this was rejected. The idea expressed was too early for the period of Theodore Roosevelt, who was more an American nationalist than an internationalist. John F. Kennedy and Lyndon B. Johnson both rose to importance as political leaders after World War II, when America had already taken on world leadership. One might think that Franklin Roosevelt was the author, but during his administration he slowly moved the United States into a position of leadership and saw the United States through the "tragedy" of World War II.

10. **(A)** The cartoon from the *World Telegram* of August 11, 1934, clearly suggests that the Republican Party, represented as the old man with the letters G.O.P. (Grand Old Party) on his vest, has no effective solution to the Great Depression. The only ideas offered are those of a return to the programs of 1929, which were in effect under President Hoover at the time of the "great crash." It might appear that the G.O.P. is being robbed by Wall Street and Rugged Individualism, but these two figures represent the G.O.P.'s major support. They are holding on to the G.O.P. for support; they are not robbing him. To be able to interpret this cartoon, one needs an understanding of the economic situation in the United States from 1929 to 1934 and to know that G.O.P. refers to the Republican Party.

11. **(D)** A careful reading of the quotation will show that the author suggests that the United States continues to be in a depression, that a veto of the tax cut would be harmful to the nation, that other nations are heavily affected by the U.S. economy, and that the unemployment rate in the country is high. The issue under discussion is a tax cut to create economic recovery at a time of high

unemployment. The author does not suggest that the political impact of the policy should be the sole guide in determining policy.

12. **(B)** The person usually given credit for the passage of the Civil Rights Act of 1964 is Lyndon Baines Johnson. In 1964 he was president of the United States. John F. Kennedy had been in favor of civil rights legislation, but couldn't get it through Congress. With the impact Kennedy's assassination had on the country, President Johnson was able to get passed not only the Civil Rights Act of 1964 but many of the things President Kennedy believed in. African Americans Adam Clayton Powell, formerly an important member of the House of Representatives, and Andrew Young, U.S. Ambassador to the United Nations under President Carter, were not involved with the congressional passage of the Civil Rights Act of 1964. George Wallace, Governor of Alabama, opposed civil rights legislation in the 1960s.

13. **(C)** The traditional interpretation of the founding of the Plymouth Bay Colony is that it was founded *primarily* for religious purposes. To some degree, the reasons were also political, social, cultural, and economic, but the religious were the most important ones.

14. **(B)** Shays' Rebellion occurred in western Massachusetts in 1786 under the government of the Articles of Confederation. It was one of the events that led to the calling of the Constitutional Convention in 1787. The Stamp Act was repealed in 1766, Daniel Boone took his first trip to Kentucky in 1767, and the Boston Massacre occurred in 1770, all before independence was declared. The Whiskey Rebellion took place in western Pennsylvania during Washington's first term as president under the Constitution. Farmers protesting a tax on whiskey were crushed by the new federal government.

15. **(C)** The XYZ Affair occurred during John Adams's administration. The other events occurred during Washington's administration. The XYZ Affair of 1797 involved a demand by French ministers for a large bribe from U.S. representatives who were in France seeking to improve relations between the two countries. Relations with France were strained as a result of Jay's Treaty and French interference with U.S. trade. Secretary of State John Jay negotiated the Jay treaty with the English in 1795. The treaty resolved issues left over from the Revolution. John Adams was elected to succeed Washington while Washington was still president. Jefferson resigned in part because his views on the Bank of the United States were rejected while Hamilton's views were accepted by Washington.

16. **(B)** The opening of the Erie Canal in 1825, providing an east-west water route through northern New York state, had an important effect on the settlement of the West, since it provided an easy water route west of the New England and New York areas. The canal increased the settlement in the Northwest territories greatly. The other events had limited impact on the pattern of western settlement.

17. **(C)** From the end of Reconstruction in 1877 to the outbreak of World War I in 1914, fundamental changes in the American system were brought about by federal legislation in all areas mentioned except civil rights.

18. **(D)** The acquisition of Pago Pago by a treaty negotiated with the chiefs of the island of Tutuila in the Samoan Islands had nothing to do with the U.S. entry into the Spanish-American War. The other choices are often given as reasons for the U.S. entry into the Spanish-American War, the sinking of the battleship *Maine* being considered the final justification for war.

19. **(B)** For this question, you need to be able to read the chart and to understand the key. The only statement that is correct is the one about more Irish coming to America in 1850–1855 than in 1885–1890.

20. **(E)** The Palmer Raids, led by the attorney general, reflected the anti-communist hysteria of the post–World War I period. The raids created a climate of opinion similar to that created by Senator Joseph McCarthy in the 1950s.

21. **(D)** The Good Neighbor Policy was the name for Roosevelt's foreign policy initiative in Central and South America. The other four choices were offered as solutions to the problems of the Great Depression. The WPA (Work Progress Administration), the AAA (Agricultural Adjustment Act), and the NRA (National Recovery Act) were part of Roosevelt's solution to the problems of the Great Depression. The "Share the Wealth" proposal was offered in opposition to Roosevelt's ideas.

22. **(D)** The areas colored black on the map represent the greatest extent of Nazi control in World War II. The names of the countries on the map should help you to identify what the black represents. The name of the city of Stalingrad may be the best clue. It was at Stalingrad that the Russians finally stopped the German advance. This question reflects how United States history became world history as the 20th century moved along. The Nazi conquests in Europe greatly affected the foreign policy of the United States and economic conditions at home.

23. **(D)** The American colonists, especially merchants from Newport and Bristol, Rhode Island, and some from Boston and Salem, Massachusetts; Providence, Rhode Island; Portsmouth, New Hampshire; and New London, Connecticut, all participated in the profitable slave trade along with many English merchants. The other statements are all true concerning the slave trade in the 18th century.

24. **(C)** Under the Articles of Confederation, the states exercised sovereignty. This was the greatest weakness of the Articles of Confederation because the central government was unable to make and enforce decisions for all of the states.

25. **(B)** Although all the choices are important for the development of factories, it was because of abundant water power that the earliest factories in the United States were located in New England. They were founded at a time when water

power was used to drive the machinery. As farming declined in northern New England with the opening of the West, and as factories grew, especially along the Merrimack River (Lowell, Manchester), many young women born on the farms found jobs in the factories.

26. **(E)** Jefferson is often considered a states' rights supporter and strict constructionist. As president, however, he often acted beyond the authority strictly given to the president in the Constitution. During his presidency, he undertook the first four events mentioned. All stretched the power of the presidency and the Constitution, especially the purchase of Louisiana. Although often a supporter of the French, he did not support the XYZ Affair.

27. **(C)** All five choices are acts passed by the U.S. Congress dealing with land. The Land Act of 1796 called for rectangular survey and sale of land at public auction at a minimum price of two dollars an acre. Townships were set at six square miles each, and they were subdivided into sections. The smallest section one could purchase under the act was 640 acres.

28. **(B)** The Social Security Act of 1935, passed as part of the New Deal, provided retirement pensions and unemployment payments. While it provided an income for the old, disabled, and unemployed, its purpose was not to control the money supply. The other four choices, the Specie Circular of 1836, the Sherman Silver Purchase Act of 1890, the Federal Reserve Act of 1913, and the establishment of the Commodity Dollar in 1933, all had as their purpose the control of the money supply in some way.

29. **(E)** If you carefully study the cartoon from *Harper's Weekly* of September 1, 1888, you can tell that the well-dressed gentleman was trying to prevent the law, as represented by the policeman, from interfering. The gentleman does not believe the police officer should interfere, but the cartoonist suggests he is prepared to do so by both the statement under the cartoon in which the well-dressed man wants to keep the police out and by the partially raised billy club ready for use. The individual being robbed in the American market is competition, and he is being robbed by American industries, which are organized as trusts. The American market is advertised as operating under freedom and equality.

30. **(A)** The American historian Frederick Jackson Turner, in his thesis on the influence of the frontier on America, stated all four points except the idea that "'The complex European life' had continual impact on America." In his article, Turner emphasized the uniqueness of America and the importance of the frontier in developing the American.

31. **(D)** The attempt to impeach Chief Justice of the U.S. Supreme Court Earl Warren during the 1950s related to domestic issues and not to issues of foreign policy. Therefore, it would not be considered part of the Cold War. The other four events involved international conflicts between the United States and its allies and the communist nations under the leadership of the Soviet Union.

32. **(B)** President Lyndon Johnson withdrew from the presidential race after his defeat in the New Hampshire primary in 1968. His withdrawal was attributed to the public's rejection of his policy in Vietnam. President Johnson had expanded America's commitment to that nation. U.S. involvement began under President Eisenhower with his support of the French in that country. U.S. forces attacked both Cambodia and Laos outside the Vietnam borders and also bombed North Vietnam. The Gulf of Tonkin Resolution authorized retaliation by President Johnson but was not a declaration of war and did not legalize the conflict internationally. One of the identifying features of the Vietnam War was the inability to identify the enemy. There were no clear battle lines.

33. **(D)** The economic program known as Reaganomics followed the theory of supply-side economics. It called first for tax cuts, which were to stimulate the economy so no revenue would be lost to the government. Reaganomics also included increased military expenditures and reduced expenditures for social services. The program resulted in unplanned massive increases in the federal debt since the economy did not respond as anticipated and the Congress did not cut social services. No cabinet-level departments were eliminated.

34. **(C)** President Clinton campaigned for Democrats in the 1994 Congressional elections, although some candidates preferred that he did not because of his lack of popularity at that time. The other four selections are true about the 1994 election.

35. **(B)** The quotation is taken from the Rhode Island colonial charter. The founders of Rhode Island were particularly concerned about both civil and religious rights. King James I believed in the divine right of kings, which is not upheld by this quotation; the Albany Plan of Union was proposed by Benjamin Franklin as the political, not religious, framework for colonial unity at the time of the French and Indian War; the trial of Peter Zenger is famous for establishing a free press and not religious liberty; and the Mayflower Compact was an oath taken by the Pilgrims to support each other and is often considered the precedent for the Constitution, a political framework of government.

36. **(C)** The statement is a definition of mercantilism. Check the Glossary for definitions of the other terms.

37. **(D)** The statement is from the Seneca Falls Convention which was held in New York State in 1848, under the leadership of Lucretia Mott and Elizabeth Cady Stanton. If you cannot identify this statement and its date, you would know it would not have been made after 1919 because in that year the 19th Amendment to the Constitution, which provided for women's suffrage, was declared ratified. The last paragraph in the statement is calling for suffrage for women and would not have been needed after 1919.

38. **(D)** The passage states the important points found in the Monroe Doctrine of 1823 that the American continents are not open for colonization and that the nations on the continents are free and independent states. Theodore Roosevelt interpreted the Monroe Doctrine to allow for the United States' intervention to maintain order in the Americas and to collect debts owed other nations. This

concept of America acting either on behalf of its own nationals or the other nations of the world to collect debts and maintain order has been called the Roosevelt Corollary to the Monroe Doctrine. It is a stretching of the original doctrine and its concept as presented in the passage. The other doctrines do not relate to the Americas so the quote would not relate to them.

39. (**D**) All of the movements are correctly linked with their leaders except for education. Although a university is named after him, Brigham Young is noted as the leader of the Mormons, not of educational reform. Horace Mann, Henry Barnard, Elizabeth Peabody, and Mary Lyon are some noted leaders of educational reform in the pre-Civil War period.

40. (**A**) The Pendleton Act (Civil Service Act of 1883) was passed as a response to the assassination of President Garfield. The act set up a three-person Civil Service Commission with the responsibility of administering competitive examinations so that federal office holders could be appointed on a merit basis. President Garfield had been assassinated by Charles Guiteau, who was a disappointed office seeker and mentally unstable.

41. (**C**) In spite of Taft's replacement of Theodore Roosevelt's "Big Stick" policy with Dollar Diplomacy, the United States continued to intervene militarily in the Caribbean (Cuba and Santo Domingo) and in Latin America (Nicaragua and Honduras). The other statements are all true concerning the concept of Dollar Diplomacy. Investments were encouraged in the Far East, especially China, and in Latin America. Because the policy was to secure a peace through business investment, less money was spent on military defense. Wilson continued the policy although philosophically he opposed it.

42. (**B**) The statement reflects the attitude toward wealth held by Andrew Carnegie. He discussed his ideas in a speech known as the *Gospel of Wealth*.

43. (**D**) Urban areas did not support Prohibition. The other four choices are characteristic of the Prohibition Era of the 1920s.

44. (**B**) The plan that Franklin D. Roosevelt introduced to force the Supreme Court to change its decisions and begin to accept the New Deal program consisted of a suggestion that the Court be increased in size. The Constitution gives to Congress the power to set the number of judges on the Court. The plan is often referred to as the Court Packing Plan. The famous "My dog Fala" speech was a humorous speech given by Roosevelt mocking the Republicans who were attacking not only his plans and policies but his family and even his dog. This was part of the presidential campaign of 1940. The president has no power to order impeachment proceedings, the president did not ignore the Court decisions but tried to get them reversed, and he did not call on the American people to elect only Democrats to Congress as a response to the decisions by the Supreme Court.

45. (**E**) All of the items except E—a major economic recession with high unemployment for all Americans—were characteristic of the period in U.S. society

between the end of World War II and the election of President John F. Kennedy. The Supreme Court knocked down segregation in the public schools in the famous *Brown v. Board of Education* decision in 1954. The McCarthy era in the late 1940s and early 1950s was another Red Scare. The start of rock and roll symbolized by Elvis Presley and the introduction of other types of popular music has changed American society considerably. Finally, the 1950s has often been characterized by historians as a period of conformity and uncritical support of government policies, a matter that is now questioned by some historians, citing *Brown v. Board of Education* and many other social developments.

46. **(B)** This is a simple chronological question dealing with a series of events. It is testing a cause-and-effect relationship. You should be familiar with all of these events involving the writing of the Constitution. The first event was the rejection of the Articles of Confederation. The last event was the Connecticut Compromise which reconciled ideas from the Virginia and New Jersey Plans. Washington was elected chair as the Convention opened.

47. **(D)** A "loose constructionist" believes that the U.S. Constitution should not be read strictly and that when you find a power that is implied by the wording of the Constitution, that power is a legitimate power for the government to exercise. The four other choices all share the concept of "strict construction" under which the Constitution must be read literally and no extension of powers made.

48. **(C)** The term *impressment* means to take by force for public service, especially naval service. As used by the United States in the period before the Revolutionary War of 1812, the term referred to the British practice of forcing American sailors into service on British warships. This British practice was one of the causes of that war.

49. **(E)** The only thing that can clearly be proven by the bar graph is that Lincoln and Wilson were both minority presidents according to popular vote, but received a majority of votes in the electoral college. The chart cannot prove that the electoral college is unjust, although many may feel that is true. Nor can it prove that Bell was a better candidate than Douglas, or that someone running in 1912 would have done as well if he had run in 1860. Finally, the chart cannot prove that popular candidates cannot win in the electoral college.

50. **(C)** The Joint Electoral Commission Report on the disputed election of 1876 between Samuel J. Tilden and Rutherford B. Hayes was accepted in 1877, making Hayes president. As part of the report, Republicans promised to withdraw federal troops from the South and appoint at least one Southerner to the cabinet. This has traditionally been interpreted to indicate the end of the political Reconstruction of the South. The South never welcomed military occupation. The other three choices all deal with post-Civil War matters but do not mark the end of Reconstruction.

51. **(B)** In the cartoon, *The Irrepressible Independent,* by W. A. Rogers, the Spoils System referred to on the Tammany booth indicates the political system of rewarding supporters with appointed offices. Tammany was a political machine that ran New York City and was noted for its system of rewarding its workers with political jobs. The other choices do not apply. This question is simply a case of knowing the definition of a political term.

52. **(D)** Helen Hunt Jackson's book *A Century of Dishonor* pricked the conscience of Americans and led to a new approach to Native Americans that was incorporated in the Dawes Severalty Act of 1887. The goal of the act was to assimilate Native Americans into the mainstream of American life by making them citizens. The other four choices were among the causes of the intense antagonisms between the Native Americans and the U.S. government that led to warfare between the two.

53. **(C)** These five events all relate to the Civil War. The event that occurred first is Lincoln's first election to the presidency in November of 1860. South Carolina seceded at the end of the year; Fort Sumter was fired upon in 1861, beginning the military activity. The Emancipation Proclamation, which freed slaves in states still in rebellion against the United States, was a wartime measure announced in 1862 and it went into effect in 1863. West Virginia was admitted to the Union as a state on June 20, 1863. (West Virginia consisted of the 50 western counties of Virginia that had refused to acknowledge the secession of Virginia from the Union.)

54. **(C)** In the cartoon from the *Saturday Evening Post* of June 6, 1914, the main point the cartoonist is making is that Theodore Roosevelt and Woodrow Wilson are again seeking popular support for their political reform programs. Roosevelt ran for president on the "Bull Moose" ticket in 1912, and in doing so split the Republican Party, which renominated President Taft. Eugene V. Debs ran as a Socialist. With these three candidates in the field, Woodrow Wilson, the candidate of the Democratic Party, was able to win, while the New Nationalism was the reform program advocated by Roosevelt, and the New Freedom was the reform program advocated by Wilson. The cartoon is not making the point that political candidates must have a named program. Many do, as did Theodore Roosevelt and Woodrow Wilson, but many do not.

55. **(D)** The Creel Committee organized during World War I by the U.S. government had propaganda as its purpose. During the war, the government was concerned about the four other issues, but other committees and commissions took care of those matters.

56. **(B)** Although all five choices present New Deal legislation, the only one dealing with banking is the Federal Deposit Insurance Corporation.

57. **(E)** The concepts expressed in the passage are those of isolationism and nationalism. Isolationism calls for separation of America from other nations. Nationalism contains the idea that your country is the best, and its sovereign will should not be compromised in any way by following other nations. The

writer is certainly in favor of freedom, but there is less emphasis on that concept than upon isolationism. Christianity, sovereignty, and socialism are irrelevant to the quotation.

58. **(A)** In the quotation the most important argument being presented is that the British Parliament has no authority to compel the obedience of any law that forces them to supply goods. The concern is that if Parliament can force the colonists to supply goods to troops, then they can force the colonists to do everything—pay taxes, clothe and house troops—and the colonists rebelled against this concept.

59. **(C)** The Constitution makes no provision about how the facts in an impeachment case are to be gathered or where or what witnesses are to be heard. The Senate and House can make their own rules on these matters. The House can approve Articles of Impeachment by a majority vote, but it takes a vote of two-thirds of the Senate to find an impeached individual guilty. If found guilty, according to the Constitution, the judgment against the president "shall not extend further than to removal from office and disqualification to hold and enjoy an Office of Honor, Trust or Profit under the United States." Article I, Section 3.

60. **(D)** Jackson refused to accept the Supreme Court decision, which led to the Cherokee Trail of Tears. The South Carolina "exposition and protest" was written but not signed by Calhoun. It supported the South Carolina legislature's resolutions declaring the Tariff of Abominations unconstitutional, unjust, and oppressive to the interest of the South. The Tariff of Abominations, passed in 1828, supported the protective concept. It was a political move by Jackson's supporters to undercut President J. Q. Adams and work for the election of Jackson. This was one step in the slow alienation of South Carolina from the Union, which culminated in secession in 1860. The Force Act was Jackson's response to the "exposition and protest." A major issue of Jackson's presidency was the rechartering of the Second Bank of the United States, which he vetoed. The Hartford Convention was called to protest the War of 1812.

61. **(D)** The "gag rule" was adopted by the U.S. Senate in 1836 to prevent debate of abolitionist proposals requesting the ending of slavery. The rule provided a complicated formula by which abolitionists could petition the Senate, but the petition would not be debated.

62. **(B)** The author of the quotation is referring to the Pan-American Union, the oldest and most successful association of sovereign governments in the world, which is now known as the Organization of American States (OAS). Its members are the nations of North and South America. The League of Nations was part of the Treaty of Versailles. NATO was formed after World War II in Europe. The Contradora Group, the most recent, was formed in 1985 to bring peace to Nicaragua and end the fighting between the Contras and the Sandinista government of Nicaragua. UNESCO is an operating arm of the United Nations.

63. **(E)** The first four answers, new business structures such as trusts, increased immigration, abundant resources, and expanding railroads all benefited the industrial revolution in the post-Civil War United States. The Interstate Commerce Commission (ICC) was meant to regulate industry for the benefit of the public, not industry.

64. **(A)** The Taft-Hartley Act of 1947 banned the closed shop, permitted employers to sue unions for broken contracts, required unions to abide by a 60-day "cooling-off period" as part of strike procedures, required unions to make public their financial statements, forced union leaders to sign a non-communist oath, and forbade unions to support political campaigns with monetary contributions. Because of these features, the act is not considered a victory for organized labor. The other four choices are. Wisconsin passed one of the first unemployment insurance laws in the country that helped workers who lost jobs or were injured; the establishment of a national minimum wage law helped increase workers' wages; the Anthracite Strike of 1902 was settled by Theodore Roosevelt in favor of the workers, using the authority of the federal government to support labor; and the Wagner Act of 1935 was one of the highlights of the New Deal labor legislation. It defined unfair labor practices on the employers' part and upheld the right of employees to join unions and to bargain collectively.

65. **(D)** William Jennings Bryan's Cross of Gold speech helped gain him the Democratic Party presidential nomination. After Bryan ran for president three times, Wilson appointed him Secretary of State, and he did testify at the Scopes Trial, but these events happened many years later. The Populists nominated him for president, but he was not a founder of the party, and Republicans never supported his views on free and unlimited coinage of silver.

66. **(A)** Keynes developed his economic theories in the post-World War I period, and they have had a profound impact on Western society since then. The general concept is that the government should interfere in the business cycle to counteract the highs and lows of inflation and deflation. To smooth out the extremes of the business cycle, the government should tax highly in times of inflation and should spend extensively in times of deflation. In theory, the high taxes will cut down the rate of inflation, and the government spending in times of deflation would create jobs and counterbalance the deflationary cycle. The government has found it much easier to spend extensively in deflationary times than it has to tax highly in times of inflation. The other choices present other economic theories. Laissez-faire economics believes that government should keep hands off all economic activity. Social Darwinists believe successful individuals who have proven they have the ability to survive, such as business leaders, should run the government. Under mercantilist economic theory the wealth of a nation is measured by the amount of gold it holds. The Federal Reserve Board sets the interest rates banks must pay to borrow money from the Federal Reserve Bank, which in theory provides some control over inflation. It

became a very popular approach to controlling inflation under Federal Reserve chairman Greenspan at the end of the 20th century and the start of the 21st.

67. **(B)** The decision in the *Brown v. Board of Education* case came in 1954. The other events in the Civil Rights Movement of the post-World War II period occurred after that date. While there had been some civil rights changes under Franklin Roosevelt and Truman involving the federal government and the armed forces, they are not given as choices. Of those given, the first event was the decision in the *Brown v. Board of Education* case which brought the issue of segregation to national attention.

68. **(C)** Both sides did make concessions during the Cuban Missile Crisis that averted a move to World War III. Both Kennedy and Khrushchev said this in reflecting upon the crisis.

69. **(D)** The chart from *Building America* dates from the Great Depression of the early 1930s. Electric lighting proves a particularly helpful clue for dating the chart. Electric lighting was not developed until the 1870s, with Philadelphia getting the first electric street lights in 1878. It had not spread widely by the time of the Populist Era in the 1890s. The New Deal through REA (Rural Electrification Administration) worked hard to bring electric power to rural areas, and it succeeded. Therefore, by the post-World War II period, there would be much more electric lighting in farm homes than is indicated by the chart. The Civil War years were the first half of the decade of the 1860s, and the Jacksonian period centered on the two terms of President Andrew Jackson, 1829–1837, both prior to the development of electric lighting.

70. **(C)** During the presidency of Ronald Reagan a plan was developed to fund the Contras in Nicaragua. It led to the Iran Contra Affair. Strategic Arms Limitation Talks (SALT) were held during Carter's presidency, and American hostages were seized after the overthrow of the Shah of Iran and the establishment of the Khomeini government. Negotiations for their release were started by Carter but the hostages were not released until the day of the inauguration of Carter's successor, Ronald Reagan. Reagan did not send troops to Iraq but supported Iraq in its war with Iran in the 1980s. Nixon is credited with the first recognition of Communist China by a U.S. president.

71. **(D)** *The Sovereignty and Goodness of God or Narrative of the Captivity and Restoration of Mrs. Mary Rowlandson* was the most popular story about Native Americans written in the English colonies. Captivity narratives telling of experiences as captives of Native Americans were very popular reading in colonial America.

72. **(C)** James Madison and Alexander Hamilton authored *The Federalist Papers* together with John Jay. They all supported the Constitution. Thomas Jefferson and Patrick Henry opposed the Constitution. Andrew Jackson and Daniel Webster were not involved in its ratification as they were members of the next generation.

73. **(C)** Changes in the number and function of executive departments must be approved by Congress, not the president alone, and no law states when the cabinet must meet. The president's cabinet is not described in the Constitution. However, the Constitution states that members of the executive branch should be appointed by the president and confirmed by the Senate. During President Andrew Johnson's administration, the Senate tried to make this constitutional provision also apply to the firing of cabinet members. This was rejected and the idea that members of the executive branch serve at the pleasure of the chief executive—the president—was reestablished and remains in force. So C is the correct answer.

74. **(D)** The office building in the center of the photograph from *Harper's Weekly*, March 9, 1912, shows the influence during the last quarter of the 19th century of the outstanding American architect, Henry Hobson Richardson. Richardson was strongly influenced by the Romanesque architecture of southern France. He is known for his use of Romanesque elements (one being the arch) and for imaginative treatment of ornament, both of which can be seen in this photograph.

Frank Lloyd Wright's work is characterized as natural. He often blended his houses into the natural surroundings and used local materials. He was deeply concerned about the materials used and about the functional qualities of his buildings. He is considered by many to be the outstanding American architect of the first half of the 20th century, with a strong influence on many others.

Eero Saarinen is remembered for his imaginative qualities, as seen in the residential colleges at Yale, which remind one of Italian hill towns. He, too, was concerned with structure and function. He is remembered as one of the outstanding mid-20th-century American architects.

Buildings in the Greek Revival style of architecture incorporate many elements of classical Greek temples. It became the style used in public buildings and homes after the establishment of the new federal government. Columns with Doric, Corinthian, or Ionic capitals; friezes and carvings with egg and dart designs; and porticoes with columns two stories high characterize this architecture.

The Georgian style was developed in England in the 18th century during the reigns of the first three Georges. In the colonies the finest public buildings, such as those at Williamsburg, the homes of wealthy colonists in Boston, Philadelphia, and Charleston, and plantation homes such as Westover in Virginia were built in the Georgian style. These constructions are all characterized by balance and symmetry and a strong emphasis on the horizontal line. In many cases, there are pediments or decorative devices above the windows and pilasters and pediments beside and above the doors.

75. **(C)** These are all famous quotes from U.S. history. The correct answer is C—Jefferson wrote this in the Declaration of Independence. The quote "Liberty and union, now and forever, one and inseparable," was said by Daniel Webster, not Andrew Jackson, who did say "Our federal union, it must be preserved." Calhoun was a states' rights advocate. His famous quotation is "The union, next to our liberty, the most dear." Patrick Henry, speaking about the rebellion against England, said, "Give me liberty or give me death." Franklin Roosevelt,

speaking about the Great Depression, stated, "The only thing we have to fear is fear itself."

76. **(A)** The last four choices correctly link the case with the decision reached. *McCulloch v. Maryland* denied the right of the state of Maryland to tax the Bank of the United States. In this famous case of 1819, Chief Justice John Marshall established the concept of loose construction of the Constitution. Although the Constitution does not give Congress the power to establish a bank, the power, according to Marshall, is implied. He went on to say that no state could tax an organ (agency) of the federal government.

77. **(C)** The quotation from John F. Kennedy's inaugural address suggests that he would have supported all four points except the establishment of a Communist government in Vietnam. He ordered troops to Vietnam to prevent that.

78. **(C)** This question requires you to know what these American authors wrote about. Of the five, Ernest Hemingway is the one who was least concerned with social criticism of America in works such as *For Whom the Bell Tolls*. On the other hand, Steinbeck, Norris, Sinclair, and Riis are noted for their writings of social criticisms. John Steinbeck in *The Grapes of Wrath* described conditions in Oklahoma and California during the dust bowl years of the 1930s. Frank Norris in *The Octopus* depicted the human drama arising from the raising, selling, and consumption of wheat. Upton Sinclair in *The Jungle* wrote of conditions in the meatpacking industry in Chicago at the beginning of the 20th century. Jacob Riis in *The Shame of the Cities* described tenement and slum life in New York, again in the early 1900s.

79. **(A)** The first oil embargo imposed by OPEC in order to raise oil prices occurred in 1973 during Nixon's second term. The effect of the embargo continued to be felt during the Carter and Reagan administrations. The other events all occurred during Carter's presidency and were important foreign policy issues of the period.

80. **(A)** The Treaty of Tordesillas in 1494 established a line to divide the Spanish and Portugueses colonies. They were the only nations involved in colonization at the time and the Pope believed dividing the world between these two nations for the purpose of colonization would avoid conflict between two Catholic nations. The way the line was drawn gave Portugal claim to Brazil. Even if you have never heard of the treaty, the date should help you eliminate items except A. The Spanish had not yet moved into South America, the French were not yet involved in the Caribbean, Georgia was not founded for another 250 years, and the Spanish had not yet attacked Mexico and the Aztecs.

## Comments on the Free-Response Questions

Comments follow on the five sample essay questions of Part A, B, and C of Section II of the exam. For each essay question, there is a general analysis that is similar to those given for the sample essay questions in each chapter of Part Two. In addition to the analyses, two sample answers—one for the DBQ (Part A) and one for the first standard essay question (Part B)—are included. In the left margin of the two sample answers there are comments on certain noteworthy elements of the answers.

You must be aware, as all of the analyses of essay questions have indicated, that there are many possible ways to answer each essay question—theses will differ, organizational schemes will differ, and the facts chosen to prove a point will differ. The two sample answers illustrate only one of the many possible ways to write good answers.

## Analysis of the DBQ (Part A)—Question 1

The DBQ is a straightforward *To what extent?* type of question (see Part Two, Chapter 7). You are asked to analyze how Supreme Court decisions and the views expressed by political leaders are related. The second sentence of the question adds a *Why?* This should present no particular problem, since it merely requires that in your answer, after you have analyzed the relationship between the Court decisions and the views of the political leaders, you explain the reasons for this relationship. You will want to keep this in mind as you analyze the question and prepare an outline of your answer.

Although the documents are chosen from 1905–1918, the time period 1900–1918 is stated in the directions. Directions are extremely important, and the time periods presented must be followed. You should give some background information from the beginning of the 20th century. The vocabulary used in the question should present no difficulties.

This DBQ asks you to deal with a perennial issue of American history, that is, do or should the decisions of the Supreme Court follow or lead public opinion? You should have discussed this matter at some time in your study so you should come to the question with some thoughts on the issue.

As indicated in Chapter 8, the DBQ on the AP examination will relate to the "mainstream" of American history. This question certainly does that, since it asks the student to focus on one crucial aspect of that important era of reform, the Progressive Era. Several of the documents are statements from presidents who led the political reforms of the age. Nothing could be more mainstream than Theodore Roosevelt and Woodrow Wilson—two presidents who would be studied in every American history course. The other documents may be less obvious and you may not have studied these particular Supreme Court cases but enough information about the cases is included for you to understand them.

Knowledge from many sources might be introduced to illustrate your understanding of the "mainstream" of American history in the Progressive Era. Information you introduce might be on the Muckrakers who, at the turn of the century, pointed out unsavory working conditions and political corruption, thus paving the way for many reforms. You might use some of this legislation such as the Pure Food and Drug Laws of T. Roosevelt's presidency to the Adamson Act (eight-hour day for railroad workers) of Wilson's presidency to illustrate one attitude expressed by legislators. On the other side, mention might be made of the attitude of Social Darwinists who supported laissez-faire government and opposed government regulation of business. Comments on Roosevelt and Wilson—their styles of leadership as president, their goals as developed in the New Nationalism and New Freedom Programs, legislation they supported and their views toward the individual—might be included to provide the background to the issues addressed in the documents.

As has been emphasized throughout the book, organizing is a crucial step in essay writing, and is particularly important in the DBQ where there are several things to analyze and connect. Of course, you must decide on a thesis before you begin to write. Comments on specific parts of the sample answer are included in the left-hand column.

## Sample Answer for the DBQ

Opening sentence introduces broad topic of the question.

Thesis on the *To what degree?* aspect of the question.

Two reasons that respond to the *Why?* part of the question follow.

*Two documents* are mentioned as evidence, and dates are given, setting the time period of the question.
Information from the "mainstream" of American history is introduced to support ideas in the documents.

Uses information in the document, but does not repeat the content of the document, thus indicating an understanding of and ability to use the information.
Poor linking of paragraphs. Ideas introduced appear separated from documents, but writer ties mainstream information to documents in last sentence to support point 1 of reasons for *Why?* part of question.

Good comment on value of sources.

A continual issue in U.S. history has been how to get the Supreme Court to work together with the executive and legislative branches and not to block their desires. This was an important issue in the years 1900–1918, when decisions of the Supreme Court were not in agreement with the views of the best-known political leaders. Two reasons can be given for this situation: first, Court members were confirmed by the conservative Senate, which was out of touch with the country and its changing political attitudes and second, the ideas of Wilson and Roosevelt were ahead of those of most political leaders.

The decisions of the Supreme Court in *Lochner v. New York* in 1905 and in *Hammer v. Dagenhart* in 1918 indicate that the Court upheld the conservative ideas of the Social Darwinists throughout the period 1900–1918. Social Darwinists applied the idea of survival of the fittest to business and wanted no government interference in the economic life of the nation. Of course, not every judge believed in Social Darwinism, as seen in Mr. Holmes's dissent in 1905 in which he is complaining about that concept. Also, a good lawyer such as Mr. Brandeis, by using special arguments, could persuade the Court to allow the regulation of the working conditions of women by a state government. But this is a major exception to the general views held by the Court.

Until 1913 the United States senators were elected by state legislatures, which were often controlled by business interests. For example, the Boston and Maine Railroad controlled the New Hampshire legislature. U.S. senators confirmed members of the Supreme Court, and the conservative views of business were thus represented both in the Senate and on the Court. This conservative view is seen in Senator Scott's statement on the working conditions he has seen—a personal view that is not a very reliable historical source, but in this case is illustrative of a widely held view.

Documents may be referred to by letter, but better to use author's name or some other specific identification from the document. Good use of "mainstream" history.

Repetition of "Roosevelt" helps link paragraphs.

*Use of abbreviation "T. R." is not formal essay style,* but permissible if time is running out.

Effective weaving together of information in documents, and knowledge *recalled* from study of main issues in U.S. history—supporting point 2 of reasons for *Why?* part of question.

Good use of document—brief quote with source stated is effective.

Repeats thesis.

Brings paper back to broad topic of opening sentence.

Document B presents a view of the Muckrakers, a group of writers who pointed out the political corruption in the cities, the power of business monopolies (Tarbell and Standard Oil), and the horror of working conditions. These writers had an impact on certain men, such as Roosevelt, who became the leaders of the Progressive Movement, a reform movement of the first two decades of this century.

Roosevelt became president by a fluke—he was on the Republican ticket to win votes and did not represent the views of the leadership. He became president when McKinley was assassinated, and he worked for better labor conditions, as can be seen in his settlement of the coal strike. But at the same time, the Court remained conservative as seen in the Lochner decision in 1905. When Taft did not support Roosevelt's ideas, T. R. ran for president in 1912 on the Bull Moose ticket. As seen in his speeches, he campaigned for the "welfare of the people" and for the judiciary to respond to the needs of all the people, and not just for special interests. Roosevelt's campaign split the Republican Party, allowing the Progressive Democrat, Woodrow Wilson, to win. Wilson, a minority president, was able to get some legislation passed to improve working conditions (Adamson Act), but the Supreme Court continued to lag behind the executive and legislative branches of government with its conservative, Social Darwinist attitude expressed in *Hammer v. Dagenhart*. This decision forbid federal regulation of child labor. The Court thus remained conservative in spite of the election of Wilson, who in speeches in 1912–1913 had expressed his desire to have the law "step in and create new conditions under which we may live."

The documents presented help to make it clear that the decisions of the Supreme Court were not in agreement with the expressed views of the leaders of the executive branch of government. The Supreme Court remained conservative while the Progressive, Woodrow Wilson, was president. The period 1900–1918 clearly illustrates the adage that the Supreme Court lags behind the people and the executive and legislative branches of government in its decisions and understanding of the needs of the people.

## Comment on the Sample Answer for the DBQ

The essay is a good example of what should be done with the DBQ. The writer makes use of all the documents except D. They are not discussed in order, but are used in different combinations to illustrate points. The writer uses considerable information from the period 1900–1918 to support the thesis and weaves it in well with the documents. He or she assumes the reader understands the content of the documents, so there is no need to summarize or quote them extensively. The writer uses one short quote from Wilson's speeches in Document F, which is an effective way to show a clear understanding of the document. In summary, the sample answer for this DBQ makes good use of the documents and includes sound information from American history to support the thesis presented. This answer would qualify for a high score on the examination.

## Analysis of the Free-Response Essays (Part B)—Question 2

The second question is a typical *Evaluate This Statement* question (see Part Two, Chapter 4). The quotation presents a most unusual interpretation of the era of the American Revolution, suggesting that the events in the West (frontier) were more "significant" for the development of the United States than events on the eastern seaboard (Boston, Philadelphia, Virginia) in the years from the Peace of Paris, which ended the French and Indian War in 1763, to the establishment of the government under the Constitution in 1788. The wording of the quotation should present no problem, and most students should quickly recall many events of the era under consideration. The question lends itself to a chronological organization, discussing events on the frontier before 1776 first, and then those after 1776, with references to events on the eastern seaboard woven in. The events you pick will be ones to support your thesis.

Remember, you are free to agree or disagree with this quotation. Most students will probably disagree, citing events such as the Stamp Act crisis; the Boston Massacre; the closing of the port of Boston; the reaction in New York to the Quartering Act; the meetings of the Continental Congresses; the writing and approval of the Declaration of Independence; the fighting at Bunker Hill, Saratoga, and Yorktown; the economic crisis under the government of the Articles of Confederation; and Shays' Rebellion, which led to the Constitutional Convention. To illustrate that there are arguments on the other side of the question, the following sample answer supports the quotation. Again, in the left-hand margin are comments pointing out good aspects of the answer. This answer presents only *one* of many possible approaches to a very interesting and provocative *Evaluate This Statement* type of question.

## Sample Answer for Standard Essay Question 2

Opening comment is broad—catches attention—flashlight beam image of Seven Steps in Essay Writing.

> The role of the historian is to determine what events of the past are significant and explain to his generation why they are.

Links opening comment to thesis, and introduces the **Topic** of the essay.

> For many years American historians have concentrated on the events that took place on the eastern seaboard between 1763 and 1788, suggesting that for American history they were the most significant events of those decades. These historians

Clearly stated **thesis** using quote from the question.

> have often ignored the events on the western frontier in those years—events that were "more significant for the development of U.S. history" than happenings in the East.

Admits evidence exists that might refute the stated thesis.

> Granted that many significant events from the Stamp Act Crisis of 1765 to Shays' Rebellion of 1786 took place in the East. Granted also that the Declaration of Independence was signed, the Continental Congresses met, and many battles of the Revolutionary War were fought in the East, but *all of these*

*Main idea of paragraph*
Introduces factual refutation of the evidence given at start of the para-

> *were affected by events in the West.* It must be remembered that the Peace of Paris in 1763 ended a war fought for control of the Northwest Territory (Ohio, Michigan, etc.) and of the

graph—important to admit and then to refute other views whenever possible.

Paragraph is structured so major point of refutation appears at the end of paragraph. Ties facts back to topic and thesis.

Word *independence* links paragraphs.

Shifts argument to events that actually took place in the West. Shows understanding of the two major laws dealing with the Northwest.

Good linkage of paragraphs as point of argument is shifted to government.

Again, ties facts to topic and thesis.

*Repeated word* again links paragraphs as several new arguments are added.

Cleverly presents many facts centered on the military significance of the West and its place in U.S. foreign policy.

Saves major point to the last paragraph so that reader is left with this crucial point of the argument in favor of the thesis.

Mississippi Valley. It was in this war that George Washington gained his colonial reputation that allowed him to become the leader of the colonial army. Without his Western military experience, where would the colonial armies have been? More significantly, the entire taxation issue that was argued in the East was precipitated by the need of the British to pay the expenses they incurred in the French and Indian War. Without that war, *a result of British policy on the frontier*, there would have been no need for the taxes—Stamp Act, Townshend Acts, Tea Act—which stirred up the East, and led to the cry, "No taxation without representation" and ultimately to independence.

One often-forgotten event leading to American independence is the British Proclamation Line of 1763, which closed the Northwest Territory to colonial settlement. American leaders such as Washington and Franklin had committed money to companies to organize this territory. When the British stopped this settlement, colonists had an important motive for leading an anti-British movement in the East. In 1774 the English made matters worse for colonial leaders when by the Quebec Act they extended the boundaries of the former French province of Quebec to include the Northwest and established a form of government for the area putting it under different laws than the British colonies.

Many of these colonies, such as Virginia and Connecticut, claimed control of the Northwest. After the Declaration of Independence, as the Continental Congress struggled to govern the colonies, Maryland refused to ratify the new government arrangement—the Articles of Confederation—until all colonies gave up their claims to Western lands. When Virginia finally did cede her claim in 1781, the Articles were ratified, and so, again, the West played a significant role in Eastern events.

Many other illustrations could be given of the *significance* of the West: the British plan to split the West from the seaboard colonies, which was frustrated by the colonial victory at Saratoga, and victories on the frontier in Carolina, which led to Yorktown. Also, during the negotiations for peace, the United States won control over the land from the Appalachians to the Mississippi because of the victories of George Rogers Clark in the Northwest. The British refused to evacuate forts and the resulting diplomatic struggle to gain control of the frontier region was the major foreign policy issue between 1783 and 1788.

All of these illustrations of the significance of the West for U.S. history pale by comparison to the great issue that was solved by the Continental Congress, that is, *how to organize and govern the frontier region*. The plan of organization was first set

Good, brief summary of important document shows writer knows the facts, not just the name of the document.

Grammatically a little confusing but presents important ideas.

Again, acknowledges events in the East, but restates thesis, and adds an interpretation of history to reinforce it.

Ends by moving back to broad topic of the opening, thus framing the essay and tying it together.

forth in the Basic Land Ordinance of 1785 and developed fully in the Northwest Ordinance of 1787. This document set the pattern for the future expansion of the United States in creating new states coast to coast. It abolished slavery in the territory and established trial by jury and freedom of religion. Nothing could be more significant to the development of the United States than the establishment both of the idea that these principles would be extended to new territory, which might have been treated as colonies, and of the plan for the expansion of the United States coast to coast.

Certainly, the East was important in American history from 1763 to 1788, but the events in the West were more significant. They provided the cause for so many events, and history is a cause-and-effect relationship. One must admit that the cause of events is more significant than the effects, and American historians should take more time to explain why from 1763 to 1788 the events of the frontier are more significant than those in the East.

## Comment on the Sample Answer for Standard Essay Question 2

This was a very good answer to the question. The writer introduces the topic with a broad statement and narrows it down to a clearly stated thesis in which the question is quoted. The thesis is the last sentence of the opening paragraph. As you are aware, you may argue on any side of the question, and in this case, the writer has taken the less accepted view. Since most individuals would believe that events in the East were more important and would be aware of these events, the writer refutes these in the second paragraph. This, then, paves the way for the positive data the writer will use. The most important point the writer has is kept for the last paragraph, which is a very effective technique. The organization used is basically chronological, but there is some movement back and forth in time as the main topic under discussion (war, government, land organization) is shifted. The conclusion restates the thesis and moves back to the more general topic introduced in the opening sentence of the essay. This frames the essay effectively. The "Seven Steps in Essay Writing" have been well used by this author, who would earn a top level grade.

## Comment on Standard Essay Question 3

This third question from the sample exam is an example of an *Assess the validity* type of question (see Part Two, Chapter 4), a type of question that has been used on many United States History AP examinations.

The first step in answering the question will be to analyze the quotation. It raises the eternal issue of democratic government—the conflict between the power of the majority and the rights of the minority. The question provides an unusual twist when it applies this issue to foreign policy. The quote states that minority rights ("views") cannot be ignored by a democratic society (the United States) when "executing foreign policy." You must decide if the statement is true or not, but, more than that, whether it is true or not for a very specific time period in American history. Once you have analyzed the quotation, you need to think about or brainstorm what factual information you could include in your answer. The time period includes the establishment of the government under Washington, Jay's Treaty with England and Pinckney's Treaty with Spain, the XYZ Affair, the Alien and Sedition Acts, the Louisiana Purchase, the Embargo of 1807, and the U.S. involvement in the War of 1812, all of which angered many. In each of these issues there were majority and minority views. You must focus on the foreign policy side of these events. You must decide if the minority views were considered and what the results would have been if they were or were not considered. Is there a lesson to draw from how the issues were handled? Your answer to this question should help supply your thesis.

To prove your thesis, you must select several issues and not try to cover everything in the time period. You might decide on a chronological approach or you might use examples where the minority views were or were not considered thus using a topical approach. In any case it is an interesting question, which raises an important issue in a slightly different way. Questions on the AP examination will often ask you to use your knowledge in a different way.

As in all essay answers, there are many ways to approach the question and no one way is best. What is important is that you use specific facts carefully selected from your study of the United States to prove your thesis.

## Comment on Standard Essay Question 4

This is a typical *In what ways?* question (see Part Two, Chapter 7). The wording of the question links economic and political history. You are given a choice of four presidential elections from which you must pick two for information to prove your thesis. One election choice is after 1970, which illustrates how this later period may be used on the AP exam. If you know nothing of the 1980 election, your choices are more limited but you can still answer the question. Many students will know something of 1980 because of current events or comparisons made to recent events when studying the past. Consider your choice of elections carefully. Each had important economic aspects. In 1896 there was depression on the farms, the Panic of 1893, and the following gold crisis. The aftermath of the Panic of 1907 and the issue of the role of government in economic activity were discussed in the 1912 election. The election of 1932 was preceded by the Stock Market Crash and start of the Great Depression. The inflationary crisis of the late 1970s and the impact of OPEC were important in the 1980 election as well as Reagan's solutions referred to as Reaganomics. Once you decide on the two elections you will discuss and the economic issues involved, you will need to consider noneconomic issues that might have been the cause for the change in political control. Among issues to consider would be U.S. expansion in the Pacific and concern over Cuba in 1896, differing views of the role of government and reform movements in 1912, the impact of the Roaring Twenties and post-World War I issues in 1932, and the aftermath of the Vietnam War and Watergate and the continuing Cold War in 1980.

You can organize the question in several ways. Least effective would be to simply write about two elections separately. More effective would be to group political and/or economic information from the two periods together.

Whether you emphasize the political or economic aspects may well depend on the emphasis given to these factors in your study of American history. The question expects you to establish a relationship between these two forces in history. Your perception of the relationship should be stated in your thesis. While deciding on your thesis, you will have recalled many events, and as always, you should use those events that you are most familiar with to prove your thesis.

## Comment on Standard Essay Question 5

This is a good question that has a clear focus on one type of information—reform. In answering this *Compare* and *Contrast* question (see Part Two, Chapter 9), the first thing you must do is to determine what reform periods you will discuss. The three choices are the Jacksonian Era (1828–1840), the New Deal (1933–1940), and the Kennedy/Johnson years (1961–1968). Are there factors that these periods have in common? How do they differ? What were the main issues addressed in each period? What role did the president play in each period? Did they respond to public pressures or did they lead? Were the reforms primarily economic, social, or political or were they a combination?

One important point to note about this question is that it involves social history. It, as does Question 4, illustrates how the AP exam has questions on different types of history. In discussing reform movements, you should mention several specific reforms of a social nature: for example, the reforms in education in the 1830s and 1840s, the laws affecting conditions of employment passed in the 1930s, the legislation concerning the improvement of the environment and civil rights passed in the 1960s. These social reforms are all interwoven with economic and political history, and you may include some economic and political history in your answer even as you focus on the social aspects of reform.

There are obviously other matters one might consider in an analysis of the question. Once you have done your own analysis, an effective thesis should follow. **The thesis must address both the comparison of the two periods and the contrast between them, as asked for in the question.**

There are many ways to organize the answer to this question. It might be chronological, with one movement following the next, or you might trace one or two issues through the two periods of reform. However you structure your answer, you must remember to include specific information on reforms in both periods.

# Practice Test B
## ANSWER SHEET

1. Ⓐ Ⓑ Ⓒ Ⓓ Ⓔ
2. Ⓐ Ⓑ Ⓒ Ⓓ Ⓔ
3. Ⓐ Ⓑ Ⓒ Ⓓ Ⓔ
4. Ⓐ Ⓑ Ⓒ Ⓓ Ⓔ
5. Ⓐ Ⓑ Ⓒ Ⓓ Ⓔ
6. Ⓐ Ⓑ Ⓒ Ⓓ Ⓔ
7. Ⓐ Ⓑ Ⓒ Ⓓ Ⓔ
8. Ⓐ Ⓑ Ⓒ Ⓓ Ⓔ
9. Ⓐ Ⓑ Ⓒ Ⓓ Ⓔ
10. Ⓐ Ⓑ Ⓒ Ⓓ Ⓔ
11. Ⓐ Ⓑ Ⓒ Ⓓ Ⓔ
12. Ⓐ Ⓑ Ⓒ Ⓓ Ⓔ
13. Ⓐ Ⓑ Ⓒ Ⓓ Ⓔ
14. Ⓐ Ⓑ Ⓒ Ⓓ Ⓔ
15. Ⓐ Ⓑ Ⓒ Ⓓ Ⓔ
16. Ⓐ Ⓑ Ⓒ Ⓓ Ⓔ
17. Ⓐ Ⓑ Ⓒ Ⓓ Ⓔ
18. Ⓐ Ⓑ Ⓒ Ⓓ Ⓔ
19. Ⓐ Ⓑ Ⓒ Ⓓ Ⓔ
20. Ⓐ Ⓑ Ⓒ Ⓓ Ⓔ

21. Ⓐ Ⓑ Ⓒ Ⓓ Ⓔ
22. Ⓐ Ⓑ Ⓒ Ⓓ Ⓔ
23. Ⓐ Ⓑ Ⓒ Ⓓ Ⓔ
24. Ⓐ Ⓑ Ⓒ Ⓓ Ⓔ
25. Ⓐ Ⓑ Ⓒ Ⓓ Ⓔ
26. Ⓐ Ⓑ Ⓒ Ⓓ Ⓔ
27. Ⓐ Ⓑ Ⓒ Ⓓ Ⓔ
28. Ⓐ Ⓑ Ⓒ Ⓓ Ⓔ
29. Ⓐ Ⓑ Ⓒ Ⓓ Ⓔ
30. Ⓐ Ⓑ Ⓒ Ⓓ Ⓔ
31. Ⓐ Ⓑ Ⓒ Ⓓ Ⓔ
32. Ⓐ Ⓑ Ⓒ Ⓓ Ⓔ
33. Ⓐ Ⓑ Ⓒ Ⓓ Ⓔ
34. Ⓐ Ⓑ Ⓒ Ⓓ Ⓔ
35. Ⓐ Ⓑ Ⓒ Ⓓ Ⓔ
36. Ⓐ Ⓑ Ⓒ Ⓓ Ⓔ
37. Ⓐ Ⓑ Ⓒ Ⓓ Ⓔ
38. Ⓐ Ⓑ Ⓒ Ⓓ Ⓔ
39. Ⓐ Ⓑ Ⓒ Ⓓ Ⓔ
40. Ⓐ Ⓑ Ⓒ Ⓓ Ⓔ

41. Ⓐ Ⓑ Ⓒ Ⓓ Ⓔ
42. Ⓐ Ⓑ Ⓒ Ⓓ Ⓔ
43. Ⓐ Ⓑ Ⓒ Ⓓ Ⓔ
44. Ⓐ Ⓑ Ⓒ Ⓓ Ⓔ
45. Ⓐ Ⓑ Ⓒ Ⓓ Ⓔ
46. Ⓐ Ⓑ Ⓒ Ⓓ Ⓔ
47. Ⓐ Ⓑ Ⓒ Ⓓ Ⓔ
48. Ⓐ Ⓑ Ⓒ Ⓓ Ⓔ
49. Ⓐ Ⓑ Ⓒ Ⓓ Ⓔ
50. Ⓐ Ⓑ Ⓒ Ⓓ Ⓔ
51. Ⓐ Ⓑ Ⓒ Ⓓ Ⓔ
52. Ⓐ Ⓑ Ⓒ Ⓓ Ⓔ
53. Ⓐ Ⓑ Ⓒ Ⓓ Ⓔ
54. Ⓐ Ⓑ Ⓒ Ⓓ Ⓔ
55. Ⓐ Ⓑ Ⓒ Ⓓ Ⓔ
56. Ⓐ Ⓑ Ⓒ Ⓓ Ⓔ
57. Ⓐ Ⓑ Ⓒ Ⓓ Ⓔ
58. Ⓐ Ⓑ Ⓒ Ⓓ Ⓔ
59. Ⓐ Ⓑ Ⓒ Ⓓ Ⓔ
60. Ⓐ Ⓑ Ⓒ Ⓓ Ⓔ

61. Ⓐ Ⓑ Ⓒ Ⓓ Ⓔ
62. Ⓐ Ⓑ Ⓒ Ⓓ Ⓔ
63. Ⓐ Ⓑ Ⓒ Ⓓ Ⓔ
64. Ⓐ Ⓑ Ⓒ Ⓓ Ⓔ
65. Ⓐ Ⓑ Ⓒ Ⓓ Ⓔ
66. Ⓐ Ⓑ Ⓒ Ⓓ Ⓔ
67. Ⓐ Ⓑ Ⓒ Ⓓ Ⓔ
68. Ⓐ Ⓑ Ⓒ Ⓓ Ⓔ
69. Ⓐ Ⓑ Ⓒ Ⓓ Ⓔ
70. Ⓐ Ⓑ Ⓒ Ⓓ Ⓔ
71. Ⓐ Ⓑ Ⓒ Ⓓ Ⓔ
72. Ⓐ Ⓑ Ⓒ Ⓓ Ⓔ
73. Ⓐ Ⓑ Ⓒ Ⓓ Ⓔ
74. Ⓐ Ⓑ Ⓒ Ⓓ Ⓔ
75. Ⓐ Ⓑ Ⓒ Ⓓ Ⓔ
76. Ⓐ Ⓑ Ⓒ Ⓓ Ⓔ
77. Ⓐ Ⓑ Ⓒ Ⓓ Ⓔ
78. Ⓐ Ⓑ Ⓒ Ⓓ Ⓔ
79. Ⓐ Ⓑ Ⓒ Ⓓ Ⓔ
80. Ⓐ Ⓑ Ⓒ Ⓓ Ⓔ

Practice Test B

# Practice Test B

## CHAPTER 14

The comments appearing in Part Three, Chapter 12 and on page 195 apply to Practice Test B. You may wish to use Practice Test A as a pre-test and Test B as a summary of your study. The two examinations provide both an effective review and a preparation for the AP examination. Again, it is suggested that in taking this exam you create a situation that is as close to that in the exam room as possible. Tear out or copy the answer sheet found at the start of the exam. Find a quiet place where you can work for more than 3 hours without interruption. Get your number 2 pencils with erasers, several pens, and some lined paper for the essays.

As in Practice Test A and on the CD-ROM model exams, the multiple-choice questions are presented in a pattern. Questions are presented in groups of from 8 to 14 questions in chronological order and then the pattern is repeated. This will help you identify the time period from which the questions come and will also help you analyze the answers to each question. Now take the exam. Afterward correct it, read the comments, and determine the time periods of U.S. history in which you are weakest. Spend extra time on them in your final review before taking the AP exam in May.

# Practice Test B

## SECTION I: MULTIPLE-CHOICE QUESTIONS

TIME: 55 MINUTES

Number of Questions—80 MULTIPLE CHOICE

**Directions:** Each of the questions or incomplete statements below is followed by five suggested answers or completions. Select the one that is best in each case and then blacken the corresponding oval on the answer sheet.

1. Which of the following should be considered as a step leading to the American Revolution?

   (A) the XYZ Affair
   (B) English control of frontier forts
   (C) the Articles of Confederation
   (D) the Boston Tea Party
   (E) the Northeast Ordinance

2. What was the key frontier post held by the British in spite of the Treaty of Paris of 1783?

   (A) Tippecanoe
   (B) Detroit
   (C) Greenville
   (D) Chicago
   (E) Erie

3. The major significance of the Whiskey Rebellion of 1794 was that it

   (A) led to the writing of the U.S. Constitution
   (B) allowed frontier farmers to share their experiences
   (C) tested the ability of the federal government to maintain order
   (D) opened the Pennsylvania frontier to settlement
   (E) focused attention on the need for Prohibition

Practice Test B

4. The Independent Treasury plan called for

(A) a bank of the United States
(B) the funding of the U.S. debt by the Treasury
(C) the use of silver coinage for debt payment
(D) the use of state banks by the Treasury
(E) the deposit of U.S. tax revenues in the Treasury rather than in banks

5. The leader of the Radical Republicans in the U.S. House of Representatives in the 1860s was

(A) Andrew Johnson
(B) Charles Sumner
(C) Thaddeus Stevens
(D) Edwin M. Stanton
(E) Ulysses S. Grant

6. One scandal connected with the Grant administration was

(A) Teapot Dome
(B) Whitewater
(C) Credit Mobilier
(D) The Tweed Gang
(E) Watergate

7. Theodore Roosevelt named a group of individuals Muckrakers after a character in Bunyan's *Pilgrim's Progress*, but the members of the group gained their real reputation as

(A) the writers of local-color novels
(B) reformers who published articles on the evils affecting America
(C) the ten richest men in America
(D) leaders of conservation movements in the West
(E) members of Roosevelt's first cabinet

8. As part of his progressive program, President Woodrow Wilson introduced the

(A) Independent Treasury
(B) Bank of the United States
(C) Specie Circular
(D) Federal Reserve System
(E) Bank Holiday

9. COMPARISON OF MANPOWER LOSSES IN WORLD WAR I

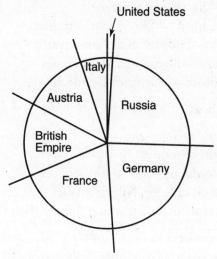

According to the chart above, manpower losses in World War I were

(A) larger for the United States than for Austria
(B) greater for Russia than for the British Empire, Austria, and Italy combined
(C) approximately the same for France, the British Empire, and Italy
(D) heaviest for the combined Central Powers of Germany and Austria
(E) approximately equal for Russia and Germany

10. One of the chief reasons Americans were willing to join the peacetime NATO alliance was of the

(A) Cuban Missile Crisis
(B) crushing of the Hungarian Revolution
(C) Berlin Blockade by the Soviet Union
(D) fall of the Berlin Wall
(E) failure of the Bay of Pigs expedition

11. An agreement by one group of legislators to support or oppose a particular bill in return for support or opposition for another bill is known as

(A) balance of power
(B) logrolling
(C) bilateral legislation
(D) a social contract
(E) a filibuster

12. A major foreign policy achievement of Jimmy Carter's administration was

(A) the withdrawal of U.S. troops from Vietnam
(B) the breakup of OPEC
(C) the overthrow of the Shah of Iran
(D) the Camp David Accords for peace in the Middle East
(E) the purchase of the Panama Canal

13. Which of the following leaders is correctly paired with the settlement he led?

    (A) John Smith—Savannah, Georgia
    (B) General Oglethorpe—Jamestown, Virginia
    (C) William Penn—Philadelphia, Pennsylvania
    (D) Roger Williams—Plymouth, Massachusetts
    (E) William Bradford—Hartford, Connecticut

14. The Albany Plan was

    (A) a plan for city development
    (B) a scheme to make money
    (C) a plan for colonial union
    (D) a plan for attack in King William's War
    (E) a plan to build a canal connecting Albany with the West

15. The Supreme Court decision in *Marbury v. Madison* established the

    (A) doctrine of judicial review of congressional legislation
    (B) principle of state control over local legislation
    (C) doctrine of Supreme Court review of state laws
    (D) principle of sanctity of contract
    (E) sanctity of congressional control of interstate commerce

16. Which of the following means of transportation was able to carry the largest amount of cargo from the East to California at the time of the gold rush?

    (A) stagecoach
    (B) railroad
    (C) horses
    (D) walking
    (E) sailing ships

17. The Reconstruction of the South after the Civil War was ended by

    (A) the Radical Republican proposals passed by the U.S. Congress
    (B) the Compromise of 1877 settling the disputed election of 1876
    (C) the establishment of local government in each seceded state
    (D) the abolishment of slavery by the thirteenth amendment
    (E) the work of the Freedman's Bureau to promote free elections

THE BATTLE OF THE BULLS AND BEARS.
"Humpty Dumpty on a wall,
Humpty Dumpty got a fall!"

Source: *Harper's Weekly*, September 10, 1872.

18. The cartoonist is chiefly concerned with making a point about

   (A) wild animal attacks on domestic cattle
   (B) earthquakes knocking down walls
   (C) the high cost of pork and flour
   (D) the high price of stocks on Wall Street
   (E) a fall in the price of gold on the Wall Street stock exchange

19. Starting with the decade of 1890 until Congress passed legislation to limit immigration in the 1920s, the largest number of immigrants came from

   (A) Ireland
   (B) Italy, Austria-Hungary, Russia
   (C) England, Germany, France
   (D) Norway, Sweden, Denmark
   (E) Poland

20. The United Nations was modeled on the

   (A) Albany Plan
   (B) League of Nations
   (C) European Union
   (D) Pan American Union
   (E) United States Constitution

21. All of the following terms became part of the American political vocabulary in the 1960s EXCEPT

    (A) *pig*
    (B) *hippie*
    (C) *dove*
    (D) *flapper*
    (E) *black power*

22. In his first year in office, President Reagan tackled the issue of inflation by

    (A) establishing a Department of Energy
    (B) encouraging Congress to pass a new tax law reducing income taxes
    (C) stopping U.S. military and economic aid to Taiwan
    (D) repealing the minimum-wage law
    (E) increasing military support for anti-terrorist activities

23. All of the following acts were part of British mercantilist policy EXCEPT

    (A) Act of Toleration
    (B) Hatters Act
    (C) Iron Act
    (D) Sugar or Molasses Act
    (E) Woolens Act

24. *Common Sense* by Thomas Paine is considered a most effective

    (A) logical argument for independence
    (B) propaganda work for independence
    (C) handbook for guerrilla warfare
    (D) condemnation of Whig philosophy
    (E) attack on the Stamp Act

25. As Secretary of the Treasury, Alexander Hamilton introduced financial measures that particularly benefited

    (A) publishers
    (B) merchants
    (C) small farmers
    (D) frontiersmen
    (E) slave owners

26. The Missouri Compromise helped to postpone the outbreak of the Civil War by

    (A) maintaining the balance of slave and free states
    (B) admitting California into the Union as a free state
    (C) reducing the tariffs on imported manufactured goods
    (D) accepting the *Dred Scott* decision that slaves were property
    (E) prohibiting all discussion of slavery by the United States Congress

27. All of the following were provisions of the Compromise of 1850 EXCEPT

    (A) admittance of California into the union as a free state
    (B) a strict fugitive slave law
    (C) establishment of Utah and New Mexico as territories with squatter
        sovereignty
    (D) the redrawing of the Texas boundary
    (E) the prohibition of the slave trade in Washington, D.C.

28. Before the Civil War, westward expansion was slowed by

    (A) the lack of a cross-continental railroad
    (B) the high cost of using the Panama Canal for sea transport
    (C) the support of Native American tribes in the Great Plains
    (D) the failure to find passable routes through the Rocky Mountains
    (E) the scarcity of game as a food source for the pioneers

Source: Los Angeles County Natural History Museum Foundation, History Fund

29. The scene in the photograph above is most likely of

    (A) Hispanic Americans in Los Angeles
    (B) San Francisco during the Gold Rush
    (C) the south side of Chicago during the days of African American migration
        to the cities
    (D) Native Americans settled in Sioux City
    (E) immigrants in New York City

30. Considered the first popular work to publicize the environmental issue, *Silent Spring* was written by

    (A) Rachel Carson
    (B) Ralph Nader
    (C) John Muir
    (D) Tom Wolfe
    (E) Jack Kerouac

31. Martin Luther King, Jr. emerged as a leader of the Civil Rights Movement as a result of his involvement in

    (A) lunch counter sit-ins
    (B) the desegregation of the U.S. Army
    (C) the March on Washington
    (D) a drive for voter registration
    (E) the Montgomery Bus Boycott

32. During the Kennedy administration the United States committed itself to

    (A) place a man on the moon
    (B) decrease U.S. involvement in Vietnam
    (C) raise taxes to finance the government
    (D) support President Castro's rule in Cuba
    (E) reduce the size of the Peace Corps

33. The decade after the end of the Cold War was a period of

    (A) confrontation between the United States and Russia
    (B) rivalry to build space stations
    (C) declining nationalism in southeastern Europe
    (D) increasing globalization of the world economy
    (E) slowing economic growth in China

34. Opportunities for women have been greatly expanded since World War II in spite of the lack of support for the

    (A) Title IX program
    (B) Equal Rights Amendment (ERA)
    (C) Family and Medical Leave Act
    (D) National Organization for Women (NOW)
    (E) Women's Liberation Movement

35. The economic and cultural life of early colonial Virginia was built upon the cultivation of

    (A) cotton
    (B) indigo
    (C) sugarcane
    (D) tobacco
    (E) rice

36. In the steps leading to the American Revolution, which of the following British acts was enacted first and created a series of crises on the issue of taxation?

    (A) Tea Act
    (B) Intolerable Acts
    (C) Stamp Act
    (D) Townshend Revenue Act
    (E) Declaratory Act

37. The following items all dealt with relations between the thirteen English colonies and the English government EXCEPT

    (A) Acts of Trade and Navigation
    (B) Stamp Act
    (C) Quartering Act
    (D) Quebec Act
    (E) Olive Branch Petition

38. "To make all laws which shall be necessary and proper for carrying into execution the foregoing powers, and all other powers vested by this Constitution in the Government of the United States" has been referred to as the

    (A) elastic clause
    (B) Bill of Rights
    (C) commerce clause
    (D) Power of the Purse
    (E) checks and balances clause

39. The Hartford Convention of 1815

    (A) nominated candidates for president
    (B) called for repeal of the Alien and Sedition Acts
    (C) was a meeting of disaffected Federalists
    (D) rejected the Treaty of Ghent
    (E) supported another invasion of Canada

40. The Kansas-Nebraska Act

    (A) incorporated the concept of popular sovereignty for Kansas
    (B) maintained the 36° 30′ line of the Missouri Compromise
    (C) provided for a strict fugitive slave law
    (D) continued the concept of balance by admitting one free and one slave state
    (E) supported the decision in the Dred Scott case

41. Cattle raising in the semiarid lands of the West increased as a result of all of the following EXCEPT

    (A) the elimination of the buffalo
    (B) the invention of the reaper
    (C) the building of the transcontinental railroad
    (D) the use of cattle drives
    (E) the development of barbed wire

42. "There is no reason why the United States should be committed to other political units or involved in entangling alliances" expresses the view held by American

    (A) socialists
    (B) immigrants
    (C) isolationists
    (D) internationalists
    (E) clergy

43. During World War I the massive depletion of resources and manpower led to

    (A) the establishment by Germany of new colonies in Africa
    (B) conditions that encouraged the rise of fascism and communism
    (C) the League of Nations overseeing the distribution of resources
    (D) the establishment of the Marshall Plan for European recovery
    (E) close cooperation between Europe and the United States

44. Just as computers have changed social patterns in the last twenty years, in the twenty years after World War II social patterns were changed dramatically by the introduction of

    (A) automobiles
    (B) microwave ovens
    (C) television sets
    (D) motion pictures
    (E) cell phones

45. The Supreme Court decision in *Brown v. Board of Education of Topeka* reversed the "separate but equal" doctrine set in the case of

    (A) *Roe v. Wade*
    (B) *Dred Scott v. Sandford*
    (C) *Marbury v. Madison*
    (D) *Plessy v. Ferguson*
    (E) *Miranda v. Arizona*

46. All of the following would be considered part of the Cold War EXCEPT

    (A) the Berlin Blockade
    (B) the Vietnam War
    (C) the founding of Israel
    (D) the fall of the Berlin Wall
    (E) Soviet invasion of Afghanistan

47. During the Clinton presidency there were several investigations of misconduct that led to

    (A) the resignation of the Independent Counsel, Kenneth Starr
    (B) the removal of Hillary Rodham Clinton from an active role in health care reform
    (C) the failure of the Whitewater Real Estate development enterprise
    (D) the impeachment of President Clinton on charges of obstructing justice and misleading testimony
    (E) the reform of the White House staff and the use of the Oval Office

48. At the Constitutional Convention there was no need to compromise on the issue of

    (A) the counting of population in the thirteen states
    (B) the method of representation in the Senate and House of Representatives
    (C) the interests of small and large states
    (D) the method of election of the president
    (E) the role of Congress in declaring war and raising an army

49. What was the first state admitted to the Union from the Louisiana Purchase territory?

    (A) Mississippi
    (B) Louisiana
    (C) Missouri
    (D) Ohio
    (E) Kentucky

50. In the Monroe Doctrine President Monroe

    (A) introduced the concept of Dollar Diplomacy
    (B) warned European nations against interfering in South America
    (C) stated the United States would collect all debts owed by South American nations
    (D) announced the United States would seize Panama to build a canal
    (E) established a free-trade area in South America

51. Which of the following events involving the secession crisis during the presidency of Andrew Jackson precipitated the crisis?

    (A) Tariff of Abominations
    (B) The Force Bill
    (C) South Carolina's nullification of U.S. tariff laws
    (D) Clay's Compromise Tariff of 1833
    (E) Calhoun's resignation as vice president

52. Jim Crow laws refer to legislation designed to

   (A) benefit railroad workers
   (B) sell western lands cheaply
   (C) deny equality to African Americans
   (D) keep immigrants from taking jobs away from Americans
   (E) provide economic opportunity for war veterans

53. Each of the following men is correctly paired with an item linked with his name EXCEPT

   (A) Joseph Pulitzer—*New York World*
   (B) Louis H. Sullivan—Skyscrapers
   (C) Thomas Edison—Phonograph
   (D) Bret Harte—*Adventures of Huckleberry Finn*
   (E) Buffalo Bill Cody—Wild West Show

54. By 1763 all thirteen English colonies in North America were either controlled by proprietors or were under the control of the King as

   (A) his private estate
   (B) economic centers
   (C) royal colonies
   (D) royal family colonies
   (E) military bases

55. Which of the following applies to the 1920s in the United States?

   (A) all people shared in the economic prosperity
   (B) prices for farm produce grew steadily
   (C) investments in the stock market were insured by the government
   (D) there were no indications an economic collapse might occur
   (E) speculation was widespread among investors

56. Which of the following legislative acts designed to regulate or control business activity was part of the New Deal legislative program?

   (A) Clayton Antitrust Act
   (B) Sherman Antitrust Act
   (C) Federal Securities Act
   (D) Federal Trade Commission Act
   (E) Pure Food and Drug Act

57. All of the following measures were enacted by Congress as part of President Lyndon Johnson's Great Society program EXCEPT

   (A) the establishment of the Department of Housing and Welfare
   (B) Operation Headstart
   (C) Voting Rights Act of 1965
   (D) The Taft-Hartley Act
   (E) Medicare

58. "It being one chief project of Satan to keep man from the knowledge of the scriptures . . . it is therefore ordered by this [Assembly] . . . that every township of fifty householders, shall appoint one within their towns to teach all such children as shall resort [apply] to him to write and read, whose wages shall be paid either by parents of such children, or by the inhabitants in general . . . provided that those who send their children be not oppressed by paying much more than they can have them taught for in other towns."

    This passage sets forth basic American attitudes concerning the

    (A) separation of church and state
    (B) power of the state over the power of Satan
    (C) political power of townships
    (D) importance of education
    (E) value of fair and equal taxation

59. Which of the following was NOT true of life in colonial America?

    (A) slavery was accepted in all thirteen colonies
    (B) subsistence farming was common, particularly in frontier areas
    (C) trade was a major source of wealth in New England
    (D) large families were important as a source of workers
    (E) women had the same legal rights as men

60. During the period of the French Revolution and Napoleonic Wars, President Jefferson was most sympathetic to the cause of

    (A) England
    (B) Germany
    (C) France
    (D) Italy
    (E) Spain

61. Which of the following would NOT be considered part of Jacksonian Democracy?

    (A) actions of Dorothea Dix to help the insane
    (B) the establishment of labor unions
    (C) the spread of free public schools
    (D) the growth of railroads
    (E) the extension of universal male suffrage

62. The "gag rule" passed by the House of Representatives in 1836 was passed to prevent

    (A) publication of Garrison's *Liberator*
    (B) Nat Turner's rebellion
    (C) debate of antislavery appeals
    (D) the growth of sweatshop factories in the North
    (E) organization of the Free Soil party

63. The United States' policy toward the Native American changed dramatically with the passage in 1887 of the Dawes Act, which

(A) treated the tribes as independent nations
(B) established new and larger reservations for all tribes
(C) granted full citizenship to all tribal members
(D) wiped out tribal ownership of property and granted 160 acres to heads of families
(E) forbade selling alcohol or guns on reservations

64. The concept that those individuals who make large sums of money should become philanthropists and spend their money for the benefit of others during their lifetime is the main message of

(A) William Jennings Bryan's Cross of Gold oration
(B) Andrew Carnegie's Gospel of Wealth address
(C) Horatio Alger's Rags to Riches stories
(D) Walter Rauschenbush's Social Gospel theory
(E) William Graham Sumner's Social Darwinism concepts

65. "For many years numerous Americans have been living in Nicaragua, developing its industries and carrying on business. At the present time there are large investments in lumbering, mining, coffee growing, banana culture, shipping and in . . . other business. In addition . . . , the Government of Nicaragua, by a treaty, granted in perpetuity to the United States exclusive rights . . . for the construction, . . . of an oceanic canal."

The above quotation is an example of the United States policy toward Latin America known as

(A) the Good Neighbor Policy
(B) the Monroe Doctrine
(C) Dollar Diplomacy
(D) Pan-Americanism
(E) Alliance for Progress

66. All of the following authors are correctly paired with one of their works EXCEPT

(A) Ernest Hemingway—*A Farewell to Arms*
(B) John Steinbeck—*The Grapes of Wrath*
(C) Eugene O'Neill—*Mourning Becomes Electra*
(D) Sinclair Lewis—*Main Street*
(E) Langston Hughes—*The Great Gatsby*

67. The Great Depression threatened the survival of the United States capitalist, free-enterprise system because

(A) there was no market for apples sold on street corners
(B) business leaders moved their headquarters overseas
(C) Communist Chinese products flooded the United States market
(D) the balance of payment favored Asian nations
(E) industry could not provide enough jobs for the unemployed

68. The first woman to serve in the United States cabinet was

    (A) Frances Perkins
    (B) Oveta Culp Hobby
    (C) Eleanor Roosevelt
    (D) Marian Anderson
    (E) Sandra Day O'Connor

69. The Supreme Court under Chief Justice Earl Warren was noted for its decisions regarding segregation and the

    (A) rights of the police to punish criminals
    (B) protection of individual rights in criminal cases
    (C) defense of the death penalty
    (D) support of presidential authority
    (E) limit of federal authority in the War on Poverty

70. All of the following are illustrations of strong conservative attitudes in American society in the years after World War II EXCEPT

    (A) the "silent majority"
    (B) the 1994 Contract with America
    (C) the presidential nomination of Barry Goldwater
    (D) the programs offered by the "Religious Right"
    (E) the pro-choice movement

71. The World Trade Organization (WTO) has the responsibility to

    (A) maintain an equal trade balance between all nations
    (B) enforce established fair trade practices between members of the WTO
    (C) control all monetary exchanges between international corporations
    (D) manage the salary negotiations between workers and owners
    (E) supervise the accounting practices of United States firms

72. The most significant difference between the Pilgrims and the Puritans is that the Pilgrims

    (A) arrived in New England first
    (B) obtained a grant of settlement from the London Company
    (C) held more radical ideas for reforming the Church of England
    (D) had a strong leader
    (E) celebrated the first Thanksgiving

73. "The object of your expedition is to . . . obtain large supplies of cattle, horses and carriages . . . during your whole progress your detachments are to have orders to bring into you all horses fit to mount the Dragoons (mounted infantrymen) . . . likewise to bring in wagons and other convenient carriages, . . . and should you find it necessary to move on before such delivery (of goods) can be made, hostages of the most respectable inhabitants should be taken to secure their (delivery) next day . . . All persons acting in Committees, or any officers under direction of the Congress either civil or military, are to be made prisoners."

    The above quotation supports all of the following statements EXCEPT

    (A) these are instructions for an expedition into enemy territory
    (B) those sending the expedition are in need of additional transport
    (C) the expedition is against forces commanded by a Congress
    (D) hostages will assure the delivery of supplies
    (E) the leader of the expedition is commanded to follow a "scorched earth" policy

74. Which of the following best describes the social structure of the colonies before the American Revolution?

    (A) It did not support the concept that "all men are created equal."
    (B) It allowed many people to rise to their fullest potential.
    (C) It reflected the social structure in England.
    (D) It did not emphasize the differences in wealth among the colonists.
    (E) It accepted all religious faiths as equally important.

75. United States historian Arthur Schlesinger called World War II the "greatest challenge democracy ever faced."

    Which one of the following events of World War II would LEAST likely be used to support this statement?

    (A) the Holocaust (killing of European Jews by the Nazis)
    (B) the ideas expressed by Hitler in his book, *Mein Kampf*
    (C) the attack on Pearl Harbor by Japan
    (D) the Allied victory in the Battle of Midway
    (E) the German defeat of France in 1940

76. Washington Irving is remembered as one of the first important writers of the newly established United States for his work

    (A) *Common Sense*
    (B) *Poor Richard's Almanac*
    (C) *The Legend of Sleepy Hollow*
    (D) *The Scarlet Letter*
    (E) *An American Scholar*

77. The National Labor Union, after winning the eight-hour day for government workers, disintegrated because of

(A) the depression of the early 1870s
(B) a Supreme Court ruling outlawing unions
(C) the opposition of President Grant
(D) the rise of the Knights of Labor
(E) the failure to admit African Americans

78. *The Jungle* by Upton Sinclair recounts the story of

(A) Theodore Roosevelt's big-game hunting in Africa
(B) life in the highly competitive electronics industry
(C) growing up on an Indian reservation
(D) corruption in the meat-packing industry
(E) working in the business world of 1950s America

*Source: Harper's Weekly*, December 13, 1862

79. The point the cartoon from *Harper's Weekly* is making centers on the

(A) way the British industrialists supplied arms and ships for the Confederacy
(B) way the Confederates could not make manacles for slaves and guns at the same time
(C) first time the Confederacy was personified in a cartoon as a man
(D) view of the Union concerning overfed British people
(E) great wealth and manufacturing skill of the British

80. All of the following occurred after the fall of the Berlin Wall in 1989 EXCEPT

(A) the beginning of *perestroika* and *glasnost*
(B) the breakup of the Soviet Union into separate nations
(C) the outbreak of warfare in Yugoslavia
(D) the Persian Gulf War
(E) the sending of U.S. troops to Somalia in the U.N.'s Project Restore Hope

# SECTION II: DBQ

The free-response section consists of two parts. All students must answer the DBQ in Part A. Parts B and C consist of four essay questions, and students must answer one question from each Part.

**You have a 15-minute reading period to read the documents and prepare your answer.**

## PART A: DOCUMENT-BASED ESSAY QUESTION (DBQ)

WRITING TIME: 45 MINUTES

**Directions:** The following question requires you to construct a coherent essay that integrates your interpretation of documents A–N **and** your knowledge of the period referred to in the question. In order to earn a high score you must cite key pieces of evidence from the documents and draw on your knowledge of the period.

1. Between 1789 and 1815 to what extent was the foreign policy of the United States driven by a concern for commerce?

### Document A

*Source:* **U.S. Constitution, 1789**

*Article I: Section 9*
The Migration or Importation of such Persons as any of the States now existing shall think proper to admit, shall not be prohibited by the Congress prior to the Year one thousand eight hundred and eight, but a tax or duty may be imposed on such Importation, not exceeding ten dollars for each Person.
No Preference shall be given by any Regulation of Commerce or Revenue to the Ports of one State over those of another: nor shall Vessels bound to, or from, one State, be obliged to enter, clear, or pay Duties in another.

## Document B

> *Source:* An Act Imposing Duties on the Tonnage of Ships or Vessels, July 20, 1790
>
> **Section 1.** *Be it enacted by the Senate and House of Representatives of the United States of America in Congress assembled,* That upon all ships or vessels which after the first day of September next, shall be entered in the United States from any foreign port or place, there shall . . . (pay) the several and respective duties following, that is to say: On ships or vessels of the United States at the rate of six cents per ton: on ships or vessels built within the United States after the twentieth day of July last, but belonging wholly or in part to subjects of foreign powers, at the rate of thirty cents per ton: on other ships or vessels at the rate of fifty cents per ton.

## Document C

> *Source:* The Proclamation of Neutrality 1793: A Proclamation
>
> Whereas . . . a state of war exists between Austria, Prussia, Sardinia, Great Britain, and the United Netherlands, of the one part, and France on the other; and the duty and interest of the United States require, that they should . . . adopt and pursue a conduct friendly and impartial toward the belligerent Powers; I therefore . . . declare the disposition of the United States to observe the conduct aforesaid towards those Powers respectfully; and to warn the citizens of the United States carefully to avoid all acts . . . which may in any manner tend to contravene such disposition.

## Document D

*Source:* **From the Letters of Thomas Jefferson**

*To Gouverneur Morris, Philadelphia, March 12, 1793:*
We surely cannot deny to any nation that right whereon our own government is founded, that every one may govern itself according to whatever form it pleases and change these forms at its own will; and that it may transact its business with foreign nations through whatever [government] organ it thinks proper, whether king, convention, assembly, committee, president, or anything else it may choose. The will of the nation is the only thing essential to be regarded.

*To Thomas Pinckney, Philadelphia, May 29, 1797:*
War is not the best engine for us to resort to. Nature has given us one—our commerce—which, if properly managed, will be a better instrument for obliging the interested nations of Europe to treat us with justice.

*To Benjamin Waring, Washington, March 23, 1801:*
. . . the will of the people . . . is the only legitimate foundation of any government, and to protect its free expression should be our first object.

## Document E

*Source:* **Jay's Treaty, signed with Great Britain, 1795**

His Britannic Majesty and the United States of America, being desirous, by a treaty of amity, commerce and navigation, to terminate their difference . . . and also to regulate the commerce and navigation between their respective countries . . . , in such a manner as to render the same reciprocally beneficial and satisfactory; . . . have agreed on and concluded the following articles:

ARTICLE I:
There shall be a firm, inviolable and universal peace, and a true and sincere friendship between His Britannic Majesty, his heirs and successors, and the United States of America; . . .

ARTICLE II:
His Majesty will withdraw all his troops and garrisons from all posts and places within the boundary lines assigned by the treaty of peace to the United States . . .

## Document F

> *Source:* **Treaty of Friendship, Limits, and Navigation, signed with Spain, 1795**
>
> There shall be a firm and inviolable Peace and sincere Friendship between His Catholic Majesty (King of Spain), his successors and subjects, and the United States and their Citizens without exception of persons and places.
>
> ARTICLE II:
> To prevent all disputes on the subject of the boundaries which separate the territories of the two, it is . . . agreed: The Southern boundary of the United States . . . , shall be designated by a line beginning on the River Mississippi . . . to the Atlantic Ocean. And it is agreed that if there should be any troops, Garrisons or settlements of either Party in the territory of the other according to the above mentioned boundar(y), they shall be withdrawn from the said territory . . .
>
> ARTICLE IV:
> It is likewise agreed that the Western boundary of the United States which separates them from the Spanish Colony of Louisiana, is in the middle of the channel or bed of the River Mississippi . . .

## Document G

> *Source:* **Treaty of Greenville, signed with Native American tribal leaders, 1795**
>
> ARTICLE 1:
> Henceforth all hostilities shall cease; peace is hereby established, and shall be perpetual; and a friendly [trade] shall take place between the said United States and Indian tribes.
>
> ARTICLE 5:
> To prevent any misunderstanding about the Indian lands relinquished by the United States in the fourth article, it is now explicitly declared, that the meaning of that relinquishment is this: the Indian tribes who have a right to those lands, are quietly enjoying them, hunting, planting, and dwelling thereon, so long as they please, without any molestation from the United States; but when those tribes, or any of them, shall be disposed to sell their lands, or any part of them, they are to be sold only to the United States; . . .

## Document H

---

*Source:* **Washington's Farewell Address, 1796**

. . . A passionate attachment of one nation for another produces a variety of evils. . . . , facilitating the illusion of an imaginary common interest in cases where no real common interest exists, . . . [and leads to] participation in the quarrels and wars of the latter without adequate justification . . .

. . . history and experience prove that foreign influence is one of the most baneful foes of republican government . . .

The great rule of conduct for us in regard to foreign nations is in extending our commercial relations, [and] to have with them as little political connection as possible . . .

Harmony, liberal intercourse with all nations, are recommended . . . But even our commercial policy should hold an equal and impartial hand; neither seeking nor granting exclusive favors or preferences; . . . define the rights of our merchants, and enable the government to support them, establishing conventional rules of intercourse, . . . but temporary, and liable to be from time to time abandoned or varied, as experience and circumstances shall dictate; . . .

---

## Document I

---

*Source:* **John Adams—Special Message to the Senate and the House, May 16, 1797**

. . . The refusal on the part of France to receive our minister is the denial of a right; but the refusal to receive him until we have acceded to their demands without discussion is to treat us neither as allies nor as friends, nor as a sovereign state.

. . . this conduct of the French Government . . . discloses sentiments more alarming than the refusal of a minister, because more dangerous to our independence and union, and at the same time studiously marked with indignities toward the Government of the United States. It evinces a disposition to separate the people of the United States from the Government, . . . have chosen to manage their common concerns, and thus to produce divisions fatal to our peace. Such attempts ought to be repelled with a decision which shall convince France and the world that we are not a degraded people, humiliated under a colonial spirit of fear and sense of inferiority, fitted to be the miserable instruments of foreign influence.

---

## Document J

*Source:* **Convention Between the French Republic, and the United States of America, December 21, 1801**

ARTICLE I:
There shall be a firm, inviolable, and universal peace, and a true and sincere Friendship between the French Republic, and the United States of America, and between their respective countries, territories, and people without exception of persons, or places.

ARTICLE VI:
Commerce between the Parties shall be free . . . and in general the two parties shall enjoy in the ports of each other, in regard to commerce, and navigation, the privileges of the most favored nation.

## Document K

*Source:* **Jefferson's third message to Congress, December 15, 1803**

Congress witnessed, at their last session, the extraordinary agitation produced in the public mind by the suspension of our right of deposit at the port of New Orleans . . . They were sensible that the continuance of that privation would be more injurious to our nation . . .

The enlightened government of France saw, the importance to both nations of arrangements as might best and permanently promote the peace, friendship, and interests of both; . . . [Therefore have agreed to] transfer to the United States . . . [the entire Territory of Louisiana]

## Document L

*Source:* **James Madison First Inaugural, March 4, 1809**

Indulging no passions which trespass on the rights or the repose of other nations, it has been the true glory of the United States to cultivate peace by observing justice, and to entitle themselves to the respect of the nations at war by fulfilling their neutral obligations with the most scrupulous impartiality. If there be candor in the world, the truth of these assertions will not be questioned; posterity at least will do justice to them.

**Document M**

*Source: The Sun, Gazette and County Advertiser,* Dover, N.H., Saturday, December 12, 1807

. . . The outrage committed on the frigate *Chesapeake* [and] . . . other acts of aggression committed within our ports and waters by British ships of war manifesting the same disregard of our national rights, and seeming to flow from the same contempt for the authority of our laws, . . . capturing American vessels within our acknowledged territorial limits . . . ; impressing seamen on board American vessels, firing on vessels and boats of all descriptions having occasion to pass near them in pursuit of their lawful trade, . . . it is [therefore] expedient to provide more effectually for the protection of our ports and harbors . . .

**Document N**

*Source:* **Amendments to the Constitution Proposed by the Hartford Convention, 1814**

. . . Third—Congress shall not have power to lay any embargo on the ships or vessels of the citizens of the United States, in the ports or harbors thereof, for more than sixty days.

Fourth—Congress shall not have power, without the concurrence of two-thirds of both Houses, to interdict the commercial intercourse between the United States and any foreign nation or the dependencies thereof . . .

# SECTION II: FREE-RESPONSE QUESTIONS 2–5

## ESSAY QUESTIONS

WRITING TIME: 70 MINUTES

> **Directions:** You are to answer *two* of the following questions—one from Part B and one from Part C. Carefully choose the question that you are best prepared to answer. Cite relevant historical evidence in support of your generalizations and present your arguments clearly and logically. When you finish writing, check your work if time permits. Make certain to number your answer as the question is numbered below. You should write your answer in pen.

**Part B:** Choose ONE question from Part B. It is suggested that you spend 5 minutes organizing your answer and 30 minutes writing it.

2. In what ways did federal legislation and federal judicial decisions between 1787 and 1860 affect the life of the African American in United States society?

3. Compare and contrast the presidencies of Jefferson and Jackson. To what extent were the presidencies of these two men revolutionary?

**Part C:** Choose ONE question from Part C. It is suggested that you spend 5 minutes organizing and 30 minutes writing your answer.

4. "The proposals of the Populists in the early 1890s were not enacted, but these proposals provided the framework for the New Deal's response to the economic and social conditions created by the Great Depression."

   Analyze the validity of this generalization.

5. Evaluate THREE of the following as a factor in establishing the United States as a leader in international affairs:

   Spanish-American War
   Opening of the Panama Canal
   Defeat of the Treaty of Versailles by the United States Senate
   Outbreak of World War II in Europe and Asia
   Vietnam War

## End of Examination

At the end of the exam you will be directed to circle on the back of your essay answer booklet the numbers of the two questions you answered.

## COMMENTS AND ANSWER EXPLANATIONS FOR MODEL EXAM B

In this section you will find answers and answer explanations for the 80 multiple-choice questions of the model exam. The explanations of the multiple-choice questions indicate which answer is most correct and, in many cases, why the other choices should be eliminated. By reading all 80 statements, you will get a quick summary of the highlights of American history.

| | | | |
|---|---|---|---|
| 1. **(D)** | 21. **(D)** | 41. **(B)** | 61. **(D)** |
| 2. **(B)** | 22. **(B)** | 42. **(C)** | 62. **(C)** |
| 3. **(C)** | 23. **(A)** | 43. **(B)** | 63. **(D)** |
| 4. **(E)** | 24. **(B)** | 44. **(C)** | 64. **(B)** |
| 5. **(C)** | 25. **(B)** | 45. **(D)** | 65. **(C)** |
| 6. **(C)** | 26. **(A)** | 46. **(C)** | 66. **(E)** |
| 7. **(B)** | 27. **(D)** | 47. **(D)** | 67. **(E)** |
| 8. **(D)** | 28. **(A)** | 48. **(E)** | 68. **(A)** |
| 9. **(E)** | 29. **(E)** | 49. **(B)** | 69. **(B)** |
| 10. **(C)** | 30. **(A)** | 50. **(B)** | 70. **(E)** |
| 11. **(B)** | 31. **(E)** | 51. **(A)** | 71. **(B)** |
| 12. **(D)** | 32. **(A)** | 52. **(C)** | 72. **(C)** |
| 13. **(C)** | 33. **(D)** | 53. **(D)** | 73. **(E)** |
| 14. **(C)** | 34. **(B)** | 54. **(C)** | 74. **(A)** |
| 15. **(A)** | 35. **(D)** | 55. **(E)** | 75. **(D)** |
| 16. **(E)** | 36. **(C)** | 56. **(C)** | 76. **(C)** |
| 17. **(B)** | 37. **(D)** | 57. **(D)** | 77. **(A)** |
| 18. **(E)** | 38. **(A)** | 58. **(D)** | 78. **(D)** |
| 19. **(B)** | 39. **(C)** | 59. **(E)** | 79. **(A)** |
| 20. **(B)** | 40. **(A)** | 60. **(C)** | 80. **(A)** |

## Multiple-Choice Answers Explained

1. **(D)** The Boston Tea Party was an important event in the series of events that led to the start of the American Revolution. The other events listed all occurred after the Revolution.

2. **(B)** Detroit was a key frontier post that the British refused to evacuate after 1783 in spite of the terms of the Treaty of Paris in that year. It was later evacuated according to the terms of Jay's Treaty.

3. **(C)** The Whiskey Rebellion of 1794 was a protest by Pennsylvania farmers over a tax on whiskey by the federal government. Its major significance was that it tested the power of the federal government to tax and president Washington sent federal troops to end the rebellion. Shays' Rebellion was a factor in the writing of the Constitution and rebellion brought farmers together, but that is not its major significance.

4. **(E)** The Independent Treasury Plan was Van Buren's answer to the concept of a Bank of the United States or the use of state banks by the federal government.

It called for depositing federal revenue directly in the U.S. Treasury, thus ignoring banks.

5. **(C)** Thaddeus Stevens was the leader of the Radical Republicans in the House. He played a key role in the impeachment of Andrew Johnson and in the development of congressional reconstruction plans. The other people listed all played important roles in government in the 1860s.

6. **(C)** A number of scandals are connected with the Grant administration. The Credit Mobilier involving railroad construction and the Whiskey Ring involving the theft of some of the whiskey tax revenue from the Treasury were major scandals in Grant's administration. Teapot Dome is a scandal connected with President Harding's administration, the Tweed Gang corruptly ran New York City and was not part of the Grant administration, Whitewater was investigated as a possible scandal under Clinton but no charges were bought against the Clintons, and the Watergate Scandal ended Nixon's presidency.

7. **(B)** Theodore Roosevelt called those "reformers who used their pens to draw attention to the evils afflicting America" "Muckrakers" after a character in John Bunyan's *Pilgrim's Progress*. The character spent so much time raking manure that he lost sight of heaven and better things. Roosevelt thought these reformers were too harsh and narrow-minded, although he supported in Congress and in the nation many of the causes these reformers supported. The other choices have no significance for the question.

8. **(D)** As part of his progressive program, President Woodrow Wilson introduced and Congress established the Federal Reserve System that still oversees the U.S. banking system. The other choices relate to banking issues at different time periods.

9. **(E)** The question is based on a pie graph in which a circle is divided into pie slices, each of which represents a percentage of the whole pie. In this chart each slice represents the number of men from the nation named killed in World War I. It provides a quick comparison of the numbers killed. It should be immediately clear from comparing the sizes of the slices that the losses of Russia were greater than those of any other nation, with the United States' losses the smallest. You are not given the actual number killed, only a comparative percentage of the total killed. To compare the percentages in each slice use a ruler, piece of paper, or pencil to measure the distance between the places where the sides of each slice meet the rim of the pie. This segment provides the basis of measurement of the size of each slice. When you do this measurement and then compare the size of the pieces, you will see that the correct answer is E—losses were "approximately equal for Russia and Germany." In fact, the official count of war dead for Russia was 1.7 million and for Germany it was 1.6 million, whereas the United States lost 49,000.

10. **(C)** The Berlin Blockade by the Soviet Union in 1948 was met by a successful airlift of supplies to the beleaguered city. This Soviet action seemed to confirm a threat to the West and to world peace by the Communist nations. As a result,

the United States joined a newly formed alliance of Britain, France, and the Benelux (Belgium, the Netherlands, and Luxembourg) nations. This alliance became NATO, our first peacetime alliance since George Washington in his Farewell Address warned the nation against entangling alliances. NATO marks a major shift in U.S. foreign policy. The other items were all Cold War events that helped to confirm the need for the NATO alliance.

11. **(B)** When legislators exchange support for each other's special bills, it is called logrolling. These terms are defined in the Glossary.

12. **(D)** The Camp David Accords, which led to the peace treaty between Egypt and Israel, were negotiated by President Carter, using his personal persuasion. President Nixon withdrew U.S. troops from Vietnam. OPEC is still in existence as this book is being written and shows no signs of breaking up. The overthrow of the Shah of Iran is not considered an achievement of the United States, and we held the Panama Canal by treaty arrangement.

13. **(C)** While all the men were leaders of colonies, the only man correctly paired with the colony he led is William Penn.

14. **(C)** The Albany Plan was drafted by Benjamin Franklin in 1754 in an attempt to get the colonies to unite for their common defense. It was not adopted, but many features foreshadowed the Articles of Confederation and the Constitution.

15. **(A)** John Marshall, a Federalist, believed in strengthening the power of the federal government and of the Supreme Court within the government. The famous case of *Marbury v. Madison* established the right of judicial review of congressional legislation by the Supreme Court. Judicial review is not stated in the Constitution. It can be implied only from other stated powers and ideas included in the document. This use of implied powers allows for a loose construction or interpretation of the Constitution.

16. **(E)** Sailing ships could carry the most cargo from the East to California at the time of the 1849 gold rush. There were no cross-country railroads. Horseback and stagecoaches had limited space, and obviously, an individual could carry fewer goods than any other option. All overland travel was subject to many difficulties.

17. **(B)** The Compromise of 1877 settled the disputed election of 1876, and the terms included the withdrawal of Northern troops from the South. This ended Reconstruction.

18. **(E)** In the cartoon from *Harper's Weekly* of September 10, 1872, the cartoonist is no doubt concerned with the high cost of pork and flour and the high prices of stocks and their fluctuations, but the real point of the cartoon has to do with a fall in the price of gold. Gold is represented by Humpty Dumpty, as the verse in the title indicates. The cartoonist is using the well-known verse about Humpty Dumpty to make his point that the fall of gold prices will lead

to a crash—an economic depression—just as the fall of Humpty Dumpty led to a broken egg that could not be repaired. This is a good example of how a cartoonist uses commonly understood imagery to make a point.

19. **(B)** Question 19 focuses on the issue of the "old" and "new" immigration. The "old" immigrants formed the majority of immigrants to the United States until 1890. They came from western and northern Europe—Ireland, England, and Germany. The "new" immigrants became the majority of immigrants after 1890 and came from eastern and southern Europe—Italy, Austria-Hungary, and Russia.

20. **(B)** The United Nations was modeled on the League of Nations.

21. **(D)** *Flapper* was a term used in the 1920s to describe the ideal young woman of the period. The other terms are all from the 1960s and have political connotations. *Pig* was used to refer to police; *hippie* was used to describe those young people in the 1960s who first adopted long hair and unisex clothing and who rejected many of the materialistic values of U.S. society; a *dove*, as opposed to a *hawk*, was against U.S. involvement in Vietnam; *black power* was the slogan of some civil rights activists.

22. **(B)** During his first year in office President Reagan successfully pressured Congress into passing a massive income tax cut—a key point of Reaganomics. It was part of his administration's attack on the high inflation rate. Reagan wanted to eliminate the Department of Energy, supported aid to Taiwan, wanted to reduce the minimum wage for teenagers, but not for all workers, and wanted to block the activities of terrorists.

23. **(A)** The Act of Toleration was first passed in Maryland in 1649, granting religious toleration in that colony. It was soon repealed. The other acts were all passed by Parliament for the purpose of controlling trade and manufacture in the colonies.

24. **(B)** Thomas Paine's pamphlet *Common Sense* is considered an excellent propaganda piece. The arguments he used in presenting his case for independence are not very logical and rely more on emotional appeal. However, they persuaded many colonists to support the rebellion.

25. **(B)** Alexander Hamilton's financial measures benefited the merchants.

26. **(A)** The Missouri Compromise in 1820 maintained the balance between free and slave states.

27. **(D)** The Compromise of 1850 was Henry Clay's (the Great Compromiser) last contribution to national unity. It temporarily resolved the free state/slave state controversy, giving both the North and South certain points they desired. Although slavery had reappeared as a divisive issue as a result of the Texas controversy and the Mexican War, the Compromise did not deal with any issue involving Texas.

28. **(A)** The lack of a cross-continental railroad slowed westward expansion before the Civil War.

29. **(E)** The photograph from the *Los Angeles County Natural History Museum Foundation* shows immigrants living in New York City. The time as revealed by the clothing is the turn of the century. Hispanic migration to Los Angeles was later than that. The population is clearly not African American. The tenement-style buildings and active life on the street all point to immigrants in New York City.

30. **(A)** Rachel Carson wrote *Silent Spring* and brought environmental issues to the attention of millions. Ralph Nader, before running for president twice, focused public attention on many questionable business and societal practices. John Muir was a naturalist and encouraged Theodore Roosevelt's interest in conservation. Tom Wolfe (*Bonfire of the Vanities*) and Jack Kerouac (*On the Road*) are post-World War II authors.

31. **(E)** All five answers relate to the Civil Rights Movement of which Martin Luther King, Jr. became the most powerful spokesman. He first emerged as a leader during the Montgomery Bus Boycott.

32. **(A)** John F. Kennedy committed the United States to placing a man on the moon before the end of the 1960s. The other four items are the opposite of what Kennedy supported.

33. **(D)** The increasing globalization of the world economy was an important trend during the 1990s, the decade after the end of the Cold War. The United States and Russia cooperated on many issues during the decade, including building an international space station. Yugoslavia, in southeastern Europe, was torn apart by strong nationalistic sentiments. The economy of China flourished in the decade.

34. **(B)** The proposed Equal Rights Amendment to the Constitution was not approved by enough states to add it to the Constitution. Many considered this a setback for women's rights. Title IX opened up athletic opportunities for women. The Family and Medical Leave Act (signed by Clinton) allowed workers to take time off from work without being fired, allowing women, and men, to meet family and medical needs. NOW supported the Women's Liberation Movement and created greater awareness of the concerns of women, and this led to greater opportunities.

35. **(D)** In the 17ᵗʰ and 18ᵗʰ centuries Virginia was economically dependent upon the cultivation of tobacco. The planter class, living on the plantations where tobacco was grown, dominated the cultural life of the colony. The other choices were important in other southern colonies.

36. **(C)** The Stamp Act (1765) was the first of these five acts enacted and started the colonists on the road to independence. The other choices occurred later

along that road and are considered steps in the cause-and-effect relationship of events that led to independence.

37. **(D)** The Quebec Act (1774) established the framework for the government of Canada, which the British acquired by the Treaty of Paris in 1763.

38. **(A)** The clause from the Constitution is often referred to as the elastic clause. It has been interpreted to give extensive powers to the federal government covering all things "necessary and proper" (for example, helpful in carrying out all the other powers given to Congress).

39. **(C)** The Federalists of New England were opposed to the War of 1812, and when it looked as though the United States would be badly defeated, they called a secret meeting at Hartford to discuss what might be done, including the possibility of secession from the union. The Convention is considered the death knell of the Federalist Party. It never again held national political power.

40. **(A)** The Kansas-Nebraska Act rejected the 36° 30′ line of the Missouri Compromise and introduced the concept of popular sovereignty to determine whether Kansas would be a free or slave state. The Compromise of 1850 included a strict fugitive slave law. The balance of slave and free states could be broken, depending on the vote taken under popular sovereignty. The Dred Scott case came three years after the Kansas-Nebraska Act.

41. **(B)** As a result of the development of barbed wire, cattle raisers could fence large areas of the semiarid lands of the West to make raising cattle more profitable and controllable. The elimination of the buffalo opened the range to cattle. Cattle drives to the railheads (shipping points) and the railroads also aided the raising of cattle as they provided an access to the large Eastern market. The reaper had no relation to cattle raising.

42. **(C)** Question 42 summarizes the view of American isolationists. It is the opposite of what internationalists believe. Socialists also support cooperation between nations. It is impossible to group immigrants and clergy together to hold any one view.

43. **(B)** The depletion of resources and manpower during World War I led to conditions that encouraged the rise of fascism and communism. The Marshall Plan and close U.S.-Europe cooperation came after World War II. The League never oversaw resource distribution, and only Italy established new colonies in Africa after World War I.

44. **(C)** In the twenty years after World War II, television dramatically changed social patterns. Motion pictures and automobiles changed social patterns before World War II and continued to do so after the war, but the TV was new and its advent affected the lives of millions very quickly. Cell phones and microwave ovens have had an impact more recently.

**Practice Test B**

45. **(D)** *Brown v. Board of Education of Topeka* reversed the "separate but equal" doctrine established by the Court in *Plessy v. Ferguson* and called for the end of segregation in schools. The Brown decision was a milestone in the Civil Rights Movement. The other choices are all landmark decisions of the Court.

46. **(C)** The founding of Israel would not be considered part of the Cold War. However, after the establishment of the nation in 1948, the Soviet Union and the United States often disagreed on policy affecting Israel and the Middle East. The alternative choices all are considered major events in the Cold War confrontation.

47. **(D)** President Clinton was impeached on charges of obstructing justice and misleading testimony. The other choices include key words—Independent Counsel, health care reform, Whitewater, and Oval Office—but the information included about them is incorrect.

48. **(E)** Delegates to the Constitutional Convention agreed that Congress would have the power to declare war and raise an army. Compromises had to be reached on the issue of the election of the president, taxation of commerce, whether slaves would be counted in determining a state's population, and the method of representation in the Senate and House that would affect the interests of large and small states. The Constitution was created by a series of compromises.

49. **(B)** The question requires that you know the boundaries of the Louisiana Purchase. It was the Mississippi River. Thus, reading the map should make it easy to determine that Louisiana in 1812 was the first state admitted to the Union for the territory acquired from France in 1803.

50. **(B)** In 1823 President Monroe warned the European powers not to interfere in South America. This, along with three other points: the Americas were not open for colonization; the American political system was different from that of Europe; the United States would not interfere in Europe or with existing European colonies, became known as the Monroe Doctrine. The other choices reflect different aspects of U.S. relations with South America.

51. **(A)** The so-called Tariff of Abominations of 1828 set off the entire tariff, state power/federal power, nullification crisis of Jackson's administration. The other four choices all represent key aspects of this controversy.

52. **(C)** The question requires you to define a common historic term. *Jim Crow* was a name given to the freed slave, just as John Doe has been used for whites. *Jim Crow* laws refer to the legislation designed to deny equality to African Americans. Such legislation was widespread and included a great variety of laws. The laws requiring separate but equal school and railroad facilities and laws denying the vote to a person unless his grandfather had voted are examples of Jim Crow laws. The U.S. Congress did not pass Jim Crow laws, but many states did. The Congress has passed laws involving the four other choices.

53. **(D)** In question 53 individuals who were important in other than political or economic areas are paired with items for which they are famous. Joseph Pulitzer helped to revolutionize the newspaper business as editor of the *New York World*; Louis H. Sullivan was a famous architect who designed the first skyscrapers; Thomas Edison invented the phonograph and many other items; Buffalo Bill Cody was a star of typically American Wild West shows. Bret Harte, although a famous author writing about the West, did not write *The Adventures of Huckleberry Finn*, which was written by Mark Twain.

54. **(C)** By 1763 the thirteen colonies were all either royal colonies controlled by the King or proprietary colonies controlled by descendants of individuals to whom the colony was granted by the King. Colonies had rudimentary forms of self-government, but final authority rested with the King or the proprietor.

55. **(E)** In the 1920s speculation was widespread among investors. The other options provide incorrect interpretations of the 1920s and in each case the opposite is true.

56. **(C)** The Federal Securities Act was part of the New Deal program. The others all came earlier. The Clayton Act and the Federal Trade Commission Act were part of Wilson's New Freedom. The Pure Food and Drug Act was passed in 1906, inspired by the Muckrakers, and the Sherman Antitrust Act was passed in 1890.

57. **(D)** President Johnson's Great Society involved many different programs including Operation Headstart, the Voting Rights Act, Medicare, and the establishment of the Department of Housing and Welfare. Although the president wanted some revisions in the Taft-Hartley Labor Act, Congress never voted for them and the act, passed over Truman's opposition in 1947, remained in force.

58. **(D)** Local financing and control of public education has been an important American attitude toward education since the Massachusetts Bay Colony passed this, the "Olde Deluder Satan" law.

59. **(E)** In colonial America women did not have the same legal rights as men. The other four choices are true.

60. **(C)** Jefferson was more sympathetic to France than to England during the French Revolution and Napoleonic Wars.

61. **(D)** The growth of railroads had a great impact on the nation. However, the railroads cannot be considered a part of social democracy, although they may have had an indirect impact by allowing individuals to move about more easily. The other four advanced the democratization of society and represent the great variety of reform movements begun in the 1820s and 1830s, which are considered a part of Jacksonian Democracy.

62. **(C)** The "gag rule" was passed by the House to eliminate the congressional debate of antislavery proposals, which Southerners feared would lead to federal acts against the interests of the South. Garrison's *Liberator* and Nat Turner's revolt helped provoke this fear, but the "gag rule" was not passed to prevent them.

63. **(D)** The Dawes Act of 1887 reversed previous policy toward Native Americans. Previously, tribes had been treated as independent nations and were placed on reservations. The Dawes Act eliminated tribal ownership of property and provided land for each head of family. It was designed to turn the natives into farmers and *eventually* into citizens. The act did nothing about guns or alcohol, but it did attempt to protect the Native Americans' claim to their 160 acres and to prepare them for citizenship. It was an attempt to deal fairly with Native Americans, but unfortunately, it was designed to turn them into whites and showed no understanding of their culture.

64. **(B)** The multi-millionaire founder of Carnegie Steel, Andrew Carnegie, set forth this view of philanthropy in his address, The Gospel of Wealth. Many 19th- and 20th-century business leaders followed this idea and gave millions to support worthy causes, from libraries to universities. The alternative answers all express important ideas. The authors were contemporaries of Carnegie. Bryan's Cross of Gold oration condemned the gold standard and won him the Democratic Party nomination for president. Alger wrote many popular stories for young people on the "rags to riches" theme. Rauschenbusch and others interpreted the Christian Gospel in terms of working actively to change and make better social conditions for the poor. Sumner applied Darwinism to the economic sphere, supporting laissez-faire and claiming that the best business-men would naturally survive in the struggle for success if no laws restricted them.

65. **(C)** The question is from a message of President Coolidge to Congress, January 10, 1927, in which he sets forth the justification for sending U.S. Marines to Nicaragua at that time. It was a move typical of Dollar Diplomacy and of the attitude of the United States toward Latin America during much of our history.

66. **(E)** The authors listed in the question are all famous writers of the period 1916–1945. Each title mentioned was written in those years, but *The Great Gatsby* was written by F. Scott Fitzgerald, not by Langston Hughes, who was noted for his poetry. Eugene O'Neill is a playwright; the others mentioned are novelists. These works all provide important insights into the attitudes of people during these years and should be read by students of United States history.

67. **(E)** The Great Depression's greatest threat to capitalism was the loss of jobs and industry's inability to supply jobs for the unemployed. The movement of business headquarters overseas, the flood of Communist Chinese products, and balance of trade favoring Asia all came in the late 20th century. A very small number of unemployed did sell apples during the depression and found a market.

68. **(A)** Frances Perkins was the first woman appointed to a cabinet post by an American president. She served as Franklin D. Roosevelt's Secretary of Labor. Sandra Day O'Connor was the first woman to serve on the U.S. Supreme Court and was appointed by President Reagan. Eleanor Roosevelt, wife of the president, was active politically and served in the United States delegation to the United Nations after her husband's death. Marian Anderson is a noted African American singer who was denied the right to sing in the hall of the Daughters of the American Revolution in Washington. President and Mrs. Roosevelt were angered by this, so Mrs. Roosevelt resigned from the DAR. Oveta Culp Hobby headed the woman's branch of the Navy during World War II.

69. **(B)** The so-called Warren Court is noted for its concern for the rights of all individuals. Many right-wing groups strongly opposed some of the decisions and called for the impeachment of the chief justice, but the Court continued to support the rights of individuals in criminal cases, such as the *Escobedo*, *Gideon*, and *Miranda* cases, and desegregation cases, such as *Brown v. Board of Education*.

70. **(E)** *Pro-choice* refers to those who support the right of a woman to choose an abortion. It is considered a liberal position. *Pro-life*, which refers to the right of the unborn fetus to live, is considered a conservative position. The other four selections all reflect conservative attitudes. The "silent majority" was President Nixon's term for those Conservatives who supported him and who were not actively involved in the agitation and turmoil of the 1960s. Barry Goldwater, a conservative Republican from Arizona, was nominated for president in 1964 and was overwhelmingly defeated, but his campaign paved the way for Nixon's victory in 1968. The 1994 Contract with America, orchestrated by House Speaker Newt Gingrich, rallied Conservatives to vote, giving Republicans control of both houses of Congress for the first time in 40 years. The "Religious Right" is synonymous with conservatism in the 1980s and 1990s.

71. **(B)** The World Trade Organization (WTO) was established to negotiate and enforce fair trade practices between the members of WTO.

72. **(C)** All the choices are true, but the most significant difference between Puritans and Pilgrims lies in their relationship to the Church of England. Some interpretations of the religious views of the Pilgrims suggest they wished to separate from the Church and start their own congregational form of worship. The Puritans were less radical and more interested in purifying or reforming the Church of England, and some recent interpretations emphasize the Pilgrims as merely more radical Puritans. It is an interesting debate considering that Congregationalism became the expression of organized religion in New England at the time of the Revolution, and early in the 19th century Unitarianism developed in the region.

73. **(E)** These instructions were given to Lt. Col. Baum by General Burgoyne before the Battle of Saratoga. Lt. Col. Baum was captured at the Battle of Bennington and these orders were found and were published in Portsmouth,

New Hampshire, in the *New Hampshire Gazette* of August 30, 1777. During the American Revolution the Continental Congress ran the war for the colonies. References to the enemy and the order to take prisoners confirm the orders are for movement into enemy territory. It is assumed in the orders that taking hostages will assure the delivery of confiscated goods. Although it is clear that one purpose of the expedition is to acquire horses, oxen, carriages, and wagons for transportation, there is no order to either take or burn everything, which is the meaning of a "scorched earth" policy, as used by Napoleon and General Sherman in his Civil War march through Georgia.

74. **(A)** The social structure of the American colonies was religiously intolerant, treated African Americans and women unequally, did not allow talent to rise easily, and, although it did not have a nobility, the social structure resembled that of England. Therefore, one could conclude that the colonial social structure did not support the concept that "all men are created equal."

75. **(D)** The Allied naval victory at Midway reversed the string of victories by Japan that had challenged democracy in the Pacific. The other choices were attacks on democracy and endangered the democracies of the West, and were part of the war or steps leading to war. The victory at Midway showed the Allies could rise to the challenge of dictatorships and the string of victories by the Axis powers (Japan, Germany, and Italy).

76. **(C)** *The Legend of Sleepy Hollow* published in 1820 established Washington Irving as the best-known author in the new nation. *The Legend of Sleepy Hollow* was one of the stories included in Irving's *Sketch Book*. Benjamin Franklin's widely acclaimed *Poor Richard's Almanac* was printed before the Revolution, as was Thomas Paine's *Common Sense*, which stirred up sentiment in favor of independence. Nathaniel Hawthorne's *The Scarlet Letter* (1850) and Ralph Waldo Emerson's *An American Scholar* (1837) were important works of the second generation of U.S. writers. This question clearly indicates the importance of knowing both dates and cultural events.

77. **(A)** The question asks about the decline of the first major post–Civil War labor union, the Nation Labor Union, begun in 1866. It was successful during the postwar boom years but collapsed when depression hit the country in the early 1870s. It set a recurring cycle for unions—success in prosperity but trouble during recession.

78. **(D)** Upton Sinclair's *The Jungle* was an example of muckraking literature. It exposed unsanitary conditions in the meat-packing industry that precipitated federal legislation.

79. **(A)** The cartoon is from *Harper's Weekly* of December 13, 1862. John Bull represents Great Britain and is shown in front of his little shop, John Bull Variety. His customer is Mr. Confederate, who represents the Confederate states. John Bull has received money in the money bag marked CAS—Confederation of American States. Mr. Confederate is loaded up with guns, pistols, swords, and, most important, a boat representative of the *Alabama*, which was a privateer

built in Great Britain and operated by the Confederacy. It did a great deal of damage to Northern shipping. The point of the cartoon is to illustrate how the British industrialists supplied arms and ships for the Confederacy. The case of the *Alabama* almost led to war between Great Britain and the Northern states. The claims against the *Alabama* were finally negotiated in 1871–1872. The cartoon required you to both interpret its parts and place them in the mainstream of American history.

80. **(A)** President Gorbachev of the Soviet Union introduced his reform policies of *perestroika* and *glasnost* soon after his rise to power in 1985. Many believe these policies led to the fall of the Berlin Wall and the end of the Cold War. Soon after, the Soviet Union broke up into separate nations. Yugoslavia also broke into separate nations and warfare between them erupted. As a result of the end of the Cold War, the still united Soviet Union cooperated with President Bush in the Persian Gulf War. The sending of U.S. troops to Somalia under the United Nations was an attempt by President Bush to respond to past Cold War issues and to establish a "new world order."

## Comments on the Free-Response Questions

Following are comments on the five free response questions from the Advanced Placement Examination Model B. There is analysis of each question, and for the DBQ, an analysis of each document.

## Analysis of the DBQ Documents

When the consultants meet to analyze the DBQ, they develop brief statements for each document that summarize the main point and the context in which the document was produced. The consultants refer to these statements often as they read and rank the examinations. As a study technique such an approach is valuable. Whenever you read documents, and especially as you prepare your answer during the 15-minute reading time on the exam, you should make notes on the key points in each document. Rather than include another sample answer to the DBQ, a brief analysis of each document is presented, followed by a list of points to note on the document. This illustrates what you should do on the exam—quickly and briefly write the key points for each document as you read them and then consider how they interrelate and connect to the mainstream history you know.

**Document A**—U.S. Constitution Article I, Section 8, and Article I, Section 9, 1787 In Section 8, the important "commerce clause" gives Congress the power to regulate commerce both internally and externally. Note the inclusion of the "Indian tribes." Section 9 refers to the slave trade—the words may hide that from the unskilled reader. Immigrants migrated to the United States of their own free will. Some made arrangements to travel as indentured servants and were imported under these agreements. Slaves were imported against their will. The clause guaranteed the federal government would not interfere with the slave trade for twenty years. This compromise allowed the slave owners to accept the Constitution.

**Points to note:**
The Constitution gives Congress power to regulate commerce.
Slave trade (importation of peoples) cannot be controlled by the Congress until 1808.
Control of commerce was a concern in 1787 at the Constitutional Convention.

**Document B**—Act Imposing Duties on the Tonnage of Ships or Vessels, 1790
The Congress quickly moved to exercise its power to control commerce by establishing duties on shipping. These duties would be an important source of revenue for the new government.

**Points to note:**
Within months of the establishment of the new government Congress exercises its power to regulate commerce.
Foreign vessels pay higher duties (50 cents per ton) than U.S.-owned vessels (6 cents per ton)—a potential for conflict.
Foreign powers are encouraged to have ships built in the United States, because duties are less than for foreign built ships.

**Document C**—Proclamation of Neutrality, 1793
As the French Revolution became more violent in the years after its start in 1789, European powers joined to restore the royal family in France. The United States had a treaty with France, which had helped us win independence. Why did Washington decide to declare neutrality and remain out of the conflict? His argument was that our treaty had been signed with the King's government and not the new revolutionary government.

**Points to note:**
The United States will not take sides in the conflict between France and the listed powers, especially, Great Britain.
Citizens are warned to avoid acts that go against neutrality.
By implication, this will affect U.S. commerce with all the listed powers as they battle for victory.

**Document D**—From the Letters of Thomas Jefferson, 1793–1801
These three letters from before and during Jefferson's presidency provide insights into Jefferson's thinking on foreign policy. The 1797 letter mentions commerce as a better tool than war to achieve justice from other nations. The other two focus on legitimate government. The "will of the people" is the guide to legitimate government, and the latter letter says its protection should be our "first object." In the first letter Jefferson indicates there is no one type of government a nation must follow but the "will of the nation" must choose it. How does one find the will of the nation? Does Jefferson base his foreign policy on commerce or on supporting the "will of the people"? With what foreign policy events was he involved?

**Points to note:**
Protection of the free expression of "the will of the people (nation?)" should be the first object of the U.S. government.
There is no one perfect form of government for all people.
Control of commerce is a better instrument than war for achieving justice.

**Document E—Jay's Treaty, 1795**

Jay's Treaty is mentioned in all textbooks. It affirmed peace with Great Britain and dealt with issues left over from the Treaty of Paris of 1783 that ended the Revolution. What was driving the need for this treaty?

**Points to note:**

The treaty mentions "commerce and navigation" twice in the opening paragraph. Withdrawal of troops and garrisons is the topic of the second article, not commerce. Peace and friendship is emphasized between Great Britain and the United States at a time Great Britain is engaged in a war in Europe against France and the United States is neutral.

**Document F—Treaty of Friendship, Limits, and Navigation, 1795**

This treaty, often referred to as Pinckney's Treaty, also affirms peace and friendship between the United States and a European power (Spain). In the two articles presented is the topic commerce or other issues? Why are the subjects of these two articles important for the United States? Is the United States concerned about territory or commerce or both? What was behind the need for this treaty?

**Points to note:**

Peace is affirmed between Spain and the United States at a time Spain is engaged in a war in Europe against France and the United States is neutral.

The southern boundary of the United States is drawn setting the line between Spanish Florida and the United States.

The western boundary of the United States is set at the middle of the channel of navigation on the Mississippi River, giving the United States the right to use the river for commerce.

**Document G—Treaty of Greenville, 1795**

Again this treaty between the United States and Native American tribes is mentioned in textbooks. It ended more than twenty years of fighting in what became the Northwest Territory and ceded lands in the southwestern corner of the territory to the United States. Although relations with the Native Americans are often considered as part of domestic history, the Indian Nations were free and independent, and a treaty with them should have been considered the same as a treaty with a European power. What was driving the United States to sign this treaty—land or commerce?

**Points to note:**

Peace with the Indian tribes is to be perpetual, and "friendly intercourse" (commerce) is to take place.

Prisoners (captives) are to be exchanged.

Land has been ceded to the United States, and if more land is to be sold, it can be sold only to the United States.

**Document H—Washington's Farewell Address, 1796**

This is another document that is widely mentioned in textbooks. Often some passages are quoted, so you may have seen some of these statements. What are Washington's views on foreign policy as seen in these sections? Would he have been driven by commerce in designing his foreign policy? What other factors were of concern to him?

**Points to note:**
Too much fondness for a nation by a country can produce many evils and lead to involvement in the affairs of that nation that are often not in the best interest of the country or people.
We should have commercial relations with other nations but limited political connections.
Commercial connections should show no favoritism and should be temporary.

**Document I**—John Adams—Special Message to the Senate and the House, 1797
This message involves the XYZ Affair, in which the French government refused to meet with U.S. delegates sent to Paris to negotiate and resolve several disagreements particularly involving trade. The French demanded payment of bribes before negotiations could start. Adams found this insulting. The United States refused to pay a bribe. In this message Adams does not even mention the issues that originally divided the two nations but focuses on the humiliation of the delegates and the insult to the United States. What is driving Adams's policy statement? The Alien and Sedition Acts were passed soon after this incident.

**Points to note:**
The French government has insulted the United States and not treated her as a sovereign nation.
The French are trying to separate the people of the United States from their government, sowing the seeds of discontent, and this is more dangerous than the insult.
The United States must show the world that we will not be insulted or treated as a colonial power.

**Document J**—Convention Between the French Republic and the United States, 1801
This convention negotiated under Jefferson's presidency ended for the moment the tension between France and the United States. After the XYZ Affair, Congress authorized the president to use the Navy to seize French shipping and it appeared we might go to war. Is he more interested in commerce or peace?

**Points to note:**
Peace and friendship are agreed upon.
Commerce shall be free, ending the seizure of ships under a 1798 act of Congress.

**Document K**—Jefferson's Third Message to Congress, 1803
At this time period the president sent an annual message to Congress indicating the state of the union. Today these messages on the state of the union are delivered as a speech before Congress. This passage is from Jefferson's third such message. He reflects on the importance of the right of deposit at New Orleans to the nation and then announces the transfer of the Louisiana Territory to the United States. Is this right of deposit and the transfer of the territory more about commerce, land, or power?

**Points to note:**
Denial of the right to deposit goods in transit at New Orleans without paying duties was a major issue in the West, which relied on the Mississippi for transportation of goods to overseas markets.
The French government has transfered the Louisiana territory to the United States. Both nations are promising to promote peace and friendship.

**Document L**—James Madison First Inaugural, 1809
In his first inaugural Madison reflects on the foreign policy of the United States. Since 1793 there had been almost continual warfare between France and the European nations. Washington had declared neutrality in 1793, and Madison is praising how the United States handled relations during those difficult years. Did "peace" drive U.S. policy during that time or was it commerce?

**Points to note:**
The United States has pursued neutrality impartially.
The policy of the United States has been to cultivate peace and observe justice and equality between combatants.
The future will prove this to be the case even if it is not believed now.

**Document M**—*The Sun, Gazette and County Advertiser,* Dover, N.H.—Saturday, December 12, 1807
This newspaper selection reflects upon the attack on the U.S. frigate *Chesapeake* by the British ship *Leopard* within the territorial limits of the United States. It was one incident in the growing tensions between the United States and Great Britain over rights of neutrals in wartime. As the Napoleonic Wars dragged on, the British tightened their attempts to control international trade. One maritime issue of concern since independence was the British seizure or impressment of seamen off U.S. ships. The British claimed that many sailors had deserted the English navy and that they were simply taking them back, but the United States disagreed. This was another concern driving U.S. foreign policy. Is this an issue of trade or national honor?

**Points to note:**
The press perceives the attack on the *Chesapeake* as aggression within the territorial waters of the United States.
The British are accused of having no respect for our laws.
U.S. seamen have been seized by the British.

**Document N**—Amendments to the Constitution Proposed by the Hartford Convention, 1814
New Englanders strongly opposed to the War of 1812 met in Hartford and proposed amendments to the Constitution. These reflect the anger of New Englanders at the foreign policy pursued by the federal government from the time of Jefferson on, when the government tried various methods of controlling trade to avoid war. Both embargos and interdictions needing only a majority vote of Congress had been used by the federal government in the period 1797–1812. Are New Englanders more concerned about commerce or national honor?

**Points to note:**

Amendment Three would deny Congress the use of embargos, thus limiting Congress's control of commerce.

Amendment Four also limits Congress's power over commerce by requiring two-thirds approval for any stopping of commerce between the United States and another nation.

## Analysis of the DBQ (Part A)—Question 1

The DBQ question is another *To what extent . . .* question. The topic focuses on U.S. foreign policy in the first twenty-six years of the nation. During twenty-two of those years the European powers were involved in war—The French Revolution and Napoleonic Wars—and the United States attempted to maintain neutrality until war was declared on Great Britain in 1812. You are asked to determine whether commerce (trade and exchange of goods) was the issue that determined or drove U.S. foreign policy in those years. Commerce certainly was important, and many of the documents mention commerce whether the document be the U.S. Constitution (Document A), an act imposing duties on shipping (Document B), a treaty (Document E), or an attempt to amend the Constitution (Document N). Recalling the "mainstream of U.S. history" in these years there are many times that commercial activity—whether a proclamation of neutrality or an embargo—was the focus of debate in the government. However, other issues are also referred to in the documents.

Land is mentioned as a concern or the focus of several documents. The Treaty of Greenville (Document G), the Treaty of Friendship (Document F), and Jefferson's Third Message to Congress (Document K) indicate the concern of the new nation for its borders and control of land. What would have happened if the United States had not acquired the Louisiana Territory? The honor of the nation is another issue raised by the documents. The Farewell Address (Document H), Adams's Special Message to Congress (Document I), Madison's First Inaugural (Document L), and the news story (Document M) all suggest that honor and/or the integrity of the nation are of key importance. Jefferson in his letters (Document D), although mentioning managing commerce as an alternative to war, is concerned about the legitimacy of foreign governments and that they express the will of the people or the nation—what we today would call democracy. Did this idea that the newly free United States should be a beacon of freedom for the world affect U.S. foreign policy in the years 1789 to 1815?

As stated many times, there is no one answer for free response questions. Your answer will depend on the emphasis you place on these different documents and what aspects of the history of the era you wish to emphasize. If you were a New Englander depending on trade for your living, you would no doubt see trade and commerce as crucial in foreign policy and you'd emphasize Washington's neutrality, Adams's negotiations with France, the tensions with England over impressment, and finally, the Hartford Convention's proposal to limit Congress's control of commerce as key elements in U.S. foreign policy. However, if you were a frontiersman in Ohio, the treaty with the Indians giving land, the purchase of Louisiana, and the right of deposit would be key factors for you. What is your interpretation of the period?

This question introduces many documents that are mentioned in most textbooks. This is somewhat unusual but brings to the forefront the mainstream of U.S. history and forces you as the writer to fill in the background to these events. Events from that mainstream that relate to this question are neutrality; the Barbary Pirates; treaties with Indians, Great Britain, and Spain; settlement of boundaries with Great Britain and Spain; impressment; questions of national honor and the rightful place in the world of the newly independent and democratic states; the influence on the French of the American Revolution, Citizen Genet; the Alien and Sedition Acts, the XYZ Affair; financial stability of the new nation; tariffs; the embargo; and the War of 1812. All of these events connect to U.S. foreign policy. As you decide your thesis, you must pick information from these events to support it and to enhance the information you choose to use from the documents.

### Comments on Question 2 of Section II—Part B

This is a straightforward *In what ways . . .* type of question, and these were discussed in Chapter 7 in Part Two. There is a clear time period. The Constitution was written in 1787. The Constitutional Convention debated the issue of slavery at length, and in Article I, Section 9 the Constitution prohibited any congressional interference with the slave trade until 1808. The document also counted a slave as three-fifths of a person in counting the population of states to determine representation in the Congress. These two points provide a starting place for a discussion of this question. Lincoln was elected in 1860, and that set the stage for the Civil War. In between those dates what federal legislation or judicial decisions had an effect on the life of the African American? This requires factual recall. Among the major legislation and decisions you should consider are the following:

The Constitution (mentioned above)

The Abolishment of the Slave Trade in 1808

The Missouri Compromise of 1820 (keeping the balance between slave and free states and prohibiting "forever" slavery north of the line 36° 30′)

"Gag Rule," 1835

Compromise of 1850 (including the fugitive slave bill)

Kansas-Nebraska Act, 1854 (replacing the 36° 30′ line of the Missouri Compromise with the concept of "popular sovereignty")

Dred Scott Supreme Court Decision, 1857

In addition to the above, three items discussed in Congress are relevant to the question.

Tallmadge Amendment of 1819 (led to Missouri Compromise)

Wilmot Proviso of 1846 (forbidding slavery in any lands taken from Mexico in the Mexican War)

Ostend Manifesto (said the United States would be justified in taking Cuba from Spain, interpreted as a way to extend slavery)

The above are the main items from the political mainstream of U.S. history that should be included in your answer. What is clear is that none of these had a positive effect on the life of the African American. All related to slavery and its possible expansion westward. They reflect the great division in the nation over the future of slavery. During the time period, agitation in the North over the horrors of slavery gradually grew, but the federal government did not even consider abolishing slavery. A good to excellent answer would address this matter and other social and intellectual history, and would include information to illustrate that there was concern over slavery and slave conditions. Among the items you might refer to in order to make this point are the following:

Concern over the slave trade

Cotton gin and resulting expansion of the growth of cotton and the westward movement of slavery

The Vesey Conspiracy and reaction to it in South Carolina in 1822

The growing split between Northern and Southern values and society, reflected in Virginia's vote against gradual abolishment of slavery in 1832 and the tariff crisis of 1832–1833

Nat Turner's Rebellion in 1831

Growth of abolitionist sentiment as seen in publication of William Lloyd Garrison's *The Liberator* and founding of the American Anti-Slavery Society, 1833

Publication of *Uncle Tom's Cabin,* 1852

"Bleeding Kansas" and John Brown's activities leading to the raid on Harper's Ferry

These events all illustrate the temper of the nation in the years 1787 to 1860. It would be difficult to include all of these in an answer written in 30 minutes, but the idea they illustrate should be included to provide the context in which the federal government failed to act.

## Comments on Question 3 of Section II—Part B

The question combines a compare and a *To what extent . . .* question. It is on a mainstream topic—the comparison of the presidencies of Jefferson and Jackson. Both elections have been referred to as revolutionary. In fact, Jefferson used the phrase to describe the replacement of the Federalist Party by his own Jeffersonians. Today some historians see Jefferson's election as less than revolutionary. Some interpret Jackson and his administration as more revolutionary. As the student, you will have investigated both men and should have several ideas to call upon as you decide on the revolutionary nature of these two presidencies.

Jefferson spoke in states' rights terms in the Kentucky Resolutions in opposition to the Federalists' actions in the 1790s, but he acted as a nationalist in buying Louisiana, sending out Lewis and Clark, and in maintaining the navy. He also continued the Federalists' policy of negotiating to avoid involvement in the European conflict. Thus, to what extent did he continue to act like a Federalist? Were his actions truly revolutionary?

Jackson's presidency is known as the time of Jacksonian Democracy—a term that should bring many items to mind. His battles over the Bank of the United States and the Tariff Controversy with South Carolina, his handling of the Cherokee Indians and the Trail of Tears, his use of the "spoils system," and his western, "frontier" roots all provide important material for judging the revolutionary nature of his administration. The social changes that were going on during his presidency—extension of voting rights to all white males, extension of free education and growth of libraries, the beginnings of the abolitionist movement—are often cited as examples of revolutionary changes in the nation, and they form the heart of the movement of Jacksonian Democracy.

Recalling this information, it should not be difficult to form a thesis for this question and to develop an answer. One approach, and the simplest, would be to discuss Jefferson and then Jackson and conclude with a judgment on the revolutionary nature of the two presidencies. Another approach would be to consider issues such as foreign policy, domestic policy, and nationalism in separate paragraphs, discuss the actions of both men in a paragraph, and conclude with a paragraph on the revolutionary nature of the presidencies.

## Comments on Question 4 of Section II—Part C

This is the familiar type of question with a quote followed by the direction to *Analyze the validity* of the quote. The quote requires that you know the proposals of the Populist Party in the 1890s and the New Deal in the 1930s to handle the economic conditions of the time. To answer the question, you should recall the Peoples (Populist) Party Platform of 1892 (see p. 330) that was adopted at the party convention in Omaha to address issues of restricted monetary supply and agrarian (farmer) discontent. If you do not recall the platform, but have an idea of the economic conditions of the 1890s and such matters as William Jennings Bryan's Cross of Gold speech in 1896, you still could answer the question.

You must also be familiar with the main acts of the New Deal. These are often grouped under relief, recovery, and reform (see p. 340). However, for this question you will want to focus on issues of monetary and banking reform and agricultural issues, both of which were addressed by the Populists and the New Deal. Whether there is a link and the former provided the "framework" for the latter is for you to decide and express in your thesis. You'll discover that several Populist proposals, such as the direct election of senators, were achieved before the New Deal. This is an interesting question and one that requires your analytical skills as a historian.

## Comments on Question 5 of Section II—Part C

You are asked in the question to discuss three of five choices. It is always important to pick three that you can recall specific information on, but also three that you can relate to the issue of the question—the "establishment of the United States as a leader in international affairs."

The Spanish-American War in 1898 is often mentioned as the time the United States became an international force, defeating Spain quickly and acquiring an overseas "empire." However, the United States had been active in the Pacific since the clipper-ship trade with China. After the Spanish-American War, the United States could not be ignored, and President Teddy Roosevelt used that position to negotiate the Treaty of Portsmouth, ending the Russo-Japanese War, to become involved in the Algeciras Conference in 1905 that defused an international crisis in Morocco, and to send the U.S. Navy around the world. He also began the building of the Panama Canal.

The opening of the Panama Canal meant the United States could act quickly in both the Atlantic and Pacific, moving its navy from ocean to ocean, thus exercising great power. The United States also benefited from increased and easier trade between both coasts and internationally. The fact that the canal was U.S. owned and built enhanced U.S. prestige. Do you think that is enough information to make the canal a factor in establishing U.S. leadership?

The defeat of the Treaty of Versailles by the U.S. Senate was a blow for internationalists. However, it did not mean the United States would not act on the international stage. The U.S.-led disarmament talks in Washington, negotiated under the Kellogg-Briand Peace Pact, readjusted the postwar reparations in the Dawes Plan, and acted as a leader in international affairs when it suited the nation. However, many interpret the defeat of the treaty as a retreat from world leadership and a return to isolation. How do you see it, based on your knowledge and interpretation of the evidence?

The outbreak of World War II led the United States to reaffirm neutrality and isolation. The entire 1930s is seen by some as an abandonment of world leadership, as the United States might have been able to lead a coalition to defeat the Nazis as was done after the United States was attacked at Pearl Harbor. Thus the start of World War II was not "a factor in establishing the United States as a leader in international affairs." The opposing view would point to the position of the United States at the end of the war, when it was the dominant victor and led one side in the Cold War for fifty years. How you will argue will, as in every essay question, depend on your personal knowledge and interpretation of evidence.

The Vietnam War came in the midst of the Cold War when most people would see the United States as already a leader in international affairs. However, you might argue that the position of the United States in 2007 as the single world power is a result of Reagan's military buildup and the first Gulf War, both of which can be interpreted as reactions to the national mood created by the Vietnam War. Thus you could say the Vietnam War was a factor in creating the United States as the dominant world power. Or, you might argue that although the U.S. withdrew from Vietnam, it had stopped Chinese expansion, weakened the Soviet Union, and emerged as the single super power in the 1990s. On the other hand, you can always argue the negative and indicate the Vietnam War was not a factor in establishing U.S. leadership. The first four choices are often referred to in a discussion of the emergence of the United States as a world leader; the fifth is rarely included. Which three you pick will determine your thesis that must be based on an evaluation of the item as a factor in the emergence of the United States.

This is an excellent question with which to end this preparation for the Advanced Placement Examination in United States History. It requires you to do what you must do on every free-response question on the exam: analyze the question, sort and evaluate your information, develop a thesis, and write a coherent essay. Remember this when you take the examination, and good luck.

# Chronological Summary of Major Events and Developments

This summary of major events in United States history is arranged according to the time divisions of the chapters in the book.

It can serve as a quick review of United States history or as an introduction to its study. The information should jog your memory if you have finished a course in United States history or, if you are just starting your study, it will give you an indication of the type of information you need to know. It illustrates the basic factual material from the mainstream of United States history one needs, but under no circumstances should it be considered a substitute for the skills developed when reading different authors with conflicting opinions of our past.

Included in each section are the names of leaders of each era. Certain events are described briefly while others are merely listed. You are urged to add dates, people, and events to this summary as you study. The margins of this section provide space to do this.

At the end of the book is a chronological listing of events by date. These two chronologies provide an important introduction to or review of your study.

## REASONS FOR EXPLORATION

Search for a sea route to the Far East
Desire for glory and wealth
Quest for new lands
Adventure

## FACTORS FAVORABLE TO SUCCESSFUL EXPLORATION

Invention of the astrolabe and compass
Invention of the printing press
Growth of national states in western Europe
Increase of monetary resources and the use of the joint stock company as an
   economic organization
The Renaissance and revival of intellectual curiosity
Invention of gunpowder
New maps of the world showing areas of Chinese exploration and other details

# EXPLORERS AND FOUNDERS OF COLONIES

> **BEFORE 1763**
>
> Material relevant to Chapter 4.

## SPAIN

| | |
|---|---:|
| *Columbus:* First visit to America, given publicity | 1492 |
| *Balboa:* First Spaniard to see the Pacific Ocean from Central America | 1513 |
| *Magellan:* First recorded circumnavigation of the globe | 1519–1522 |
| *Cortez:* Conquered and claimed Mexico | 1519 |
| *Pizarro:* Conquered and claimed Peru | 1531 |
| *De Soto:* First European to explore the Mississippi River | 1541 |

## PORTUGAL

| | |
|---|---:|
| *Da Gama:* Reached India by sailing around Africa | 1498 |
| *Americus Vespucci:* Explored the coast of South America. America is named after him. | 1501 |

## FRANCE

| | |
|---|---:|
| *De Champlain:* Founded Quebec, the Father of New France; discovered Lakes Champlain and Huron | 1608 |
| *Fathers Marquette and Joliet:* Explored upper Mississippi River | 1673 |
| *La Salle:* Explored the Mississippi River to its mouth | 1682 |

## ENGLAND

| | |
|---|---:|
| *Cabot:* Explored the Labrador coast | 1497 |
| *Frobisher:* Explored the Labrador coast | 1576 |
| *Drake:* First Englishman to circumnavigate the globe | 1577–1580 |
| *Raleigh:* Attempted to found a colony off the coast of North Carolina | 1584 |
| *Smith:* Founder and leader of Jamestown | 1607 |
| *Bradford:* Leader of Plymouth Colony | 1620 |
| *Lord Baltimore:* Founder of Maryland | 1634 |
| *Penn:* Founder of Pennsylvania | 1681 |

## HOLLAND

| | |
|---|---:|
| *Minuit:* Founder of New Amsterdam (later New York) | 1626 |

# REASONS FOR COLONIZATION OF THE NEW WORLD

| | |
|---|---|
| Religious freedom | Farming land |
| Economic opportunity | Social change |
| Political freedom | Spreading Christianity |
| Empire building | |

## TERRITORY CLAIMED BY EUROPEAN NATIONS IN THE NEW WORLD

*Spain:* All of South America except Brazil, plus Central America, Mexico, Florida, California

*Portugal:* Brazil

*France:* All of Canada except the Hudson Bay region, plus the Great Lakes region, the Mississippi Basin, the French West Indies

*Holland:* The Hudson River Valley in New York

*England:* The eastern coast from New England to Georgia, west to the Appalachian Mountains

## ENGLAND ACHIEVES DOMINATION OF EASTERN HALF OF NORTH AMERICA

| | |
|---|---|
| English navy defeated the Spanish Armada, gaining control of the seas | 1588 |
| English drove the Dutch out of New York | 1664 |
| England defeated France at Quebec in the French and Indian War, gaining control of Canada and the lands east of the Mississippi River | 1763 |

## GEOGRAPHY AND ITS EFFECT ON SETTLEMENTS

The physical nature of the settled land usually determined the occupation and manner of life of the period.

New England: Rocky soil and long winters prevented extensive farming; wheat, corn, hay, and flax were the main agricultural products; colonists lumbered vast forests and fished off the coast; because of excellent harbors and rivers they developed trade as their chief source of income.

Middle Colonies: Level, fertile, rich land and good rainfall made for abundant farming; wheat, oats, and barley were grown in such quantity that these states were called "bread colonies."

Southern Colonies: Warm climate, long growing season, and fertile lands produced rich crops of cotton, tobacco, rice, and indigo; a good river system provided easy transportation inland; the produce was shipped to England and brought plantation owners large profits and manufactured goods in return.

Southwestern Colonies: Warm climate, dry; limited agriculture and settlement; horse and Christianity introduced to pueblo-dwelling Native Americans, which changed their lifestyle.

## EARLY SETTLEMENTS IN FUTURE UNITED STATES AND CANADA

| | |
|---|---|
| St. Augustine, Florida (Spain) | 1565 |
| Jamestown, Virginia (England) | 1607 |
| Quebec, Canada (France) | 1608 |
| Santa Fe, New Mexico (Spain) | 1609 |
| Plymouth, Massachusetts (England) | 1620 |
| New York, New York (Holland) | 1626 |

# SOME CONTRIBUTIONS OF MOTHER COUNTRIES TO NORTH AMERICA

*England:* Democratic forms of local government; tradition of hard-working, zealous individuals; English language; Protestant (Puritan) religion.

*France:* Language, culture, and religion (Roman Catholicism) of France introduced to Canada and Louisiana and to many Native Americans west of Appalachians.

*Spain:* Schools, hospitals, and printing presses established by missionaries; Spanish language in Southwest; teaching of Christianity (Roman Catholicism) and handicrafts to Native Americans.

# EVENTS THAT FOSTERED THE DEMOCRATIC IDEAL IN THE ENGLISH COLONIES

*Formation of Virginia House of Burgesses:* First representative assembly in America; the beginning of representative government in America. 1619

*Signing of the Mayflower Compact:* First agreement for self-government; bound the freemen to obey "just and equal laws." 1620

*New England Town Meeting:* Taught people to express themselves openly and helped further self-government. after 1629

*Petition of Rights and Bill of Rights:* Established certain rights of English subjects in relation to the Royal Power in England. The colonists later claimed these rights also. 1628, 1689

*Colonial Government:* The governor of each colony, whether a royal or charter colony, had to consult advisors before taking action.

*Control of Purse:* The settlers of most colonies voted for members of a legislature, which in turn determined the governor's salary. When this control was threatened, the colonists felt threatened.

*Fundamental Orders of Connecticut:* The first written constitution in America. 1639

*Formation of New England Confederation:* Connecticut, New Haven, Plymouth, and Massachusetts formed a league of friendship for defense, offense, and advice. This was a first step toward the later union of states. 1643

*Passing of Maryland Toleration Act:* Guaranteed religious freedom to all Christians. 1649

*Bacon's Rebellion:* Virginia farmers revolted against corrupt and oppressive government. 1676

*Formation of New York Chapter of Liberties:* This document granted freedom of religion to all Christians and gave all freeholders the right to vote. 1683

*Zenger Case:* Set a precedent that led to the establishment of freedom of the press. 1734

## SOME IMPORTANT INDIVIDUALS OF THE PERIOD OF EXPLORATION AND COLONIZATION

| | | |
|---|---|---|
| Jeffrey Amherst | Anne Hutchinson | Mary White Rowlandson |
| Edmund Andros | Thomas Hutchinson | William Shirley |
| Nathaniel Bacon | Cotton Mather | Miles Standish |
| Edward Braddock | Montezuma | George Washington |
| Charles II | King Philip | William and Mary of England |
| John Cotton | Pocahontas | Roger Williams |
| Jonathan Edwards | Queen Elizabeth I of England | John Winthrop |
| Thomas Fairfax | Queen Isabella of Spain | John Witherspoon |

## CAUSES OF THE AMERICAN REVOLUTION

*Mercantilism:* Theory that colonies existed only for the profit of the mother country; caused discontent among American businessmen and traders.

> **1763–1789**
>
> Material relevant to Chapter 5.

*Navigation Acts:* Controlled colonial commerce with England and other countries.                                                    1660, 1663, 1673

*Concept of the Rights of English subjects:* Colonists believed their traditional rights as Englishmen, such as those stated in the Magna Carta, in the Petition of Rights, and English Bill of Rights, were being denied by Parliament.

*Aftermath of the French and Indian War:* British had acquired a large debt they felt the colonists should help pay; also, they acquired all of Canada, which they had to rule.                                                    1763

*The Proclamation of 1763:* Tried to stop colonization of the West by closing the land between the Alleghenies and the Mississippi to protect the Native Americans from exploitation by the settlers until treaties could be negotiated.                                                    1763

*The Sugar Act:* Taxed sugar to raise revenue, which threatened to destroy the profitable triangular trade between Britain, the colonies, and the West Indies.                                                    1764

*The Stamp Act:* The colonists were forced to pay a tax on all papers—pamphlets, calendars, almanacs, etc.—for the purpose of raising money to support the British army in the colonies. It was during this controversy that Patrick Henry said, ". . . Give me liberty or give me death!"                                                    1764

*The Quartering Act:* Required the colonists to quarter (house) British troops while they enforced unfavorable acts and "protected" the colonies.                                                    1766

*Writs of Assistance:* Allowed British officials to enter any home to search for smuggled goods, which contradicted the traditional right of English subjects to protection of their homes.

| | |
|---|---|
| *The Townshend Acts:* Placed a tax on imported paper, lead, glass, tea, and painter's colors in order to pay the salaries of the governors and judges in the colonies, which would eliminate colonists' control of the purse. | 1767 |
| *The House of Burgesses:* The colonial assembly was arbitrarily dissolved by the governor of Virginia. | 1769 |
| *The Boston Massacre:* Some Boston townspeople were fired upon by a group of British soldiers. Several people were killed. The reason for the firing of weapons was complex, including the overreaction of the troops to taunts by the colonists, but the "massacre" became a focus for colonial anger. Reflecting the complexity of the situation, the patriot, John Adams, defended the troops at their trial. | 1770 |
| *The Boston Tea Party:* Enraged by the monopoly of the tea trade held by the East India Company and by the English refusal to rescind the tax on tea, about 50 men disguised as Indians boarded the tea ships at the wharf and emptied the tea into the harbor, defying the law and English authority. | 1773 |
| *The Intolerable Acts:* The British government, in retaliation for the Boston Tea Party, closed the port of Boston until the tea was paid for, revised the charter of Massachusetts so that the Council would be appointed by the king, and forced the colonists of Massachusetts to house British soldiers. British officers were allowed to be tried in England for crimes of violence. | 1774 |
| *Summary View of the Rights of British America:* Expressed views of the colonists in opposition to England and called for the ending of slavery—written by T. Jefferson. | 1774 |

## SOCIAL CONDITIONS AT THE TIME OF THE REVOLUTION

Differences in the colonies continued up to and after the Revolution. These were often rooted in geography and the reasons for settlement. Class structures had developed in all the colonies by the time of the Revolution and there were tensions between settlers on the frontier and those in the more settled regions. In spite of the class divisions, there was no agreement within classes over their attitudes toward the mother country. For instance, prosperous merchants in Portsmouth, New Hampshire, both supported and organized against England. Similar divisions could be found throughout the colonies and the classes.

## IMPORTANT EVENTS OF THE REVOLUTIONARY PERIOD

| | |
|---|---|
| *First Continental Congress:* All colonies except Georgia were represented; they pledged to boycott all English goods if England did not settle existing disagreements. | Sept., 1774 |
| *Battle of Concord and Lexington:* Minutemen and Massachusetts militia, forewarned by Paul Revere and William Dawes, routed English in the first battle of the Revolution. | April, 1775 |

*Second Continental Congress:* Met in Philadelphia, attended by all 13 colonies; made provisions for raising a colonial army, issuing and borrowing money; appointed George Washington as commander-in-chief of the army; drafted the *Articles of Confederation,* (not approved until 1781) an agreement among the states outlining the operation of the united government.                              1775

*Declaration of Independence:* Signed by John Hancock, president of the Second Continental Congress, and all the members present, stated the equality of all people, declared the right of the people to rebel when denied life, liberty, and the pursuit of happiness by their governments.                                              July 4, 1776

*Treaty of Paris:* England recognized the independence of the colonies and ceded land from Canada to Florida.                            1783

## IMPORTANT BATTLES OF THE REVOLUTION

*Battle of Trenton and Princeton:* After New York was captured, Washington had fled to Pennsylvania. He recrossed the Delaware River and won these two victories, which made it clear the war would continue.                                          1776–1777

*Battle of Saratoga:* The colonists stopped England's attempt to split New England off from the other colonies. Considered the turning point of the war when Americans proved they could defeat the best soldiers in the world, which persuaded the French to sign a treaty of alliance with the colonists.                                   1778

*Battle of Yorktown:* Washington cornered a British army on land, while Admiral de Grasse, a French ally, prevented British reinforcements from landing by sea. As a result, Lord Cornwallis surrendered the British Army, bringing the war to an end.                   1781

## DEVELOPMENT OF THE CONSTITUTION

*The Articles of Confederation:* America's first Constitution, written by the Continental Congress and adopted by the states, had the following weaknesses:

Each state, regardless of size, had only one vote.

Congress could make laws, but there was no executive to enforce them.

Amendments could be adopted only by unanimous vote.

There was no national court to settle arguments between states.

Congress could not regulate commerce between states, collect taxes, or force states to contribute to government needs.

Congress could only ask states for troops, but could not raise an army.                                                   1781

*Shays' Rebellion:* Farmers in western Massachusetts rebelled against the state government, citing economic conditions that were driving them to bankruptcy. The rebellion was crushed but clearly illustrated the political and economic weaknesses of the country and of the *Articles of Confederation.*

*Annapolis Convention:* Several states met at Annapolis, Maryland to consider ways of improving trade and making changes in the Articles. They issued a call for a meeting that became the Constitutional Convention.                                                                    1786

*Constitutional Convention:* Convened at Independence Hall, Philadelphia, to revise *Articles of Confederation* but decided to draw up a completely new document.                                                    May, 1787

## COMPROMISES REACHED IN FORMING THE CONSTITUTION

*The Great Compromise:* Resolved the conflict between large and small states by providing equal representation in the Senate and representation based on population in the House of Representatives.

*Three-fifths Compromise:* Resolved the conflict between slave and free states by counting five slaves as three people in determining each state's representation in the House of Representatives.

*Commerce Compromise:* Resolved the conflict between agricultural and manufacturing states by permitting Congress to tax goods entering but not leaving the country.

*Indirect Vote for President:* Resolved the conflict between aristocrats and democrats by having the president elected by electoral college.

## THE GREAT ARCHITECTS OF THE CONSTITUTION

Known as *The Founding Fathers,* the men most responsible for its adoption were George Washington, James Madison, Alexander Hamilton, Gouverneur Morris, Robert Morris, Benjamin Franklin, and George Mason.

## BRANCHES OF THE GOVERNMENT

Authority was vested in three branches that acted as a check on each other:

*Legislative:* The House of Representatives and the Senate make laws according to the power granted in Article I Section 8. These powers include making laws concerning such items as money, commerce, courts, war, the armed forces, immigration, and taxation. The Congress may override a presidential veto of passed legislation by a two-thirds vote. The Senate confirms presidential appointments and treaties.

*Executive:* The president, who heads the executive branch, enforces the laws, conducts foreign policy, and negotiates treaties with the "advice and consent" of the Senate. The president is commander-in-chief of the army and makes appointments of judges and members of the executive branch with the approval of the Senate.

*Judicial:* Supreme Court, and such lesser federal courts as Congress establishes, determine the constitutionality of laws and the interpretation of the Constitution. Federal judges are appointed by the president and confirmed by the Senate.

## THE BILL OF RIGHTS

A written guarantee of the people's liberties, these were added to the Constitution as the first ten amendments in 1791. Several states refused to ratify the Constitution unless a Bill of Rights was added immediately. The Bill of Rights guaranteed:

1. Freedom of speech, press, religion.
2. The need for a militia and thus the right to bear arms.
3. That people would not be forced to quarter soldiers.
4. Protection against illegal search.
5. The right to know reasons for arrest.
6. The right to a quick trial by a jury of peers.
7. The right to trial by jury in civil cases involving more than $20.
8. Protection against cruel and unusual punishment and excessive bail.
9. That no rights not listed in Constitution should be therefore denied.
10. That the people and states would retain powers not assigned to the federal government.

## SOME IMPORTANT INDIVIDUALS OF THE REVOLUTIONARY PERIOD: 1763–1789

| | | |
|---|---|---|
| Abigail Adams | Elbridge Gerry | Gouverneur Morris |
| John Adams | Nathan Hale | Robert Morris |
| Samuel Adams | Alexander Hamilton | James Otis |
| Ethan Allen | John Hancock | Thomas Paine |
| Crispus Attucks | Patrick Henry | William Pitt |
| Daniel Boone | Sir William Howe | Edmund Randolph |
| General Edward Braddock | John Jay | Paul Revere |
| John Burgoyne | Thomas Jefferson | Benjamin Rush |
| George Rogers Clark | John Paul Jones | Daniel Shays |
| John Singleton Copley | Ann Lee | John Trumbull |
| Lord Cornwallis | Richard Henry Lee | George Washington |
| Benjamin Franklin | James Madison | Martha Washington |
| Joseph Galloway | George Mason | |

## THE GROWTH OF POLITICAL PARTIES

*Bank of the United States:* Hamilton and Jefferson submitted papers to President Washington explaining their position on a National Bank. This involved their interpretation of the Constitution—strictly for Jefferson, loosely for Hamilton—since there was no mention of a bank in the Constitution—only the right to issue currency. Gradually, others expressed opinions on the Constitution, and out of this discussion came the first two political parties in the nation.

*The Federalists:* Following the ideas of Alexander Hamilton, they became the political party representing investors, merchants, and manufacturers. It is viewed as the more conservative of the two parties. John Adams is considered the first Federalist president, although Washington was inclined to support Hamilton's views. The Federalists were in power until 1800.

**1789–1824**

Material relevant to Chapter 6.

*The Anti-Federalists, or Republicans:* Led by Thomas Jefferson, the party represented the farming population, small business people, and some city workers. At the time it was the more liberal of the two parties and was dominant from 1800 to 1824. The leaders of the Republican Party grew increasingly conservative and finally it was absorbed by the Whig Party.

*Disappearance of Federalist Party:* It passed from the political scene in 1816. The Federalists lost credibility after the Hartford Convention and they opposed the War of 1812, which lost them support outside of New England.

*The Democratic Party:* It emerged with the election of Andrew Jackson in 1828; it represented the Western and Southern farmers and workers of the East; it became the more liberal party.

*The Whig Party:* It was formed after the Federalist and the Republican parties disappeared; Henry Clay, former Federalists, and some conservative Republicans organized the opposition to the Democratic Party in the form of the newly created Whig Party.

## THE ESTABLISHMENT OF THE FEDERAL GOVERNMENT

President Washington developed the concept of a *cabinet* to advise him. Alexander Hamilton, Secretary of the Treasury, supported a *loose interpretation* of the Constitution to give power to the government in Washington. Thomas Jefferson, Secretary of State, supported a *strict interpretation* of the Constitution to give more power to the people and the state governments. These interpretations continue to divide people today. Congress passed laws establishing the framework of the government, including the *Judiciary Act of 1789*, which established the federal court system.

*Whiskey Rebellion 1794:* Washington used state and federal troops to crush a farmers' rebellion in Pennsylvania, giving strength to the federal government.

*Treaties with England (Jay's Treaty) and Spain (Pinckney's Treaty):* The two treaties avoided war, established the borders of the United States with the colonies of Spain and England, gave the new nation international status, and laid the foundations for trading relationships.

*Reaction to Wars of the French Revolution:* Washington declared neutrality of the United States in reaction to the outbreak of war in Europe. He stated that the Treaty of Alliance with France, signed in 1778, which had brought support to the colonists and had been signed with the royal government of France, was no longer valid since the King had been overthrown. Many citizens were inclined to support France, but the United States government struggled to maintain its neutrality in spite of events such as the XYZ Affair and the actions of Citizen Genet. The neutrality allowed the new nation to grow without involvement in war.

*Washington's Farewell Address 1797:* In it Washington called for no foreign alliances, two terms for the president, and no factions (parties) in political life.

*Chief Justice John Marshall:* Appointed to the Supreme Court, Marshall led the Court in interpreting the Constitution to give power to the federal government.

# SOME IMPORTANT SUPREME COURT DECISIONS

*Marbury v. Madison* (1803) established that the Supreme Court had the power of judicial review.

*Dartmouth College v. Woodward* (1819) established the point that the charter of a private corporation is protected by the Constitution.

*McCullough v. Maryland* (1819) interpreted the elastic clause giving the federal government power to do those things not denied it in order to achieve legitimate goals. Also established the idea that the elastic clause applied to federal-state relations, thus extending the power of the federal government.

*Gibbons v. Ogden* (1824) established the concept of federal control over interstate commerce.

# THE WAR OF 1812

*Causes*

Election to Congress of War Hawks from western states (example: Henry Clay from Kentucky) who wanted war with England to gain control of western lands and defeat the Native American tribes.

In the Northwest Territory and on the frontier, British furnished Native Americans with arms and encouraged them to attack settlers who were encroaching on tribal lands and breaking treaty agreements.

Economic warfare of the British and French symbolized in such acts as the British Orders in Council, Jefferson's Embargo of 1807, and the Non-intercourse Act of 1809.

British attacked U.S. ships and impressed American sailors into service in their crews.

British seized American ships.

British fired on frigate *Chesapeake,* killing three American sailors.

*Important Events of the War*

Captain Perry's naval victory on Lake Erie, reported with the famous words, "We have met the enemy and they are ours." Victories of the *USS Constitution* (*Old Ironsides*) at sea.

The capture of Washington, D.C., and the burning of the White House by the British.

The writing of the *Star-Spangled Banner* by Francis Scott Key as the British bombarded Fort McHenry in Baltimore, Maryland.

Battle of New Orleans, won by General Andrew Jackson ("Old Hickory") after the treaty ending the war had been signed.

*Results of the War of 1812*

The United States Merchant Marine was almost destroyed.

Development of national pride and increase of national unity (although the *Treaty of Ghent* [1814], did not reflect a victory, it established clearly our complete independence from Britain).

Increased western migration when unemployment spread in the East as a result of the destruction of United States commerce.

Manufacturing developed in different areas of the United States since Britain's wartime embargo prevented imports.

## THE MONROE DOCTRINE

After Napoleon's defeat in 1815, *Russia, Prussia,* and *Austria* formed the Holy Alliance to crush rebellions against any monarchy wherever they might arise. Spain sought their help to regain its South American possessions lost due to popular revolts of the people led by Simón Bolivar and José de San Martín.

Russia was claiming the Oregon Territory, which both the United States and Britain were also claiming.

The British, in order to protect their trade, suggested joint action with the United States against European encroachment in the Americas, but this was rejected by the United States. Instead, to prevent European expansion in the Americas, President James Monroe, in an address to Congress in 1823, stated what became known as the Monroe Doctrine. The Doctrine, which became a cornerstone of American foreign policy, stated:

1. No part of North or South America was open to further European colonization.
2. European attempts to interfere with any existing American (North or South) governments would be considered unfriendly acts.
3. The United States would not interfere with existing European colonies.
4. The United States would not interfere in the affairs of Europe.

## THE ERA OF GOOD FEELING

The Federalists lost support as a result of not fully supporting the War of 1812. After the war the Republicans were in control of the nation. Henry Clay from Kentucky and John C. Calhoun from South Carolina soon emerged as national leaders. Clay, the "Great Compromiser," tried to reconcile the sectional differences with his "American System"—a protective tariff to aid manufacturers and better transportation (internal improvements), paid for with money from the tariffs, to aid farmers. Presidents Monroe and J. Q. Adams vetoed all bills for such improvements. Henry Clay offered the Missouri Compromise in 1820 to admit Maine (free) and Missouri (slave) as states, thus reconciling differences between the North and the South.

## SOME IMPORTANT INDIVIDUALS OF THE PERIOD 1789–1824

| | | |
|---|---|---|
| John Adams | Citizen Genet | James Monroe |
| John Q. Adams | Alexander Hamilton | Charles Wilson Peale |
| Abigail Adams | William H. Harrison | Charles C. Pinckney |
| Aaron Burr | Washington Irving | Sacajawea |
| John C. Calhoun | John Jay | Winfield Scott |
| Samuel Chase | Thomas Jefferson | Tecumseh |
| William Clark | Meriwether Lewis | Mersey Warren |
| Henry Clay | Dolley Madison | George Washington |
| George Clinton | James Madison | Eli Whitney |
| Albert Gallatin | John Marshall | |

## THE GROWTH OF SECTIONALISM

*The Industrial North.* As trade and manufacturing became the most important activities of the northern section of the United States, the North developed the following political and economic needs:

<table>
<tr><td>

**1824–1850**

Material relevant to Chapter 7.

</td></tr>
</table>

A national bank that would guarantee uniform and stable currency.

The end of the sale of cheap lands in the West to workers needed for northern industry.

A high protective tariff to protect native manufactured products against foreign competition.

Internal improvements (roads and canals) to link the markets and raw materials of the West to the markets and manufacturing of the Northeast.

The prevention of the spread of slavery and the slave-based economic system to new western territories where it would compete with wage labor and provide less of a market.

*The Slave South.* With the invention of Eli Whitney's cotton gin in 1793, unskilled slave labor became increasingly important to plantation owners whose main crop, cotton, produced almost all of southern wealth. The economic and political needs of the South were:

Cheap western lands in which more cotton could be grown.

The extension of slavery to these lands.

No internal improvements (roads and canals) because they benefited only the Northeast and West and were to be paid for by tariffs.

No high tariffs since they raised the price of manufactured goods, which the South imported from Britain, to whom cotton was sold in payment.

*The Farming West.* Since agriculture was the principal activity and chief source of wealth in the West, its needs were:

Access to cheap land for expansion.

Cheap money (much money in circulation even though, as a result, the value of that money in terms of purchasing power is lessened), which meant opposition to the national bank that was controlled by eastern business interests.

Extension of voting rights to all, regardless of property holdings.

Internal improvements (roads and canals) to transport produce to the market.

## JACKSONIAN DEMOCRACY

While the issue of slavery dominated the social issues in the pre-Civil War era, there were many other issues, many of which had important consequences for the United States. Many of these issues have been grouped under the term Jacksonian Democracy, but they were not confined to the years of his presidency.

The election of Jackson, first president from the frontier region, marked a revolution in thought. Life on the frontier was dangerous and difficult. Clearing land, creating farms, forming communities, dealing with the Native Americans—all these factors required self-reliance, initiative, and a will to work. Ancestry and education alone counted for little. These qualities placed an emphasis on the individual's abilities and, according to the later historian, Frederick Jackson Turner, created the American character. These qualities led to the political idea of the "spoils system," which Jackson employed. The spoils system held that every individual had the ability to run the government. It emphasized the equality of all but was limited in those days to white males. This emphasis on the individual is the root of democracy and provided the philosophical base for Jackson's Democratic Party and the social relations of the era.

Issues of the pre-Civil War period grouped under Jacksonian Democracy were:

*Education:* Horace Mann in Massachusetts introduced from 1837 to 1848 many curriculum changes emphasizing useful skills and the first requirement for a minimum school year—six months. Emma Willard established the first high school for women in Troy, New York, in 1821.

*Mental Health:* Dorothea Dix was a leader in reform of prisons and insane asylums. In 1843 she published the *Memorial to the Legislature of Massachusetts* which was an indictment of the living conditions and treatment of the insane in institutions in Massachusetts. She later published similar reports on conditions in several other states. Her actions led to changes in treatment of the insane as well as of prisoners and to the enlargement or establishment of state supported hospitals for the insane in 15 states and Canada.

*Voting Rights:* During the Jackson period, white males throughout the nation were able to vote as property requirements were dropped. A women's movement calling for the right to vote (women's suffrage) and giving them the legal rights of men developed. Leaders included Angelina and Sarah Grimke and Elizabeth Cady Stanton and Lucretia Mott. The latter two organized the Seneca Falls Convention in 1848, which issued a Declaration of Independence for women modeled on the U.S. Declaration.

*Temperance:* Susan B. Anthony became a leader of the movement to abolish the use of alcohol. According to the temperance leaders, drinking hurt families and limited the potential of the individual.

*Religious Revival—the Second Great Awakening:* Underlying many of the reform movements was a revival of interest in religion. This interest focused on the Bible and the need for every individual to read and interpret it. Revivals have been an important aspect of religion, especially Protestantism, throughout United States history.

*Intellectual Developments:* In addition to the social and intellectual developments suggested above, the 1830s saw the emergence of **Transcendentalism**. Considered the first truly American philosophical movement, Transcendentalism developed in New England and was centered in Concord, Massachusetts. Ralph Waldo Emerson is considered the most important spokesperson for the movement. In his essay *On Nature* and lectures he extolled nature, the individual, and self-reliance—characteristics that are considered typical of the American (see Alexis de Tocqueville's *Democracy in America*). Transcendentalists believed the most important truths went beyond human reason and that each individual had divine possibilities within. This led them to support social reforms and later, abolition. Brook Farm, a cooperative effort, is one manifestation of the movement as are the works of Henry David Thoreau (*On Civil Disobedience, Walden*) and the writings of the Alcotts.

## SECTIONAL COMPROMISES

As each section tried to gain control of the federal government to pass bills advantageous to itself, bitterness between the sections increased and problems could be settled only by compromise. Some of the more important compromises were:

*Missouri Compromise* (1820): Since, if there were more free states than slave states, the North would gain political control of Congress, the South opposed the admission of free states unless they were balanced by the admission of an equal number of slave states. Likewise, the North opposed the admission of slave states. When Missouri requested admission to the Union in 1818 as a slave state, Henry Clay, (the "Great Compromiser") proposed the Missouri Compromise, which states that:

Missouri would be admitted as a slave state, Maine, separated from Massachusetts, would be admitted as a free state.

Slavery would be prohibited in the Louisiana Territory north of the 36° 30′ parallel. (Missouri was to be the one exception.)

*Compromise Tariff of 1833*: When the North pushed a high tariff through Congress in 1828, the South was angry. When the tariff was slightly modified and general duties lowered only a little in 1832, South Carolina, led by John Calhoun, threatened secession and refused to obey the law. After negotiating a new tariff acceptable to the South, Clay saw it pushed through Congress as well as a bill (Force Act) that would allow the president to use troops to collect the tariff. The compromise avoided civil war in 1832–1833.

*Compromise of 1850*: When California asked for admission in 1850, the balance between the North and South was once again endangered. The Compromise of 1850, called the Omnibus Bill, and also written by Henry Clay, provided that:

The people of Utah and New Mexico would vote to determine whether they should be free or slave states (this idea became known as popular or "squatter" sovereignty).

California would be admitted as a free state.

The Fugitive Slave Law would be strengthened.

Slave trading would be prohibited in the District of Columbia.

# IMPORTANT MILESTONES IN EXPANSION 1787–1853

*Northwest Ordinance of 1787:* Adopted by the government under the Articles of Confederation, it made provision for lands north of the Ohio River and east of the Mississippi conquered by George Rogers Clark in the Revolution. It stated that

No more than five and no less than three states were to be formed from this Northwest Territory.

Inhabitants of a territory would be admitted as a state on equal terms when its population reached 60,000.

Slavery was prohibited in the territory.

*Louisiana Purchase:* Extending from the Mississippi River to the Rocky Mountains and from Canada to the Gulf of Mexico, this vast territory was purchased from Napoleon for $15 million during Jefferson's administration in 1803.

*Florida Purchase:* American settlers in western Florida revolted against Spain in 1810, and the land was annexed in 1812 and added to the state of Louisiana. In 1819 the United States purchased the eastern part of Florida from Spain for $5 million.

*The Oregon Territory:* Originally claimed by Britain, United States, Spain, and Russia; by 1818 the other two countries ceded rights to the United States and Britain, which occupied it jointly.

Marcus Whitman led American settlers into the area in 1840. A dispute developed over the territory as American settlers moved in. In 1844 the slogan "fifty-four forty or fight," which meant the United States would take over all the Oregon territory, helped elect James Polk president.

In 1846 a compromise was worked out with Britain and a treaty signed that gave the United States rights to the land south of the 49th parallel and Britain the land north of it.

*Gadsden Purchase:* A small strip of land, now incorporated in Arizona and New Mexico, was purchased from Mexico in 1853 to provide a good southern railroad route to the West. Its purchase completed the territory of what became the 48 contiguous United States (the lower 48).

*Manifest Destiny:* Many Americans hoped that war with Mexico (1846) would unite the nation and prevent the sectional conflicts from breaking up the Union. Many also believed that it was our *Manifest Destiny* to expand the borders of the nation to include all of North America. They held that this expansion would bring benefits to all peoples. Unfortunately, the war added to sectional divisions as New Englanders did not support it. The peace treaty added new territory that had to be organized as states. This created both economic tensions and problems over the spread of slavery to the new areas.

# MEXICAN WAR

*Annexation of Texas:* There were conflicts for a number of years between Mexican and United States settlers in Texas based on disagreements over the border between the land of the Louisiana Purchase and the nation of Mexico. The U.S. settlers requested aid from the federal government but it was rejected. Finally, Texas settlers organized an attack on Mexico and claimed the Rio Grande as the border. Led by General Sam Houston, the settlers defeated the Mexican leader, Santa Anna, in 1836, and Texas was granted its independence from Mexico and established as a republic. In the following nine years there were various attempts to have Texas join the Union or ally with Britain. Finally, in 1845 Texas was admitted as the 28th state of the United States.

*Outbreak of War:* In 1846 war broke out between the United States and Mexico—Mexico being angered by United States annexation of Texas and the claims of Texas to all land north of the Rio Grande. The United States, under the generalship of Winfield Scott and Zachary Taylor, won a series of battles in Mexico. California was captured under the combined efforts of Stephen Kearny, John Sloat, and John Fremont.

*The Treaty of Guadalupe-Hidalgo:* Signed in 1848 it provided that the regions of Mexico called New Mexico (present-day Utah, New Mexico, Colorado, and Arizona) and Upper California (present-day California) were ceded to the United States.

The Rio Grande was fixed as the southern boundary of Texas.

The United States agreed to a payment of $15 million for the territory.

## SOME IMPORTANT INDIVIDUALS OF THE PERIOD 1824–1850

| | | |
|---|---|---|
| John Q. Adams | John C. Fremont | Edgar Allan Poe |
| John Jacob Astor | Margaret Fuller | James K. Polk |
| John James Audubon | William Lloyd Garrison | Winfield Scott |
| Thomas Hart Benton | Angelina Grimké | John Slidell |
| Nicholas Biddle | Sarah Grimké | Father Junipero Serra |
| John C. Calhoun | William H. Harrison | Elizabeth Cady Stanton |
| Kit Carson | Sam Houston | Zachary Taylor |
| Henry Clay | Andrew Jackson | Henry David Thoreau |
| Samuel Colt | Henry Wadsworth Longfellow | Nat Turner |
| James Fenimore Cooper | Mary Lyon | John Tyler |
| Charlotte Cushman | Horace Mann | Martin Van Buren |
| Dorothea Dix | Samuel F. B. Morse | Daniel Webster |
| Frederick Douglass | Lucretia Mott | Brigham Young |
| Ralph Waldo Emerson | William S. Mount | |

## EVENTS LEADING TO THE CIVIL WAR

*North-South Hostility over Regional Differences:* Disagreement over tariffs and the economic systems of the two areas was a basic cause of the hostility. As new territory was added to the Union, the question of the extension of slavery became crucial to the South for both economic and political reasons.

*The Abolitionists:* In 1831, William Lloyd Garrison began publication of *The Liberator,* a paper calling for the abolition of slavery. The Abolition Movement began a slow but steady growth in the North. Important leaders of the movement were ex-slaves Frederick Douglass, who spoke widely and effectively of the slave experience, and Harriet Tubman, who organized and ran an Underground Railroad leading escaped slaves from the South to freedom in the North. Led by William

Lloyd Garrison, publisher of *The Liberator*, Frederick Douglass, and many others, the Abolitionists argued for an end to slavery.

**1850–1877**

Material relevant to Chapter 8.

*Abolition of Slavery in the British Empire* (1833): This was the culmination of a movement led by religious leaders, intellectuals, and some industrialists. It reflected changing attitudes toward slavery.

*Slave Rebellions*: There were many rebellions in the South. Those led by Denmark Vesey and Nat Turner terrified slave owners and alerted Northerners to the many horrors of slavery.

*Wilmot Proviso*: Introduced into the House of Representatives in 1846 at the time of the Mexican War, the Proviso focused attention on the question of extension of slavery. The Proviso stated there would be no slavery in any territory acquired from Mexico as a result of the war, thus blocking Southern ideas for expansion. It passed the House but was defeated in the Senate.

*Free Soil Party*: This "third party" in the election of 1848 supported the idea of popular sovereignty and wished to keep slavery out of the western territories. It helped to make slavery a national political issue.

*National Fugitive Slave Law*: This law, which the South demanded, pointed out vividly to Northerners some of the evils of the slave system as they saw slaves who had escaped being taken back, often in chains, to their owners. The original law was strengthened in the Compromise of 1850.

*Uncle Tom's Cabin*: The famous novel (1852) by Harriet Beecher Stowe awakened Northern sympathy for the slaves.

*The Underground Railroad*: Organized by Abolitionists, it helped slaves escape to the North. Harriet Tubman was one of the famous and effective operators of the railroad.

*Compromise of 1850*: California's application for statehood in 1849 as a state without slavery created a crisis in Congress. Admittance would upset the balance of free and slave states in the Senate. Again, Henry Clay worked out a compromise that delayed secession and war. The Compromise included several points: 1—California would enter as a free state. 2—Popular sovereignty would be applied to the territories of New Mexico and Utah. 3—The slave trade would be banned in the nation's capital. 4—Congress had no power to end the slave trade between states. 5—Strengthened the Fugitive Slave Law, making it easier for Southern slave owners to get their escaped slaves returned to them. 6—Settled the border dispute between New Mexico and Texas.

*Kansas-Nebraska Act*: In 1854 this act repealed the Missouri Compromise and stated that each new state created from the territory of the Louisiana Purchase would decide whether to be free or slave. Both Northerners and Southerners financed settlers in both the Kansas and Nebraska territories to support their positions on slavery. Small-scale civil war broke out in both areas as they struggled to decide on a slave or a free status.

*Dred Scott Case*: In 1857, when a slave named Dred Scott demanded freedom because his master had moved from a slave state (Missouri) to a free state (Illinois), the case was taken all the way to the Supreme Court. The Court in *Dred Scott v. Sandford* decided that slaves were property that could be taken anywhere and that the Missouri Compromise was unconstitutional.

*John Brown's Raid:* In 1859 an Abolitionist, John Brown, led a raid on an arsenal at Harper's Ferry in Virginia. He planned to seize arms, distribute them to slaves, and lead them in a revolt for freedom. He was captured, tried, and hanged.

*The Election of 1860:* The Democratic Party split into two parts over the slavery issue. These were:

> *The northern wing,* which ran Stephen Douglas on a platform of popular sovereignty to determine free or slave status.

> *The southern wing,* which ran John C. Breckenridge on a policy based on the Dred Scott decision that slaves were property protected everywhere by the Constitution.

The remnants of the Whig and American parties nominated John Bell on a platform that condemned sectional parties and called for upholding the Constitution and the laws of the land.

The recently formed Republican Party nominated Abraham Lincoln on a platform that stated:

> Kansas was to be admitted as a free state.

> Slavery was not to be extended to the territories.

> Free farming land was to be given to those settling in the West.

> A high protective tariff was to be maintained.

In the four-party race no one won a majority. Lincoln was elected by the electoral college system, even though he received no more than 40 percent of the votes cast.

*Southern Secession:* With Lincoln's election, seven states (South Carolina, Texas, Louisiana, Mississippi, Alabama, Florida, and Georgia) seceded from the Union. They created The Confederate States of America with Jefferson Davis as president. Their constitution stated that:

> There would be no Supreme Court.

> States would have more rights than the central government.

> Slavery was lawful.

*Lincoln's Inaugural Address* (1861): Lincoln refused to accept the dissolution of the Union, and stated that war or peace was in the hands of the South.

*Fort Sumter:* On April 12, 1861, Southern forces fired on Fort Sumter in the harbor of Charleston, South Carolina. The federal fort had been built years before to guard the harbor and was occupied by federal troops. Lincoln was determined to hold onto federal property in the seceded states and would not acknowledge the secession. Civil war therefore began. Virginia, Tennessee, Arkansas, and North Carolina seceded and joined the Confederacy.

## BASIC CAUSES OF THE WAR

*Economic:* The northern manufacturers needed a high tariff, skilled labor, internal improvements, and a national bank. The southern planters needed low tariffs, slave labor, state banks, and opposed internal improvements.

*Political:* Northerners opposed the extension of slavery to new states because they wanted political control of Congress, which made laws. Most Southerners favored the extension of slavery because they, too, wanted to control Congress. Many Northerners believed the Constitution had created a Union—"one nation, indivisible"—that could not be dissolved. Southerners believed the states that made the Union could unmake it and secede.

*Moral:* Abolitionists and others felt that slavery was an evil and must be eliminated. The South defended slavery by claiming it was established by God and quoted Bible passages to prove it.

## MAIN EVENTS OF THE CIVIL WAR

*Blockade of the South:* In order to cut the South off from supplies, the North blockaded the coast from Virginia to Texas. The blockade also succeeded in preventing the Confederacy from exporting cotton and tobacco. The iron-clad Confederate ship *Merrimac* attempted to break the blockade, but was prevented from doing so by the iron-clad Union ship, *Monitor.*

*Capture of Vicksburg:* Union forces captured Forts Henry (Kentucky) and Donelson (Tennessee) in 1862, which opened up the Mississippi River valley to invasion by the North. General Grant captured Vicksburg (Mississippi) in 1863, cutting off the West from the rest of the Confederacy since New Orleans (Louisiana) had been captured by the Union in 1862.

*Emancipation Proclamation* (effective January 1, 1863): Lincoln's famous proclamation freed all slaves residing in states that had rebelled against the Union. This was a military move to help win the war. Lincoln offered other plans for dealing with the problems of slavery after the war.

*The Battle of Gettysburg* (1863): After defeating invading northern armies, General Robert E. Lee invaded the North and was himself defeated at Gettysburg (Pennsylvania) in the crucial battle of the war.

*Capture of Atlanta* (1864): General Sherman captured Atlanta (Georgia), and, in a famous march through Georgia, destroyed everything in his path that might help the enemy. This action, plus the capture of Vicksburg, cut the South into three sections.

*Surrender at Appomattox* (April 1865): Lee surrendered after steadily losing ground and after finding himself unable to lift the siege of Petersburg (Virginia). Petersburg fell to Grant on April 2. Lee then abandoned Richmond (Virginia), the Confederate capital, and fled west only to surrender a week later on April 9. This essentially ended the war, although some fighting continued until the end of May.

## RESULTS OF THE CIVIL WAR

*Northern Business and Industry:* It grew and prospered during the war, and replaced Southern agriculture as the principal activity of this country.

*Homestead Act* (1862): The act provided free land in the West for those who settled on it and developed it. The South had not supported such legislation before the war.

*Pacific Railroad Acts* (1862 and 1864): Prior to the war southern routes for a transcontinental railroad were considered. The route approved after secession went from St. Louis to San Francisco. It would tie the industry of the East to raw materials and farm products of the West. The acts granted rights of way and land to the builders, thus providing government subsidies for the road's construction.

*Constitutional:* The federal government was proven more powerful than any state government. No state could secede from the Union. Three amendments to the Constitution (Thirteen, Fourteen, and Fifteen) ended slavery and gave equal protection of the laws and the vote to all males.

*Destruction of the Southern Plantation Economy:* Based on slavery, it was destroyed forever. It was replaced by sharecropping.

*Wartime Rights of Civilians:* The Supreme Court in *ex parte Milligan* upheld the Constitutional rights of a civilian during wartime. The case established civilian rule as primary over military government even in times of war.

## RECONSTRUCTION

*Issue I:* Readmission of rebel states to the Union.

> *Solution:* Lincoln's plan was to readmit states when 10 percent of the voters pledged loyalty to the United States and agreed to the abolition of slavery. After his assassination, northern members of Congress, called Radical Republicans, became harsher, passed the *Reconstruction Acts of 1867*, which treated the South as a conquered province. To gain admittance the seceded states had to ratify the Fourteenth Amendment and meet other requirements. Northern troops occupied the Southern states until a state met all conditions of readmission. The last occupation troops were withdrawn in 1877.

*Issue II:* Guarantee of civil rights to African Americans.

> *Solution: The Civil Rights Bill of 1866* was aimed at undoing the effects of Black Codes established by southern governments. The Fourteenth and Fifteenth amendments were to guarantee the civil rights of the former slaves. None of these actions were successful in protecting civil rights. The Supreme Court limited the application of the Civil Rights Bill to national issues. Southern legislators maintained some Black Codes and found other ways, including the later Jim Crow laws, to restrict the rights of the freed slaves.

*Issue III:* Government of rebel states.

> *Solution:* Former slaves, but not Confederate leaders, were allowed to vote at state party conventions and in elections until states were readmitted, after which the states again set their own rules as to who could vote. Immediately after the war many of the state governments passed important social legislation dealing with schooling and other issues.

## RESULTS OF RECONSTRUCTION

Reconstruction problems focused on the issue of whether the southern states were ever out of the Union. The Radical Republicans held that they were, and so developed plans to readmit the states that differed from Lincoln's plan, as he believed the states had always been part of the Union, even if in rebellion. The freed slaves were often treated as pawns in the game of power politics, especially by northerners who came south (Carpetbaggers). In many southern states ex-slaves held important political offices and helped to write new enlightened state constitutions.

*Formation of the Solid South:* The federal occupation troops were recalled from the South by President Hayes (1877) after he was declared the winner of the disputed presidential election of 1876. After 1877, and the withdrawal of all federal troops from the South, for many years the southern states voted for the Democratic Party on almost all occasions, as a result of the whites' dislike of Radical Republicans. This concept of the Solid South was still a consideration in elections in the immediate post-World War II period.

*Thirteenth Amendment:* 1865—Abolished slavery in the United States.

*Fourteenth Amendment:* 1868—African Americans were made citizens of the United States. It guaranteed that no state could deny life, liberty, or property without due process of law.

*Fifteenth Amendment:* 1870—Stated that no state can deny the right to vote on account of race, color, or previous condition of servitude.

*Ku Klux Klan:* It was formed to control ex-slaves and to "keep them in their place" and not allow them to change the basic political and social structure of the South. The Klan grew, especially after 1877.

*New Constitutions of Southern States:* Established free public schools for all children, abolished imprisonment for debt, abolished property qualifications for voting and jury duty.

*Railways, Highways, and National Banking System* strengthened the federal government.

*Prevention of Voting* (after 1877): To counteract the influence of ex-slaves, the South tried to deny them political rights by state measures that limited voting privileges to those:

Who could pass literacy tests

Who could pay a poll tax

Who owned property

Whose grandfather had voted

## WESTWARD EXPANSION

*Frontier:* From the founding of the first colonies until the Census Bureau in 1890 stated that there was no longer an area or line of unsettled land left in the United States, there had been Americans living on the frontier. The first frontier was just inland from the coastal areas, and by the time of the Revolution, it was across the Appalachians and heading into Kentucky and the Northwest Territory. With the purchase of the Louisiana Territory from France in 1803, the United States came into possession of land from coast to coast. Jefferson sent Lewis and Clark to explore this territory and soon after other explorers, followed by trappers, were discovering the rivers and mountains of the West. Manifest Destiny and expansion were important in the 1840s and led to the Mexican War, and the acquisition of the southwest, and to the settlement of the Oregon Dispute. With the discovery of gold in California in 1849, a rush of miners came to California and the area was admitted as a state as part of the Compromise of 1850. Subsequent discoveries of gold and silver in Nevada and Colorado led to more mining towns that flourished until the minerals ran out and then slowly became ghost towns. The mining frontier died slowly and was replaced by cattlemen and then farmers, and by 1890, the frontier had disappeared.

*Railroads:* During the Civil War, Congress passed legislation giving large grants of land and money to two companies, the Union Pacific and the Central Pacific, to build a cross-country railroad. Completed in 1869 largely by immigrant laborers including the Chinese, the railroad had a great impact on the nation. It made possible extension of cattle raising, which was started by the Spanish much earlier. The cattle frontier, with its long drives of cattle to the railheads where they could be shipped to profitable markets, flourished. Free-ranging cattle dominated the plains as the buffalo were destroyed and the Native Americans were defeated and moved to reservations. The railroads advertised for settlers, led to the growth of cities where lines crossed, and slowly tied the nation together, replacing travel on the Oregon Trail and other wagon routes that had served as the road West since the beginning of the settlement of Oregon.

*Homestead Act:* Passed in 1862, the act opened western land to settlement. If one staked a claim and made improvements over a five-year period, 160 acres would be yours. The opportunity brought many West in the post-Civil War period.

*Barbed Wire:* With the invention of barbed wire and the overgrazing of the plains, the cattle frontier faded and farmers created large fenced ranches for cattle-raising and large farms for grain. Other inventions (reaper, plow) aided the growth of these huge farms which became the symbol of American productivity.

*Life on the frontier:* Frontier life throughout history was rough. From the beginning, land had to be cleared, travel to areas of settlement was hard, and only tough, self-reliant individuals could survive. This was true of colonial yeoman, pre-civil war miners, cowboys, and farmers. Women on the frontier faced a lonely, hard-working life. The treeless prairies, the rugged mountains, and the wind created situations that were new and different from what the settlers were used to in the East or in Europe. Mining towns on the frontier were often violent places, and many of the stories of the Wild West are true.

## SOME IMPORTANT INDIVIDUALS OF THE PERIOD 1850–1877

| | | |
|---|---|---|
| Louisa May Alcott | Rutherford B. Hayes | Thaddeus Stevens |
| Horatio Alger | "Stonewall" Jackson | Lucy Stone |
| Clara Barton | Andrew Johnson | Harriet Beecher Stowe |
| John Brown | Robert E. Lee | James E. B. Stuart |
| Jay Cooke | Abraham Lincoln | Charles Sumner |
| Jefferson Davis | George McClellan | Roger B. Taney |
| Stephen Douglas | Herman Melville | Samuel Tilden |
| Mary Baker Eddy | Francis Parkman | Sojourner Truth |
| Millard Fillmore | Matthew C. Perry | Harriet Tubman |
| Jay Gould | Franklin Pierce | William "Boss" Tweed |
| Ulysses S. Grant | Dred Scott | Walt Whitman |
| Horace Greeley | William T. Sherman | |

# THE INDUSTRIAL REVOLUTION

**1877–1916**

Material relevant to Chapter 9.

The Industrial Revolution was a change from hand manufacturing, which was done in homes, to machine manufacturing done in a factory. The Revolution was stimulated in the United States by:

*Growing trade*, especially after the Revolutionary War removed British restrictions on American industry. Markets for exported goods were soon found. The United States was also free to import under our own tariff regulations.

*Invention of the cotton gin* by Eli Whitney in 1793 provided northern textile plants with an abundance of raw material. It also established the idea of interchangeable parts in manufacturing, which standardized products.

*Power* from swift-running rivers was easily available, especially in New England and along the Fall Line of the Appalachian Mountains.

*Coal, iron ore, and lumber* in abundance and near population centers.

*Napoleonic Wars, War of 1812, and British blockade* all forced manufacturing to grow, since we could not rely on imports.

*Westward expansion* opened new markets throughout the 19th century, while immigration and population growth created new demands.

*Labor shortage* and wartime needs during the Civil War led to increased use of machinery.

*Building of roads, railroads, and canals* made transportation of raw materials and finished products easier and stimulated manufacturing in industrial centers.

# INFLUENCE OF GEOGRAPHIC FACTORS ON INDUSTRIAL AND AGRICULTURAL DEVELOPMENT

The United States can be divided into four major geographic areas: the Atlantic coastal plain, the Appalachian highlands, the great central plain, the Cordilleran highlands.

*Atlantic Coastal Plain:* East of the Appalachian Mountains.
First area settled by English colonists.
Suitable for growth of manufacturing cities because of:
    Power available from rivers flowing down from Appalachian Mountains.
    Rivers that also allow for some transportation inland (such as the Hudson River).
    Excellent harbors.
Long, narrow plainland between mountains and the Atlantic provides excellent areas for farming to supply food to large population centers.

*Appalachian Highlands:* From Adirondack Mountains through Allegheny and Cumberland plateaus to central Alabama in the South.
Mountain area, originally dense forest, provided protection for colonists during the Revolutionary War.
Rich mining areas—coal and iron—in mountainous parts of Pennsylvania, West Virginia, and Alabama.
Valley areas are suitable for farming.

*The Great Central Plain:* From the Appalachians to the Rockies, and from Canada to Mexico, this is the largest region, comprising almost half of the land in the United States. Richest agricultural region in the world because of great fertile plains. Lush land for stock grazing from North Dakota to Texas.

Mississippi River, great North-South waterway, drains the area and supplies excellent transportation, along with its tributaries such as the Ohio and Missouri Rivers.

*Cordilleran Highlands:* From Rocky Mountains to the Pacific Ocean.

Mountainous area rich in lumber and mineral resources.

Fertile valley and lowland area near the Pacific is suitable for fruit orchards and farming.

## 18TH-CENTURY INVENTIONS THAT SPURRED INDUSTRIAL REVOLUTION

*Flying Shuttle:* John Kay (English), increased speed of weaving.                1733

*Spinning Jenny:* James Hargreaves (English), spun several threads at one time.                1765

*Water Frame:* Richard Arkwright (English), machine operated by water power spun thread very fast.                1769

*Steam Engine:* Invented by Thomas Newcomen (English) in 1703, and improved by James Watt (English) in 1769, ushered in the Age of Steam. The use of steam power transformed:

> *Transportation* because of application to water and land travel.

> *Factories,* which were no longer dependent on water power, and so could produce at much greater rates of speed and could be located in different areas nearer to raw materials and away from waterfalls.

## IMPORTANT 19TH- AND 20TH-CENTURY INVENTIONS AND DISCOVERIES

*Industry:* Many inventions transformed the American way of life. Among them were:

| | |
|---|---|
| *Colt Revolver:* Samuel Colt | 1831 |
| *Electric Dynamo:* Michael Faraday | 1831 |
| *Rubber:* Charles Goodyear | 1837 |
| *Kerosene:* Abraham Gesner | 1850s |
| *Electric Lightbulb:* Thomas A. Edison | 1879 |
| *Zipper:* Whitcomb L. Judson | 1893 |
| *X-Ray:* Wilhelm Roentgen | 1895 |
| *Radio Vacuum Tube:* Lee De Forest | 1907 |
| *Bakelite* (Plastic begins synthetics revolution): Leo Backeland | 1909 |
| *Cellophane:* Jacques Brandenberger | 1912 |
| *Liquid Fuel Rocket:* Robert Goddard | 1926 |

| | |
|---|---|
| *Synthetic Superpolymer* (Nylon): Wallace Carothers | 1937 |
| *Mark I* (computer): Howard Aiken | 1937 |
| *Controlled Nuclear Fission:* Enrico Fermi | 1942 |
| *Power-Producing Nuclear Fission:* United States Atomic Energy Commission | 1951 |
| *Solar Battery:* Bell Telephone and Air Research Development | 1954 |
| *Microwave (Radar) Oven:* Raytheon | 1955 |
| *Velcro:* Georges de Mestral | 1956 |
| *Demonstration of Laser Action:* Theodore Maiman | 1960 |
| *Astroturf:* Monsanto Chemical Company | 1965 |
| *Calculator (pocket):* Jack Kilby, Jerry Merryman, James Van Tassel | 1967 |
| *Kevlar (Bullet Proof Vest):* Stephanie Kwolek (Dupont) | 1976 |

*Agriculture:* Until 1800, all farm work was done by hand with the help of draft animals and using primitive tools that had changed very little over the centuries. The following inventions revolutionized farming in the 19th century:

| | |
|---|---|
| *Cotton Gin:* Eli Whitney | 1793 |
| *Iron Plow:* Charles Newbold | 1797 |
| *Reaper:* Cyrus McCormick | 1834 |
| *Modern Steel Plow:* James Oliver | 1868 |

*Transportation and Communication:* Inventions also drastically changed the speed of travel and communication. Outstanding ones were:

| | |
|---|---|
| *Steamboat:* Robert Fulton | 1807 |
| *Locomotive:* George Stevenson | 1830 |
| *Screw Propellor:* John Ericsson | 1831 |
| *Telegraph:* Samuel Morse | 1844 |
| *Sleeping Car:* George Pullman | 1867 |
| *Air Brake:* George Westinghouse | 1872 |
| *Telephone:* Alexander Graham Bell | 1876 |
| *Automobile:* developed by Henry Ford and others | 1895 |
| *Motion Pictures:* C. F. Jenkins | 1896 |
| *Airplane:* Wright Brothers | 1903 |
| *Radio:* R. A. Fressenden | 1906 |
| *First Rocket:* Robert Goddard | 1926 |
| *Diesel tractors and trains* | 1930s |
| *Helicopter:* I. Sikorsky | 1939 |
| *Electric Computer:* American Industry | 1940s |

*Television:* Philo Farnsworth (1921), C. F. Jenkins, V. Zworykin, RCA, and CBS                                                    1941

*Jet Planes:* Lockheed Company                                                    1942

*Transistor:* William Shockley and Bell Telephone Team                                                    1948

*UNIVAC (Universal Automatic Computer):* Eckert-Mauchly Corp.                                                    1951

*Duplicating Machine* (Xerox)                                                    1959

*Microchip (I. C. Chips):* Robert Noyce (Fairchild Co.), Jack Kilby (Texas Instruments, Inc.)

*Manned Space Flight (NASA)*                                                    1961

*Facsimile Machine (fax)*                                                    1970

*Microsoft Basic:* William Gates, Paul Allen                                                    1974

*Personal Computer—Floppy disk:* Steve Wozniak                                                    1978

*First Space Shuttle*                                                    1981

*Compact Disk:* Sony and Phillips Companies                                                    1983

*Cellular Telephone:* Bell's AmeriTech Mobile Communications Lab

*Start of assembly of international space station:* U.S. (NASA) and Russia (organizers)                                                    1998

*Mining and Smelting:* As steel became increasingly important in manufacturing, the following processes developed:

*New method of making steel from iron:* William Kelly                                                    1851

*Bessemer Process:* Henry Bessemer, used blast of hot air to remove impurities from molten iron.                                                    1856

*Open Hearth Method* used more of the iron effectively.                                                    1868

*New steel alloys* with special strengths were developed to aid the growing industrial demands of car, plane, and rocket industries.

*Health:* New discoveries and treatments revolutionized health care in the 20th century. A few key developments were:

*Yellow Fever Epidemic in New Orleans:* controlled through work of Walter Reed and others—vaccine developed.                                                    1905

*Penicillin:* Discovered in 1928, penicillin comes into use through efforts of Howard Florrey and Ernst Chain, marking revolution in treatment of bacterial-based disease.                                                    1940s

*Double Helix:* Francis Crick and James Watson                                                    1953

*Salk Vaccine:* Eliminates polio as a health threat in U.S. for those vaccinated.                                                    1955

*MRI (Magnetic Resonance Imaging):* Allows diagnosis of many medical problems without intrusion.                                                    1970s

*Human Genome Institute:* Founded as part of the National Institute of Health (NIH), the entire human genome has been analyzed with great potential for treatment of disease.          1997

## CONTRIBUTION OF IMMIGRANTS TO THE UNITED STATES

*Immigration:* All Americans are immigrants. Even the ancestors of the Native Americans came as immigrants from Siberia across the Bering Sea. All immigrants both as groups and as individuals have contributed to the development of the nation. The Native Americans cultivated plants, developed a special understanding of their relationship with the environment, and aided the first white settlers. The first settlers on the coast carved cities and farms out of forests. The slaves gave their labor to produce much wealth and capital for the later industrial development of the nation. Chinese laborers built the great railroads through the Rockies. Later immigrants from Europe supplied labor in the early factories and mines of the Northeast, working under poor conditions to build the wealth of America. After the Civil War, immigration increased greatly and the U.S. was considered the melting pot of peoples. How closely this idea was achieved is debatable, but for generations it was the stated goal of the nation—*e pluribus unum*—from many, one. In more recent years the concept of pluralism has replaced the melting pot image. Pluralism suggests greater emphasis on the many, the *pluribus,* but pluralism still holds that the many peoples make one nation. Some individual contributions by immigrants to the United States illustrate how beneficial this immigration has been to the nation and how diversified the peoples have been.

## SOME WELL-KNOWN IMMIGRANTS

| | |
|---|---|
| *British West Indies:* | Alexander Hamilton (politics) |
| *Canada:* | James J. Hill (railroads) |
| *China:* | Yung Wing (diplomacy) |
| | Poon Chew Ng (publishing) |
| *Denmark:* | Jacob Riis (social reform and literature) |
| *England:* | Alexander Graham Bell (invention) |
| *Germany:* | Walter Damrosch (music) |
| | Albert Einstein (science) |
| | Carl Schurz (politics) |
| *Greece:* | Dimitri Metropoulos (music) |
| *India:* | Ananda Keutish Coomaraswamy (philosophy) |
| *Ireland:* | Augustus St. Gaudens (sculpture) |
| *Italy:* | Arturo Toscanini (music) |
| | Amadeo P. Giannini (banking) |
| *Jamaica:* | Marcus Garvey (civil rights) |
| *Japan:* | Hideyo Noguchi (medicine) |
| | Yamasaki (architecture) |
| | Jokicho Takamine (medicine) |
| *Lithuania:* | Sydney Hillman (labor) |
| *Mexico:* | José Limón (dance) |

| | |
|---|---|
| *Russia:* | David Sarnoff (television) |
| | Mark Rothko (painting) |
| | Al Jolson (entertainment) |
| *Santo Domingo:* | John James Audubon (ornithology) |
| *Scotland:* | Andrew Carnegie (industry) |
| *Switzerland:* | Louis Agassiz (zoology) |
| *Yugoslavia:* | Michael Papin (X-ray) |

## OTHER FACTORS

*Resources:* America has been blessed with rich deposits of oil, coal, iron, and other minerals needed for industry. Farmlands are rich and can produce almost every type of product needed for manufacture, except natural rubber. There have been abundant water resources and the nation is blessed with a variety of climates, none of which is truly oppressive.

*Psychological Factors:* Open lands, political freedom, inventiveness, and individualism were factors that created a climate of opinion that encouraged industrial growth.

## RESULTS OF EARLY INDUSTRIAL REVOLUTION

*Growth of great cities*, as people changed their occupation from farming to manufacturing.

*Rapid growth of city population*, causing slums and increased crime rate.

*Bad working conditions* shared by many people, leading to development and growth of trade unions.

*Trade unions* that organized laborers to demand such items as shorter working days, safer working conditions and insurance to cover injuries.

*Greater interest* in social reforms and politics to provide solutions to problems.

*Demand for political parties* to change programs to meet new problems created by industrial change.

*Increase of America's productivity* and power.

*Imperialism*, as leaders and the people perceived a need for colonies as sources of raw materials and markets for finished products in competition with other industrializing nations.

*Increased militarism*, as international competition grew.

*Speeding up of transportation*, bringing people closer together.

*Increased need* for education.

*More foods and materials* available to a greater number of people.

*New giant industries* (railroad, oil, steel, sugar, aerospace, computers).

*Transformation in farming* techniques.

*Increased standard* of living of most people in industrialized societies.

*Rising expectations* of most people to share in the "good life" produced by material plenty.

# EFFECTS OF INDUSTRIAL REVOLUTION ON AMERICAN LIFE

*New Production Methods*: Large-scale production in factories produced new techniques of organizing work. These were:

*Division of labor*: Each worker performs one small task over and over again.

*Assembly line*: Each worker adds one part to the product being made as it moves along from worker to worker.

*Standardization of parts*: Many parts of each machine and the same part in different machines are made the same in shape and size so that, when defective or worn out, individual parts can be easily changed and replaced with new parts or parts from another similar machine. The parts are thus interchangeable.

*Business Combines*: Until the Civil War, most factories were small but afterward they began growing larger and larger; railroads opened up new markets; the heavy flow of immigrants provided cheap labor, and discovery of new mineral resources increased tremendously the supply of raw materials. As a result, factories increased in size, hiring many more workers and buying more machinery. Individual capitalists were unable to finance these huge projects, and new business forms were created. They were:

*The Corporation*: A company sells shares of stocks; shareholders elect the management (the Board of Directors), casting one vote, usually, for each share of stock owned; the management then selects the officers of the company who run the business on a day-to-day basis but who are responsible to the Board of Directors and ultimately to the shareholders.

*The Trust:* As industries grew, many related corporations such as sugar refineries merged into one large combination, run by a Board of Trustees.

Shareholders assigned their share in the corporation to trustees who managed the new trusts as Boards of Directors did for the corporation. The trustees were often members of the Board of Directors of the corporations. Often the creating of a trust was the work of an individual such as John D. Rockefeller who created the Standard Oil Trust to control the industry.

*Advantages of the trust*: Huge amounts of raw materials can be purchased more economically.

Large-scale manufacture creates more efficient production and distribution. The industry can make gainful use of by-products.

*Disadvantages of the trust*: Drives out small business and destroys competition. Regulates prices often unfairly through price cutting wars.

Concentrates great wealth and power in the hands of a few.

May control an industry by achieving a vertical or horizontal control. A *vertical trust* or organization is one where the trust owns or controls everything—raw materials, manufacturing, distribution facilities—needed by the company. A *horizontal trust* or organization is one where the trust owns either all the raw materials or all the manufacturing or all the distribution facilities of an industry.

*Other related forms of business organization were the pools and holding companies. Pools* were combinations of businesses that agreed to control prices; *holding companies* were arrangements in which a company controlled a portion of the stock in other corporations (for example, U.S. Steel Corporation).

*Development of Trade Unions.* The early factory system was responsible for many evils such as:

Use of child labor.

Low pay and a long working day.

Unsanitary working conditions.

Forced purchase at company stores.

There were no laws to restrain abuses by employers or to protect workers. Workers in America had found as early as 1793 that they could best achieve their demands and changes in working conditions by uniting. Gradually, large unions grew. The most important were:

*Knights of Labor.* Organized in Philadelphia, 1879, by garment workers, it aimed at organizing all workers into one large union. Although it reached a membership of 700,000, poor leadership and internal disputes caused its gradual collapse.

*American Federation of Labor* (AFL): Founded in 1886, it soon replaced the Knights of Labor; it organized skilled workers according to their trade, or craft. Craft unions in different cities united to form national craft unions in different fields (carpenters, painters, and so on). Thus the AFL is an organization of many craft unions united under a single leadership. Noted early leaders of the AFL: Samuel Gompers, one of the founders; William Green, who succeeded on Gompers's death and remained in charge from 1924 to 1952; George Meany.

*Congress of Industrial Organization* (CIO): In the early 1930s the AFL formed a Committee of Industrial Organization to consider the establishment of industry-wide—rather than craft—unions. It met with limited success and there were internal disagreements. In 1936 the Committee broke away from the AFL to create a union (CIO) based on all the workers in a particular industry—for example, all workers in the steel industry became members of the Steel Workers Union. The CIO gained recognition for its new unions through a series of sit-in strikes in the late 1930s. The AFL and CIO reunited as one union in 1955.

*Growth of cities:* As industries grew, cities grew with the arrival of increasing numbers of immigrants from Europe and from rural areas of the country who came in search of employment. Their needs were many and some were met by churches following the concept of the *Social Gospel.* Hull House, founded by Jane Addams in Chicago, is an example of the type of organization that was started in many cities to address the needs of immigrants. Also, help came from political organizations led by city bosses who, while aiding immigrants, often used their power in corrupt ways. This led to periodic cries for reform of the city political machines such as Tammany Hall in New York. Immigrants usually settled in areas in the cities where they found friends or relatives from the old country. Crowding led to slums and tenement living, with families crowding into one room without running water and sharing kitchens and baths. Still, for many, the United States seemed a land of opportunity.

*Social Darwinism:* Darwin's theory of Evolution—especially the idea of the survival of the fittest—became popular among some business and political leaders and philosophers (Herbert Spencer in England and William Graham Sumner in the United States). His theory was used to justify and/or explain the success of certain business leaders and trusts. It was used to justify government policies of laissez-faire, as they held that economic conditions were the result of a natural process and should not be interfered with by government.

## THE POPULIST MOVEMENT

With the disputed election of 1877 settled in favor of Hayes, the Reconstruction Era ended. The nation's interests turned to issues of economics. As business grew, wealth accumulated in the hands of businesspeople and bankers. Agricultural prices began a decline in 1884, which again intensified farm protests. Sectional antagonism intensified. A number of previous attempts to help the farmer's cause were revitalized, such as the Granger Movement, with little impact. Finally in 1892, several years of efforts to unite labor and farmers led to the formation of a third political party—the People's or Populist Party. Holding its first national convention in Omaha, the Populist Party produced a platform (Omaha Platform) that proposed significant reforms. To address the farmer's need for inflation and cheap money the Populists called for the coinage of silver at a 16 : 1 ratio with gold. The Platform also called for a graduated income tax, direct election of senators, a shorter work day and restrictions on immigration. In the presidential election James B. Weaver came in third behind Cleveland (Dem.) and Harrison (Rep.). Eventually the major features of the Omaha Platform were adopted by the federal government.

In 1896 the Populists nominated William Jennings Bryan for president. He was also the nominee of the Democrats who were won over to the 16 : 1 ratio for the coinage of silver by Bryan's stirring *Cross of Gold Speech,* one of the most famous speeches in U.S. history. His campaign, while extensive, focused on the issue of the coinage of silver, which was considered the best way to help the farmers and workers as it would create an inflationary pattern. Bryan lost to William McKinley (Rep.) and with the return of better economic conditions and the start of the Spanish-American War the Populist Party declined and eventually died.

## THE PROGRESSIVE MOVEMENT

The Progressive movement developed at the turn of the century, largely as a response to problems created in urban areas by industrial growth. The Progressives worked within the established party framework, with the exception of Theodore Roosevelt's "Bull Moose" party in 1912. They achieved a variety of reforms ranging from the Pure Food and Drug Laws (1906) under Theodore Roosevelt (Rep.) to the establishment of the Federal Reserve System (1913) under Woodrow Wilson (Dem.). Theodore Roosevelt and Woodrow Wilson were both leaders of the Progressive movement as was Robert La Follette of Wisconsin. They illustrate the range of participation in the movement.

Others involved in the movement were writers and publicists whom Theodore Roosevelt referred to as "Muckrakers". These writers focused the public's attention on certain areas that needed change. Among the leaders of the Muckrakers were Lincoln Steffens (*Shame of the Cities*—corruption), Ida Tarbell (*History of the*

*Standard Oil Company*—Rockefeller's oil trust), and Upton Sinclair (*The Jungle*—meat-packing industry).

The movement died with the U.S. entry into World War I but not before it had made profound changes in America's business and political life. The Progressive Movement is one example of a period of reform. They occur periodically throughout United States history. Other examples are Jacksonian Democracy, the New Deal, and the Great Society.

## LEGISLATION AND SUPREME COURT DECISIONS RELATED TO INDUSTRIAL GROWTH AND THE PROGRESSIVE MOVEMENT: 1877–1916

*Munn v. Illinois:* In this Supreme Court case the Court declared that the state, not the federal government, had the right to regulate business. Therefore, citizens had to resort to the polls and control of state government rather than to the federal courts for redress in cases involving control and regulation of business. The case has been grouped with several other cases as the Granger Cases; cases that worked against the interests of the people and in favor of business. These attitudes eventually led to the Populist movement.          1877

*Civil Rights Cases:* In these cases the Supreme Court declared that the Fourteenth Amendment applied only to state actions involving infringement of civil rights. If one individual infringed on another's rights as guaranteed by the Fourteenth Amendment, it was an individual offense and redress had to be found in the state courts. Federal law and the Fourteenth Amendment did not apply. The reaction of Congress to this interpretation of its limited powers was to pass no further civil rights legislation until the 1950s.          1883

*Wabash, St. Louis and Pacific Railroad Company v. Illinois:* In this famous case the Supreme Court declared that the state of Illinois could not regulate interstate commerce. A state could only regulate intrastate commerce. This created a great need for federal legislation, which came in the Interstate Commerce Act.          1886

*Interstate Commerce Act:* This act set up fair rate schedules for railway freight, prohibiting special rates to trusts and the charging of higher rates for short hauls than for long hauls. It also established the Interstate Commerce Commission (ICC) to enforce the act.          1887

*Sherman Antitrust Act:* Aimed at breaking huge trusts into smaller units, it failed because it was not enforced and because some administrations favored big business.          1890

*Plessy v. Ferguson:* In this Supreme Court decision the court validated the principle of separate but equal facilities for African Americans established by the Jim Crow laws. These laws created a two-tier system of rights for African Americans and whites. The Jim Crow laws created a subservient class who had poor educational opportunities. The civil rights system of America was based on the concept of separate but equal until the 1950s.          1896

*Pure Food and Drug Act:* This act prohibited the sale of impure food and medicine; four years later the act was amended to include the prohibition of false advertising.

1906

*Department of Labor:* This was created to give labor representation in the cabinet.

1913

*Federal Reserve Act:* This act set up a system of Federal Reserve banks under the joint control of the people, government, and the banking industry to regulate and control credit.

1913

*Clayton Antitrust Act:* This act prohibited unfair agreements that might diminish competition; established a Federal Trade Commission (FTC) to investigate charges of unfair competition and prosecute such cases; prohibited competing businesses from having the same men on Boards of Directors.

1914

*Conservation of Resources:* Greedy lumber cutting depleted woods without replanting; unintelligent farming ruined soil; inefficient mining methods wasted oil and gas; indiscriminate hunting and fishing decimated wildlife. Under President Theodore Roosevelt, a conservation program to end these abuses was begun. The following measures were aimed at conserving our national resources:

*National forests:* Under Roosevelt, millions of acres were set aside as forests; timber cutting was regulated so that there would be a continuous supply.

*Hunting licenses:* In order to regulate killing of game, laws were passed by states requiring hunters and fishermen to purchase licenses.

*Reclamation Law of 1902 known as the Newlands Act:* Irrigation projects were made possible by the act. Projects were initiated aimed at controlling floods (which washed away valuable topsoil and caused much other damage), improving navigation and producing electric power for outlying areas, and reclaiming wastelands. The most important projects were: Boulder Dam in Arizona and Nevada, Grand Coulee Dam and Roosevelt Dam in Washington, Shasta Dam in California, Fort Peck Dam in Montana, Garrison Dam in North Dakota.

1902

*National Park Service:* The service was established to oversee and operate the national parks. Yellowstone, the first national park, had been established in the Wyoming Territory in 1872. The movement for more national parks was part of the conservation effort begun under Theodore Roosevelt.

1916

## AMERICAN EXPANSION IN THE POST-CIVIL WAR PERIOD

In the post-Civil War period, Americans continued to move westward and settle the frontier. The railroad made settlement easier and opened new markets for eastern products and western raw materials and food. The movement led to warfare with the Native Americans and fighting on the plains continued until late in the century. The Dawes Act (1887) was an attempt to replace the tribal organization of the Native

Americans by eventually making them citizens of the United States. In 1890 the Census Bureau reported there was no longer a definable frontier line as the country was settled coast to coast, although there were large areas with very few white settlers. The historian, Frederick Jackson Turner, developed an important thesis on what the "closing of the frontier" meant, stating that the formative years of American history were over. However, the nation continued to grow and expand. The growth of cities became the chief focus of domestic growth while expansion overseas became very important, especially after 1890.

## THE GROWTH OF GREAT CITIES IN THE 19TH CENTURY

Cities were founded by the earliest colonists. Transportation facilities—harbors, rivers, river fords, and later canal and railroad lines—were important in determining the location of many cities. The nearness of raw material and a power supply, the availability of a labor supply, and the convenience of cheap transportation also were important factors in city location and growth.

*Some Major U.S. Cities*
BOSTON
Became an early shipping center because of Massachusetts Bay; proximity to the mouths of the Mystic and Charles rivers

CHICAGO
Railroad center; chief market for agricultural products of the central plains; approximate geographic center of great coal mining and steel manufacturing areas; harbor on Lake Michigan

DENVER
Junction of South Platte River and Cherry Creek; center of the Rocky Mountain states; access to mineral resources and oil

DETROIT
Center of a network of waterways made it a terminal for shipping on the Detroit River, River Rouge, St. Clair, Lake Erie, and Lake Huron; easy access to coal and steel by river and rail transport made it the birthplace of the automobile industry in the late 19th century

NEW ORLEANS
Located near the mouth of the Mississippi River and close to the Gulf of Mexico; proximity to external shipping (Gulf of Mexico) and internal transportation facilities (Mississippi River) made it the center of cotton and later oil industries

NEW YORK
Great natural harbor; juncture of Hudson River with Atlantic Ocean; waterway to the Midwest created by linking Hudson River to the Great Lakes via the Erie Canal

PHILADELPHIA
Junction of Schuylkill and Delaware rivers; proximity to coal fields; Pennsylvania Railroad gave it a link to the West

PITTSBURGH

Junction of Ohio, Allegheny, and Monongahela rivers; proximity to both coal and iron ore, making it convenient for growth of the smelting industry; oil and natural gas fields nearby

SAN FRANCISCO

Proximity to Sacramento and San Joaquin rivers; located on the Pacific Ocean, with one of the world's finest harbors; near great gold fields

SEATTLE

Located on Puget Sound and Lake Washington; the gateway to Alaskan gold fields; great shipping center for the Pacific; the center for the lumber and salmon fishing industries

## OVERSEAS EXPANSION 1867–1917

*The Alaska Purchase:* Called "Seward's Folly," Alaska was purchased from Russia upon the urging of Secretary of State Seward in 1867 for $7.2 million.

*Annexation of Hawaii:* Discovered by an Englishman, Captain James Cook, in 1778, Hawaii first attracted the interest of the United States in 1820 when missionaries went there. In 1884 the United States leased Pearl Harbor as a naval station. In 1889 the native queen was overthrown by a rebellion, and the new government petitioned the United States to annex the islands. In 1898 Congress approved annexation.

*Pacific Islands:* In 1867 the United States annexed uninhabited Midway Island as a coaling station.

In 1889, by negotiation with European nations, the United States acquired Tutuila, Pago Pago for its valuable harbor.

*The Panama Canal Zone:* With seaports on both the Atlantic and Pacific and trading interests in both oceans, the United States needed a way to get its navy from ocean to ocean without sailing around South America or Africa. A canal providing a short water passage between the two oceans was the ideal solution. Such a canal was first attempted by a French company, but it failed.

The United States under President Theodore Roosevelt in 1903 offered $10 million and a yearly rental of $250,000 to Colombia for use of land for 99 years in the province of Panama where a canal could be built. The Colombian government refused the offer.

In November 1903 the Panamanian people rebelled, and with United States support, set up an independent government. Fifteen days later the new republic of Panama accepted the same terms offered to Colombia and gave the United States the right to build a canal and exclusive control of a Canal Zone in perpetuity. The United States paid Colombia $20 million as redress for the loss of her Province of Panama and Colombia recognized the independence of the Republic of Panama. The canal was dug and opened for traffic in 1914.

*Virgin Islands:* These islands, purchased from Denmark in 1917, provided a defense for the Panama Canal. They provided naval bases on the perimeter of the Caribbean Sea.

# SPANISH-AMERICAN WAR

*Steps Leading to War.* In 1895 Cuban patriots led a revolt against harsh Spanish rule and were crushed and severely punished, with many Cubans put into what we would consider concentration camps. Sensational American newspaper stories demanded intervention, as did American business owners who had considerable investments in Cuban sugar and tobacco.

In February 1898 the American battleship *Maine* was mysteriously blown up while in the harbor of Havana. The slogan "Remember the Maine" aroused the American public as did articles in the "yellow press."

*The War.* In April 1898 Congress declared war on Spain. An American army landed in Cuba and soon destroyed Spanish resistance. Meanwhile, the Spanish fleet bottled up in the harbor of Santiago, was thoroughly beaten while trying to escape. The Under Secretary of the Navy Theodore Roosevelt, before leaving to lead a contingent of the Army in Cuba at the Battle of San Juan Hill, arranged for the U.S. Navy in the Pacific to be ready to attack the Philippines in case of war with Spain. When war came, the fleet attacked the Spanish Fleet in the Philippines and occupied Manila. Spain then sought peace.

*The Treaty of Paris.* Signed in December 1898, it ended the war. It contained the following provisions:

Puerto Rico, Guam, and the Philippines were ceded to the United States.

Cuba was granted independence. The United States was to supervise this independence.

The United States paid $20 million to Spain for the Philippines.

# SOME IMPORTANT INDIVIDUALS OF THE PERIOD 1877–1916

| | | |
|---|---|---|
| Jane Addams | Henry Ford | Joseph Pulitzer |
| Susan B. Anthony | James A. Garfield | Jacob Riis |
| Chester Arthur | Samuel Gompers | John D. Rockefeller |
| Ethel Barrymore | Benjamin Harrison | Theodore Roosevelt |
| Edward Bellamy | Rutherford B. Hayes | Augustus Saint-Gaudens |
| William Jennings Bryan | William Randolph Hearst | Margaret Sanger |
| Andrew Carnegie | Winslow Homer | Louis H. Sullivan |
| George Washington Carver | Charles E. Hughes | William H. Taft |
| Mary Cassatt | Helen Hunt Jackson | Ida Tarbell |
| Willa Cather | Sarah Orne Jewett | Samuel Tilden |
| Grover Cleveland | Robert La Follette | Mark Twain (Samuel |
| Eugene Debs | Mary Elizabeth Lease | Clemens) |
| Emily Dickinson | Margaret Mead | Cornelius Vanderbilt |
| Dorothea Dix | Frank Norris | Booker T. Washington |
| W. E. B. DuBois | Frederick Olmstead | Frances Willard |
| Isadora Duncan | John J. Pershing | Woodrow Wilson |
| Thomas Eakins | Gifford Pinchot | |

## HIGHLIGHTS OF U.S. FOREIGN POLICY TO WORLD WAR I

**1916–1945**

Material relevant to Chapter 10.

Throughout its history the United States has had contact and involvements with foreign nations. Our interest in South America stems from the founding of the nation. Interest in the Pacific was officially acknowledged as early as 1785, when still governed under the Articles of Confederation, Americans began trading with China, and, of course, the United States introduced Japan to modern times with the "opening" of Japan by Perry in 1853. There have always been foreign policy relations with Europe, but many have suggested the United States followed a policy of isolation from Europe during most of the 19th century. The War of 1812, efforts to keep England and France out of the Civil War, and the Spanish-American War are three among many possible indications that U.S. isolation from Europe was only a theory in the 19th century, and in fact, the United States interacted with other nations in pursuit of her national interests.

During the first 35 years of the nation's history several actions were taken that provided a foundation and attitude for much of United States foreign policy.

*Proclamation of Neutrality* by President Washington stated that the United States would be neutral in the war between England and France. This established the tradition of U.S. neutrality in European affairs.                                                                  1793

Washington's *Farewell Address* urged America not to sign an alliance with any nation.                                                                 1796

*Jefferson's Inaugural Address* promised that the United States would seek peace, commerce, and friendship with all nations, but would enter into entangling alliances with none. This became the basis of U.S. foreign policy until after World War II when the NATO alliance was established. Since then, the United States has signed many treaties allying itself with foreign nations, establishing a multilateral approach to international affairs.                                                                 1801

The *Monroe Doctrine* states an idea that guided U.S. policy toward the Americas. President Monroe promised that America would stay out of European affairs, and demanded that European countries stay out of the affairs of North and South America. Later presidents added their own interpretations to this basic policy as it applied to South America.                                                                 1823

## INVOLVEMENT IN THE AMERICAS AND THE PACIFIC

*Involvement in the Americas* even preceded the Monroe Doctrine. In the post-Civil War period U.S. interest in the Americas became focused on Central America and new markets. Concern over Cuba culminated in the Spanish-American War. Desire to maintain "order" and keep European powers out of the area led to the sending of U.S. Marines to several nations. A highlight of U.S. involvement was the support of Panama's revolution and the building of the *Panama Canal* (completed in 1914). Involvement in the Mexican Civil War after 1911 almost led to a second war with Mexico.

*Involvement in the Pacific* became important for the United States after the Civil War with the rapid industrial growth that followed. Acquisition of islands as coaling stations (Samoa) and interest in new markets (Hawaii) illustrate this early involvement. Later the proclaiming of the *Open Door Policy* in China in 1899, U.S. involvement in the *Boxer Rebellion* in China in 1900, and the fact that President T. Roosevelt arbitrated the Russo-Japanese War in 1905 (for which he won the Nobel Peace Prize) showed continued concern for the U.S. position in Asia and the free access to markets. The *Spanish-American War* marked the emergence of the United States as a great power on the international scene. U.S. interest in Asia was seen by the acquisition of the Philippines at the end of that war.

## WORLD WAR I

*Causes:* Sparked by the assassination of Archduke Ferdinand of Austria-Hungary on June 28, 1914, World War I was really caused by imperialistic and economic rivalries.

*Why America Joined:* Although President Wilson urged a policy of neutrality, Americans sold arms to the Allies, and in 1917 the United States abandoned its neutral position. The following events caused the United States to enter the war:

Sinking of the *Lusitania* by German submarines aroused public opinion.

The use of unrestricted submarine warfare (sinking ships without warning) by Germany. Such warfare was stopped temporarily after U.S. protest.

Arms sales and loans to the Allies led business to support them.

Anti-German propaganda by the Allies was effective.

Discovery of the Zimmermann Note, which demonstrated that Germany planned to urge Mexico to attack the United States.

On April 5, 1917, after Germany resumed unrestricted submarine warfare, sinking U.S. ships and those of other neutral nations despite a U.S. note of warning, Congress declared war.

*The War:* An army of 4 million troops was raised by a draft (Selective Service). Many volunteered. Bond drives helped to pay the huge expense of financing the war. These bonds were called Liberty Bonds.

The nation was mobilized for a total war effort including a *War Industries Board* and a *Committee for Public Information.*

American naval power broke Germany's blockade of England and helped destroy its fleet of submarines.

Two million American soldiers in the *American Expeditionary Force* (AEF) and, under General John J. Pershing, added to the forces of the Allies, crushed Germany on land, and participated in battles at *Belleau Wood, Chateau-Thierry, St. Mihiel,* and the *Argonne Forest.* Fighting in World War I occurred in the Middle East, where Turkish lands were conquered and boundaries arbitrarily drawn to make the nations that are in the region today, and in Africa and the Pacific, where the Allies, especially Britain and France, conquered German colonies.

An armistice was signed on November 11, 1918.

*Wilson's Fourteen Points:* Wilson's plan for a peace treaty included fourteen points that he hoped would prevent future wars. Some important points were:

Reduction of armaments.

An end to secret treaties.

Freedom of the seas.

An equitable solution to the colonial problem.

Self-determination of peoples.

Establishment of a League of Nations to arbitrate problems among nations peacefully.

*Treaty of Versailles:* Largely ignoring the Fourteen Points and intending to make Germany powerless to wage war forever, the Allies formulated a treaty that was signed June 28, 1919. Some of its important provisions were:

*Surrender of German Territory:* Cession of Alsace-Lorraine on the border of France and Germany to France; cession of other territories and colonies to other European allies and Japan. The colonies were to be administered by the various victorious nations under *mandates* of the League of Nations.

*Reparations:* Germany was forced to compensate the Allies for war damages.

*Allied Occupation:* The Allies occupied the Rhineland region in Germany, between the Rhine River and the French and Belgian borders.

*War Guilt:* Germany was forced to admit guilt for starting the war.

*A League of Nations:* Designed to provide a forum for the nations to discuss issues of conflict and prevent war, the League failed to act effectively in disputes and proved to be ineffective in preventing the outbreak of World War II. Although the League was Wilson's idea, the U.S. Senate voted not to accept the treaty. The failure of the United States to join is considered one reason for the League's failure.

## THE 1920s

*"Return to Normalcy:"* The war caused many dislocations. The Republicans under Harding won the election of 1920 with the slogan "return to normalcy," but it was not achieved. There were many social changes that could not be reversed. African Americans had moved north to urban areas, finding work in factories and a social life in places such as Harlem in New York. Harlem became the center of intellectual ferment for these newcomers, and the resulting flowering of music, poetry, and literature has been acknowledged as the *Harlem Renaissance.* Many women had taken jobs during the war only to lose them and their financial independence with the return of over four million troops. These veterans came home with new attitudes toward life and their roles and expectations. The automobile became readily available to many and changed social patterns of dating and vacations and also created the opportunity for the growth of suburbs as well as economic opportunities with gas stations, motels, and road building.

*The Roaring Twenties:* In the immediate postwar period there were many problems of adjustment to peace. Jobs were hard to find for many returning veterans. Farm prices were depressed and remained so during the entire period until the New Deal. Industry slowly recovered, prosperity returned, and there was an economic boom but it is now clear that the prosperity was not evenly distributed. There was a great land boom in Florida in which many people lost money and heavy speculation on the stock market culminated in the crash of October 1929.

Prohibition was in effect and led to the growth of crime as criminal leaders like Al Capone organized others to supply illegal alcohol. New attitudes towards sex and morality, the growth of "speakeasies" (bars), and the development of jazz and the blues have led scholars to refer to the decade as the "roaring twenties."

*Expatriates:* A group of alienated American citizens settled in Europe in the 1920s. Known as the "lost generation," these expatriates as well as several who remained in the United States added to the intellectual and artistic life of the decade. They supported painters, among them Picasso, but more importantly they wrote literature that has become American classics—Ernest Hemingway *(Farewell to Arms* and *For Whom the Bell Tolls)* and T. S. Eliot *(The Waste Land)*. At home, Sinclair Lewis *(Babbitt, Main Street)*, F. Scott Fitzgerald *(The Great Gatsby)*, and Eugene O'Neill in his plays portrayed the values of money and success that were driving the nation. The sharpest critic of the postwar social milieu was Baltimore-based news reporter, H. L. Mencken, whose cynicism and satire spared no group or individual.

*The Red Scare* of the early 1920s was a reaction to communism, which Americans came to fear after a Communist government was established in the Soviet Union and a Communist-led uprising occurred in Germany. Attorney General Palmer and J. Edgar Hoover made reputations for themselves attacking the communist threat but the actual threat to the nation was exaggerated.

*Republican Administrations:* The Harding Administration (Republican), elected in 1920, supported a return to prewar attitudes and foreign policy positions. The United States Senate had turned down the Treaty of Versailles with its League of Nations. The Republicans returned to *isolationism,* as the policy of ignoring Europe was called. The administration ended with several scandals, such as Teapot Dome, and this discredited the federal government. Harding died in office. His successors, Coolidge and Hoover, basically followed the pattern of support of business and little government regulation begun by Harding. In foreign policy, although they professed a policy of isolationism, they supported negotiations over reparations from Germany and sent military forces to Central American nations on several occasions to protect the status quo and American business interests.

## THE GREAT DEPRESSION AND THE NEW DEAL

Although a decade of good times and prosperity for some followed World War I, the United States was engulfed in a major depression at the end of the 1920s. Causes of the depression included:

*High tariffs* aimed at eliminating European competition from American markets but the reduced trade made it impossible to sell U.S. goods abroad.

*Speculation* in real estate and stocks caused artificial rises in prices.

*Overproduction and unemployment* caused in part by replacement of workers with machines.

*War debts* absorbed European purchasing power, lessening foreign trade.

*Too much credit* on easy terms caused financial collapses when borrowers were unable to pay back their loans.

*The stock market crash* of October 1929 is considered the starting point of the Great Depression. The federal government under President Hoover took little action to correct the economic problems believing the economy would adjust naturally without interference and that the states or local charity should help the jobless until the economy again was operating fully. It reflected the laissez-faire attitudes and Social Darwinist philosophy that had prevailed in the Republican Party in the 1920s. After two years with no economic improvement, Hoover did support some federal help (Reconstruction Finance Corporation).

The *Great Depression* impacted everyone. Thousands were out of work. Many women took menial jobs to support families where there was no work for the men. Over 50% of African-American men were unemployed. Mexican Americans who had recently moved from farm work to factories were seen as a threat and the government sent thousands back to Mexico.

In the *election of 1932* Franklin D. Roosevelt, a Democrat, defeated Herbert Hoover. As a candidate, Franklin D. Roosevelt promised action to combat the depression. The actions became incorporated in what is known as the *New Deal*—another period of major reforms. The various measures of the New Deal taken to combat the depression have been grouped by some historians in the general categories of the "3 Rs"—relief, recovery, reform. Some historians reject this classification as some acts fit in more than one category. However, the "3 Rs" provide one organizational scheme for categorizing the many New Deal measures. Examples of each type of legislation are:

1. *Relief*—direct giving of goods, clothing, shelter, and jobs to the unemployed. *Works Progress Administration (WPA):* The federal government gave employment to men on work projects it initiated.

2. *Recovery*—laws aimed at curing the poor state of the economy at that moment. *Home Owners Loan Corporation (HOLC):* Government made loans available to homeowners to prevent loss of their homes to mortgagees.

   *Agricultural Adjustment Act (AAA):* Reduced amount of crops planted to create artificial shortages and stimulate prices.

3. *Reform*—long-term changes in the economy designed to prevent future depressions.

   *Tennessee Valley Authority (TVA):* Comprehensive development of the production of electricity and the control of flooding in the Tennessee River valley. Opposed by many as socialism—government involvement, development, and ownership of industry—the TVA was approved by the Supreme Court. The electricity produced proved vital to the development of the atomic bomb by the United States in World War II.

   *Reciprocal Tariff Act:* Removed barriers to trade by lowering tariffs through negotiation.

   *National Industrial Recovery Act (NIRA):* Codes of fair practices including rights of workers were drawn up by each industry involved in interstate commerce. The codes were administered by the National Recovery Administration (NRA). The Supreme Court, interpreting the Constitution very strictly, declared this and some other early New Deal legislation unconstitutional.

*Supreme Court Controversy:* Roosevelt attempted in 1937, after his overwhelming reelection, to change the composition of the Supreme Court. Roosevelt was upset by the failure of the Court to approve much of his legislation. Congress refused to support his "court packing" plan. With the death of several judges, Roosevelt was able to appoint new judges who supported his legislation and interpreted the Constitution more loosely.

*Recession of 1937*: In the first few years of the New Deal economic conditions improved in the nation. In 1937 recovery staggered and there was a little recession. With the coming of World War II the American economy improved rapidly and the Great Depression quickly receded from view.

*Organized Labor*: The American Federation of Labor (AFL) had organized only skilled workers. In 1935 the AFL created a Committee for Industrial Organization, headed by John L. Lewis, to organize unskilled and semiskilled workers. The committee left the AFL in 1936, and in 1938 formed its own labor organization, the Congress of Industrial Organization (CIO). Instead of dividing workers by craft, the CIO divided them by industry. For example, all workers in the automobile industry, whether skilled or unskilled, became members of the United Automobile Workers. The CIO made quick progress in organizing previously unaffiliated industrial workers in such fields as steel, textile, shipbuilding, and rubber. The CIO used "sit-in" strikes as a tool to gain recognition from industry.

Movies and radio provided a way to escape the problems of the time. Shirley Temple, age five when she first became a movie star, smiled, danced, and sang, cheering many. *Snow White and the Seven Dwarfs* introduced the full-length animated film and *The Wizard of Oz* starring Judy Garland provided escape. The greatest movie success of the 1930s was *Gone With the Wind*—an epic of the Civil War that took people away from the reality of the 1930s to show another time of crisis in which the heroine, Scarlett O'Hara, showed optimism that tomorrow would be better.

The WPA paid artists to paint and many public buildings benefited from the creation of murals on their walls. The government sent photographers (Dorothy Lange) to record life in the Depression and the Dust Bowl, providing a moving, explicit record of the impact on the people of those events. The author, John Steinbeck, in *Grapes of Wrath*, told the story of the Dust Bowl and its impact on Oklahoma farmers.

## IMPORTANT LEGISLATION AND SUPREME COURT DECISIONS 1916–1945

| | |
|---|---|
| *Adamson Act*: Provided for eight-hour day for railroad workers. | 1916 |
| *Norris-LaGuardia Anti-Injunction Act:* Limited power of courts to issue injunctions and curtail workers' rights to strike and picket. | 1932 |
| *New Deal Legislation*: (See acts mentioned above). Acts were passed dealing with many issues from agricultural reform to workman's compensation; they changed the American economy. A number of the programs were reversed during President Reagan's terms in office. | 1933 |
| *Federal Communications Commission (FCC)*: Regulates communication by telephone, telegraph, radio, and television. | 1934 |

*Securities and Exchange Commission (SEC)*: Protects investors by establishing fair procedures in sale of stocks; in 1935 the SEC was

| | |
|---|---|
| given power to regulate financial practices of public utilities involved in interstate commerce. | 1935 |
| *Schechter Poultry Corp. v. U.S.*: The Court declared the National Industrial Recovery Act unconstitutional since the creation of the codes delegated the legislative authority of Congress to another body. | 1935 |
| *National Labor Relations Act (called Wagner Act)*: Safeguarded labor's rights to organize and bargain through unions and incorporated many protections for labor that had been developed in the NRA Codes. | 1935 |
| *Social Security Act*: Established a federal-state system of unemployment compensation and old age pensions paid for by a federal tax on employee's income and employer's total payroll. | 1935 |
| *U.S. v. Butler*: The first Agricultural Adjustment Act was declared unconstitutional. | 1936 |
| *NLRB v. Jones and Laughlin Steel Corp.*: The Court, in a 5-4 decision upheld the National Labor Relations Act. This reversed the Court's trend of declaring New Deal legislation unconstitutional. | 1937 |
| *Fair Labor Standards Act:* Established minimum wage and work week of 40 hours with time and a half for overtime. | 1938 |
| *Serviceman's Readjustment Act (GI Bill):* Addressed the issue of demobilizing the 12,000,000 servicemen who had fought in World War II by providing loans to veterans for housing and education. | 1944 |

# WORLD WAR II

*Background:* Many interrelated incidents and complex problems led to the outbreak of World War II.

The failure of the United States to join the League of Nations weakened the effectiveness of the organization in dealing with international crises. The League did have some successes in the area of social work on health issues. In the 1920s the U.S. led efforts to bring about disarmament (Washington Conference) and, after the Great Crash, to negotiate the amount of reparations to be paid to the Allies by Germany, but failed to cancel the Allies' wartime debt owed to the U.S., intensifying the worldwide economic crisis.

*Rise of Fascism:* In 1922 Mussolini, leader of the Italian Fascists, took power. Pursuing a militaristic policy as a solution to Italy's economic problems, he attacked Ethiopia in 1935. The League of Nations failed to intervene and Italy annexed Ethiopia and later Albania.

In 1931 Japan, led by a military dictatorship, attacked China and annexed Manchuria. In 1937 Japan invaded China. China lost Shanghai and coastal areas to the Japanese but continued fighting.

Germany, under Hitler, who took power in 1933, also embarked on a militaristic program to address economic problems. The three Fascist powers—Germany, Italy, and Japan— formed an alliance known as the Axis. Hitler denounced the Treaty of Versailles. He seized the industrialized Ruhr in 1936 and annexed Austria in 1938.

Hitler and his Nazi Party made vicious attacks on Catholics and Jews and suppressed all who did not agree with his policies. Yet the League of Nations and the World War I Allies did not join together to stop any of the aggressive moves of the Axis powers. The former Allies were all facing hard economic conditions as a result of the Depression. Their governments could not agree on policy and there was a strong isolationist sentiment in the United States. In 1938 England and France negotiated the Munich Agreement with Hitler hoping to bring "peace in our time" by allowing Hitler to take the Sudetenland from Czechoslovakia but Hitler soon broke the agreement. Hitler invaded Poland in September 1939.

*The War Before the Entry of the United States:* France and Britain declared war on Germany to help Poland resist the attack, but they failed. Germany speedily conquered Norway, Denmark, the Netherlands, Belgium, and then France. Great Britain and the British Commonwealth together with governments in exile from the conquered countries and the colonies of these countries continued the war. England withstood a massive air onslaught by the Germans in 1940. Finally in June, 1941, Hitler broke a treaty with the Soviet Union and attacked, bringing the Soviets into the war on the side of the Allies—those fighting against Germany and Italy and later Japan. In spite of severe losses China continued to resist the Japanese forces. The feuding Chinese Communist and Nationalist forces joined in the resistance.

*American Involvement in the War:* There was strong opposition to any United States involvement in Europe. Many groups organized to support isolationism. The best known public hero (first solo flight across the Atlantic) of the 1930s, Charles Lindbergh, led an organization, America First, that essentially supported the policies of Hitler and called for separation from European affairs. On the outbreak of war in Europe in 1939, a policy of neutrality was declared by President Roosevelt. It was later repealed and replaced by the Lend-Lease Act, which gave the president power to sell or lease war equipment to any country whose defense he deemed important to the preservation of American safety. The U.S. became "the arsenal of democracy," and supplied Great Britain with arms after the fall of France in 1940.

*America Enters:* Relations between the United States and Japan became very strained in the 1930s. Negotiations were undertaken in Washington to address these differences. Then, on December 7, 1941, the Japanese air force and navy, in a surprise attack on Pearl Harbor, destroyed a large part of the American fleet that was stationed there. The United States became a participant in World War II when, the next day, Congress declared war on Japan, and three days later, Germany and Italy declared war on the United States.

*Wartime Government Agencies:* The government quickly organized for full-scale war while military forces were rapidly built up. A number of agencies were established to run the war. Among them were:

*War Production Board (WPB):* Organized industry so that war materials could be produced at the highest level of efficiency.

*Office of Price Administration (OPA):* To prevent inflation and a black market, the OPA set prices and rationed goods such as oil and sugar, meat and other food. This assured a fair distribution of the limited consumer supplies and assured the needs of the military would be met.

*War Labor Board (WLB):* Settled disputes between business and labor without strikes so that production would not be interrupted and morale would be high.

*Fair Employment Practices Committee (FEPC):* Aimed at insuring morale and maximum use of the labor force by preventing employer discrimination against workers because of race or religion. The efforts of this committee laid the foundation for the Civil Rights Movement of the 1950s.

*Office of War Information (OWI):* Issued patriotic material and served as the propaganda branch of the government. Its goal was to maintain morale by warning people against defeatist and harmful propaganda.

*Allied Wartime Cooperation:* During the war the allied leaders, Churchill (England), Stalin (Soviet Union), De Gaulle (Free France), Jiang Jieshi (China), and Roosevelt (United States) held a series of conferences (Casablanca, Cairo, Teheran) to plan war strategy, and at Yalta (1945) to plan for the postwar world. Different combinations of these Big Five leaders attended these meetings, which made it possible for the war effort to be unified. These wartime conferences set the precedent for postwar summit meetings.

*The War in Europe:* In November, 1942, General Eisenhower, Commander of Allied Forces, landed with Allied armies in French West Africa and captured Morocco and Algeria. In 1943 Sicily and then Italy were invaded.

The final phase of the war began on June 6, 1944, with the Allied invasion of the Normandy peninsula in France. Caught between an attack by Soviet troops on the east and Allied troops on the west, German resistance crumbled after a final attempt to stop the invasion in the Battle of the Bulge in December, 1944. On May 1 it was announced that Hitler had committed suicide, and on May 7, 1945, the Germans surrendered unconditionally.

*The War in Asia:* After Pearl Harbor Japan quickly captured the Philippines, Guam, Wake, Hong Kong, and Singapore. The crippled U.S. fleet was unable to stop the occupation of these and other islands. By the spring of 1942, the tide began to turn with aid from Australia and New Zealand.

Important naval victories in the Coral Sea and at Midway (the "turning point of the war") shattered most of the Japanese fleet. This was followed by a series of American victories in hotly fought battles on Pacific islands. Guadalcanal, the Aleutians, and Bougainville fell in 1943; the Marshalls, Saipan, the Philippines, Corregidor, and Iwo Jima in 1944 and 1945.

Meanwhile, China continued to fight Japan on the mainland, and following the agreement signed at Yalta, Russia invaded Japanese-held lands in Manchuria on August 8, 1945. On August 6 and 9, 1945, atomic bombs were dropped on the Japanese cities of Hiroshima and Nagasaki. On the 14th of that month, the Japanese agreed to unconditional surrender. The official surrender document was signed on board the U.S.S. *Missouri* on September 2, 1945, ending World War II. The fighting in Europe had already ended.

# SOME IMPORTANT INDIVIDUALS OF THE PERIOD
## 1918–1945

| | | |
|---|---|---|
| Marian Anderson | Adolf Hitler | Paul Robeson |
| Stephen V. Benet | Herbert Hoover | Eleanor Roosevelt |
| Mary Bethune | Charles E. Hughes | Franklin Roosevelt |
| Louis D. Brandeis | Al Jolson | George H. "Babe" Ruth |
| Willa Cather | Robert LaFollette | Carl Sandburg |
| Charles Chaplin | John L. Lewis | Alfred E. Smith |
| Winston Churchill | Charles Lindbergh | Joseph Stalin |
| Calvin Coolidge | Henry Cabot Lodge | Gertrude Stein |
| Charles De Gaulle | Joe Louis | John Steinbeck |
| T. S. Eliot | Douglas MacArthur | Jim Thorpe |
| Albert Einstein | George Marshall | Edith Wharton |
| Dwight Eisenhower | Georgia O'Keeffe | Wendell Willkie |
| F. Scott Fitzgerald | A. Mitchell Palmer | Frank Lloyd Wright |
| Clark Gable | George Patton | Richard Wright |
| Greta Garbo | Frances Perkins | Mao Zedong |
| Warren Harding | John Pershing | |
| Ernest Hemingway | A. Philip Randolph | |

# THE IMMEDIATE POSTWAR PERIOD

The problem of demobilizing 12 million servicemen and women and returning them to civilian life was addressed by the *Serviceman's Readjustment Act of 1944*, commonly known as the G.I. Bill of Rights. Among its provisions were:

> **1945–2007**
>
> Material relevant to Chapter 11.

Government-financed job training and education for discharged servicemen and women.

Unemployment payments for veterans.

Loans to veterans for business, farm, and home construction.

With the end of rationing and price control, prices rose rapidly. There was a period of inflation, but a postwar depression, which many people had feared, was avoided. No truly satisfactory solution for the problem of inflation was found, and inflationary pressure continued to affect the nation for many years.

# FOREIGN POLICY ISSUES

*The United Nations*

Meetings at Bretton Woods in 1943 and at Dumbarton Oaks in 1944 laid the basis for a worldwide organization dedicated to finding peaceful solutions to international problems. On April 25, 1945, delegates from 50 nations met in San Francisco to draw up the charter for a new organization, the United Nations, to replace the League of Nations. The main provisions of the charter were:

Member nations would not help an aggressor nation.

Member nations would settle disputes peacefully.

Member nations would use neither force nor the threat of force to settle disputes.

Member nations would use the armed might of an international police force to fight against aggressors.

*The Charter of the United Nations* created the following governing bodies:

*General Assembly:* Composed of delegates from each member nation, it discusses and recommends solutions to international problems, but must refer all solutions regarding the use of force to the Security Council. Each nation has one vote.

*Security Council:* Consists of 15 members, five permanent members—the Big Five: (the victors in World War II over Germany and Japan) the United States, Great Britain, France, China (the government of Jiang Jieshi on Taiwan held the seat until 1972 when the People's Republic was given the seat), the Soviet Union (replaced by Russia in 1991)—and ten nonpermanent members elected for a two-year term by the General Assembly. Decisions may be passed by the vote of nine members, but must include all of the Big Five. That gives any one of the great powers veto power over the Council's decisions.

The Council bears primary responsibility under the UN Charter for the maintenance of international peace and security. Situations may be brought to its attention by any nation and the Council can investigate it or initiate action. Peacekeeping missions are voted on by the Security Council.

*The Economic and Social Council:* Studies and makes suggestions for economic and social betterment of countries.

*The Secretariat:* The UN's administrative arm, headed by the Secretary General, who is elected by the General Assembly. Its task is to carry out those policies adopted by the Assembly and Council. It oversees peacekeeping forces. The headquarters is in New York City. Other offices are in Geneva, Switzerland, former headquarters of the League of Nations; The Hague, the Netherlands, seat of the International Court of Justice, and other cities.

There are many other important organizations and committees connected with the United Nations. Among the more important are:

International Court of Justice, International Labor Organization, and World Health Organization.

## THE COLD WAR

At the end of World War II, previously amicable relations between the United States and the Soviet Union deteriorated. President Truman, who had become president after the death of Roosevelt in April 1945, reacted quickly, and the basis of the U.S. post-World War II foreign policy was set by the end of 1947. The focus was a struggle with the Soviet Union to block their expansion while protecting the interests of the United States and its allies. Nuclear weapons held by both sides after 1948 deterred a "hot war" between the superpowers. The antagonisms remained between the two superpowers until the mid-1980s although there were times of improved relations such as the period of *détente* under President Nixon. With the introduction of the policy of *glasnost* by President Gorbachev in 1985, relations between the two powers changed rapidly. Presidents Reagan and Gorbachev held several summit meetings and negotiated arms reductions. With the fall of the Berlin Wall in 1989 and the subsequent breakup in 1991 of the Soviet Union into the *Union of Independent States*, the Cold War was declared ended.

# MAJOR COLD WAR EVENTS

While all these events of the Cold War dealt with international issues, they all had complex and far-reaching impacts on domestic political, economic, and social issues.

*Truman Doctrine:* Truman announced a pledge of aid to the governments of Greece and Turkey, which he believed were being threatened by Soviet-led Communist interests. The doctrine was later interpreted to mean the United States would oppose the overthrow of any democratic government. 1947

*"X" Article:* George Kennan of the State Department published an article in the magazine *Foreign Affairs* that outlined as the goal of U.S. policy the containment of the Soviet Union to prevent its expansion and spreading doctrines of communism. Known as the *Containment Policy,* it was adopted as the basis of U.S. Cold War policy and underlay many of the events of the Cold War. 1947

*National Security Act:* This act established the National Security Council as an advisory body to the president and the CIA as an information-gathering/spying organization. 1947

*Marshall Plan:* Secretary of State Marshall's European Recovery Program, known as the Marshall Plan, made provision for United States' financial assistance to European countries whose economies had not recovered from World War II. Offered to all European nations, the plan was rejected by Communist countries. 1947

*Berlin Blockade:* The Soviet Union blocked land access to Berlin and the United States responded with an airlift of supplies. 1948

*North Atlantic Treaty Organization (NATO):* NATO, the first U.S. peacetime military alliance, reversed George Washington's advice of 1797 to avoid permanent alliances. NATO was designed to block or contain Communist, especially Soviet, expansion in Europe. 1949

*Communist Victory in China:* After a struggle dating back to the 1920s, the Chinese Communists under Mao Zedong defeated the Nationalist forces of Jiang Jieshi. The Nationalists fled to Taiwan, establishing a government there that was recognized as the government of China by the United States and the UN until the Nixon administration reversed the policy and officially recognized the mainland government of Mao Zedong. In the early 1950s this "loss of China" was a divisive issue in U.S. domestic politics. 1949

*Korean War:* Communist North Korea attacked South Korea; the United States and other nations under the United Nations flag fought for three years to block the aggression. The armistice terms essentially restored the status quo. Communist North Korea continues as a threat to international security, having announced in 2003 that it had developed nuclear bombs. 1950–53

*Southeast Asia Treaty Organization (SEATO):* Designed to contain Communist, especially Chinese, expansion in Asia. 1954

*Fall of Dien Bien Phu* and *Geneva Conference on Vietnam*: After the French lost their important base at Dien Bien Phu to the Vietnamese Communists, at Geneva, a peace plan was developed for the region. It was rejected by Ngo Dinh Diem, premier of South Vietnam.                          1954

*Involvement in Vietnam*: The United States became more and more involved in Vietnam as U.S. foreign policy focused on the containment of Communism in Southeast Asia (see Vietnam War on pp. 352–353).                          1955

*Hungarian Revolt*: Hungary's attempt to throw off Soviet domination was crushed by Soviet military intervention.                          1956

*Aswan Dam*: Foreign aid became a tool of the Cold War. The United States and Great Britain offered to help Egypt build a high dam at Aswan to aid economic development of the nation. They later withdrew the offer and Egypt received funding from the Soviet Union.                          1956

*Suez Canal Seized*: In an attempt to raise money for development, Egypt seized the Canal. France, England, and Israel invaded Egypt to regain control of the Canal. They were stopped by the United States and the USSR. This provided a rare example of superpower Cold War cooperation.                          1956

*Eisenhower Doctrine*: Approved by Congress, this permitted the United States to extend economic and military aid to Middle Eastern countries that wanted it because they believed they were threatened by Communists.                          1957

*Lebanon*: United States sent troops to keep Communists from seizing power.                          1958

*U-2 Spy Plane*: The Soviets shot down a U.S. spy plane over Soviet territory, which ended a move toward rapprochement at the end of Eisenhower's presidency.                          1960

*Independence of African Nations*: In 1960 the United Nations admitted 13 new African nations to membership. Civil War broke out in the Republic of the Congo and the United Nations intervened. Many of the nations were caught in the Cold War and played both sides against each other, seeking financial and military aid from both sides.                          1960

*Cuban Revolution*: Castro's guerrilla troops seized control of Cuba from the U.S. supported dictator. Relations with the United States rapidly deteriorated as Castro established a Communist state in Cuba. Many Cubans fled to the United States and finally the United States broke diplomatic relations with Cuba.                          1961

*Bay of Pigs*: Unsuccessful attempt by Cuban refugees backed by the United States to invade and overthrow Castro's Communist regime in Cuba. The attempt was supported by the new Kennedy administration.                          1961

*Berlin Wall*: East Germans sealed off their part of Berlin from the West. The wall became the symbol of the Cold War.                          1961

*Cuban Missile Crisis:* Soviet attempt to set up intermediate range missiles in Cuba was blocked by a U.S. blockade and political maneuvering. Nuclear war was narrowly avoided as the U.S. and Soviets negotiated a compromise.

1962

*Hot Line Agreement:* Established direct rapid communication between Moscow and Washington, suggesting cooperation was possible between the superpowers. First used during the Six-Day War of 1967 between Israel and its Arab neighbors.

1963

*Limited Nuclear Test Ban Treaty:* After many years of bomb testing and unilateral stopping of tests, a treaty was signed banning the testing of nuclear weapons in the atmosphere, in outer space, or underwater. Underground tests were permitted.

1963

*Dominican Republic Intervention:* President Johnson sent U.S. troops into the Dominican Republic to crush a "band of Communist conspirators" who the president claimed had gained control of a revolution against an authoritarian president.

1965

*Outer Space Treaty:* Banned military bases, weapons, and weapons tests in space and established principles for peaceful development of space.

1967

*Pueblo Seized:* A U.S. intelligence-gathering ship was seized off Korea. After a U.S. officer signed a statement accepting guilt for spying, the ship was released by the North Korean government.

1968

*Nuclear Nonproliferation Treaty:* The treaty banned the spread of nuclear weapons among signatory nations. It approved of access to nuclear energy for peaceful uses.

1969

*Nixon's Visit to China:* A new era in relations was confirmed with President Nixon's visit to the People's Republic of China. The U.S. accepted the People's Republic, not Taiwan, as the holder of the Security Council seat.

1972

*Moscow Summit:* President Nixon visited Moscow and signed several agreements including the ABM (Anti-Ballistic Missile) Treaty. An easing of Cold War tensions was obvious and was given the name *détente* by the press.

1972

*Yom Kippur War and Shuttle Diplomacy:* After the overwhelming Israeli victory in the Six-Day War of 1967 an uneasy truce settled in the Middle East. War erupted again in October 1973, which resulted in a costly Israeli victory. Secretary of State Kissinger undertook a series of visits to the Middle East ("Shuttle Diplomacy"), which resulted in cease-fire agreements between Israel and Syria. The Soviet Union sought influence in the Middle East to balance that of the United States and Israel. Arms were sold to both Arab nations and Israel by the United States and to the Arab nations by the Soviet Union, which led to further Cold War tensions.

1974

*SALT II Agreement:* The agreement limited the number of missiles and long-range bombers held by the United States and the Soviet

Union. President Carter asked the Senate to delay ratification after the Soviet Union invaded Afghanistan.

1979

*Afghanistan Invasion:* The Soviet Union sent troops into Afghanistan to maintain Soviet influence over the government. President Carter responded with a grain embargo, cutting off Soviet food supplies from the United States. With the advent of *glasnost,* an agreement involving the Soviet Union, the United States, and various Afghan factions was negotiated and Soviet troops were withdrawn. The United States ignored fighting in Afghanistan among warlords and the Islamic Taliban until September 11, 2001, and the start of the war on terrorism when an invasion was launched to drive out the Taliban and destroy the bases of al-Qaida.

1979

*Iran-Iraq War:* War broke out between these two oil-producing Muslim nations on the Persian Gulf. Both the United States and the Soviet Union had important interests in the region and the conflict added tensions to relations between the superpowers. The war became a stalemate with neither side able to win. With the change in U.S.-Soviet relations after 1985, a cease-fire was finally negotiated in 1988.

1980

*The "Evil Empire":* In a speech President Reagan declared his view of the Soviet Union as the "evil empire" responsible for the evils of the world. The policy dominated his administration's foreign policy in the first five years and led to such policies as the Anti-Soviet trade boycott that followed Reagan's declaration that the Soviet Union was responsible for repression in Poland.

1981

*El Salvador/Nicaragua:* Early in the Reagan years guerrilla movements in El Salvador and their relationship to the Sandinista-controlled government of Nicaragua, considered communist by the U.S. administration, became a major foreign policy concern of the Reagan administration with many Cold War ramifications. The administration established a guerrilla organization, the Contras, in Nicaragua to oppose the Sandinista government, and asked Congress for funding, which was alternately given and denied.

1981

*Invasion of Grenada:* The Cubans and Soviets appeared to be building a major airstrip on the island of Grenada. Reagan ordered an invasion "to protect" Americans there. A new anti-communist government was then established.

1983

*Iran-Contra Affair:* Denied funding for the Contras, the Reagan administration developed a complex plan to free the American hostages held in Lebanon by selling arms to Iran thus getting Iran's support to release the hostages. The monetary profits were then used to fund the Contras fighting against the Sandinista government of Nicaragua. The plan was developed secretly and lacked congressional approval. Several individuals involved in the plan, including President Reagan's National Security Advisor, Admiral Poindexter, and White House Aide Marine Lt. Col. Oliver North, were indicted on several counts of lawbreaking. Found guilty, on appeal the judge dismissed charges because testimony freely given before Congress by North and

Poindexter was used to convict them thus encroaching on their Constitutional rights. The investigation ended inconclusively.

1987

## END OF THE COLD WAR

*Glasnost and Peristroika*: Mikhail Gorbachev emerged as the leader of the Soviet Union after several older Communist leaders died having served brief terms as head of the Soviet government. As a member of the younger generation, Gorbachev addressed domestic reform (peristroika) and changes in foreign policy (glasnost). His goal was to create limited reforms while maintaining Communism, but changes came rapidly in foreign affairs yet too slowly for many within the Union. The reform movements led to the collapse of the Soviet Union and the fall of Communism in Eastern Europe.

1985

*Fall of the Berlin Wall*: President Gorbachev refused to suppress reforms and changes in Eastern European nations militarily as had been done during the Cold War. Changes in Poland led by *Solidarity*, a nationalist, anti-communist labor union, and the *"Velvet Revolution"* in Czechoslovakia are examples of the changes. Finally, the East German government announced in November that the Berlin Wall, symbol of the Cold War, would be torn down and Germans could travel freely between East and West. Within a year the two Germanys voted for reunification, thus ending the division created by the "Iron Curtain" after World War II.

1989

*Persian Gulf War*: (first Iraq War) Iraq invaded Kuwait and the United States led a multinational effort through the United Nations to reverse the aggression. While not supplying troops, the Soviet Union and China supported the move in the Security Council. After considerable debate in the country, on January 12 the Senate narrowly passed (52-47) the *Resolution on Use of Force Against Iraq*, which authorized the use of U.S. military force.

*Operation Desert Shield*: Designed to protect the Gulf states immediately after Iraq's attack. Desert Shield became Operation Desert Storm—the first Iraq War (see p. 354).

1990

*United Nations Negotiated End to Military Conflicts*: With the Cold War ending, an end to several international conflicts with roots in the Cold War were negotiated including an end to the war in Afghanistan and an agreement ending the conflicts in Cambodia and El Salvador.

*Commonwealth of Independent States*: The Soviet Union broke up into its separate states. A loose confederation, the Commonwealth of Independent States was formed. The Communist Party was declared unconstitutional in Russia and other states, thus ending the 74 years of Communist rule.

1991

*Nuclear Arms Negotiations:* With the breakup of the Soviet Union, four successor states held nuclear weapons. Tentative agreements were reached that would reduce arms by half. Russia was identified as the sole successor nuclear power. In spite of negotiations and agreements the future of Soviet nuclear weapons still remains unclear. Russia was allotted the Soviet Union's seat in the Security Council.                                                                        1991

*Rising Nationalism and Continued Economic Instability:* Russia and most of the other successor states to the Soviet Union struggled with economic reform made more difficult by high inflation, a rising crime rate, and intense nationalistic sentiments. Russia's invasion of the Muslim region of Chechnya provoked a continuing conflict that became involved with the war on terrorism.                                   1994

## VIETNAM WAR

*Background:* Starting in 1945, Vietnam became a battleground in the U.S. effort to contain Communism. The United States encouraged and gave limited support to the French in their fight against the Communist Viet Minh. When the French were defeated at Dien Bien Phu in 1954, their withdrawal was negotiated in the Geneva Accords and the nation was split into North and South. The United States secretly aided South Vietnam in a small way under Eisenhower. As war between the Communist North Vietnamese and their Viet Cong allies and the South Vietnamese intensified, the United States continued to expand its involvement to block Communism's spread. The *"domino theory"*—if one nation in Southeast Asia goes Communist, the others will also—was followed in establishing U.S. policy.

*United States Involvement:* President Kennedy insisted it was the Vietnamese's war to "win or lose" but he increased U.S. aid and sent in more troops. President Johnson continued the policy and after a confusing incident in the Gulf of Tonkin involving U.S. naval vessels, he obtained support from Congress for the *Gulf of Tonkin Resolution,* which gave the president full power to protect South Vietnam from further aggression and to protect U.S. forces. Johnson used the Resolution as a declaration of war.

*Fighting the War:* Lyndon Johnson's support for the war put a strain on his Great Society program. Protest against U.S. involvement grew steadily and led to Johnson receiving less than a majority of the votes in the New Hampshire primary in 1968. He then withdrew from the presidential race. Hubert Humphrey, Johnson's vice president, was unable to extricate himself from the taint of war support. Nixon won the election and sought ways to end U.S. involvement in the Vietnam War. The massacre of civilians by U.S. troops at My Lai in 1969 and the shooting of student demonstrators by the National Guard at Kent State intensified U.S. protests against the war.

*End of the War:* Nixon desired to end the war but "with honor." Negotiations were begun. He authorized the invasion of Cambodia in 1970, and in 1972 he ordered the bombing of North Vietnam to put pressure on North Vietnam to negotiate. A reduction of U.S. forces was begun with the South Vietnamese gradually taking over responsibility for defending their nation. After lengthy negotiations that began in 1969 a settlement was reached in 1973, and U.S. forces were completely withdrawn. In 1975 the governments of South Vietnam, Cambodia, and Laos all fell to the Communists. In 1974 President Ford offered clemency to Vietnam War draft dodgers and in 1977 President Carter granted a full pardon to Americans who fled to Canada rather than be drafted to fight.

*Effect of the War on the United States:* The war created inflationary pressures and increases in the debt as Johnson tried to maintain both his Great Society program and fight the war (guns and butter). To deal with the problems, Nixon called for reductions in domestic programs. This war, which some Americans see as the first war the United States "lost," continues to have a profound effect on the nation. Many refugees, including the so-called "boat people," fled Vietnam and some have found asylum in the United States. Many veterans, seeing the lack of support from the nation, felt alienated. During the Reagan and Bush administrations contacts with the Communist government of Vietnam gradually increased but relations remained strained over the issue of missing American soldiers. The "lessons of Vietnam" were referred to in debates over policy for Central America in the 1980s, but there was often disagreement as to what these lessons were—to interfere or not to interfere in foreign civil wars, to fight against native Communist movements or not, to subsidize guerrilla warfare in other nations or not, the validity of the "domino theory." President Bush seized the victory in the Persian Gulf War as a way of "putting Vietnam behind us." He claimed the successful United States intervention in the Middle East to stop aggression proved that the United States could pull together as a nation in support of a cause and be successful in a war. Immediately after the Persian Gulf War the president received the strong support of the American people and he announced the tragedy of Vietnam had been replaced by a new sense of American spirit and nationalism. In the 1992 presidential election campaign Bill Clinton's failure to serve in Vietnam was made a major issue by the Republican Party. After his election in 1993 Clinton stopped the government policy of blocking Vietnam's access to international trade loans and in 1994 ended the embargo on trade with Vietnam. There was progress on the issue of missing servicemen (MIAs) as Vietnam joined the search for remains. Finally, in 1995, following an agreement on seized property and the opening of liaison offices in Hanoi and Washington, Clinton recognized the government of Vietnam. Some Republicans opposed the move but the majority of business and political leaders supported normal relations with Vietnam.

The war continues to impact national affairs. In the presidential election of 2004, the Democratic Party nominee was John Kerry, a decorated Vietnam War veteran. A group of fellow veterans organized a campaign supported by the Republican Party to discredit the heroism of Kerry. It had an important impact on the election, losing Kerry a number of votes.

## MIDDLE EAST

*Israeli-Palestinian Wars:* The nation of Israel was established by U.N. vote in 1948. The first of six wars between the Palestinians and Israelis immediately began. The conflict in the Middle East continues to the present, with U.S. involvement a continuing factor. The United States has been a strong ally of Israel while trying to negotiate a resolution to the conflict.

*U.S. Involvement:* Beginning with the Eisenhower Doctrine (1957) the United States sent troops to the Middle East on several occasions. In 1957 troops helped crush a rebellion in Lebanon. Reagan sent marines to pacify Lebanon but withdrew them (1983) after 241 marines were killed in a terrorist attack on their barracks. The U.S. has bases in Saudi Arabia and other Gulf states.

*Camp David Accords:* (1978) President Jimmy Carter invited President Anwar Sadat of Egypt and Prime Minister Menachem Begin of Israel to Camp David, where agreements were reached. Egypt and Israel signed a peace treaty—the first Arab nation to recognize Israel.

*Iran-Iraq War:* (1978) The U.S. backed Saddam Hussein of Iraq in this long war, which included the use of poison gas by Iraq. Iran was led by Khomeini, who established the first Islamic fundamentalist state and supplied support for the Palestinians and terrorists in Lebanon.

*Palestine Liberation Organization (PLO) and Israel's Invasion of Lebanon:* (1982) Failing in war, the PLO mounted terror attacks on Israel with support from Iran and Lebanon. Israel invaded Lebanon but was forced to withdraw after years of fighting. The Palestinians began sustained attacks (the Intifada) on the Israeli forces occupying the West Bank. In 1988 President Reagan opened a limited dialogue with the PLO.

*Persian Gulf War* or *first Iraq War:* (1990–1991) Iraq invaded Kuwait to control her oil production. President George H. W. Bush organized a multilateral coalition through the United Nations to drive Iraq out of Kuwait in Operation Desert Storm. An armistice called for the disarmament of Iraq's weapons of mass destruction, supervised by U.N. weapons inspectors. Saddam Hussein failed to cooperate; inspectors were withdrawn in 1998; Britain and the United States bombed military targets. George W. Bush reopened the issue in 2002 as part of his war on terrorism.

*Oslo Accords:* (1993) This agreement reached between Israel and the Palestinians outlined negotiating steps to achieve peace. First step was a peace treaty between Jordan and Israel (1994). Negotiations continued throughout Clinton's presidency with limited success and ended when President Arafat rejected an Israeli offer (1999).

*Second Intifada:* Beginning in 2000, violence again flared in the Palestinian territories as Palestinians attacked Israeli forces in the West Bank. Israel reoccupied the area and later withdrew. The violence slowly ebbed as elections were held in the Palestinian territories, and some talks were held between Israeli and Palestinian leaders after the death of Yasir Arafat. In 2006 the Palestinians, in a major election showing democracy at work, rejected the Fatah party of Arafat and gave a majority to Hamas, a political party with humanitarian aspects that was considered a terrorist organization by the U.S. and Israel. In spite of the Israeli troop withdrawal from the Gaza area and the building of a wall to separate Israeli and Palestinian territory, the situation remains volatile with links to the broader Middle East. President Bush periodically states the U.S. will take a more active role in resolving the tensions but, as of this writing, there has been limited activity. The administration has called for a separate Palestinian state, but has stated the Palestinian solution should be part of a broad Middle East settlement.

*Afghanistan War:* (2002–) Responding to the September 11, 2001 attack on the United States, war was first fought against al-Qaida and the Taliban in Afghanistan. Success came quickly and a new elected government was established. However, the situation never stabilized. United States responsibility for Afghanistan was turned over to NATO forces in 2006 but U.S. troops are still an important part of the mission to rebuild the nation and defeat the growing insurgency led by members of the Taliban. After the initial success that had the strong support of United States citizens,

President Bush focused the war on terrorism on Iraq, whom he accused of developing weapons of mass destruction and being a supporter of terrorists.

*Second Iraq War* (2003–) See page 366.

## DOMESTIC ISSUES

## MAJOR LEGISLATION AND SUPREME COURT DECISIONS—1945–2007

| | |
|---|---|
| *Taft-Hartley Law:* Aimed at making unions more responsible in relations with management, it prohibited unfair labor practices. | 1947 |
| *Presidential Succession Act:* Revised the 1886 law and made the Speaker of the House and then the president pro tempore of the Senate successors after the vice president. | 1947 |
| *National Security Act:* Reorganized the army, navy, and air force and established the cabinet-level Department of Defense, the National Security Council, and the CIA. | 1947 |
| *Internal Security Act (McCarran Act):* Required registration of Communists and all Communist front organizations. | 1950 |
| *Department of Health, Education and Welfare:* Created new cabinet-level department to handle these areas of social concern. | 1953 |
| *Atomic Energy Act:* Permitted private power companies to own reactors for the production of electric power. | 1954 |
| *Brown v. Board of Education:* Supreme Court decision reversed the concept of separate but equal in race relations and ordered the integration of schools to provide equal educational opportunities for blacks and whites. | 1954 |
| *Highway Act:* Established the federal interstate highway system. | 1956 |
| *Civil Rights Act:* First act dealing with civil rights and their guarantee passed by Congress since Reconstruction. Established a six-person Commission on Civil Rights to investigate civil rights violations. | 1957 |
| *Peace Corps:* Program to aid economically undeveloped countries by sending volunteers to help in the development of their economy by doing many things from teaching farming techniques to building schools. | 1961 |
| *Gideon v. Wainwright:* The Supreme Court determined that a lawyer must be provided by the state for all those charged with committing a felony. | 1963 |
| *Escobedo v. Illinois:* The Supreme Court ruled that if requested, a lawyer had to be present during police interrogation before an indictment is made. | 1964 |
| *Voting Rights Act:* Act guaranteeing to all the right to vote in federal elections—directed toward southern blacks who flocked to register supported by federal marshals. | 1965 |

*Medicare Act*: Provides medical service to those over 65 under the administration of the Social Security System.                                    1965

*Office of Economic Opportunity (OEO)*: Catchall office set up to operate Job Corps, Operation Head Start, and other parts of Johnson's Great Society program to benefit depressed areas and underprivileged persons.                                                                      1965

*Elementary and Secondary Education Act*: Provided federal money for certain programs in public and parochial schools to improve the quality of education in the United States.                                         1965

*Water Quality Act*: Allowed federal government to set water purity standards for states to force industry to clean up the lakes and rivers of the nation.                                                             1965

*Freedom of Information Act*: Made certain documents and records available to citizens who asked to see them, including some secret documents.                                                                 1966

*Civil Rights Act*: Directed toward eliminating racial barriers in most of the nation's housing.                                                  1968

*Consumer Credit Protection Act (Truth in Lending)*: Requires lenders and retailers selling merchandise on credit to make full disclosures of the total cost of such credit to the consumer.                           1968

*Washington Omnibus Anti-Crime Law (No-Knock Law)*: Designed to give more authority to police enforcement officials in the District of Columbia and to serve as a model of tough reform police laws for the nation.                                                               1970

*Environmental Policy Act*: Established a commission in the White House to report on environmental quality and to oversee the enforcement of environmental legislation.                                          1970

*Furman v. Georgia*: The death penalty was held unconstitutional. Later decisions modified this opinion to make it permissible in some circumstances if applied fairly.                                             1973

*Roe v. Wade*: Declared state laws denying abortion during the first trimester of pregnancy unconstitutional as a violation of a woman's right to privacy in determining to end a pregnancy.                       1973

*Energy Policy and Conservation Act*: Set control limits on car exhaust and gave the president more control over energy policy.                1973

*Department of Energy*: In response to the OPEC energy crisis of the 1970s, the Department of Energy was created, taxes on oil increased, and conservation measures were instituted.                               1977

*Civil Service Reform Act*: These measures were part of President Carter's attempts to streamline and increase the efficiency of the government's bureaucracy. The act reduced the Civil Service.                1978

*Air Transport Deregulation Act*: Airline fares and routes were no longer to be controlled by government regulation.                           1978

*Bakke v. Board of Regents*: The Supreme Court held that Bakke, a white who had been denied admission to medical school in California, had been discriminated against since his scores were higher than those of persons admitted to positions at the school reserved to minorities. The Court also upheld the University of California's use of race as a criterion for admission to achieve a mixed student body.

1978

*Department of Education*: As part of the streamlining efforts of President Carter, the various government offices dealing with education were consolidated in one department.

1979

*Peacetime Draft Registration*: Draft registration was required of 18-year-olds to have the country prepared for any international emergency. No one, however, was actually drafted into the armed services.

1980

*Toxic Waste Superfund*: Established to treat quickly dangerous spills of toxic wastes and to clean up toxic waste dumps.

1981

*Economic Recovery Tax Act (ERTA)*: A supply-side tax program (the Reagan tax cuts) that reduced taxes and cut the budget, changing the long-standing taxing policies of the government.

1981

*Anti-Drug Legislation*: Each session of Congress from 1982–1989 passed drug legislation reflecting the continuing concern with drug use and traffic. The 1989 law established a cabinet-level position of *Director of National Drug Policy* (Anti-Drug "Tsar") to coordinate President Bush's war on drugs. The 1989 legislation included the death penalty for major drug trafficking and the 1988 law required schools to implement programs aimed at preventing illegal substance use and provided assistance to Colombia, Peru, and Bolivia to fight drug traffickers.

1982

*Clean Water Act*: Authorized a 10-year extension of the federal program for subsidizing building of sewer plants. It was passed over President Reagan's veto.

1987

*Savings and Loans (S & L's) Bailout Legislation*: Congress provided funds and approved a program to buy or shore up financially failing S & L's.

1987

*Repeal of the Catastrophic Health Care Act of 1988*: In a major change of policy and under heavy pressure from AARP (American Association of Retired Persons), Congress repealed the expansion of the Medicare program that it had passed the previous year. This was the first time Congress had repealed a major social benefit it had enacted. The act had extended Medicare to cases of long-term hospital care and catastrophic illness to be paid for by a surtax on Medicare enrollees. Their objection to this tax led to the repeal of the law.

1989

*Board of Education of Oklahoma City v. Dowell*: Supreme Court held that a school district could end busing to achieve integration if it had done "everything practical" and the schools were single race because of local housing patterns. The case illustrated the continuing importance of the courts in the struggle for civil rights.

1990

*Americans with Disabilities Act:* The act prohibits discrimination against disabled persons in employment, public services, and accommodations, and requires that telecommunication be made accessible to those with speech and hearing impairments. Employers are required to make reasonable accommodations for disabled workers.

1990

*Immigration Bill:* The first major revision of immigration policy in 25 years changed visa requirements, allowed for more immigrants, especially those with education and skills needed in the United States, and made it harder to exclude foreigners because of their sexual persuasion.

1990

*Clean Air Act:* After 10 years of inaction the 1977 Clean Air Act was revised and updated with support from President Bush. Deadlines for control of harmful emissions by cities and motor vehicles were revised. Provisions to control acid rain and chlorofluorocarbons, which harm the earth's ozone layer, were also made.

1990

*Rust v. Sullivan:* The Supreme Court by a 5-4 vote upheld regulations issued in 1988 by the Department of Health and Human Services that barred federally funded health and family planning clinics from providing information on abortion. It was one more case in the ongoing struggle over abortion rights fought out in the courts.

1991

*Civil Rights Act (Job Bias Bill):* After several years of debate and struggle between Congress and President Bush, the president signed a bill that reversed several recent Supreme Court decisions that had made it more difficult to achieve redress in cases of job discrimination in employment.

1991

*Planned Parenthood v. Casey:* The Supreme Court by a 5-4 vote upheld several Pennsylvania laws restricting a woman's access to abortion, but the Court affirmed the basic right to abortion established in *Roe v. Wade.*

1992

*Family and Medical Leave Act:* The act provides up to 12 weeks of unpaid leave in any 12-month period for workers giving birth or adopting a child, to care for a seriously sick child, spouse, or parent, or in case of workers' illness. It applied only to companies employing 50 or more people.

1993

*National Service Trust Act (Americorps):* A federal program was established to allow students to receive financing for college or technical training in return for one or two years of public service in education, environment, public safety, or other areas of need. Students receive $5,000 per year of service. After their victory in 1994, Republicans moved to abolish the program. Under George W. Bush they reversed their position and supported the idea of service, although they found it difficult to increase the funding because of tax cuts and the war on terrorism. 1993

*NAFTA (North American Free Trade Agreement):* The pact between the United States, Canada, and Mexico was to eliminate or reduce tariffs and other restrictions on investment and trade over a 15-year period beginning on January 1, 1994. 1993

*Handgun Violence Prevention Act:* The so-called Brady Bill imposes a five-day waiting period for the purchase of a handgun. The act was the result of twelve years of lobbying by Reagan's press secretary, who was disabled in the 1981 attempted assassination of President Reagan. 1993

*Anti-Crime Act:* The bill, the first passed in six years, called for spending $30 billion over six years divided among enforcement (100,000 more police), prison construction, and prevention measures. The bill also extended the death penalty to more than 50 crimes and required that released sex offenders had to notify authorities of their address and communities were to be notified of it. 1994

*GATT (General Agreement of Tariffs and Trade):* The agreement, negotiated over several years and known as the Uruguay Round, was designed to liberalize existing national and international trade regulations, eliminate quotas and tariffs, and introduce measures to increase trade. GATT established the WTO (World Trade Organization), a new organization responsible for implementing the agreement. 1994

*Clinton Vetoes Stopgap Spending Measures:* Budget disagreements between Democratic President Clinton and the Republican-controlled Congress led to two government shutdowns and a standstill in legislation. 1995

*Telecommunications Act:* This act expanded competition in telephone long-distance service and allowed cable companies to compete for regional calling; relaxed restrictions on TV station ownership; deregulated cable rates. 1996

*Antiterrorism Act:* This act appropriated $1 billion to fight terrorism over four years; denied entry into the United States to members of any terrorist groups, and permitted prosecution of anyone making donations to such groups; required an ID to purchase any plastic explosives. 1996

*Welfare Reform Act:* This act "ended welfare as we know it." Block grants for welfare were given to states; five-year limit on grants to individuals; welfare participants to be cut 50 percent by 2000. 1996

*Health Insurance Portability Act:* This act permits individuals changing jobs to keep their health insurance. 1996

*Illegal Immigration Bill:* This bill has penalties for smuggling or providing false documents; it expanded the border patrol and fence in San Diego. 1996

*Balanced Budget Agreement:* Democrats and Republicans finally agreed on the plan to create a balanced budget by 2002. (The goal was achieved by 1998 due to the booming economy.)    1997

*NATO Expansion Act:* This act approved the admission of the former communist nations of Poland, Hungary, and the Czech Republic into NATO, thus changing its complexion and focus.    1997

*Transportation Equity Act:* With this act, $173 billion was approved for highways, $41 billion for mass transit plans, and $2 billion for highway safety.    1998

*Impeachment:* House voted to impeach President Clinton on two charges—perjury and obstruction of justice.    1998

*President Clinton Acquitted:* The Senate, acting as the jury in the impeachment trial of President Clinton, found him "not guilty" on all counts. House members acting as prosecutors obtained only 45 votes on the first charge (perjury) and 50 on the second (obstruction of justice), thus failing to win the necessary two-thirds (67) votes of the Senate.    1999

*Bush v. Gore:* The Supreme Court's 5–4 decision gave Florida's electoral votes to George W. Bush, thus giving him the presidency. Gore won the popular vote but Bush won in the Electoral College by four votes.    2000

*Tax Reform Act:* Referred to as the "Bush tax cuts," this Republican-sponsored bill returned the "surplus to the people." It incorporated a $1.35 trillion 10-year tax cut that reduced the projected budget surplus by nearly half.    2001

*Airline Bailout Act; Airline Security Act; U.S. Patriot Act:* These three acts were Congress's first responses to September 11. The first gave financial aid to the airlines that had been hurt by the curtailment of travel after the attack, as well as aid to the families of the victims. The second set up the agency to administer airport security, and the third gave new powers to the Department of Justice to limit civil rights in the war on terrorism.    2001

*Education Reform Bill:* Labeled "No Child Left Behind," the measure calls for extensive testing of students to hold schools "accountable" in assuring each child can read and do math.    2002

*Campaign Finance Reform:* Led by Republican John McCain a bill restructuring how campaign contributions can be made by business and individuals was finally passed and signed.    2002

*Vote on Iraq:* Responding to the president's request, the Senate overwhelmingly supported a measure giving the president the power to use whatever force was necessary to destroy any weapons of mass destruction held by Iraq. The measure encouraged consultation with the United Nations.    2002

*Homeland Security Bill:* The largest government reorganization in fifty years brought together many departments dealing with immi-

gration and terrorism in a new cabinet-level department. The bill
excluded the CIA and FBI from the department.                    2002

*Atkins v. Virginia:* Execution of mentally retarded found to be "cruel
and unusual" punishment. *Ring v. Arizona:* Jury, not judge, must
decide critical sentencing issues in death penalty cases.

*Supreme Court Decisions:* In *Lawrence v. Texas* the Court declared
unconstitutional a Texas law making sodomy a crime; in *Gratz v.
Bollinger* the use of race as a factor in admission to the University of
Michigan was declared unconstitutional but in *Grutter v. Bollinger* a
different use of race was accepted in admission to the University of
Michigan Law School.                                            2003

# PRESIDENTIAL ADMINISTRATIONS 1945–2007

*Harry Truman:* (Democrat) Truman became president upon the death of Franklin
Roosevelt in April 1945. Not well informed by Roosevelt on issues, he quickly took
control supporting the establishment of the United Nations at the San Francisco
Conference, making the decision to drop atomic bombs on Japan (Hiroshima and
Nagasaki), and presiding over the end of World War II. His foreign policy focused
on containing the perceived Communist threat, which became the key element of
the Cold War. He announced the Truman Doctrine of containment, supported
Foreign Aid (the Point Four Plan) and the Marshall Plan, and responded to
Communist North Korea's invasion of South Korea by sending troops and appealing
to the United Nations. In a very close election in 1948, he won a second term,
defeating Governor Thomas Dewey of New York. His stance on the Communist
threat and his support of labor in vetoing the Taft-Hartley law (passed over his veto)
gained him support.

*Dwight D. Eisenhower:* (Republican) Eisenhower defeated Adlai Stevenson in the
1952 election. The Korean War was a major issue in the campaign. Eisenhower's
foreign policy was one of Cold War confrontation and brinkmanship. John Foster
Dulles served as a forceful secretary of state. Domestically, after Joseph
McCarthy's "witch hunts" against the domestic threat of Communism ended and
he was censured by the Senate, the Eisenhower years were quite peaceful. The
Civil Rights Movement was stimulated by the *Brown v. Board of Education*
Supreme Court decision on school integration. Eisenhower gave only moderate
support to the movement but did finally send federal troops to support the inte-
gration of the high school in Little Rock, Arkansas. His administration held to a
high standard of honesty in government. Sherman Adams, his White House
Chief of Staff, was asked to resign after it was revealed he had accepted a vicuna
coat as a gift. The most far-reaching domestic legislation of his presidency was the
National Highway Act, which set up the interstate highway network.

*John F. Kennedy:* (Democrat) Kennedy was elected president in 1960 by a narrow
margin over Richard M. Nixon. He was the first Catholic to win the office and
the youngest ruler of a major world power. His administration supplied much
polish and glitter, but little substantial domestic legislation. Kennedy's administration is most noted for foreign policy developments, among them the Alliance
for Progress, the Peace Corps, the Bay of Pigs, the Cuban Missile Crisis, the start
of the Space Race, and the extension of the U.S. commitment to Vietnam.

Kennedy was assassinated on November 22, 1963 in Dallas, Texas and Vice President Lyndon Johnson became president.

*Lyndon Johnson:* (Democrat) In the aftermath of Kennedy's tragic death, Johnson initiated a number of domestic reforms including a Civil Rights Act.

*The Civil Rights movement* was an important aspect of the Kennedy/Johnson years. Supreme Court decisions, congressional legislation, and the efforts of many workers and leaders led to a great breakthrough in the extension of rights to African Americans. However, the assassination in 1968 of Martin Luther King, Jr., a believer in nonviolent protest, was followed by outbreaks of violence, and the movement lost momentum. More militant leaders called for Black Power. The eventual success of the movement inspired many other minority groups to seek power, with the result that Mexican-Americans (Chicanos), Native Americans, homosexuals (Gay Power), and women organized to have an impact on political affairs.

Johnson initiated a *War on Poverty* in an attempt to eradicate poverty in America and create a Great Society. In many ways it was an updating and extension of Franklin Roosevelt's New Deal. It began well and included such diverse programs as Head Start and Medicare, but implementation of the Great Society was hampered by increased involvement in and the cost of the war in Vietnam.

The Vietnam War came to dominate Johnson's presidency. Student unrest in the mid-1960s reflected a change in attitude among some young people and culminated in antiwar protests. President Johnson announced he would not run for a second term. Unrest took many forms, including the "hippie" movement, greater use of illegal drugs, establishment of communes, antiwar demonstrations, and violence at the Democratic Convention in Chicago in 1968. One hero of the movement, Robert Kennedy, was assassinated in Los Angeles in 1968 while campaigning for the Democratic presidential nomination, removing an important political leader of the protest.

*Richard M. Nixon:* (Republican) Elected president in 1968, Nixon promised to "bring the nation together." Antiwar protests increased and there were periodic outbursts of antiwar violence, such as Kent State, 1970, during his presidency that led his administration to seek ways to prevent it. He negotiated an end to the war in Vietnam.

As the Vietnam War was winding down, the Nixon administration made moves to reverse the policies of the previous 25 years. His actions collectively have been referred to as *détente.* Some observers saw this as the beginning of the end to the Cold War. Nixon's negotiations with the Soviet Union and recognition of the People's Republic of China were the most important developments in foreign policy during his administration.

Domestically, Nixon pursued a conservative political agenda, trying to cut federal programs under a program of *New Federalism. Watergate* was the most memorable event of his presidency domestically. Nixon was concerned by the antiwar protests and the possibility of a Democratic victory in 1972. He approved of "dirty tricks" including a break-in at the Democratic Headquarters in the Watergate apartment complex in Washington. A cover-up unraveled through newspaper exposés, the appointment of a special prosecutor, and grand jury inquiries. Meanwhile Vice President Spiro Agnew was forced to resign as a result of illegal acts involving his personal taxes. Finally, tape recordings of White House meetings revealed that Nixon was aware of the break-in and cover-ups of illegal acts. Congress began impeachment proceedings and President Nixon resigned in August 1974. He was the first president to be forced from office. He was succeeded by Gerald Ford, who had been chosen to succeed Agnew as vice president, following the procedure set forth in the Twenty-fifth Amendment, which was ratified in 1967. Nelson Rockefeller, four-term governor of New York, was chosen as vice president following the same procedure.

*Gerald R. Ford:* (Republican) President Ford, the first man to come to the presidency by appointment rather than election, served the remaining years of Nixon's term. Ford continued the policy of *détente,* holding a summit conference in Vladivostok in 1974 and visiting China in 1975. The aftermath of Watergate, including Ford's pardon of Nixon, colored his administration. There was high inflation and Ford introduced his WIN (Whip Inflation Now) policy to combat it with limited success. OPEC (Organization of Petroleum Exporting Countries) and its oil pricing policies affected domestic affairs and led to large increases in oil costs. Ford was defeated in his reelection campaign by Governor Jimmy Carter of Georgia.

*James E. Carter:* (Democrat) Jimmy Carter considered himself a "born again" Christian. Elected in 1976 as an "outsider," President Carter found it difficult to be effective in dealing with the established bureaucracy of Congress and government. He wanted to streamline the government and make it more efficient. He began the deregulation of business (Air Transport Deregulation Act), which intensified under Reagan. Domestic issues of inflation and energy crises, together with the international crisis of the Iranian Revolution and the seizure of American hostages, clouded his administration. His foreign policy focused on the issue of human rights. The highlight of the administration of Jimmy Carter was the establishment of the *Camp David Peace Accord,* which finally brought peace in the Middle East between Israel and Egypt, although it did not solve all of the outstanding issues in the area. He also negotiated a new treaty with Panama, which gave that nation control over the Panama Canal.

*Ronald Reagan:* (Republican) Viewed by many as an extreme conservative Republican, Ronald Reagan overwhelmed Jimmy Carter in the election of 1980. The Republicans gained control of the Senate; Reagan's goals were to reduce inflation, reform the tax structure, reduce taxes, deregulate business and industry, cut social welfare programs, and build up the military. A major debate developed about the need for a balanced budget and military versus social welfare expenditures. *Supply-side economics,* the philosophical position behind the Reagan economic reforms, did not operate as expected and a huge government budget deficit and a large trade deficit developed, although the inflation rate slowed dramatically. Reagan appointed Conservatives to the Supreme Court and the Court's views on privacy, especially the right to abortion, began to shift.

Reagan's foreign policy centered on the concept of the Soviet Union as an "evil empire" responsible for the Cold War and world unrest. This view guided Reagan's foreign policy in such matters as his support of the Contras against the Sandinista government of Nicaragua and his policy of peace through strength. He introduced SDI—*Strategic Defense Initiative,* commonly known as Star Wars—which antagonized the Soviets but led to negotiation with them for a disarmament agreement. When Mikhail Gorbachev came to power, his policies of glasnost improved relations. Negotiations led to summit meetings at Geneva, Reykjavik (Iceland), and Washington, where in 1987 an Intermediate Range Missile Treaty (INF) was signed marking the beginning of a new phase of the Cold War.

The release of the American hostages by Iran on Reagan's inauguration day led Democrats to investigate an "arrangement," but nothing was proven. The Israeli invasion of Lebanon, which left that country divided, led Reagan to send in marines, who were later withdrawn after 237 were killed in a terrorist bombing of their barracks. The Iran-Iraq War led to unrest in the Persian Gulf and caused Reagan to put the American flag on Kuwaiti oil tankers and escort them through the Gulf with U.S. Navy ships in order to assure the flow of oil to Europe and Japan.

*George H. W. Bush:* (Republican) [Bush 41—i.e., the first president Bush, George H. W. Bush, was the forty-first President of the United States, and so some have referred to him in this way since the election of his son, George W. Bush or Bush 43—the forty-third president of the United States.] In 1988 Reagan's vice president, George Bush, overwhelmingly defeated Democrat Michael Dukakis, governor of Massachusetts, in a negative campaign that addressed such issues as the environment, crime, patriotism, and family values. The public's alienation from politics grew during Bush's term reinforced by the deadlock between the Democratic Congress and the Republican president, the battle over conservative Supreme Court appointments such as Judge Clarence Thomas, the Savings and Loan Associations, a type of bank, financial bailout by the federal government, continued investigations of the Iran-Contra Affair, and several scandals involving Congress (Keating Five, House of Representatives Post Office and Bank Scandals).

The administration, led by Vice President Quayle, supported the conservative agenda of pushing family values and overturning *Roe v. Wade*. Bush supported a Clean Air Act but did not support the UN. Conference on the Environment and Development (Rio Conference). What began as a mild recession continued to worsen and was seen as a depression by 1992. Differences between Congress and the president led to near deadlock in response to the economy, and the trade and budget deficits continued to grow. Bush was unable to present a balanced budget to the Congress.

President Bush had extensive foreign policy experience and used it to deal directly with world leaders. His great success was the *Persian Gulf War* or *first Iraq War* (1991). After Iraq, led by its president, Saddam Hussein, had seized the country of Kuwait Bush organized Operation Desert Shield through the United Nations. Then Operation Desert Storm forced Iraq's withdrawal from Kuwait. Bush gained strong public support for his war actions, but it quickly evaporated as the recession developed.

Bush developed a close relationship with Gorbachev and his successors as the Soviet Union collapsed. The end of the Cold War heightened the domestic argument over military defense vs. social welfare spending. Outbreaks of fighting in former states of the Soviet Union and in Yugoslavia based on nationalistic interests indicated the "New World Order" proclaimed by President Bush after the success in the Persian Gulf War would not be peaceful. Other foreign policy events included the invasion of Panama to seize accused drug dealer General Manuel Noriega and the opening of essentially unsuccessful Arab-Israeli peace talks.

The election of 1992 saw third-party candidate, unknown businessman H. Ross Perot win 20 percent of the vote in many states. Bill Clinton and Al Gore (Democrats) won with 43 percent of the vote, defeating Bush and Quayle.

*William Jefferson Clinton:* (Democrat) Clinton focused his campaign on the saying "It's the economy, stupid," but Congress failed to enact his major economic proposals. However, the economy boomed during his eight years, led by the computer industry. A budget crisis in 1995 led Clinton to shut down government operations that led to budget agreements and the first budget surplus in thirty years. Legislation passed under Clinton included Welfare Reform that reduced time on welfare; an education bill, Goals 2000, that set standards for subject areas; an anti-crime bill that increased the number of police; a family and medical leave bill; a reform of the IRS; and the Brady Bill, which restricted the sale of handguns.

Health care reform was a major legislative defeat. A committee headed by Hillary Rodham Clinton offered a plan for comprehensive health care, but the medical and insurance company opposition defeated the measure in 1994. Clinton was forced to compromise on his order to include gays in the military and a "don't ask, don't tell" policy was adopted. Republicans won control of both the House and Senate in 1994 with a specific campaign platform, the Contract with America. The victory established divided and confrontational government. However, Clinton and Gore won reelection in 1996, although the Republicans controlled Congress.

Investigation of possible scandals involving the Clintons and several members of his cabinet dominated the Clinton years, culminating in an impeachment proceeding in 1999 that found the president innocent on charges of perjury and obstruction of justice. Early in Clinton's administration a special prosecutor, Kenneth Starr, was appointed to investigate the Clintons' involvement in a land development scheme on the Whitewater River in Arkansas. Other possible scandals involving the White House travel office and a White House intern, Monica Lewinsky, became part of the Whitewater investigation. Democratic fund raising in 1996 and the final presidential pardons were also investigated, as were several congressional scandals—one involving Newt Gingrich, Republican Speaker of the House. The "politics of personal destruction" appeared to dominate Washington during the 1990s.

Clinton pursued an active international foreign policy, seeking resolution to crises in the Balkans, examples being the Dayton Accords on Bosnia and cooperation with NATO in Kosovo, and bringing peace to Northern Ireland. Trade initiatives led to the passage of NAFTA (North American Free Trade Agreement), more trade with China, the passage of GATT, and increased globalization and use of the Internet. Clinton actively pursued peace in the Middle East following the Oslo Accords, but he failed as he had in Somalia, from which he withdrew U.S. troops.

*George W. Bush:* (Republican) [Bush 43—i.e., the second President Bush, the forty-third president] George W. Bush gained the presidency as a result of a Supreme Court 5–4 decision, *Bush v. Gore*, which ended a vote recount in Florida and gave him the state's electoral votes, assuring him of a four-vote victory in the Electoral College. Al Gore won the popular vote and had contested irregularities in the Florida voting. Bush chose several leaders of his father's administration for top positions, including Vice President Dick Cheney, Defense Secretary Donald Rumsfeld, Secretary of State Colin Powell, and National Security Advisor Condoleezza Rice. Several advisors, including Paul Wolfowitz and Paul Nitze, referred to as neoconservatives or neocons took a new view, termed *unilateralism,* of U.S. foreign policy, rejecting the multilateralism of the post–World War II period. These leaders believed the United States should use its power as the world's only superpower to achieve what the United States considered best for itself. Following this concept the administration withdrew from the Antiballistic Missile Treaty to develop SDI (an antimissile shield to protect the United States), refused to sign the Anti-Land Mines Treaty and the U.N. Convention on the Rights of Children, rejected the Kyoto

Accords on Global Warming, as they were not in the economic interests of the United States, and refused to join the U.N. War Crimes Tribunal.

Congress passed a massive $1.35 trillion tax cut following the supply-side theory of the Reagan years and an education bill, No Child Left Behind, that focused on testing and accountability. After several years of debate an energy bill with emphasis on new technology was finally passed and a major addition to Medicare, a prescription drug option for seniors, was approved in 2005. In spite of talk on the need to address economic issues affecting Social Security and Medicare as a result of the coming retirement of the Baby Boom generation and Republican control of both Houses until the 2006 election, legislative success was limited as the administration focused on foreign policy. The defining event of the Bush administration was the terrorist attacks on the World Trade Center and Pentagon on September 11, 2001.

Congressional responses to September 11 included passage of the Patriot Act curtailing civil rights, the Airlines Security Act, the establishment of the Homeland Security Department, and the Senate's approval of the use of force against Afghanistan and Iraq. To mid-2007 the Congress approved all funding requests for the wars in Afghanistan and Iraq to "support our troops" in spite of growing public and congressional concerns.

Bush proclaimed a war on international terrorism and identified Osama bin Laden and his Al-Qaida network as behind the attack. The United States gained international sympathy and attacked Afghanistan's Taliban leaders, who supported bin Laden. The Taliban fell, but nation rebuilding in Afghanistan is ongoing. In January 2002 Bush defined Iraq, Iran, and North Korea as an "axis of evil" and shifted the focus of the war on terrorism to Iraq, its president, Saddam Hussein, and weapons of mass destruction.

The United States sent troops to the Persian Gulf and, failing to get U.N. support for a deadline for Iraq to disarm after a massive bombing attack, invaded Iraq with a handful of allies in March 2003. Military success came quickly with the disintegration of the Iraqi army and the fall of the capital, Baghdad. On May 1st Bush flew to the deck of a returning aircraft carrier and proclaimed "mission accomplished" in Iraq. It soon became obvious that the U.S. had not planned an occupation policy and did not have enough troops to maintain order once the Iraqi army was disbanded. In spite of the writing of a Constitution and the democratic election of a government, an insurgency began between the Shia and Sunni religious sects with car bombings, shootings, and death squads operating freely. U.S. troops, at first the main victims of roadside bombs, became less a target and by the end of 2006, many were referring to the situation as a civil war with the U.S. caught in the middle. Bush's popularity had dropped from 80% approval after September 11th to under 30% at the time of the 2006 congressional election in which his handling of the war became a major issue. Democrats captured both Houses and several governorships. Nancy Pelosi, a Democrat from California, was elected Speaker of the House, the highest position in the federal government ever held by a woman. She and the Democrats have called for greater Congressional oversight of the Executive and the taking of more responsibility for government policy, but has restrained from calling for inquiries into how the U.S. got involved in the Iraq fiasco. The Democrats have asked for new policies; Bush responded with a call for more troops to pacify Baghdad.

Other foreign policy issues of the Bush years include the confrontation with North Korea over its development of nuclear bombs and long-range missiles, and nuclear power developments in the Islamic Republic of Iran. Iran has been accused of supporting terrorist groups in the Middle East, particularly Hamas in Palestine and Hezbollah in Lebanon, both of which have attacked Israel. There are also issues with drug production in South America and Afghanistan and with the election of leftist leaders in Venezuela (an important supplier of oil to the U.S.) and Bolivia. Trade deficits, especially with China, continue to be of concern for the United States economy.

A recession began in 2001, ending the long bull market. The computer industry and e-commerce were hit hard. Compounding the problem were several business scandals, including the bankruptcy of Enron and Global Crossing. The recession, combined with the tax cuts and the cost of the war in Iraq, eliminated the projected budget surpluses in 2002. The country slowly emerged from the recession but job creation has lagged while the productivity of workers has increased. Many jobs continue to be created in the service industries.

Bush and Cheney narrowly defeated the Democratic candidates, John Kerry and John Edwards, in the 2004 election. With Bush ineligible to run and Cheney having announced he would not run, the presidential election of 2008 began in early 2007 with over a dozen candidates announcing they would run. Democrats Hillary Rodham Clinton, Barack Obama, and John Edwards were considered the top Democratic candidates and John McCain, Rudolph Giuliani, and Mitt Romney the top Republicans, a year before the party nominating conventions were scheduled in mid-2008.

## SOCIAL AND CULTURAL ISSUES 1950–2007

Social, intellectual, and cultural issues all interrelate and have varying impacts on political and economic life of a nation. Some of the more significant issues are mentioned here first by decade and then by movements.

*1950s:* The 1950s are often considered a time of conformity suggested in works such as *The Man in the Grey Flannel Suit* and *The Organization Man*. Then there's Benjamin Spock, whose views on child care were closely followed by eager parents. However, it was also the decade of the *Brown v. Board of Education* decision that helped ignite the Civil Rights Movement and the birth of rock and roll in the black community. The introduction of television into many homes may have emphasized conformity as millions watched the same few channels and ate their dinners off TV trays in front of the screen. The significance of this major technological advance can not be underestimated, as it impacted the lives of everyone, bringing everything from entertainment to presidential debates into homes.

Movie idols of the decade, Marilyn Monroe (the new sex symbol) and James Dean (the alienated star) suggest two different sides of the time. Jack Kerouac's *On the Road* revealed the life of the Beat Generation—travel, drugs, sex—and *Catcher in the Rye* (1951) is the classic story of the alienated teenager while the best seller, Kinsey's *The Sexual Behavior of the American Male*, illustrated life was not what many thought. Music, with the arrival of Elvis Presley and rock and roll, took a new turn that separated generations.

The automobile, an important part of society since Ford introduced the assembly line in 1913, became more important and this led to the rapid growth of suburbs and the decline of the inner cities which became centers of poverty and neglect.

*1960s:* The 1960s are considered a decade of protest and rebellion symbolized by Civil Rights Marches, draft card burning rallies, and the Woodstock festival. The assassinations of John F. Kennedy, Malcolm "X," Martin Luther King, Jr., and Robert Kennedy, and the stalemate of the Vietnam War impacted everyone. The counterculture movement led by the hippies and "flower children" were described in popular film, *Easy Rider* (1969) and books, Thomas Wolfe's *Electric Kool Aid Acid Test* (1968) and in the music of the Rolling Stones and Janis Joplin. Joan Baez and Bob Dylan were leaders of a folk music revival that created memorable protest music.

The availability of new methods of contraception including the *pill* made possible a sexual revolution and women and men considered themselves liberated from the restraints imposed by fear of pregnancy which had tremendous impact on traditional values and family. Betty Friedan in *The Feminine Mystique* (1963) laid the foundation for the women's liberation movement that questioned the traditional role of women in western society.

Michael Harrington's *The Other America* (1962) reported on the continuing poverty in the "affluent society," the title of a book (1958) by John Galbraith that gave a name to the growing wealth of the nation. Johnson's *Great Society* program and *war on poverty* were in part reactions to Harrington's book. Rachel Carson's *The Silent Spring,* documenting environmental damage, is considered the start of the present environmental movement.

*1970s:* Thomas Wolfe described the 1970s as the age of the "me" generation and described the life of the Yuppie—the young urban professional and successor to the hippie—in his novel, *The Bonfire of the Vanities* (1984). He saw them as focused on self and money after the previous decade of protest and attempts to change—much of it unachieved. The popular movies of the time, George Lucas' Star Wars series, *Jaws* (1975) and *Raiders of the Lost Ark* (1981) that made Harrison Ford a role model, suggest self indulgence and escape into fantasy. *Apocalypse Now* (1979) at the end of the decade indicated that the Vietnam War was still an important issue for the nation.

The Supreme Court decision, *Roe v. Wade,* which made abortion legal, divided the country into pro-life and pro-choice groups that are still arguing the issue. It became a major political matter with related ramifications on the rights of homosexuals and traditional family values. Religious leaders, from Jerry Falwell to Billy Graham, *How to Be Born Again* (1977) spoke strongly for conservative values. Their ideal was a father who supported the family and mother who cared for the children, an ideal that was less and less the norm with soaring divorce rates, premarital sex, unwed mothers and single parents supporting children of divorce. However, family values had strong appeal and were capitalized on by the Republican Party. Nixon first described those quiet voters who did not protest but adhered to the values of their religion as the "moral majority," a phrase used often in the decade. Another aspect of the decade is revealed in the first world Earth Day in 1970.

*1980s:* The 1980s were a period of conservative leadership epitomized by the very popular president, Ronald Reagan. There were undertones of protest, especially against his military buildup. The yuppie mentality was slowly replaced by what has been identified as Generation X—a group that was cynical and focused on self, continuing a national focus on self-improvement as seen in a growing interest in matters of health and exercise—jogging, running, and biking. MTV was added to TV viewing options. The music of Madonna, "the material girl," reflected the materialistic goals of the age, as did the extremely popular Michael Jackson whose album, *Thriller* (1982) sold 40,000,000 copies. Rap was becoming the new music media of protest and 1986 saw the first platinum rap album, *Raising Hell.*

The identification of AIDS, first seen in large numbers in the gay and drug communities, created new tensions over sexual behavior and added to the cynicism of the period. AIDS galvanized the gay community. ACT-UP and changes in lifestyle resulted, slowing the spread of AIDS. There is still no cure for it and it continues to spread.

The decade saw the rapid growth of computer use in games and the introduction of the laptop. Society was slowly adapting personal computers, laying the foundation for a great economic boom driven by technology. Cable TV with CNN leading the way made more and more channels available and the *couch potato*, one who spent the day watching TV, became a model in contrast to the *health nut*, providing another division in society.

*1990s and 2000s:* The 1990s were dominated by the technology boom that made fortunes for many and accentuated the growing division between the poor and wealthy in the country. Salaries of CEOs skyrocketed and the difference between the hourly wage of the worker and the salary of the CEO became a concern. By 2007 one CEO who was relieved of his position was then given a separation package worth $200,000,000—even failures were rewarded in this environment. Several cases of deliberate falsification of economic information (ex. Enron-2001) by CEOs and/or corporate management revealed another aspect of this division of wealth as well as moral and ethical failings of the business community. Profits for shareholders as well as personal gain appeared to be the motivation in these cases. Executive leaders were tried and some were sent to prison. New laws and regulations addressed some of the issues.

The Internet grew rapidly and became essential for business and research. Cell phones added to the technology that became both a symbol of affluence and a necessity for communication. Computer technology, instant messaging, and photography exemplified the rapidity of technological advance. Ipods in the 21st century became one of the inventions driving a second technology boom after the first crashed at the turn of the millennium. Society was at the point where one was able to always be in touch with others but not in face-to-face relationships.

Rap music came to dominate popular music but opera began a comeback, suggesting an interest among many people in more traditional forms of expression. The movie about AIDS, *Philadelphia* (1993), indicated the willingness of the industry to deal with social subjects. Several others followed including *Schindler's List* (1994), a protrayal of the Holocaust, and *A Beautiful Mind* (2001), a film about schizophrenia. The *Harry Potter* books brought exciting reading to a generation but created a backlash from those who saw it as glorifying witchcraft and the devil—an indication that society was contentious and divided on every issue.

**Movements:** The last 60 years has seen innumerable movements develop that have affected United States society. Among them have been:

*McCarthyism*—The anti-communist "crusade" led by Senator Joseph McCarthy reflected the fear of the early Cold War.

*Civil Rights*—The movement was given impetus by the *Brown v. Board of Education* decision on integration of schools and grew under the leadership of Martin Luther King, Jr. to focus on ending all aspects of segregation. There were many spin-offs from the Civil Rights Movement including:

*Women's Liberation*—The movement focused on changing the role of women in society, giving them equal rights with men in the workplace and throughout society.

*Gay rights*—The movement of homosexuals and lesbians to achieve equal rights and acceptance in society.

*Chicano Power*—The movement of Mexican Americans for acceptance and equality.

*Abortion*—The decision in *Roe v. Wade* led to two very vocal and committed movements. A Pro-Choice group that supported a woman's right to choose an abortion and a Pro-Life group that believed human life began at conception and that abortion was murder.

*Environment*—Given emphasis by Rachael Carson's book, *The Silent Spring*, the environment became a concern for many and led to a movement for clean air and water, protection of threatened species, and many other issues including global warming.

*Globalization*—By the end of the 20th century, industrialization had become international. Trade agreements had been negotiated among almost all nations under the auspices of the World Trade Organization. The speed of transportation and communication (e-mail, cell phone, fax), growing markets in Asia, Africa and South America, and the low costs of manufacturing in many countries created a truly world economy.

*Immigration*—While not an organized movement as are the others, immigration has been a topic of concern since World War I. After World War II, increased immigration from Asia and Africa changed the nation and there has been continual concern over illegal immigrants particularly from the Americas.

## SOME IMPORTANT INDIVIDUALS OF THE PERIOD
## 1945–2007

| | | |
|---|---|---|
| Madeline Albright | Martha Graham | Nancy Pelosi |
| Muhammad Ali | Alan Greenspan | Adam Clayton Powell |
| Woody Allen | Joseph Heller | Colin Powell |
| Neil Armstrong | Hubert Humphrey | Elvis Presley |
| Leonard Bernstein | Saddam Hussein | Ronald Reagan |
| Humphrey Bogart | Jesse Jackson | William Rehnquist |
| David Brinkley | Lyndon B. Johnson | Condoleezza Rice |
| H. Rap Brown | Helen Keller | Nelson Rockefeller |
| Warren Burger | Edward M. Kennedy | Donald Rumsfeld |
| George H. W. Bush | John F. Kennedy | Eleanor Roosevelt |
| George W. Bush | Robert Kennedy | Dean Rusk |
| Jimmy Carter | Ayatollah Khomeini | Jonas Salk |
| Rosalynn Carter | Billy Jean King | Alan B. Shepard |
| Cesar Chavez | Martin Luther King, Jr. | Frank Sinatra |
| Dick Cheney | John Lennon | George Steinbrenner |
| Bill Clinton | Douglas MacArthur | Gloria Steinem |
| Hillary Rodham Clinton | Malcolm X | Adlai Stevenson |
| John Foster Dulles | Nelson Mandela | Robert Taft |
| Bob Dylan | George Marshall | Clarence Thomas |
| John Edwards | Thurgood Marshall | Harry Truman |
| Dwight Eisenhower | Joseph McCarthy | Donald Trump |
| Jerry Falwell | Arthur Miller | Ted Turner |
| William Faulkner | Marilyn Monroe | Kurt Vonnegut |
| Geraldine Ferraro | Toni Morrison | George Wallace |
| Gerald Ford | Ralph Nader | Andy Warhol |
| Betty Friedan | Richard M. Nixon | Earl Warren |
| William Fulbright | Barack Obama | Tennessee Williams |
| Bill Gates | Sandra Day O'Connor | Wendell Willkie |
| Newt Gingrich | Jacqueline Kennedy | Oprah Winfrey |
| Ruth Bader Ginsburg | Onassis | Richard Wright |
| Mikhail Gorbachev | J. Robert Oppenheimer | Andrew Young |
| Albert Gore | Rosa Parks | |
| Billy Graham | H. Ross Perot | |

# Chronology of Important Dates

The following Time Line of United States History provides an overview that should prove useful in a quick review. You may wish to add your own dates to this Time Line as you study.

about 50,000 years ago — First Native Americans cross land bridge from Siberia

about 500 A.D. — Pueblo culture develops in southwestern United States

1492 — Columbus's first voyage to America

1497–98 — Voyage of John Cabot

1519–21 — Magellan circumnavigates the globe

1565 — St. Augustine founded by Spanish

1580s — Failure to establish permanent colony at Roanoke by Sir Walter Raleigh

1607 — Colony founded at Jamestown by English

1608 — Santa Fe founded by Spanish

1609 — Quebec founded by French

1619 — House of Burgesses

1619 — First slaves brought to Virginia

1620 — Mayflower Compact — colony at Plymouth

1630 — Boston founded

1634 — Maryland founded

1638 — New Sweden founded by Swedes

1639 — Fundamental Orders of Connecticut

1642 — Ye Olde Deluder Satan Act in Massachusetts (education)

1664 — Dutch driven from New York

1675 — King Philip's war

1682 — Pennsylvania founded

— Mary Rowlandson's "Captivity account"

1689–97 — King William's war

1692 — Salem witch trials

1696 — Navigation Acts restated

1702 — Cotton Mather publishes *The Ecclesiastical History of New England*

1702–13 — Queen Anne's War

1718 — San Antonio founded

1730s — Beginnings of the Great Awakening

1733 — Molasses Act
— Georgia, last of original 13 colonies, founded
1739–42 — War of Jenkin's Ear
1740–48 — King George's war
1754 — Albany Plan of Union proposed
— Fort Necessity (Pitt) built
— Jonathan Edwards, noted preacher and writer, dies
1754–63 — French and Indian War
1759 — Fort Ticonderoga captured
— Quebec captured
1763 — Treaty of Paris — France loses Canada and Northwest Territory
— Pontiac's Rebellion
— Proclamation of 1763
1764 — Sugar Act
1765 — Quartering Act
— Stamp Act/Stamp Act Congress
1766 — Stamp Act repealed
— Declaratory Act passed
1767 — Townshend Acts passed
— New York Assembly suspended
— Nonimportation of British goods
1768 — Massachusetts Assembly dissolved
— Troops stationed in Boston
1769 — San Diego founded by the Spanish
— First California mission
1770 — Townshend Acts repealed
— Tea Tax maintained
— Boston Massacre
1772 — Massachusetts Committee of Correspondence
— *Gaspée* burned
1773 — Boston Tea Party
1774 — First Continental Congress
— Intolerable Acts
— Quebec Act
— Galloway's Plan of Union
— *Summary View of the Rights of British America* and "Novanglus" Letters
1775 — Battles of Lexington and Concord
— Lord North's Conciliation Plan
1776 — Second Continental Congress
— Declaration of Independence
— *Common Sense* by Thomas Paine published
1778 — Battle of Saratoga
— France becomes U.S. ally
1781 — Battle of Yorktown
— Articles of Confederation ratified
1783 — Treaty of Paris
1785 — Basic Land Ordinance
1786 — Annapolis Convention
1786–87 — Shays' Rebellion

1787 — Constitutional Convention
— Northwest Ordinance
1788 — Nine states ratify Constitution
— *Federalist Papers* written
1789 — George Washington elected first president
— 13 states join federal union
1790 — Alexander Hamilton's financial program
1791 — Bill of Rights adopted
— Bank of the United States chartered
— Benjamin Franklin's *Autobiography* first published
1792 — Gilbert Stuart portrait of George Washington
1793 — Proclamation of Neutrality
— Citizen Genêt affair
1794 — Whiskey Rebellion
1795 — Jay's Treaty
— Pinckney's Treaty
1796 — John Adams elected second president
1797 — XYZ Affair
1798 — Alien and Sedition Acts
— Kentucky and Virginia Resolutions
1800 — Thomas Jefferson elected third president
1801 — John Marshall Chief Justice
1803 — Louisiana Purchase
— *Marbury v. Madison*
1804–07 — Lewis and Clark Expedition
1807 — Embargo
— Fulton invents the steamboat
— Aaron Burr conspiracy trial
1808 — James Madison elected fourth president
— Slave trade stopped by congressional law
1810 — Annexation of West Florida
— *Fletcher v. Peck*
1812–15 — War of 1812
1815 — Battle of New Orleans
— Hartford Convention
— Treaty of Ghent
1816 — James Monroe elected fifth president
— Second Bank of the United States chartered
1817 — Rush-Bagot agreement
1818 — Convention of 1818
1819 — Washington Irving's *Sketch Book* published (includes *Legend of Sleepy Hollow)*
— Knickerbocker School of New York writers
— *McCulloch v. Maryland* and *Dartmouth College v. Woodward*
— Economic Panic of 1819 – first economic crisis for new nation
1820 — Missouri Compromise
— Greek Revival architecture dominates
1821 — *Cohens v. Virginia*
— Second Great Awakening begins

1823 — Monroe Doctrine
1824 — John Quincy Adams elected sixth president
1825 — Erie Canal opened
    — *Self Portrait in His Museum* painted by Charles Wilson Peale
    — New Harmony, Indiana founded
1828 — Tariff Act
    — Andrew Jackson elected seventh president
1830 — Webster-Hayne debate
1831 — Alexis de Tocqueville visits United States
    — Peggy Eaton Affair
    — Nat Turner slave rebellion
    — Maysville Road bill vetoed
    — William Lloyd Garrison publishes *The Liberator*
1832 — Tariff Act
    — Nullification controversy
    — Jackson vetoes bill to recharter Second Bank of the United States
    — Telegraph invented
    — Reaper invented
1834 — Whig Party formed
1836 — Texas Revolution
    — Martin Van Buren elected eighth president
    — Ralph Waldo Emerson's *Nature* published
    — Transcendentalism
1837 — Panic of 1837
    — Gag Rule in Congress
    — Specie Circular
    — *Charles River Bridge v. Warren Bridge*
    — Boston police force established
1840 — William Henry Harrison elected ninth president
    — Independent Treasury Act
1841 — Harrison dies; John Tyler becomes tenth president
1842 — Webster-Ashburton Treaty
1844 — James K. Polk elected eleventh president
    — Oregon Dispute
1845 — Texas annexed
    — Native American political party founded
1846 — Oregon settlement
1846–48 — Mexican War
1848 — Treaty of Guadalupe Hidalgo
    — Gold discovered in California
    — Zachary Taylor elected twelfth president
    — Seneca Falls Convention
    — Brook Farm established
    — Cunard Company steamship service to England begins
1849 — California gold rush
1850 — Taylor dies; Millard Fillmore becomes thirteenth president
    — Compromise of 1850
1851 — Melville's *Moby Dick* published
1852 — Harriet Beecher Stowe's *Uncle Tom's Cabin* published

— Franklin Pierce elected fourteenth president
1854 — Republican Party formed
— Kansas-Nebraska Act
— Japan reopened by Admiral Perry
1856 — Violence in Kansas
— James Buchanan elected fifteenth president
1857 — *Dred Scott v. Sandford*
1858 — First transatlantic cable
— Lincoln-Douglas debates
1859 — John Brown's raid on Harper's Ferry
— First oil well drilled
1860 — Abraham Lincoln elected sixteenth president
— South Carolina secedes
1861 — Confederacy formed
— Fort Sumter attacked
— Morrill Tariff
1862 — Morrill Act
— Pacific Railways Act
1863 — Emancipation Proclamation
— Battle of Gettysburg
1864 — Homestead Act
— Sherman's march through Georgia
1865 — Wade Davis Bill
— Lee surrenders
— Lincoln assassinated; Andrew Johnson becomes seventeenth president
— Thirteenth Amendment (abolished slavery)
1866 — Civil Rights Act
— *Ex parte Milligan*
— National Labor Union formed
1867 — First Reconstruction Act
1868 — President Johnson impeached
— Fourteenth Amendment (equal protection of the laws)
— Ulysses S. Grant elected eighteenth president
1869 — Wyoming Territory gives women right to vote
1870 — Ku Klux Klan formed
— Fifteenth Amendment (no discrimination in voting)
1871 — Tweed Ring in New York
1873 — The "Crime of '73"
— Slaughterhouse cases (first under Fourteenth Amendment)
1874 — Women's Christian Temperance Union formed
1875 — Rutherford B. Hayes elected nineteenth president
1876 — Centennial Year celebrations
Battle of the Little Big Horn – Custer's "Last Stand"
1877 — Last federal troops removed from South
— *Trinity Church Boston* designed by Henry Hobson Richardson
— *Munn v. Illinois*
1878 — Bland-Allison Act
— Pago Pago naval base established
— Knights of Labor formed

1879 — Standard Oil Trust formed by John D. Rockefeller
— Thomas Edison perfects the incandescent lightbulb
— Henry George's *Progress and Poverty* published
1880 — James A. Garfield elected twentieth president
1881 — James A. Garfield assassinated; Chester A. Arthur becomes twenty-first president
1883 — Pendleton Civil Service Act
— Civil Rights cases
1884 — Grover Cleveland elected twenty-second president
1885 — Mark Twain's *Huckleberry Finn* published
1886 — American Federation of Labor formed
— Haymarket Riot
1887 — Interstate Commerce Act
— Dawes Act
— Right to Pearl Harbor naval base acquired
1888 — Benjamin Harrison elected twenty-third president
1889 — Oklahoma opened for settlement
— Andrew Carnegie's *Gospel of Wealth* speech
— Hull House founded by Jane Addams
— First Pan-American Conference
1890 — Frontier "closes" according to Census Bureau
— Sherman Antitrust Act
— Sherman Silver Purchase Act
— Battle of Wounded Knee
1892 — Bering Sea Dispute
— Homestead Steel strike
— Populist Party nominates James B. Weaver for presidency
— Grover Cleveland elected twenty-fourth president
1893 — Panic of 1893
— Anti-Saloon League founded
1894 — Eugene V. Debs leads Pullman strike
— Carey Act passed (Reclamation)
— *Chicago Stock Exchange* building designed by Louis Sullivan
1895 — Venezuela Boundary dispute
— *U.S. v. E. C. Knight Co.*
— Booker T. Washington's *Atlanta Exposition* speech
1896 — William McKinley elected twenty-fifth president
— *Plessy v. Ferguson*
1897 — Diesel engine invented
1898 — Battleship *Maine* sunk
— Spanish-American War
— Edward Bellamy's *Looking Backward* published
1899 — Open Door Policy announced
1901 — President McKinley assassinated; Theodore Roosevelt becomes twenty-sixth president
1902 — Newland Act passes (conservation movement)
— Owen Wister's *The Virginian* published
— Anthracite coal strike
1903 — Panama Revolt

— First World Series baseball game
1904 — Roosevelt Corollary to Monroe Doctrine
1905 — Russo-Japanese War ended by Treaty of Portsmouth
— *Lochner v. New York*
1906 — Pure Food and Drug Law passed
— Hepburn Act
1907 — Gentlemen's Agreement with Japan
1908 — William Howard Taft elected twenty-seventh president
— White House Conservation Conference
— *Muller v. Oregon*
1911 — U.S. Intervention in Nicaragua
1912 — Woodrow Wilson elected twenty-eighth president
1913 — Underwood Tariff passed, reducing tariff rates
— Federal Reserve Banking Act
— Sixteenth Amendment (income tax)
— Seventeenth Amendment (direct election of senators)
— *Cliff Dwellers* by George Bellows painted
— First moving assembly line at Ford Motor Co.
1914 — Federal Trade Commission established
— Clayton Antitrust Act
— World War I begins in Europe
— Panama Canal opened
1915 — Sinking of the *Lusitania*
— Reelection of Woodrow Wilson in "He kept us out of war" campaign
1916 — Mexican border campaign by U.S. Army
— Keating-Owen Child Labor Act passed
— National Defense Act
1917 — United States enters World War I
— Virgin Islands purchased
— Law limiting European immigration passed
1918 — Wilson announces 14 Points
— World War I ends
— *Hammer v. Dagenhart*
1919 — U.S. Senate rejects Treaty of Versailles
— Eighteenth Amendment (Prohibition)
— Palmer raids
— *Schenck v. U.S.*
1920 — Warren G. Harding elected twenty-ninth president
— Nineteenth Amendment (vote for women)
— Prohibition begins
— Sinclair Lewis' *Main Street* published
— First commercial radio broadcast
1921 — Quota system for immigration introduced
— Washington Disarmament Congress
1923 — President Harding dies; Calvin Coolidge becomes thirtieth president
— Ku Klux Klan exposés
— *Adkins v. Children's Hospital*
1924 — National Origins Act passed
— Dawes plan on German reparations

— Harding administration scandals revealed

1925 — Scopes "Monkey" trial

— *The Great Gatsby* by F. Scott Fitzgerald published

1926 — *Eleven A.M.* by Edward Hopper painted

1927 — Geneva Disarmament Congress

— Kellogg-Briand Peace Pact

— Sacco-Vanzetti case

— *The Jazz Singer* — first talking motion picture

1928 — Herbert Hoover elected thirty-first president

— *Strange Interlude* by Eugene O'Neill performed

1929 — Stock market crash, start of the Great Depression

— Ernest Hemingway's *A Farewell to Arms* published

1931 — Hoover debt moratorium

— Japan invades Manchuria (start of war in Asia)

— Eugene O'Neill's *Mourning Becomes Electra*

1932 — Franklin D. Roosevelt elected thirty-second president

— Reconstruction Finance Corporation established

— Glass-Steagall Act

1933 — New Deal Begins: First AAA, NIRA, TVA, FERA, HOLC, FDIC, CCC, SEC, FHA

— Twenty-first Amendment (ends Prohibition)

— Good Neighbor Policy announced

1934 — Philippine Independence Act passed

— Nye Committee munitions investigations

1935 — "Second New Deal"

— Social Security Act

— *Schechter v. U.S.*

1936 — *U.S. v. Butler*

1937 — Supreme Court "packing" plan

— *Falling Water* house designed by Frank Lloyd Wright

— *NLRB v. Jones and Laughlin Steel Corp.*

— United Auto Workers Union stage sit-down strikes

1938 — Second Agricultural Adjustment Act

— Fair Labor Standards Act

1939 — Limited national emergency declared as World War II begins in Europe

— Neutrality Act

— New York World's Fair

1941 — Four Freedoms speech

— Atlantic Charter

— Lend-Lease Act

— Japanese attack Pearl Harbor

— United States enters World War II

— Film, *Citizen Kane,* produced by Orson Welles

1942 — Bataan and Corregidor captured by Japanese

— Battle of Midway

— U.S. forces invade North Africa

— Price control and rationing

1943 — Invasion of Philippines

— Invasion of Sicily and Italy

1944 — D-Day invasion of France
— Battle of the Bulge
— G.I. Bill
— *Korematsu v. U.S.*
1945 — End of World War II: Germany (May) and Japan (August) surrender
— President Franklin D. Roosevelt dies; Harry Truman becomes thirty-third president
— Atomic bombs dropped on Hiroshima and Nagasaki
— Yalta Conference
1946 — First meeting of General Assembly of United Nations
— Cold War begins
— Philippine independence
— Churchill describes "Iron Curtain" in speech in Europe
— Benjamin Spock's *Baby and Child Care* published
1947 — Truman Doctrine
— Marshall Plan
— Taft-Hartley Act
— *Cathedral* by Jackson Pollock painted
— Jackie Robinson becomes first African American player on major league baseball team
— *To Secure These Rights* (Civil Rights) published
1948 — Berlin Blockade and airlift
— Organization of American States formed
— Hiss case
— *Sexual Behavior in the American Male* by Kinsey published
1949 — NATO formed
— Fall of mainland China to Chinese Communists
1950 — McCarran Internal Security Act
1950–53 — Korean War
1951 — Japanese Peace treaty
— West German Peace contract
— Internal Security Act (McCarran Act)
— Twenty-second Amendment (two terms for president) ratified
— J. D. Salinger's *Catcher in the Rye* published
1952 — United States explodes first H-Bomb
— Dwight D. Eisenhower elected thirty-fourth president
— Ralph Ellison's *Invisible Man* published
1953 — Execution of convicted spies Julius and Ethel Rosenberg
— Department of Health, Education, and Welfare created
— *Gentlemen Prefer Blondes* makes Marilyn Monroe a star and sex symbol
1954 — *Brown v. Board of Education*
— Senator Joseph McCarthy censured by Senate
— SEATO formed
— Dien Bien Phu captured by Vietminh
— Atomic Energy Act
— Elvis Presley introduces his style of rock and roll
1955 — Summit conference at Geneva
— Austrian Peace Treaty
— AFL and CIO merge to form AFL-CIO

— Montgomery, Alabama, bus boycott; Martin Luther King, Jr. emerges as leader

— *Rebel Without a Cause* introduces James Dean as new Hollywood star

1956 — Suez crisis

— Hungarian revolt

— Federal Aid Highway Act

— Allen Ginsberg's poem *Howl* introduces the "Beat Generation"

— Elvis Presley emerges as new rock star and symbol of changing music styles

1957 — Eisenhower Doctrine

— *Sputnik* (first earth orbiting satellite) launched by Soviet Union

— Civil Rights Act

— Little Rock, Arkansas, school integration riots

— Defense Reorganization Act

— Jack Kerouac's *On the Road* published

1958 — John Kenneth Galbraith's *The Affluent Society* published

— Postwar Baby Boom peaks

1959 — St. Lawrence seaway opened

— *Black on Maroon* by Mark Rothko painted

— Xerox machine available for public use

1960 — Kennedy and Nixon engage in first televised presidential election debate

— John F. Kennedy elected thirty-fifth president

— U-2 incident

— John Updike's *Rabbit Run* published

1961 — Berlin Crisis

— Bay of Pigs

— First man in space

— Advisory group sent to South Vietnam

— Peace Corps formed

— Twenty-third Amendment (District of Columbia voting rights)

— *Mapp v. Ohio*

— Civil Rights Movement organizes Freedom Riders

— Eisenhower refers to *Military Industrial Complex* in farewell speech

1962 — Cuban Missile Crisis

— Trade Expansion Act

— Michael Harrington's *The Other America* (poverty) published

1963 — President Kennedy assassinated; Lyndon Johnson becomes thirty-sixth president

— Supreme Court (Warren Court) declares prayer in public schools unconstitutional and supports rights of criminal suspects

— Civil Rights March on Washington

— Martin Luther King's *Letter From a Birmingham Jail* published

— Betty Friedan's *The Feminine Mystique* published

1964 — Civil Rights Act passed

— War on Poverty begins; Economic Opportunity Act

— Warren Commission report on Kennedy assassination

— Twenty-fourth Amendment (No Poll Tax)

— *Escobedo v. New York*

— The Beatles tour the United States
1965 — U.S. Troops engage in combat in South Vietnam
— Voting Rights Act
— Great Society programs: Elementary and Secondary School Act; Medicare; Water Quality Act: Omnibus Housing Act; Higher Education Act
— Assassination of Malcolm X
— Selma to Montgomery, Alabama, Civil Rights March
— Riots in the Watts District of Los Angeles
— Malcolm "X" assassinated
— *Sixteen Jackies* by Andy Warhol painted
1966 — Department of Transportation
— NOW (National Organization for Women) founded
— Freedom of Information Act
— *Miranda v. Arizona*
— Black Panthers organized
1967 — Urban riots (Detroit, Newark, Rochester, Milwaukee, Washington)
— Twenty-fifth Amendment (presidential succession)
— Organized draft card burning protest in New York City
— "Summer of Love" proclaimed by Hippies in San Francisco
1968 — Dr. Martin Luther King, Jr., assassinated
— Robert Kennedy assassinated
— Riots at Democratic Convention in Chicago
— Richard M. Nixon elected thirty-seventh president
— Columbia University students seize the campus (SDS)
— Non-Proliferation Nuclear Treaty passed by United Nations
— Anti-Vietnam War protests
— *U.S.S. Pueblo* seized by North Korea
1969 — Men land on the moon
— My Lai massacre revealed
— Nixon "Silent Majority" speech
— Woodstock rock concert
— Stonewall Riot (Gay Rights) in New York City
— *La Grande Vitesse* sculpture by Alexander Calder
1970 — U.S. troops invade Cambodia on orders of President Nixon
— Independent U.S. Postal Service established
— Environmental Protection Agency (EPA) established
— First worldwide Earth Day celebration
1971 — Twenty-sixth Amendment (voting age)
— Amtrak (train) service initiated
— *Pentagon Papers* published
— New Economic Program — price control
1972 — Watergate break-in by agents of the Republican White House; "cover-up" begins
— Death penalty decisions (*Furman v. Georgia* and others) of the Supreme Court
— President Nixon visits Communist China
— Senate passes Equal Rights Amendment (ERA) but it is not ratified by states

— SALT disarmament treaty signed

— OPEC Oil Embargo

— War Powers Act

1973 — Vice President Agnew forced to resign; Gerald Ford chosen as vice president by Nixon with congressional approval

— *Roe v. Wade*

— Wounded Knee incident

— Existence of White House tapes revealed as part of Watergate investigation

— "Saturday Night Massacre"—Resignation of Attorney General Eliot Richardson and Special Prosecutor Archibald Cox over Watergate

— United States negotiates withdrawal from Vietnam

1974 — Presidential impeachment hearings

— *U.S. v. Nixon*

— President Nixon resigns presidency; Gerald Ford becomes thirty-eighth president

— Nelson Rockefeller confirmed as vice president

— Ford pardons Nixon

— Ford Vietnam War amnesty program

— Oil shortages due to embargo and OPEC

— Privacy Act

1975 — Oil price controls ended

— President Ford visits mainland China

— Government of South Vietnam surrenders to the North Vietnamese

— Former Attorney General Mitchell and Nixon presidential aides Haldeman and Ehrlichman sentenced to prison for roles in Watergate scandals

1976 — Bicentennial Year

— 200-mile fishing limit proclaimed by United States

— Supreme Court upholds busing in Boston to achieve integration

— Copyright Revision Bill

— Jimmy Carter elected thirty-ninth president of the United States

1977 — Carter opens presidency by granting a pardon to draft evaders and proposing a large government spending program to reduce unemployment

— Trans-Alaska pipeline opens

— Clean Air Bill

— President Sadat of Egypt visits Israel

— Government Reorganization Bill

— Government Ethics Law (includes provision for Independent Council)

— Billy Graham publishes *How to Be Born Again*

1978 — California tax cut (Proposition 13) approved by voters

— Air Transport Deregulation Act

— Civil Service Reform Act

— *Bakke v. University of California*

— Humphrey-Hawkins Employment Bill

— Camp David meetings (Israel-Egypt peace talks) and accord

1979 — U.S.-China diplomatic recognition finalized

— Egypt-Israel Peace Treaty

— Three-Mile Island nuclear plant accident
— Iranian students seize U.S. embassy in Teheran and take employees hostage
— Boat people leave Vietnam
— *Apocalypse Now* – major film presentation on Vietnam
— Moral Majority established

1980 — Inflation continues as consumer prices rise 13.3 percent
— Attempt to rescue Iranian hostages fails
— John Anderson announces independent race for the presidency
— Peacetime draft registration is begun
— Ronald Reagan elected fortieth president
— Alaska Wilderness Act

1981 — Inflation continues as consumer prices rise 12.4 percent
— Reagan supply-side economic plan reduces taxes, cuts welfare benefits, and increases spending for defense
— Soviet grain embargo lifted by President Reagan
— AIDS identified
— United States increases aid to El Salvador
— MTV channel opens

1982 — Inflation rate slows as unemployment reaches post-World War II record
— Equal Rights Amendment to Constitution (ERA) defeated
— U.S. troops ordered to Lebanon due to civil war and fight between Israel and PLO
— Congress passes budget with a projected deficit of $100 billion
— START talks open
— Reagan introduces Strategic Defense Initiative (SDI or "Star Wars")
— *USA Today* begins publication

1983 — U.S. troops invade Grenada
— Terrorists bomb U.S. Marine barracks in Beirut, Lebanon, killing 237
— Congress passes bill to reform Social Security System
— Unemployment rate goes over 10 percent

1984 — Ronald Reagan and George Bush overwhelmingly reelected, defeating Democrats Walter Mondale and Geraldine Ferraro, first woman vice presidential candidate for a major party
— Record deficit in balance of trade payments

1985 — Gramm/Rudman Act (balanced budget)
— Mikhail Gorbachev becomes leader of Soviet Union and introduces reforms (glasnost and peristroika); summit meeting in Geneva between Mikhail Gorbachev and Ronald Reagan
— Supreme Court bars "moment of silence" in schools
— S & L (savings and loan) failures upset economy

1986 — *Challenger* space shuttle explodes
— Chernobyl nuclear power plant accident in Soviet Union
— Iran-Contra affair revealed

1987 — Iran-Contra congressional hearings
— Stock Market collapses with over 500-point loss on the Dow Jones in one day
— INF Treaty signed
— Congress approves S & L bailouts program

— Clean Water Act passed over Reagan's veto

— Toni Morrison's *Beloved* published

1988 — George H. W. Bush (Bush 41—Republican) elected forty-first president with Dan Quayle as vice president

— Anti-Drug Act passed (fourth act in six years)

— Peace accord signed in Nicaragua and Sandinistas are voted out of office

1989 — Fall of Berlin Wall

— United States invades Panama to seize accused drug dealer General Noriega

1990 — Second Earth Day celebration heightens environmental concerns

— Clean Air Act renewed

— Non-Communist governments established in all of Eastern Europe

— Cold War ends

— Americans with Disabilities Act

— Fox Network established

— P.C.s and laptops lead technology revolution

1991 — Kuwait freed as Iraq invaded by UN coalition led by United States (Operation Desert Storm); fighting ends with armistice and Saddam Hussein still in control

— Soviet Union breaks up—replaced by Commonwealth of Independent States

— Clarence Thomas approved as judge of United States Supreme Court in spite of charges of sexual harassment

— Cambodian Peace Accords; El Salvador Peace Pact; Afghanistan Peace Agreement; Namibia Accord—all arranged through United Nations with U.S.-Russian cooperation

— Last U.S. hostages freed in Lebanon

— *Rust v. Sullivan* Supreme Court decision upholds *Roe v. Wade*

— Cable Television Deregulation Act

1992 — UN Conference on Environment and Development (Rio Conference)

— Legislative stalemate as President Bush continues to veto Democratic legislation

— Rodney King case followed by riots in Los Angeles

— Bill Clinton (Democrat) elected forty-second president of the United States with Al Gore as vice president, defeating George H.W. Bush and Dan Quayle (Republican) and H. Ross Perot and James Stockdale (Independent)

1993 — NAFTA (North American Free Trade Agreement) approved

— Bio-Diversity Treaty signed

— Israel–PLO Oslo Peace Accords signed

— Whitewater investigation begins

1994 — GATT (General Agreement on Tariffs and Trade) approved

— Jordan–Israel sign peace treaty

— Brady Bill (arms registration) passed

— Republicans gain control of Senate and House of Representatives in mid-term election: Republican Contract with America

— Steven Spielberg wins Academy Award for *Schindler's List* (Holocaust)

1995 — O. J. Simpson acquitted of murder of Nicole Simpson and Ronald
Goldman
— Oklahoma City Alfred P. Murrah Federal Building bombed; Timothy
McVeigh and Terry Nichols later found guilty
— Clinton and Congress approve closing of 79 military bases
— Welfare Reform Bill "ends welfare as we know it"
— Dayton Accords signed; commitment of U.S. troops to peacekeeping in
Bosnia
— Clinton and congressional disagreements over budget lead to
government shutdowns in November and December; public supports
Clinton stance; budget finally passed in January 1996
— Beginning of Monica Lewinsky–Bill Clinton affair

1996 — Telecommunications Overhaul Bill
— *Romer v. Evans* (gay rights)
— Late Term Abortion Bill vetoed
— Antiterrorism Bill
— Health Insurance Portability Bill
— Illegal Immigration Bill
— Clinton–Gore (Democrat) reelected with 49.2% of the vote over Bob
Dole–Jack Kemp (Republican) and Ross Perot (Reform)

1997 — "Politics of self destruction" dominate political life in Washington
— Balanced budget by 2002 plan approved
— Arab-Israel talks at impasse; civil war in Zaire; Northern Ireland peace
talks
— U.S. refuses to sign Land Mine Treaty
— Thailand currency devaluation precipitates Asian financial crisis
— U.S. economy continues to boom

1998 — House of Representatives impeaches President Clinton
— First budget surplus in 30 years; Clinton calls for surplus to be used for
Social Security; Republicans call for tax cuts
— NATO expansion approved; Hungary, Czech Republic, Poland to join
— India and Pakistan explode atomic bombs
— United States and Britain bomb Iraq; UN arms inspection teams
withdraw
— Many states settle with tobacco companies after national settlement
fails to win congressional approval

1999 — Senate holds impeachment trial; Clinton cleared on all charges
— NATO bombs Yugoslavia (Serbia and Kosovo); peace agreement
reached; NATO sends in troops
— *Alden v. Maine, College Savings Bank v. Florida* (interpretation of
state sovereignty)
— *Murphy v. U.P.S.* (limits Americans with Disabilities Act)
— Senate rejects Nuclear Test Ban Treaty

2000 — Drunk Driving Bill
— George W. Bush (Bush 43) (Republican) elected forty-third president
of the United States with Dick Cheney as vice president, defeating Al
Gore and Joseph Lieberman (Democrat) in closest election in U.S.
history; Gore wins popular vote—Bush wins Electoral College vote
— *Bush v. Gore* settles disputed Florida presidential vote

— Dow Jones drops 6.2 percent as bull market ends
— DVD technology readily available replacing VCRs

2001
— Tax Reform Act
— United States withdraws from Antiballistic Missile (ABM) Treaty
— September 11 (9/11) terrorist attacks on World Trade Center and Pentagon
— War on terrorism proclaimed
— War in Afghanistan
— Antiterrorism Bill
— Airline Security Act
— Computer industry suffers major losses
— Enron bankruptcy reveals business scandals
— Kyoto Treaty rejected by Bush administration

2002
— Campaign Finance Reform Bill
— Education Reform Bill (No Child Left Behind)
— Bush 43 labels Iraq, Iran, and North Korea an "axis of evil"
— U.N. weapons inspectors return to Iraq; Security Council votes Resolution 1440—"one final chance for Iraq to disarm"; U.S. sends troops to Persian Gulf
— Rebuilding begins in Afghanistan
— Budget surplus disappears with tax cuts and recession
— *Spiderman* takes top place as money winner

2003
— United Nations rejects United States, Britain, and Spain's proposal for deadline for war in Iraq
— United States, Britain, and "coalition of the willing" attack Iraq to topple government of Saddam Hussein and destroy any weapons of mass destruction (WMDs); war begins March 19; Bush declares war over on May 1 after Baghdad falls; guerilla-type war breaks out in Iraq
— North Korea announces it has nuclear weapons; Bush refuses direct talks
— Medicare Prescription Drug Law approved
— Five year, 15 billion plan to fight HIV/AIDS approved
— Ten year, 330 billion dollar tax cut and 150 billion dollar appropriation for Afghanistan and Iraq Wars approved
— Supreme Court declares Texas sodomy laws unconstitutional (*Lawrence v. Texas*) and Campaign Finance Law constitutional

2004
— Bush and Cheney (Rep.) defeat John Kerry and John Edwards (Dem.) for presidency in tight race decided by the vote of Ohio; Republicans retain control of Congress
— Sudan accused of genocide in Darfur—limited international response
— Bush administration questions science behind Endangered Species Act and other legislation
— Bush limits federal funding of stem cell research
— Federal legislation recognizes fetus as distinct entity separate from mother
— Global "black market" in nuclear weapons revealed led by A. Q. Khan of Pakistan

— Committing of abuses of detainees by U.S. forces at Abu Ghrarib
prison in Baghdad revealed

— Explosion in the use of blogs changes politics (ex. Howard Dean
campaign for presidency), business, and popular culture, reducing
influence of the elite leader group and permitting greater participation
by the public

2005 — Hurricane Katrina causes devastation along Gulf Coast and destroys
much of New Orleans; slow response of federal government criticized

— Kansas State School Board replaces evolution with 'intelligent design'
as state science requirement

— Widespread debate on issue of availability of emergency contraception

— Suit by 8 states over funding by federal government of mandates in
No Child Left Behind law

— Independent Commission on 9/11 finds fault with both Clinton and
Bush administrations and that the U.S. is still not secure

— White House leak of CIA agent's name investigated; Howard Libby,
advisor to Vice President, later found guilty of perjury; Bush immediately commutes his prison sentence

— Energy bill passed (includes extension of Daylight Saving)

— Transportation bill passed

— Bush advocates 'globalization of democracy' in State of Union Address

— Harriet Miers, Supreme Court nominee, withdraws under fire; Samuel
Alito approved as Justice by Senate; Democrats and Republicans reach
compromise on filibustering of court nominees

— Celebrity culture dominates U.S. news reporting

2006 — Democrats regain control of both Houses of Congress; Iraq War
policy the major issue as President's approval rating falls below 30%

— Supreme Court strikes down Bush administration system for holding
and trying detainees at Guantanamo; administration claims Geneva
Convention does not apply to prisoners taken in the war on terror

— Bush calls for new research on alternative energy sources and for new
nuclear power plants to lessen dependency on oil

— Funding voted for development of vaccine for Avian flu

— Facebook and MySpace encourage cyberspace socializing and raise
issues of personal privacy

— South Dakota law declaring abortion illegal rejected in state
referendum

— Border Security Bill addresses issue of illegal immigrants by focusing
on border patrol and fence

— Pension Plan Overhaul law passed

— Patriot Act reauthorization approved

2007 — Nancy Pelosi elected first woman Speaker of the U.S. House of
Representatives

— Over a dozen individuals including Democrats Hillary Rodham
Clinton, wife of former President Clinton, and Senator Barack
Obama, and Republicans Senator John McCain and former NYC
Mayor Rudolph Guiliani indicate they will seek their party's
nomination for November 2008 presidential election

— Iraq and Afghanistan war financing approved by Congress without
  deadline for troop withdrawal after bitter debate
— Bush's approval rating hits new low as opposition to Iraq policy grows
— Bush orders "surge" in numbers of U.S. troops to end Iraq "Civil War"

# Glossary

The words listed in this glossary are ones you should have encountered during your study of United States history. Read the list and see how many are familiar. It is important to know the vocabulary of history, so be certain you understand those words that are new to you.

**Abolitionist** — before the American Civil War, one who believed in the abolition of slavery

**Abrogation** — the terminating or voiding of a treaty or agreement

**Absolutism** — control of a people or nation with no checks on the authority of the ruler

**Admiralty Court** — a court that has jurisdiction over maritime cases

**Aggression** — attack on or invasion of territory of another country

**AIDS** — Acquired Immune Deficiency Syndrome — A fatal disease first diagnosed in 1981 that has become a worldwide epidemic and for which a cure is being sought

**Alien** — someone not a citizen of the country

**Alliance** — a formal temporary union of two or more countries

**Amendment** — a change or proposed change in a bill or in the Constitution

**Amnesty** — the act of forgiving a large group en masse

**Anarchy** — a government without law or order, or in which no central authority is obeyed; a state of society in which law and order are absent

**Appeasement** — the act of giving in to a potential enemy in the hope that the enemy's appetite for further plunder or aggression will be filled

**Appropriation** — setting aside funds for a particular use, especially as applied to government expenditures

**Arbitration** — settlement of a dispute by a hearing before one or more persons chosen by the conflicting parties

**Aristocracy** — the theory or practice of government rule by an elite considered to be the best. In common historical usage it implies an inherited nobility

**Armistice** — a cease-fire in anticipation of negotiations for a more durable peace

**Assassination** — the killing of a politically important individual by surprise attack

**Autocracy** — government by one person who exercises supreme authority

**Automation** — use of machines to take the place of labor

**Autonomy** — the right of self-government within a framework of a larger political unit

**Axis** — the alliance of Germany, Italy, and Japan in World War II

**Baby Boom** — the sudden precipitous rise in the birth rate after World War II that lasted through the 1950s. The Baby Boomer generation is made up of individuals born in these years

**Balance of Payments** — specie, credit, or exchange of goods needed by one nation to clear its accounts with another nation over a set trading period

**Balance of Power** — policy that attempts to balance a nation's power either by alliances or by national action against a combination of nations that might threaten the nation's national interests

**Bear Market** — a period of declining prices on the stock market or any market

**Belligerent** — a country that is at war or is openly supporting another country at war

**Bicameral** — a legislature that has two chambers or houses; for example, the United States Congress is bicameral, having a House of Representatives and a Senate. Nebraska's legislature is unicameral, having but one legislative chamber

**Bilateral** — two-sided, as opposed to unilateral, onesided, or as compared to a multilateral, many-sided action or treaty

**Bimetallism** — backing a nation's currency with use of both gold and silver

**Black Code** — a series of laws relating to the control and dehumanization of African Americans during the Reconstruction period and after, largely in Southern states

**Black Power** — a political and social concept that African Americans should exercise control over their destiny without pressure from members of the majority; assumes the group needs political and economic independence to achieve this goal. The concept can be applied to other groups, such as Chicano Power

**Bloc** — a group of politicians or political parties temporarily joined to work for the same goal

**Blockade** — use of ships or troops to prevent entrance to or exit from a country

**Bloody Shirt** — term used as a symbol of the rebellion of the Confederate states by the Republican Party to discredit the South in the years after 1865

**Blue Laws** — laws written to enforce moral behavior

**Boondoggling** — word invented during the New Deal period and used primarily by conservative forces to describe what they termed wasteful expenditure of public money

**Bourbon** — very conservative Southern Democrat

**Bourgeoisie** — the middle class — particularly merchants and industrialists in that period when nobility was the upper class; used by Marx in his analysis of the class struggle

**Boycott** — to refuse to have business dealings with a nation, firm, or person

**Brinkmanship** — a term coined in respect to the foreign policy approach of Secretary of State John Foster Dulles, and used since to describe a gambler's attitude in the management of foreign relations. Dulles said that one must be prepared to go to the "brink," presumably atomic war, if a nation were to be taken seriously in international affairs

**Budget** — a financial statement that estimates and limits future expenses

**Bull Market** — a period of increasing prices on the stock market or any market

**Cabinet** — advisory council of a president or other ruler; usually appointed

**Capital** — money that can be used for building factories, railroads, etc.

**Capitalism** — the economic system in which means of production and distribution are privately owned under competitive conditions

**Carpetbagger** — a northerner who traveled to the former Confederacy during the Reconstruction period to participate in the political reorganization of the South, often for profit

**Cartel** — a business monopoly that extends beyond national boundary lines

**Catch-22** — a situation in which a decision is required and whatever decision is made will work against you because of regulations and circumstances. It came into common usage as a result of a war novel, *Catch-22*, by Joseph Heller in which the hero is caught in an impossible situation

**Caucus** — a private meeting of leaders of a political party to determine policy; often used to refer to those members as a group, i.e. the Black Caucus in the United States Congress

**Cavalier** — a supporter of Charles I of England, particularly a soldier defending his reign; now someone of aristocratic leaning

**Charisma** — magnetic personality, charm, leadership, attractiveness; often used in reference to political candidates

**Charter** — a document issued by a government or ruler granting rights and privileges to an individual or group

**Charter Colony** — a corporate colony operating under a charter obtained from the king by a company's stockholders

**Chauvinism** — extreme or exaggerated patriotism or commitment to a position; it comes from Nicolas Chauvin, who supported Napoleon in the extreme

**Chicano** — individuals of Mexican ancestry; Mexican Americans

**Civil Rights** — the liberties and privileges of citizens, especially those granted in the Bill of Rights

**Closed Shop** — a factory or place of business at which only union members may be employed

**Coalition** — a temporary union of individuals or political parties to attain some common aim

**Cold War** — a state of hostility between nations not involving physical contact. Applied specifically to U.S.–USSR relations between 1946 and 1990

**Collective Bargaining** — settlement of labor management disputes by discussion between representatives of the workers and the employer

**Colony** — an inhabited region politically dependent on and dominated by a more powerful nation

**Collective Security** — combining nations in an effort to provide greater protection from aggression

**Communism** — an economic system in which all means of production and distribution are owned and controlled by the government

**Compact** — an agreement, a contract

**Computer** — a machine that can solve problems very quickly because of its ability to do calculations fed into it by operators

**Conscription** — compulsory enrollment for military service; draft

**Conservation** — official care and protection of natural resources

**Conservative** — in politics, one who wishes to keep conditions basically as they are with little or no change

**Continental** — a soldier in the Revolutionary army; paper money issued by the Continental Congress, which continually depreciated in value

**Contras** — those forces opposing the Sandinista government of Nicaragua and funded and supported by the Reagan administration

**Convention** — a body of delegates meeting for a particular reason

**Copperhead** — a Northerner in sympathy with the South and active in its cause, or one in favor of a negotiated peace with the South

**Corporation** — a firm (usually in business) operating under a government charter that legally authorizes it to act as a single person with all the rights of a person under the law, but actually composed of two or more people who share ownership

**Counter Culture** — movement of the 1960s that focused on opposition to the Vietnam War and values of current society. Hippies and the "flower children" of the Haight-Ashbury section of San Francisco are examples of its members. Jimi Hendrix and Janis Joplin in their rock music expressed many of the movement's values as did the Beatles, and John Lennon in his phrase, "... give peace a chance"

**Coup d'Etat** — a sudden, forceful overthrow of government at the top

**Creationism**—the idea popularized by Christian Fundamentalists that an intelligent designer following a plan created the world. The proponents believe the Theory of Evolution is too haphazard to explain the wonder and variety of the earth and so Creationists reject the Darwinian theory

**Culture** — the way of living and ideas a people share

**Darwinism** — Charles Darwin proposed his theory of Evolution, incorporating ideas of the "survival of the fittest" and "natural selection" in the mid-nineteenth century. It was controversial and at first rejected by many, especially Christians who believed the story of creation as presented in the Bible. Over time it has found general acceptance as a way to explain a variety of phenomenon, from the variety of creatures on earth to the geological formations that make up earth. In the late 20th century the theory was again questioned by Christian fundamentalists who proposed the idea of Creationism as an explanation for the creation of the earth

**Delegate** — a representative of a group to a meeting or convention

**Democracy** — government by the people, by majority vote

**Depression** — time of unemployment and financial collapse. The depression that began in 1929 was so long and severe that it is known as the Great Depression

**Desegregation** — ending of segregation, usually by integration

**Despot** — a ruler with absolute power, usually a tyrant

**Detente** — a relaxing and easing of tensions between nations used particularly in reference to the foreign policy of President Nixon in relation to the USSR

**Deterrence** — measures taken by one country to discourage attack by other nations

**Dictator** — a ruler who has supreme and absolute power; one who has usurped that power by force or legal trickery

**Diplomacy** — the conduct of negotiations to achieve agreements between countries; international contacts

**Discrimination** — a majority's denial of advantages to certain minority groups

**Displaced Persons (DPs)** — those uprooted from their native land by war and forced to move elsewhere

**Divine Right** — the belief—especially prevalent in the 16th and 17th centuries in Europe—that kings ruled and held power because of God's will

**Dollar Diplomacy** — a type of economic imperialism whereby the United States sought to insure its investment abroad, particularly in Latin America, by using military power or threat of military power to support United States business interests

**Due Process** — traceable in English and American legal tradition to Magna Carta, due process has come to mean the procedure guaranteed to all citizens, that affords them their "day in court"

**Duty** — a tax, usually on imports

**Ecology** — the study of the relationship between individual organisms and their environment

**Edict** — an order issued by a governmental authority that has the same effect as a law

**Electoral College** — the procedure by which the president and vice president of the United States are elected. Every state has as many votes in the electoral college as it has senators and representatives combined, and the electors are voted for at the November presidential election every four years. The electors collectively (the college) then vote for president and vice president

**Embargo** — a government order preventing the movement of merchant ships and/or the prohibition of trade

**Emigrants** — those who leave their country to settle in another

**Empire** — many lands ruled by one ruler or nation

**Entente** — an agreement temporarily uniting two or more countries, usually informal and unsigned

**Entitlements** — programs such as Social Security to which the recipients believe they have a right

**Environment** — surroundings; all the conditions around us

**Equality** — everything being equal or everyone having the same rights

**Ethnic Cleansing** — the expulsion, imprisonment, or killing of ethnic minorities by a dominant majority group. It drew world-wide attention to Rwanda and Yugoslavia in the 1990s, but throughout history it has been used by dominant groups to establish their control over an area

**Evangelicals** — those Christians who are committed to the so-called "traditional" Christian beliefs and see themselves as "saved" and/or "born again." Evangelicals understand the Bible in a literal way believing, it to be the word of God, and accept everything in it as true. In that sense they are Fundamentalists. The popularity of the evangelical viewpoint grew greatly in the period after 1970 with the emergence of several leaders that became politically active. Their voice and viewpoint became an important factor in many social issues from abortion to gay rights

**Evolution** — the theory that the present condition of the earth and its inhabitants has developed over billions of years by a natural process that includes the "survival of the fittest" and "natural selection." Charles Darwin, in his work *The Origin of Species* is credited with presenting the theory

**Excise Tax** — an internal tax on the manufacture, sale, or consumption of goods, such as tobacco, alcohol

**Executive Agreement** — an agreement between the president and the head of a foreign country

**Expansion** — as applied to countries, the acquisition of additional territory

**Exports** — goods sent out of the country for sale in another country

**Extraterritoriality** — the state or privilege of exemption from the laws of local courts, particularly in the case of diplomatic representatives to a foreign country

**Fair Deal** — the slogan used to describe the domestic program of President Truman

**Fascism** — a political philosophy, movement, or regime that exalts a nation and/or race above the individual and that stands for a centralized, autocratic government headed by a dictatorial leader, severe economic and social regimentation, and forcible suppression of all opposition. The term Fascist was applied specifically to the regime established by Mussolini in Italy before World War II

**Featherbedding** — retaining workers on unnecessary jobs, or paying workers more than necessary to do a job, or hiring more workers than necessary to do a job

**Federal** — the central government or authority as contrasted with state or local government

**Federalism** — a system of government in which a central authority divides or shares power with its regional parts

**Feudalism** — the social structure of the Middle Ages, based on the relation of a lord to his vassals, who held land (called fiefs) granted by the lord in return for obedience and loyalty

**Fifth Columnist** — a traitor who aids the enemy

**Filibuster** — private imperialistic adventure by unauthorized individuals out for their own profit and in some cases their own sovereignty; extended debate in the U.S. Senate designed to prevent a vote on a bill of which the filibusterer (speaker) disapproves but the majority of Senate members approves

**Flapper** — phrase used to describe the "liberated" woman of the "roaring twenties"

**Fourteen Points** — Wilson's statement of war aims, delivered to Congress during the course of World War I. Among the points were freedom of the seas, self-determination of subject peoples, reduction of armaments once the war was successfully ended, and, most important, a League of Nations to keep the peace in the postwar world

**Frontier** — that boundary or border of a country that faces either another country or unsettled land; also the concept of newness or challenge as in John F. Kennedy's New Frontier

**Gay Rights** — a movement demanding civil rights for homosexuals—gay men and lesbians

**Genocide** — the deliberate murder, or attempted murder, of a whole people; may be based on racial, ethnic, religious, cultural, or political concepts

**Ghetto** — place where people of one minority group live together

**Glasnost** — an opening up in Russian; it refers specifically to both the economic and political opening within the USSR under President Mikhail Gorbachev in the 1980s and the opening in foreign policy that permitted greater contacts with the West and relaxed control over Eastern Europe. Together with peristroika these actions led to the end of the Cold War

**Good Neighbor Policy** — part of the New Deal's foreign policy, which aimed at strengthening United States ties with Latin America

**Great Society** — name given to the program of domestic reforms instituted by President Lyndon Johnson

**Guerrilla** — one who carries on or assists in an irregular war

**Guild** — an association of persons in the same trade or craft, formed for mutual aid and protection

**Hegemony** — leadership, paramount influence, or military-economic overlordship of one nation over another, or over other nations or regions

**Holding Company** — a company that usually does not produce anything or perform any service except to control other companies through the ownership of controlling shares of stock

**Holocaust** — mass slaughter of European civilians during World War II, especially of Jews, who the Nazis considered to be members of inferior races. Over six million Jews were killed in gas chambers or as a result of forced labor and starvation (see Ethnic Cleansing)

**Hostage** — a civilian seized by a group or individual and held captive to force an enemy to negotiate and make changes in policy; a form of blackmail

**Immigrants** — those who come to make their home in a new country

**Impeach** — to indict a public official for misbehavior; the case is then tried before a jury assigned to the case. In the case of the impeachment of the U.S. president, the Senate serves as the jury

**Imperialism** — a government policy of annexing territory by force or political pressure, or gaining political control over weaker lands

**Implied Powers** — powers suggested but not specifically listed in the Constitution and exercised by the national government and its three branches

**Imports** — goods brought into one country from another

**Impressment** — the practice of the British of forcing American sailors into service on British warships under the assumption that they were escaped British seamen

**Inalienable** — nontransferable, irrevocable. As associated with rights it means that there are certain rights that humans cannot cancel; they are God-given, or derived from nature

**Industrial Revolution** — that phase of economic development characterized by a change from home to factory production and use of non-human sources of power (water, coal) to run machines

**Inflation** — a large rise in prices due to an increase in the money supply and/or expansion of credit

**Injunction** — a court order preventing a person or group of people from carrying on some activity; usually applied to an order preventing a union from picketing

**Insurgent** — a rebel

**Integration** — bringing together or making as one; unification; applied especially to blacks and whites in a number of social areas

**Internationalism** — an ideology that emphasizes the unity of the world's peoples, and that deplores restrictive national boundaries and competing national sovereignties

**Iran-Contra** — name given to the policy followed secretly by the Reagan Administration to sell arms to Iran to help free hostages in Lebanon while using the profits from the arms sales to support the Contras in Central America

**Isolationism** — a foreign policy that shuns alliances and compacts with other countries

**Jihad** — the interpretation of an idea found in the Koran and followed by some Muslims of fighting to support and spread the Islamic faith. Those who fight are referred to as Jihadists

**Jim Crow Laws** — laws enforcing segregation of African Americans and whites, following the concept of separate but equal

**Jingoism** — supermilitaristic patriotism

**John Birch Society** — a pro-American, anti-Communist organization founded after World War II by Robert Welch, an ultraconservative retired businessman from Massachusetts. The Society was organized in semi-secret cells and used vicious and ruthless tactics in its fight against Communism

**Journeyman** — worker who is learning a craft under a master; such individuals work for a daily wage

**Judicial** — that branch of government related to the courts and their decisions concerning the legality of laws and acts

**Judicial Review** — the power of a court to accept appeals of legislative and executive action and decisions of lower courts with the possibility of modifying or nullifying such action as being "unconstitutional"

**Jury** — a group of people in a court who hear and decide a case

**Keynesian Economics** — ideas of John Maynard Keynes, British economist. Essentially Keynes believed in government spending during depression periods and retrenching with economy budgets and high taxation during periods of boom

**Ku Klux Klan** — formed in 1867 by southern whites to help them establish their prestige and power over the freedmen. It was organized in secret groups and terrified the countryside with threats, lynchings, and burnings. It declined after federal laws were passed later in the century but resurfaced in the 1920s as an anti-Communist organization that saw threats to traditional small town American values from Roman Catholics, Jews, and organized labor. It continues as a small, often vocal, anti-minorities organization

**Labor Theory of Value** — a central part of Karl Marx's scientific socialism was also expressed by John Locke. Marx contended that economic value is derived from labor acting on materials of production and that no true economic value is achieved by moving funds among banks or by buying and selling businesses

**Labor Union** — organization of workers to improve their wages and working conditions

**Laissez-faire** — noninterference by government in private enterprises

**Lame Duck** — an elected official (congressperson, etc.) defeated in an election but continuing to serve because his or her successor is not scheduled to take office until a later date

**Law and Order** — a vaguely defined political concept held by those who oppose violence and anarchy; an important campaign issue in many elections in the late 20th century

**Legal Tender** — any kind of money that is declared official by an act of government

**Legislative** — branch of government concerned with making laws

**Liberal** — in politics, an individual who is not tied to tradition or party lines and welcomes experimentation with new ideas; its root is *liber* meaning free

**Logrolling** — mutual assistance in the passage of legislation so that one member of Congress votes for a colleague's bill in return for similar assistance in his or her desired legislation

**Lynching** — execution or killing by a mob, with no proper trial

**Majority** — more than half of the votes, or the larger part of the population

**Mandate** — a vote of confidence from the people. A mandate also refers to a colony held in trust by a major power under the League of Nations

**Manifest Destiny** — the belief that it was the destiny of the United States to expand to the natural boundary of the Pacific

**Marxism** — the economic and political theories of Karl Marx as interpreted by Lenin, Stalin, Mao Zedong, and many others. The main features of Marxism are world revolution, removal of the exploiting class, a dictatorship of the proletariat during the transition period of the "withering away" of the state, and a goal of the classless Communist society where everyone shall contribute according to his or her abilities and take according to his or her needs

**Master Craftsman** — a worker who has learned a trade and produced a masterpiece to become a member of a guild

**Masterpiece** — an object produced by a journeyman. If approved of by the guild, the journeyman would be admitted into the guild as a master

**Me Decade** — a term used by the novelist Thomas Wolfe to describe the personal attitude that many believe was the primary focus of individuals in the 1970s. They argue that many adults concentrated on individual self-expression and personal improvement, rejecting the intense political and social involvements of the 1960s

**Megalopolis** — a very large urban region

**Mercantilism** — the practice of achieving a favorable balance of trade (exports exceed imports) through government acts to benefit the commercial interests of the country (example: English Navigation Acts of the 1680s)

**Metropolitan Centers** — big cities with smaller cities around them

**Middle Class** — that part of society between the affluent upper class and the poor lower class

**Migrant** — person moving from one place to another

**Militarism** — the overvaluing of the military establishment, its leaders, their aims, and ideals, also, the substitution of military for civilian control of the state

**Militarist** — one who believes in an aggressive foreign policy backed up with well-prepared armed forces

**Military Industrial Complex** — a phrase used by President Eisenhower to refer to the relationship between the military and business in the United States; he warned against their power in his Farewell Address to the nation

**Monarchy** — system of government with a king as ruler

**Monopoly** — control of the entire supply of some product, giving the power to set prices and/or limit production

**Moratorium** — a period of suspended activity

**Most-Favored-Nation Clause** — a common treaty provision that grants to the recipient all privileges granted to any other nation by the granting nation; often applies to trading agreements

**Mother Country** — the nation that sends out settlers to found a colony and the nation to which that colony owes allegiance

**Muckraker** — one who exposes, usually in writing, misdeeds in business or political activities, hoping to bring reform. The term was first used in this way by Theodore Roosevelt

**Multilateralsim** — (Multinationalism) the concept in foreign policy that nations should work together to achieve political, economic, and social goals. The United Nations, NATO, and Operation Desert Storm are examples of multilateralism. The concept was the basis of U.S. foreign policy from World War II to the inauguration of George W. Bush.

**National (or Public) Debt** — the sum total of all financial obligations that result from borrowing by a nation-state

**Nationalism** — ardent and sometimes excessive devotion to national interests and prestige

**Natural Law** — rules that appear to be true and are argued as true because they are either rational or because they are ordained by God

**Natural Right** — a right assumed to be protected by natural law

**Nazism** — the German variation of fascism established by Adolf Hitler in the 1930s. The Nazis considered the Germans a superior race and sought domination over Europe and extermination of those they considered of inferior races such as Jews, gypsies, homosexuals, and East Europeans especially the Slavs of Poland and the USSR

**Negotiation** — in international affairs, the practice of settling disputes by means other than the resort to armed force, by using judicial or arbitrational or diplomatic mechanisms; in domestic affairs, the settling of disputes by discussion and compromise

**Neoconservatives** — the name given to a group of like-minded individuals (Neocons) who held positions of power in the administration of George W. Bush. They rejected multilateralism as an approach to foreign policy and believed the United States as the sole super power should use its power to impose its values and ideas on the world to make it a better place. They believed they were instrumental in leading the United States into war in Iraq in 2003 and that every nation, given the opportunity, would welcome a democratic government

**Neutral** — a country that neither assists nor allies itself with another country at war

**Neutralism** — a nonpartisan or nonattached view of policy in regard to competing systems or states

**Neutrality** — the policy of a nation that seeks to maintain impartiality between two opposing states or groups of states, but at the same time to fully protect its own international rights

**New Deal** — the domestic reform program of President Franklin Roosevelt

**New Federalism** — President Nixon's domestic program, which centered on returning some power to the states at the expense of the national government under the assumption that the federal bureaucracy had grown too large and unresponsive to local needs; also endorsed by President Reagan

**New Freedom** — the domestic and foreign policy programs of Woodrow Wilson

**New Frontier** — the domestic and foreign policy programs of President John F. Kennedy

**New Nationalism** — slogan for the reform program of Theodore Roosevelt and the Bull Moose Party

**Nonviolence** — a peaceful form of protest connected with Gandhi and Martin Luther King, Jr.

**Nullify** — to cancel or destroy the legal effectiveness of a law, tradition, or agreement

**Oligarchy** — government by a few

**Open Door** — American foreign policy in regard to Asia that was initiated by Secretary of State John Hay on September 6, 1899. The policy was to persuade nations having interests in Asia, and particularly having business in China, to deal with China as an equal. The policy sought equal commercial opportunity for all nations and the abolition of restrictive spheres of influence as well as other supranational privileges such as extraterritoriality

**Open Shop** — factory in which employment is not dependent upon being a member of a union

**Ordinance** — a rule or regulation issued by a nonsovereign body (usually a city, country, or township)

**Panic** — financial crisis followed by unemployment and hard times, but not as severe as a depression

**Patronage** — appointing people to government positions as a reward for political services while disregarding merits such persons might have for the jobs assigned

**Peristroika** — a rebuilding in Russian; it refers specifically to the rebuilding of the Soviet economic system by President Mikhail Gorbachev in the 1980s. It does not imply any movement towards democracy in the political area but simply a restructuring of the economy. Its implementation hastened the end of the Cold War.

**Petition** — a written plea from an individual or organized group protesting some wrong, personal or societal, in hopes of gaining a redress

**Plebiscite** — a vote by the people of the country on some measure submitted to them for acceptance or rejection. It was originally considered an extension of the democratic principle, but has recently been used by dictators to gain support for their autocratic decisions

**Plutocracy** — government by the wealthy

**Police Power** — the broad power of government to regulate and restrain the life, liberty, and property of individuals and groups in order to protect and promote peace, order, health, safety, good morals, and general welfare

**Policy** — the course followed by a government or one of its representatives

**Pollution** — the fouling of the environment; something unclean or poisonous

**Pork Barrel** — the money and public works Congress distributes and the spending of public money through logrolling techniques to benefit particular localities and enhance the election possibilities of representatives at the expense of the general public good

**Poverty** — lack of money or goods; condition of being poor

**Precedent** — in American and British law, it is a previous ruling in law that is so important it must be taken into account in subsequent cases; these later decisions usually abide by the earlier decision

**Prejudice** — dislike for a person or group without reason

**Pro-choice** — the position that abortion should be a woman's choice and not subject to restrictions established by government

**Proclamation** — a public announcement of official policy

**Pro-life** — the position that abortion is not a right and the Supreme Court decision of *Roe v. Wade* should be overturned

**Propaganda** — ideas, beliefs, and information either untrue or exaggerated spread by an organized group or government

**Proportional Representation** — a system of electing legislators that results in representation approximately proportionate to the strength of each political party as determined in a vote

**Proprietary Colony** — a colony run and controlled by an individual or group of individuals as their private estate, such as, William Penn's Pennsylvania

**Protective Tariff** — a tax on imported goods designed to increase their price to the level of similar home-produced goods

**Protectorate** — a country protected by a more powerful state that shares in its government

**Protestant Ethic** — the extolling of work and the abhorrence of waste by Calvinists and their descendants; connected in the United States with the Puritans

**Purge** — to free a state or party of disloyal elements

**Quorum** — the minimum number of members who must be present in order for a business to be transacted by a group, usually of elected representatives

**Racism** — the doctrine that some races are inherently superior to others because of supposed cultural and intellectual inheritance

**Radical** — one who favors basic changes in the structure of society

**Ratify** — to approve a bill or law

**Reactionary** — one who favors a return to an older, more conservative way of life

**Reaganomics** — President Reagan's plan of reduced taxes to stimulate economic activity and cut inflation; supply-side economics

**Rebate** — a percentage of the cost returned ostensibly for services performed or commodities sold

**Recall** — a petition signed by a large percentage (usually 25 percent) of the voters that recalls an elected representative from his or her position and thus leaves vacant the office held; usually the official so removed may run again

**Recession** — panic or slight depression

**Referendum** — a petition signed by a small percentage (usually 10 percent) that requires the public be given a chance to vote (in a special election) on a law passed by a legislative body, thus rejecting or confirming public support for the law

**Religious Right** — the conservative, fundamentalist, "born again" side of Protestantism in America first organized in the mid-20th century

**Renaissance** — a rebirth of interest in culture, especially as applied to art and literature in the 14th to 16th centuries in western Europe. The term has been used for other periods of rebirth such as the 12th-century Renaissance in France or the Harlem Renaissance of the 1920s in New York City

**Reparations** — payment in compensation for damages, caused usually as a result of war or war-connected activity

**Representative** — a person elected to represent others; a member of the U.S. House of Representatives or some other legislative body

**Republic** — a nation in which the people elect representatives to govern; from the Latin *res publica*, or public thing

**Resources (natural)** — the natural wealth of a country— minerals, farmlands, forests, etc.

**Revenue** — money a government collects by taxes and duties

**Revolution** — a sudden end of one government and the start of a new one; any dramatic and somewhat sudden change

**Roaring Twenties** – phrase used to describe the economic, literary, and social aspects of the 1920s that included gangsters, speakeasies and illegal alcohol, short skirts, risqué dancing (ex. Charleston), the Harlem Renaissance, and writings of F. Scott Fitzgerald, as well as a booming stock market until the "Crash" in 1929

**Royal Colony** — a colony directly controlled by a king and governed by the king's appointed representative

**Rule of Law** — a fundamental principle of American and British legal systems and constitutional government. It involves three points: (1) the absolute supremacy of law over arbitrary power—no person is above the law, not even the chief executive; (2) equality before the law; (3) the Constitution is the supreme law of the land and the protective force of inherent or natural rights

**Satellite** — an object orbiting another and commonly used to describe objects sent into space from earth. The term has also been used to refer to nations that are dependent on another country for defense or political direction

**Scalawag** — contemptuous name for a Southern white who cooperated with Northerners or blacks during Reconstruction

**SDS (Students for a Democratic Society)** — a youth group formed in the 1960s to force changes upon United States society by political and/or violent means

**Secession** — withdrawal of a constituent member from a political group

**Sectionalism** — devotion to the interests of a state or some particular section of it over and above the interests of the country itself

**Sedition** — actions that encourage disrespect for law and government that fall short of treason but go beyond normal legal and political opposition

**Segregation** — as applied to African Americans and whites—isolating one group from the other

**Serf** — in feudal society, a peasant permanently attached to land owned by a lord

**Settlers** — those who make their home in a new, usually sparsely settled area

**Sharecropping** — a type of farm tenancy in which the tenant agrees to share part of the crop in lieu of rent and often to receive seed and other necessary capital goods

**Silent Majority** — a term used by President Nixon to refer to those Americans who opposed the actions of protestors and activists of the late 1960s and supported "law and order"

**Social Contract** — a theory that primitive societies were first brought into being by a voluntary agreement between the ruled and the elected ruler in order to provide for mutual protection and welfare

**Social Darwinism** — a loose adaptation of Darwin's theories of evolution to social conditions. Social Darwinists held that since human society had evolved naturally, any interference with existing conditions by the government was against evolution. Thus they supported the laissez-faire attitude toward economic conditions. The wealthy were wealthy by the process of natural selection and survival of the fittest.

**Social Gospel** — a late 19th-century movement that emphasized social responsibility as the way to salvation, i.e. applying the teachings of Jesus as presented in the four gospels in the Christian bible, to social conditions. They built churches in the slums and supported settlement houses and help for immigrants, the poor, and the oppressed.

**Socialism** — belief in a society based on government ownership and control of many means of production and distribution especially of major production (coal, steel) and utilities (railroads, electricity)

**Sovereignty** — supreme power. In the United States ultimate sovereignty is vested in the people and exercised by the federal government, which they control. Under the Articles of Confederation it was in the hands of several states, and prior to the American Revolution, in the British Crown. In the United States, each level of government exercises degrees of sovereignty, but since the Civil War ultimate sovereignty has rested in the federal government.

**Soviet** — Russian word for "council"

**Specie** — money in the form of coins, usually gold or silver

**Speculation** — legal gambling on stocks, real estate, farm commodities, etc.

**Sphere of Influence** — a geographic area in which a nation seeks to dominate to the point of securing preferential treatment of a political, economic, and even social nature

**Spoils** — in politics, the influence and jobs the winning party distributes to its workers

**Spoils System** — the awarding of government jobs or the granting of favors or advantages by government officials to political partisans and workers

**Square Deal** — the slogan used to describe the domestic program of President Theodore Roosevelt

**Squatter Sovereignty** — (similar to popular sovereignty) the professed right of settlers in an area to determine for themselves solutions to key problems affecting them

**Status Quo Ante Bellum** — the situation as it existed before a war, especially used to refer to the period before the U.S. Civil War

**States' Rights** — a belief that the federal government should be limited so that the individual states may exercise more power; it supports the concept of state as opposed to federal sovereignty

**Statute** — a law. One may distinguish four important types of legal restraint that are embodied in American and British legal systems: *Statutory law* is law established by a legislative body with the approval of the executive (or passed over his veto). *Common law* is the so-called unwritten law that has been established by custom, tradition, or precedent. *Constitutional law* is the overriding legal principles embodied in the basic governing document (such as the U.S. Constitution); *ordinances* are rules or regulations established by bodies—cities, counties, townships—not having full sovereignty, but existing as subdivisions of a sovereign body

**Strict Construction** — philosophy that holds that the Constitution should be narrowly or literally interpreted, which leads to the concept that government should be limited

**Strike** — walkout by workers, or general refusal to work, in the hope of forcing an employer or government body to offer better contract terms or change policies

**Suburb** — residential neighborhood at the edge of a city

**Suffrage** — the right to vote

**Surtax** — an additional tax added to the normal tax

**Tariff** — taxes, usually referred to as duties, imposed by governments on imports and exports

**Tenement** — unsafe, unsanitary, and crowded apartment building

**Theocracy** — a church-ruled government, local, regional, or national

**Third World** — a term used to designate nonwestern nations that have not industrialized

**Totalitarianism** — a government whose leadership excludes all opposition and opposing political parties and exercises complete control over all phases of national life

**Transcendentalism** — a philosophical movement starting in New England (Ralph Waldo Emerson's *On Nature* [1836] is considered one of the best statements about Transcendental ideas) that held the most important truths went beyond human reason and had divine possibilities in them and nature could help us to understand these truths

**Treaty** — a formal agreement between two or more countries

**Trust** — an organization composed of different companies united under one board of trustees, whose purpose is to eliminate competition and thereby control an industry by creating a monopoly

**Underground Railroad** — an escape route for Southern slaves fleeing to the North and Canada in the years prior to the Civil War

**Unification** — as applied to nations, the process of joining different self-governing states into one central government

**Unilateralism** — the concept in foreign policy that a nation should strive to achieve its national goals without regard to the opinions and concerns of other nations and that a nation should use its power as it sees fit. The Republican administration of George W. Bush switched the basis of U.S. foreign policy from multilateralism to unilateralism under the influence of a group of Neoconservatives (see Isolationism)

**Union Shop** — a limited closed shop

**Unwritten Constitution** — customs, traditions, and practices in government that have become the way of life of a society

**Urban** — having to do with a city

**Vassal** — in feudalism, one who swears loyalty to a higher lord in return for protection and privileges

**Veteran** — one who has served in the military forces

**Vigilantes** — individuals who band together without the support of the law to enforce a particular code of behavior

**Violence** — attacks that harm or damage a person or thing. Politically it is usually associated with anarchy and revolution and often is a result of poverty or extreme, either conservative or radical, ideology

**Veto** — to refuse approval, usually of a bill, law, or motion, or to forbid

**Watergate** — a term used to refer to the scandals of the Nixon Administration that led to his resignation as president. The scandal began with a break-in at the Democratic Party headquarters in the Watergate Building—a condominium complex—in Washington, D.C.

**Whitewater** — a term used to refer to the investigation of the activities of President and Mrs. Clinton in a land development scheme in Arkansas. The Whitewater investigation by special prosecutor Kenneth Starr was expanded to include several other suspected scandals, such as Travelgate and the Monica Lewinsky affair.

**Women's Liberation** — a women's movement stimulated by Betty Friedan's book, *The Feminine Mystique,* which held that middle-class values stifled women; passage of the ERA (Equal Rights Amendment) was a goal

**Welfare State** — the set of government supports established by law that provide care for the disabled, elderly, poor, and unemployed who are unable for one reason or another to care for themselves in an industrialized society

**Woodstock** — a rock festival held at Woodstock, NY in 1969 that has come to symbolize the "counter-culture" movement of the 1960s that focused on opposition to the Vietnam War and the values of society. Their dream was to have a society based on peace, love, drugs, and rock music

**Writ** — a formal written document or order issued under seal in the name of the sovereign or of a court or judicial officer commanding the person to whom it is directed to perform or refrain from performing an act specified therein

**Xenophobia** — a fear or hatred of foreigners

**Yellow Journalism** — used particularly to describe a newspaper style of the 1890s; the style sensationalized the news, especially scandals, to attract readership

**Yeoman farmer** — originally a farmer in England who worked his own land. In United States history Yeoman refers to the 19th- century, self-sufficient, often frontier-based farmer whom Thomas Jefferson idealized as the epitome of American freedom and defender of liberty

**Youth Groups** — organizations of young people, often for political action

# Index

The following documentation applies if you purchased
**AP United States History, 8th Edition** with CD-ROM.

Please disregard this information if your version does not contain the CD-ROM.

## SYSTEM REQUIREMENTS

The program will run on a PC with:
Windows® Intel® Pentium II 450 MHz
or faster processor, 128MB of RAM
1024 × 768 display resolution
Windows 2000, XP, Vista
CD-ROM Player

The program will run on a Macintosh® with:
PowerPC® G3 500 MHz or faster processor,
128MB of RAM
1024 × 768 display resolution
Mac OS X v.10.1 through 10.4
CD-ROM Player

## INSTALLATION INSTRUCTIONS

The product is not installed on the end-user's computer; it is run directly from the CD-ROM. Barron's CD-ROM includes an "autorun" feature that automatically launches the application when the CD is inserted into the CD drive. In the unlikely event that the autorun features are disabled, alternate launching instructions are provided below.

**Windows®:**
Insert the CD-ROM. The program will launch automatically. If it doesn't launch automatically:
Click on the Start button and choose "Run."
If your CD-ROM drive is mapped to (D:), type AP_US_History.exe and click "OK" or replace *D*: with the appropriate drive letter.

**Macintosh®:**
Insert the CD-ROM.
Double-click the CD-ROM icon.
Double-click AP_US_History icon to start the program.